JOHN BETJEMAN

Coming Home

An anthology of his prose 1920–1977

Selected and introduced by
Candida Lycett Green

Methuen

Published by Methuen

Copyright in the compilation and introduction © Candida Lycett Green, 1997
Illustrations © Endellion Lycett Green, 1997

Copyright in the writings, verses and illustrations of John Betjeman is vested
in the Estate of Sir John Betjeman.

Candida Lycett Green has asserted her right under the Copyright, Designs and Patents
Act, 1988 to be identified as the author of this work.

First published in the United Kingdom in 1997 by Methuen,
Random House, 20 Vauxhall Bridge Road, London SW1V 2SA

Random House Australia (Pty) Limited
20 Alfred Street, Milsons Point, Sydney,
New South Wales 2061, Australia

Random House New Zealand Limited
18 Poland Road, Glenfield,
Auckland 10, New Zealand

Random House South Africa (Pty) Limited
Endulini, 5A Jubilee Road, Parktown 2193, South Africa

Random House UK Limited Reg. No. 954009
A CIP catalogue record for this book
is available from the British Library

ISBN 0 413 71710 0

Typeset in Janson by Deltatype Ltd, Birkenhead, Merseyside
Printed and bound in Great Britain by
Mackays of Chatham PLC, Chatham, Kent

In memory of Myfanwy Piper

Contents

Preface

By the end of his life in 1984, my father, John Betjeman, had become widely celebrated as a poet and television broadcaster. But his articles, lectures, radio talks and contributions to books were seldom mentioned and his newspaper journalism was unregarded. Yet the former had been an important part of his output since he began working on the *Architectural Review* in 1930 and the latter had been his consistent financial mainstay: for fifty years he was never without a regular job in the field. He had neither capital nor built-in pension and needed to work until the end in order to subsist. He fell into his jobs through circumstance rather than by design and was willing to work for almost anyone who paid him. He had no political leanings. He worked for Conservative, Labour and Liberal newspapers and magazines.

If I have felt hesitant about making a selection of his prose it is because JB himself never really considered it to be of lasting value. If I had suggested even contemplating republishing any of his newspaper journalism, he would have thought me mad. But now that some time has elapsed, I have come to feel that perhaps he would not mind so much my including in this volume what are, in fact, mere drops in the ocean of half a century's journalistic output, in order to evoke a more vivid picture of the times in which he was writing and his response to them. But I am also proud of, and want to boast about his consistent and extraordinary vision and prescience. He loved and valued certain buildings like St Pancras Station decades before they were generally appreciated and he recognised virtue in people and things where others didn't. Over the years I believe he extended our idea of what is beautiful.

Some of his articles could have been written yesterday. A piece he wrote for the *Architectural Review* in 1931 when he was twenty-five, for instance, is as topical today as it was then: 'The revolting phrase "The Battle of the Styles," wherein architecture is now considered a fighting ground between old gentlemen who imitate the Parthenon and brilliant young men who create abstract designs, can only have been

coined by the stupid extremists of either side. There is no battle for
the intelligent artist. The older men gradually discard superfluities.
The younger men do not ignore the necessary devices of the past.
Both sides find their way slowly to the middle of the maze, whose
magic centre is tradition.'

The prose in this book is arranged chronologically. I have prefaced
each section with a short description of what was happening in JB's
working life together with the briefest of notes on his abiding concern
– the face of England. In editing the two volumes of his *Letters* I tried
to paint a personal portrait of my father, based on my own memories
of him. Here I have tried to make the descriptions impersonal and
down to earth. I merely want to present a factual background so that
the prose falls into context.

The pieces I have selected divide roughly into five main categories.
The first were written – whether for periodicals, books, newspapers,
radio or television – to convey JB's pleasure at seeing and discovering
places, literature and people. I think his generosity of spirit in wanting
to share his excitement bursts through much of his writing in a clear
and simple way. He never tried to impress people with his knowledge;
'I do not remember to have laughed so much at a new funny book as I
have done at *Lucky Jim* by Kingsley Amis, since when I first read
Evelyn Waugh's *Decline and Fall* . . .', he wrote when the novel first
came out in 1958 – a time when most reviewers were writing self-
consciously complicated pieces. His approach was always straightforward, his enthusiasm infectious. 'Golf is a beautiful game,' he wrote in
Time and Tide, when reviewing *A History of Golf in Britain* by Bernard
Darwin, 'It tests the nerves and then it soothes them. It can be played
alone (which is how I like playing it best) when the player can quietly
cheat to himself. It encourages an eye for landscape. It turns a dreary
stretch of clay or the coniferous aridity of some sandy waste into an
enchanted kingdom of contours, hazards and distances.'

When writing about what might on the face of it be quite an
ordinary place, he could add another dimension and a mystery – he
particularly enjoyed bringing places and people from obscurity and
shining a spotlight on them. The 1890s composer Theo Marzials
typified the kind of forgotten character by whom JB was fascinated. It
was so like him to want to find out about Marzials' background and
circumstances and to travel on a long voyage of discovery to a village
in Devon where people still remembered him in his last days. This
resulted in an evocative character sketch of a great unsung Englishman
who might otherwise have remained in darkness.

The second category of JB's writing is the everyday slog: written to order to impart information and to entertain. During the thirties, forties and fifties this involved the reviewing of over 500 films and 3,000 books; in the fifties and sixties the writing of regular opinion columns for *The Spectator* and *The Daily Telegraph*. It was work which, more often than not, he didn't feel like doing. In fact he always dreaded writing his regular pieces. Nevertheless, even when he was in his early thirties, at an age when most young journalists would want to keep in with their editors, JB never hesitated to let his fancy take wing if a topic appealed to him. He also seemed to take pleasure in exceeding the boundaries. He was never scared of being sacked and sometimes was. 'No, I refuse to use that word nostalgic,' he said on air on Christmas Day 1947, when the BBC had just introduced his broadcast entitled 'Christmas Nostalgia.' 'Nostalgia sounds like neuralgia. And it is a smart new word, smacking of psychological slang.'

Reading through his many film reviews for the *Evening Standard* it is easy to see when he got bored with talking of film stars and would write instead about an architectural jaunt to a cinema miles out in the outer London suburbs – or he would interview an unknown music-hall star – hardly part of his editor's brief. Thirty years later JB was writing his regular, rather grown-up column for *The Daily Telegraph* called 'Men and Buildings', for which he had to produce the requisite 800 words once a month. The best of these pieces contain flashes of vision and passion; but in others his style often becomes mechanical and it is easy to detect where he has filled in with irrelevant waffle in order to make up the length.

The third category of writing resulted from the crusading and lobbying role which came to occupy an increasing amount of JB's time and energy (as well as often informing his regular journalism). Once he was established with the BBC and had gained an appreciative band of listeners, he used many of his radio broadcasts to put over how strongly he felt about the slow erosion of the fabric of England. He began in the early thirties and continued for the rest of his life. He wrote and spoke about every aspect, from his horror of concrete lamp-posts wrecking market towns in the magazine *Lights and Lighting*, to his sadness at the bleakness of the new Paternoster Square in *Private Eye*. For a mass of people who cared about such things, he became a champion and educator. His knowledge – he never forgot anything – seemed fathomless. Ever looking ahead with the grand vision of England in his eye when politicans took a short-term view, he often foresaw disasters, such as Doctor Beeching's axing of so much of our railway network. JB was never far from the cutting edge of radicalism. His bravery knew no bounds, for he not only took on individuals, including Prime Ministers, but whole Government departments.

The fourth category was the writing of film scripts for architectural and topographical documentaries. It was an art in which, by the sixties and seventies, he was almost unsurpassed. He became deeply involved in the creation of each film, from the choosing of locations and camera angles to the recording of wild track, and his careful script evolved as the film proceeded right through to its final editing stage. If you look at the films now, the commentaries seem to be organically interwoven with the images, as is the case in few other comparable films.

The fifth category of pieces within this collection is the short stories. Five are included here, the first published in 1929 and the last in 1951. All are shot through with JB's quirky humour and imagination and reflect many of his passions and predilections.

Of course these categories overlap in many cases, but threaded all through there is an openness and a continuing sense of wonderment. I have selected pieces from each period not necessarily because they are well written in every case but because they illustrate a particular passion. In 1952 his old friend Myfanwy Piper selected her own preferences which were published in a volume entitled *First and Last Loves*. Her choice was spot on. Similarly, John Guest made a brilliant selection of prose to include alongside the poetry in *The Best of Betjeman* in 1978. Many of their choices are included in my selection because they are too good to miss. But I have a wider canvas.

In the end it was his fundamental interest in human life which made him such an extraordinary and sympathetic writer. This shone through in whatever he wrote about, perhaps never more so than in this extract from *The English Town in the Last Hundred Years*.

'I only enjoy to the full the architecture of these islands. This is not because I am deliberately insular, but because there is so much I want to know about a community, its history, its class distinctions, and its literature, when looking at its buildings, that abroad I find myself frustrated by my ignorance. Looking at places is not for me just going to the church or the castle or the "places of interest" mentioned in the guide book, but walking along the streets and lanes as well, just as in a country house I do not like to see the state rooms only, but the passage to the billiard room, where the Spy cartoons are, and the bedrooms where I note the hairbrushes of the owner and the sort of hair-oil he uses. My hunt in a town is not just for one particular thing as an antiquary might look for Romanesque tympana, an art historian for a particular phase of baroque, or an architect for le Corbusier, but it is for the whole town . . . I like to see the railway station, the town hall, the suburbs, the shops, the signs of local crafts being carried on in the backyards. . . . For architecture means not a house, or a single building or a church, or Sir Herbert Baker, or the glass at Chartres, but your surroundings; not a town or a street, but our whole over-populated island.'

JB was inspired by the people, buildings and landscapes of Ireland, of Europe, and of Australia – as this volume testifies. But it was above all this island where he felt at home. The prose he wrote evoking many aspects, public and private, of its people, its poets, its landscapes and its buildings, from the Orkneys to his beloved Cornwall, complements the poetry which has immortalised so many of its foibles, joys, tragedies and glories.

Candida Lycett Green
April 1997

Acknowledgements

I would like to thank the staff at Colindale Library, the Royal Institute of British Architects Library, Neil Somerville at the BBC Archives in Caversham, Colin Stevenson at the London Library, Anthony Spink, Peregrine St Germans, Amabel Lindsay, Jonathan Stedall, Billa Harrod, Andrew Parker Bowles, David Manson and Mike Bushell.

Especial thanks to Nickie Johnson for speed-of-light word processing, Nathan Mayatt for being kind, Endellion for her lovely drawings, Richard Ingrams for wise counsel, Alan Bell for scholarly supervision, Geoffrey Best for tremendous help, my goddaughter Nell Stroud for her clear judgement, my father's godson Matthew Connolly for his quiet brilliance, Michael Earley and Helena Beynon at Methuen for great patience, Peter Gammond, editor of *The Betjemanian*, without whom I would have been sunk, and lastly to Geoffrey Strachan my editor, Desmond Elliott my agent, and Rupert my husband, for their putting up with me.

The editor and publishers have taken all possible care to secure permissions for the extracts used in this volume, and to make the correct acknowledgements and apologise for any errors or omissions. If any errors have occurred, they will be corrected in subsequent editions, provided notification is sent to the publisher. The dates given below indicate those of original publication.

Gentlemen's Follies from *Country Fair (The Country Life Annual,* 1938)

Museums Should be more Attractive, Goodbye to Films, Extracts from Film Reviews from *Evening Standard,* 1934, 1935

Outline and Skyline, Glasgow, The Outer Isles, Elusive Ralph Hodgson, The Rhyme and Reason of Verse, Sheffield, The Buchanan Plan, Non Conformist Architecture, The Ideal Town, Garden Suburbs, The Demolition of Euston Arch from *The Daily Telegraph,* 1953, 1958, 1959, 1960, 1961, 1962, 1964, 1971

A New Westminster, City and Suburban pieces from *Spectator,* 1955, 1956, 1957

The Literary World, High Frecklesby has a Plan, The Lecture from *Punch,* 1953, 1954, 1955

Bristol: An Unspoiled City, The Country Town, How to Look at Books, How to Look at a Church, Some Comments in Wartime, Back to the Railway Carriage, Cooke of Cookesborough, Coming Home, Sabine Baring-Gould, Seeking Whom He May Devour, Aberdeen Granite, Evelyn Waugh, Hawker of Morwenstowe, Church of St Protus, St Mark's, Swindon, Bournemouth, Christmas Nostalgia, Theo Marzials, Polzeath, St Endellion, Childhood Days, South Kentish Town, Augustus Pugin, Kelmscott, Sir Henry Newbolt, The Whitsun Weddings, Thank God it's Sunday, Metroland, A Passion for Churches from BBC, 1937, 1938, 1939, 1940, 1943, 1945, 1946, 1947, 1948, 1949, 1950, 1951, 1952, 1962, 1964, 1972, 1973, 1974

Winter at Home, Aspects of Australia from *Vogue,* 1962

A Hungarian at Eton and Oxford from *The Times,* 1977

The Death of Modernism, Obituary of Frederick Etchells from *The Architectural Review,* 1931, 1973

Maurice Bowra from *Hugh Lloyd-Jones,* 1974

Hardy and Architecture from *The Genius of Thomas Hardy* from *Margaret Drabble,* 1976

Trebetherick from *Both Sides of Tamar* from *Michael Williams,* 1975

Illustrations

========

One:

1920 to 1935

One
1920–1935

JB began to earn his living through writing, at the height of Britain's economic crisis in 1929. His own personal economic crisis started when he was an undergraduate at Oxford and lasted for the rest of his life. This meant he was never able to let up. His confidence had gradually grown from having essays and poems praised and even printed in school magazines, both at the Dragon School in Oxford and Marlborough. By the time he went to Magdalen College, Oxford he felt self-assured and contributed poems and prose pieces to *The Isis* and *The Cherwell*. As his Oxford guru Maurice Bowra pointed out early on, nobody else was remotely like him in their writing or choice of topics.

JB's interest in what was thought to be unusual architecture was already keen and his fascination with the dim and obscure heartfelt. The surroundings of his childhood home in Highgate, the walks on Hampstead Heath, and tram rides and grand railway termini, made indelible impressions. From the Dragon School, set among laburnum and cherry blossom-ed North Oxford streets of spacious Victorian houses, he had ventured out on a bicycle to look at ancient churches. From Marlborough he had found remoter country towns and villages. Exploring his surroundings – whether on the underground to outer London suburbs in the winter holidays or to inland valleys in Cornwall in the summer – became a passionate hobby. With university friends his explorations took him farther afield to country houses in unknown counties. His enthusiasm never waned – whether for eccentric architects or unusual religious sects – and he desperately wanted to impart it to the world.

J. C. Squire, a famous literary figure of the day, who edited *The London Mercury*, spotted this and published his first story 'Lord Mount Prospect' in 1929. JB's first job was as assistant editor on the *Architectural Review* at the age of twenty-three. He earned £300 a year. Bursting with youthful arrogance, he nonetheless toed the line of the

editor, Christian Barman, embracing modern architecture and the
Bauhaus. This grounding, which came at a great architectural turning
point in English taste, was to give him a catholic outlook and a
valuable footing for the rest of his life. From his wide knowledge he
was able to form clear views of what he did and didn't like. He singled
out individualistic architects like Baillie Scott and Charles Voysey. '. . .
Only in England is Voysey not taken at his true value . . . like other
truly modern architects, he is strictly traditional. In common with
them are his attempts to evolve from tradition, not to copy, and to him
"collectivism is the Coward's Cloak".'[1] JB began an article about the
architect James Wyatt: 'On the fifth of September, 1813, a coach
spilled over on the Bath Road on the Savernake Forest side of
Marlborough and spilled out the brains of James Wyatt. Perhaps for
the sake of ARCHITECTURE this was well, for he was so far gone in
Gothic Revival that he would never have built a Classical house
again. . . .'[2]

Lord Beaverbrook, the quirky and independent newspaper magnate,
liked his writers to be as quirky as himself. He spotted JB's article
'Peers without Tears' (written as a freelance for the *Evening Standard*),
which had been sparked off by a debate about reforming the House of
Lords. It eulogised obscure peers such as Lord Roden '. . . who is
extremely interested in high explosives and blows up bits of his
estate. . . .'[3] Beaverbrook wanted JB on his staff and offered him £800 a
year to be film critic on the *Standard*.

The rage for talking pictures had only just begun to hit England and
JB went into writing about them with a fresh and completely
uncluttered mind. He rated Alfred Hitchcock, American gangster
films, '. . . cars racing round corners, dingy rooms with bowler-hatted
thugs swigging whisky and playing dice . . .', and Warner Brothers
musicals which '. . . resemble more often than not a sort of drunkard's
dream. . . . Girls' legs forming a starfish in a bathing pool: Ruby
Keeler's face set in a star repeated twenty times on different parts of a
black screen. The effect is sometimes that of a surrealistic photo
montage. . . . To the average Englishman coming out of a lavish
American musical into the quiet of an English country town, what he
has seen seems to be sheer madness'.[4] He loved Myrna Loy, Claudette
Colbert, Marlene Dietrich, Elizabeth Bergner, Greta Garbo, Kather-
ine Hepburn and Mae West – the last of whom he worshipped. He
interviewed Mary Pickford on the radio and when he went to
interview Jean Parker who was famous for hating parties, he was as
always self-deprecating, 'Even I was a nasty shock to her. When I first

came in with my yellow face, bald head, and bogus "Hail fellow, well met" manner, she was alarmed. She sat staring at me out of enormous blue eyes in stricken silence...."[5]

JB was no run-of-the-mill film hack. He began to pick films for their directors rather than their stars, which was an unusual thing to do in those days, and quite often when he couldn't think of anything to say he would write a little poem (usually saying it was by Wordsworth or Byron). To alleviate the monotony of studio gossip, first nights and viewing rushes, he started going to see new or celebrated cinemas outside central London in such places as Streatham, Hammersmith, Kilburn, Stepney, Acton, Ealing, Northfields, Edgware, Tooting, and Wood Green, and made observations on the districts in which cinemas did their business. He parodied his rivals, 'I am able to reveal exclusively to readers of the *Even*ng N*ws* that Clark Gable, who played with such conspicuous success in *Some Other Tiger*, *No Other Lady*, *Not that Elephant*, *Whirlwind*, *Hurricane*, *Tempest*, *Thunder*, *Cloudburst*, *Tornado Typhoon* ... is to play the lead in Wolf Chastity Pictures' forthcoming production *Macbeth*, Mr Ben Kosh, their chief publicity manager over here informs me.'[6]

By the end of his stint of seeing over five hundred films, in most cases each worse than the last, his greatest interest was in the emergence of the documentary film. His friend Arthur Elton, with whom he had been at Marlborough, worked for the Ministry of Labour, making films about unemployment in Welsh mining villages. The revelation of ordinary Britain in short black and white films excited JB most and these were to influence him and help him when he later began his television career.

His first book of poems *Mount Zion* was published in 1931, by his excessively rich Oxford friend Edward James, and together they chose the entire design from the typeface to the coloured paper. This stoked up JB's interest in typography and layout which had already been awoken both by his work on the *Architectural Review* and his love of the well produced second-hand books which he had begun to collect.

The *Shell Guides* which Jack Beddington the publicity manager of Shell, employed him to mastermind after he left the *Architectural Review* in 1934, combined both innovative layout and a new kind of topographical writing. JB wrote, 'The *Guides* came into existence chiefly because there seemed no half-way house in modern topographical literature between the fulsome paean of a town clerk's brochure and the exhaustive and sometimes exhausting antiquarian accounts published either in local pamphlets or in Methuen's *Little Guides*....

The *Shell Guides* had at once to be critical and selective. They had to illustrate places other than the well-known beauty spots and to mention the disregarded and fast disappearing Georgian landscape of England. . . .'[7] In those days all but the finest Georgian architecture was generally looked down on or ignored by the authors of guide books.

1. 'Charles Francis Annesley Voysey, the Architect of Individualism', *Architectural Review*, October 1931.
2. *Architectural Review*, March 1932.
3. 'Peers Without Tears', *Evening Standard*, 19 December 1933.
4. 'Costumes, settings, backgrounds', *Footnotes to the Film*, ed. Charles Davy (Lovat Dickson, 1937).
5. *Evening Standard*, 15 July 1935.
6. 'Shakespeare on the Screen', *Press Gang*, ed. Leonard Russell (Hutchinson, 1937).
7. *A Shell Guide to Typography*, 1937.

A Stained Glass Window

Printed in The Draconian,
September 1920, when JB was fourteen.

The sun was sinking in an almost cloudless sky, as the old man, with his head reverently bowed, passed up the sombre nave of the lofty cathedral. Before him in all its magnificence stood the high altar, the candles already lit for evening service. He turned and faced the west window, through which the parting rays of the sun were shining. Seen from the choir, the colours melted into one another like clouds gathering in the sky. Among beautiful foliage and soft green grass sprinkled with daisies, stood the figure of St Francis with uplifted cowl of poverty.

There was St George with uplifted sword aiming a great blow at the dragon, which writhed at his feet spitting fire and clouds of inky smoke. Above these two panels were emblazoned the coats of arms of rich benefactors, in gold and red, with Latin inscriptions and strange proverbs. In the centre, on a lonely hill with the turrets of Jerusalem in the distance, the Crucifixion.

The sun disappeared behind the house-tops and the pictures faded. The bells echoed down the aisles, and the old man took his accustomed seat.

Our Lovely Lodging-houses!

Printed in The Isis, *October 1926,*
when JB was twenty.

Let us open that yellow 'grained oak' front door whose upper panels of stained glass foretell what may be ecclesiastical within. The clouds of Irish stew make the gloom more impenetrable and the elaborate bamboo umbrella-stand more emphatic than ever. Clutching the rather greasy knob of the pitch pine bannisters, we ascend to the front room.

Two ill-proportioned staring plate-glass windows gape at the Gothico-Norman architecture of the red and grey brick houses opposite, framed in coffee-coloured lace curtains neatly looped with pale blue ribbon. The interspace of the windows contains a lithograph of Our Lord on one of the mountains around Palestine. Its colours are dimmed by the begonias and roses in a reddish-brown relief on a green background which constitute the wallpaper. Although its floral effect may be interesting, even valuable, this paper does not serve to lighten the room. However, it forms a good set-off for the most prominent feature, the chimney-piece. The grate is framed in richly-coloured tiles and an unobtrusive mantelpiece is hung with red cloth fringed with bobbles and draped in semi-circles.

Indeed may the landlady be proud of the overmantel which surmounts the slab. It is a Jacobean-classical structure which wriggles its way to the ceiling shooting out mirrors and brackets left and right and terminating in a debased broken pediment that nibbles the insignificant plaster cornice. And what a wealth of art this overmantel holds! The upper brackets, supported on pillars like stretched sweets, are riddled with Goss china in the form of ships, swans and lighthouses emblazoned with the arms of Whitby, Leamington and Ashton-under-Lyne; the lower brackets contain vases for a single carnation in the irreproachable manner of the eighties and little 'quaint' brass figures which betray a later stage of artistic development. The central mirror on the mantel itself reflects a black cat calendar for 1924 and a goo-goo baby doll that were given by a former undergraduate tenant to the landlady, together with the two Bonzo pictures on the east wall.

Of the other furniture of the room little may be said. A slender stand of deal, after an Edwardian design, supports a beaten copper bowl from which flops a magnificent aspidistra. A cupboard into which nothing will fit is painted black and picked out in gold; it supports a fumed oak bookshelf in the Elliston and Cavell manner. The pictures – photographs and oleographs – are either sacred or military. The chairs have sweetly pretty red, yellow and olive green covers and are of beech after an 1890 Jacobean-Rococo-Gothic design.

To an undergraduate who is in the least susceptible to hideousness, this compulsory residence will prove so restless that he cannot work in it, or else it will eat into his very soul, so that an overmantel is a thing to be tolerated – even liked. He cannot move the furniture for fear of offending the landlady, had he the money to buy new. It would, surely, not be difficult to make it compulsory for landladies to put up plain papers, to remove overmantels and aspidistras, and gradually to replace all their furniture with something unobtrusive, were it even 'arts and crafts'.

But no. That brings us even more horrible vistas . . . I can imagine a landlady getting a mania for art cushions and craft salt-cellars . . . the first bright yellow and black, the second unpourable but well meaning . . . Ugh! Then there would be orange-coloured napkins draped over the electric light. And as for calendars – well, a black cat is one thing, but a fabulous beast with art feet and craft tail is indisputably another. We could never stand all that. For at least, now, we are stimulated by the horror of what we see. We are not slowly and insidiously having our mentalities gutted by the atrocious abortions of feeble-minded young ladies working in community schools.

So it's a bad business, whatever happens. Surely the powers that be are under obligation to us to see that something is done?

Oh, YOU DELEGATES OF LODGINGS – STIR YOUR-SELVES! Or are you a council of landladies?

Lord Mount Prospect

Whenever I sit down to my solitary meal of an evening, I am put in mind of the many obscure Irish peers who are sitting down to theirs. Some, perhaps, in a room over the stables, gaze at the moonlit ruins of what once was a stately mansion; others sip port as the Adam decoration peels off the ceiling and falls with an accustomed thud to the floor. The wind sighs and sings through the lonely Irish night round the wet walls of every house and down each grass-grown drive until it causes even the stable bell to tinkle, although the clock has long ago ceased to work. Such thoughts as these divert me and such thoughts as these produced the narrative which I am about to relate.

It was after a dinner where the food and the wine and the guests were well selected, where there was an absence of academic friction and where an aromatic content had settled in upon us, that the germ of an important society came into being. Did we not follow a tradition handed down in our Universities by Wesley, Heber, Tennyson and Wilde? The Society for the Discovery of Obscure Peers was militantly charitable from its outset. It was produced in the glow caused by good food and drink, it was later to burst with good intentions that would fall on Ireland like Golden Rain. A desultory conversation upon the acute condition of that country had led up to speculations upon its grander inhabitants. There was that comforting lightness about the talk which unites the intelligent.

How kind it would be, we considered, if we were to arrange a dinner for the obscurer Irish peers! It was very sensibly suggested that some of them might not be able to afford the fare to England so that a meal in their own country should be arranged, if their own country could provide it. With such a spirit of unselfishness the society was formed, an example not so much of the waste of talent and pettifogging machinations of the pedant, as of the oblique large-heartedness that typifies a University. The following rules, unwritten but telling, were composed:

1. *Who's Who* shall be accepted as the Truth.

2. Any distinction, regarded by the Society as distinguished, disqualifies the peer.

This rule would not affect, for instance, Lord Pentagon who states in *Who's Who* that he is vice-Chairman of the Ballysligo Branch of the Church of Ireland Jubilee Fund Administrative Committee.

3. A peer who is known to a member of the Society is disqualified.
4. A younger brother or son and heir does not count.

The method of selecting an object for our charity was similar to that used by those with simple faith in the Bible and who have no doubts about the Minor Prophets. *Who's Who* was opened at random. The nearest peer who conformed to the Society's rules was chosen and every effort was made to get into touch with him.

The usual device was to write and say we were interested in electrical matters and proposed erecting a plant on his estate. This plan was abandoned after the trouble with Lord Octagon. He replied on crimson notepaper and said he would be delighted to see his correspondent.

Our member set out for the west of Ireland. Octagon Abbey was a glorious extravaganza of the eighteenth century. Within it sat Lord Octagon surrounded by Indian relics collected by his ancestors and by himself. At great expense he had had electric eels imported into his own fishponds. His knowledge of electricity was amazing. With fanatical fervour he explained his device for breeding the eels and conserving their electricity by means of a plant which he intended our member to establish at the edge of the ponds. It was three months before Lord Octagon could be induced to abandon the scheme, three months of anxiety for members, both at home and abroad.

Then there was the other plan of introduction: – 'Would you be so good as to allow me to consult your library, where I believe there are some valuable sixteenth-century editions of Virgil?' Lord Santry, who is one of our staunchest supporters, replied in the kindest way. He welcomed the request of the member chosen for the task. Soon after his arrival at Cahir Santry, our member was informed of his host's translation of the libretto of all the Savoy operas into Latin Hexameters. The first three volumes have cost the society more than it can reasonably be expected to pay.

I suppose we had collected something like ninety peers and were considering the extension of our membership in order that a successful dinner might be provided when the problem of Lord Mount Prospect arose.

It was not usual for our letters to be disregarded. Persons as lonely as the objects of our charity become excited even on the receipt of an advertisement. For weeks and weeks they gaze out of their castles at the surrounding swamp, unable, probably, to reach the nearest village owing to the torrents of rain and the floods which mirror the leaden sky. Then, when Summer comes, and with it a ray of sunlight, they are overjoyed to get a letter from the outside world.

But not so Lord Mount Prospect. The *Who's Who* was loose in the binding and the pages torn and thumbed like a directory outside a public telephone box when we discovered his name. In truth, the mission of the society was nearly accomplished; there were few obscure peers left and the fervour and charity which had started our project was waning under disillusion. For the most part our peers were happy in their gloomy mansions, they showed real pleasure as the footman brought in the oil lamps and they could settle down to a long evening of cutting out jigsaw puzzles or pasting half-penny stamps on to a fire screen.

We were, then, somewhat disappointed to find the name of Lord Mount Prospect: but even the most lukewarm among us was stimulated by the odd way in which he announced himself.

MOUNT PROSPECT (10th Visc:) cr: 1684. Archibald Standish CosPatrick Reeve. b: 1849. An Ember Day Bryanite. Address: – Mount Prospect, County Galway.

What is an Ember Day Bryanite? With trembling hands we turned to Haydn's *Dictionary of Dates*. Allow me to quote from Haydn's *Dictionary of Dates* (1871):

EMBER DAY BRYANITES is the name given to an obscure sect which was founded by William Bryan, a tailor of Paternoster Row, London, and his cousin John Reeve, a chandler in the city of Exeter. These two declared to the world in 1717 that they were the two witnesses mentioned in Rev. XI.3. 'And I will give power unto my two witnesses and they shall prophesy a thousand, two hundred and three-score days, clothed in sackcloth.' They hold many curious beliefs among which the chief is that God came down in person on to the cross and left Elijah as vice-regent in Heaven. They believe in a bodily resurrection and the sleep of the soul. They declare that the sun is four miles from the earth. The sect was still in existence according to the census in 1851.

That spirit of research and curiosity which made possible the forthcoming adventure prompted me to visit a deserted part of North London during the autumn of last year. Could it be that Ember Day Bryanites were still prophesying away up the Caledonian Road? Could it be that even now tired charwomen and weary tailors dressed themselves in sackcloth to listen? Under 'Places of Worship' in the *London Directory* I wondered at the hopeful signs I found. Last and almost least beneath 'Other Denominations', below the Particular Baptists, and the Peculiar People, below the Sandemanians and Independent Calvinistics, came the glorious words, 'Ember Day Bryanite' and the address, 'Hungerford Green, Barnsbury, N.1.'

Fortified with a long and beautiful lunch which lasted until the time when the others have tea I trod out into the Sunday evening. There was a waiting hush about the Gothic Revival steeples which pricked the starlit London sky: the well-lit thrills of evensong were hardly in preparation and electric light had not yet thrown up the full richness of nineteenth-century glass which was to stream on to the pavement without.

But what a change met my eye as I left the black brick station, vast and deserted, near the Caledonian Road and saw the fervour of North London's religious life! Above the noise of tram-car bells, above the gear changing of the cheaper motor cars, for this day no longer commercial, and back from the deep joys of Epping and Chingford, above the rich peal of a parish church and the insistent tinkle of a chapel-of-ease urgently in need of funds could be heard quavering sopranos and the cockney hoarseness of men and women pronouncing a warning of the wrath to come. There they stood, amid listless little groups, gathered inside turnings off the main road. Some political, many religious and most neither the one nor the other but vaguely connected with anti-vivisection or the suppression of the Jews, they prophesied with equal fervour of a doom hanging perilously near us.

Small wonder that my progress was slow towards the pleasant little hill embellished with low stucco houses that led up to Hungerford Green! Small wonder that I almost changed my mind as I caught the bright eyes of a thin bearded gentleman proving the inevitability of another deluge. The silence of the empty streets upon the hill enveloped me with the uneasy comfort of a blanket. Only the knowledge of my curious goal urged me on.

Hungerford Green was attractive enough. It was a relic of successful Regency commerce. Two-storeyed houses, once 'tight boxes, neatly sashed', surrounded an oblong space of burnt grass with a curious pavilion in the middle, some conceit of a former merchant aping the gazebos of the great and good. The railings round the grass were sadly bent to make loopholes for dogs and children, the noble urns of ironwork were battered: from all over Hungerford Green came the whooping of hymns loud enough to stream through ventilating spaces in the pointed windows of Baptist and Wesleyan chapel. The worn grass was bright with the rays of gaslight from the places of worship, with an additional brightness from the outside lamp of a more prosperous chapel where electric light had been installed.

Joyous opening strains of an hearty nonconformist service! How anxious was I to know under what gas or electric light Ember Day Bryanites, possibly in sackcloth, were even now praising the Lord! And so, reining my enthusiasm with happy delay, I asked a girl whether she knew which was the chapel of the Ember Day Bryanites. She burst into those whooping shrieks maid-servants affect on a round-about. A sympathetic but dreary woman beside her, yellower and more miserable, suggested that perhaps I meant the Baptist Chapel. When I replied that I did not, a sad long nasal negative streamed out of her mouth and nose.

With no faint heart I walked round the green, yet fearful of breaking silence with irreligious feet, and I scanned the names on black and gilded notice boards. 'Congregational', 'Primitive Methodist', 'United Methodist', 'New Jerusalem', 'Presbyterian Church of England', and the last was the last of the lighted chapels which made glorious Hungerford Green. It could not be that the directory was wrong or that my eyes had betrayed me.

There in the remotest corner of the place was the black pedimented outline of an enormous building, more like a warehouse than anything else. As I approached I saw a space of green before it boldly sheltering a struggling plane tree. But the gates of the pathway were padlocked and a street lamp showed that the path was almost grass. No light or sound came from the great edifice in front, the hymns of the neighbouring chapels had died down to spontaneous prayer and only the Sunday roar of North London disturbed the air.

I scaled the rusty railing that protected the grass before the chapel building. The plot was bigger and darker than I had supposed and the chapel loomed so large and high on my approach that it was almost as if it had moved forward to interrupt me. It was plain and square with a coating of plaster which had peeled in many places and fallen on to the untidy grass below.

I could just discern a printed notice about an electoral roll, years old and clinging limply to its inefficient paste. The double rows of windows were bolted and boarded up. The great doors were shut. But beside them was a wooden notice board with the remains of lettering still upon it. I struck a match and read:

> THOSE WHO ARE CHOSEN FOR HIS
> COURTS ABOVE WILL MEET HERE
> (GOD WILLING) ON THE LORD'S
> DAY AT 11 A.M. AND AT 6.30.
> Holy Supper by Arrangement.

The Lord had received his Ember Day Bryanites.

Meanwhile the Society had not been idle in its attempts to form an acquaintanceship with Lord Mount Prospect nor had it failed to follow them with experiments more daring. The silence of his Lordship and the mystery which surrounded his name made even the idea of his existence uncertain. A member had written, after a careful study of the geological and political maps of County Galway, professing an interest in the peat bog which extended for some miles round Mount Prospect. His personal and delicately worded letter had evinced no reply. Undeterred by this he had stolen some paper from the *Methodist Recorder* and written to suggest an Union of the Methodist and Ember Day Bryanite churches. He had been equally unsuccessful.

Notwithstanding, he conceived a bolder proposition. It is a general rule that Irish peers are interested in natural history; at considerable expense and with no little trouble, a large rhinoceros, stuffed and redecorated during the latter part of the last century, was moved with little regret from the spacious hall of a member's country mansion. It was packed by a firm which was intimately connected with the Natural History Museum and transported to Ireland. The duty levied by the Free State government was enormous.

Three months later the rhinoceros was returned. The workmen had been unable to find the road to Mount Prospect and had wandered about Galway for the greater part of a fortnight. Being English they found it hard to get into communication with the inhabitants. When they finally discovered the way to Lord Mount Prospect's estate they were unable to reach it.

Although it was high summer (the flies and the other insects must have been unpleasant, while even the peat bogs must have been withered in their very channels), the swamps around Mount Prospect were impassable. In a letter, the contractors attempted to describe, in what terms commercial language will allow, the state of things which their employees had encountered. There were large bridges along the road which had either been blown up in the 'trouble' or fallen into ruin; vehicular traffic had not been known to go to His Lordship's estate within the memory of the said natives, and so the firm regretted inability re animal as per contract and would beg to return the same to hand.

The news of the final extinction of the Ember Day Bryanites in London, which I was able to bring before the Society, filled all with gloom and disappointment, but it did not quench the re-awakened ardour. A letter was sent to every obscure peer befriended by the Society, seeking information, in a tactful manner, of Lord Mount Prospect. Only three had heard his name, none had seen him and only one supplied information. This was Lord Octagon whose tales were clearly untrue.

We pictured fearful scenes in the silent mansion of Mount Prospect – a skeleton sitting in a ruined dining room grinning over a now very aged glass of port, a corpse rotting between sheets of coroneted Irish linen.

The natural course was to go to the *Daily Express* and suggest a 'scoop' which would at the same time replenish the funds of the Society. A lord who was the very reverse of all that we stood for kindly undertook the unearthing of Lord Mount Prospect. For a week he was mentioned in the social columns. The Dragoman saw him at Tooth's Galleries looking at a fascinating exhibition of the etchings of the insides of railway engines by Frank Brangwyn. He met him at a party in St John's Wood where everyone was dressed as a clergyman, later in the same evening he met him at another party where everyone was dressed as a policeman.

Possibly some of my readers may remember what happened after this. He was removed to the front page of the paper. He had been about to make an ascent in a balloon from Sydenham when he was kidnapped. 'THE MISSING PEER' was billed all over London for three days. But the 'scoop' failed. No reply came from Lord Mount Prospect safe in his castle in Ireland.

The wet weather had by now settled down and it was hopeless to attempt the journey through Galway until the next summer. At

Christmas a present of handkerchiefs was sent, purporting to come from a poor relation in Harringay. But it, too, met with no response. After this the practical efforts of the Society ceased until next year should render personal investigation possible.

'Oh! *My* prestidigitation
Is the bulwark of the nation
And *I* like my new creation
  As Mi-Lord High Conjurer-er-er.
  Chorus:
    'Oh! *His* prestidigitation
    Is the bulwark of the nation
    And *he* likes *his* new creation
      As The Lord High Conjurer-er-er-er-er.'

With an irregular rattling the persons behind the scenes tugged the curtain across the stage. The applause was deafening and for the fifth time the curtain was pulled apart; and for the last time, for the temporary nature of the fittings had caused it to stick and there stood the actors, sweat glistening through their grease paint, their smiles happy.

There was a renewed burst of clapping; the spirit of fun was not dead yet. For a sixth, seventh and up to an eleventh time the enraptured audience called for an encore of that wonderful final chorus. The curtains stood ominously apart. The humourless stage manager turned out the lights on the stage. Peers and their wives in the front, army men, clergymen and their families in the back, retained the calm of good breeding until the lights were switched on in the hall.

We had known that Gilbert and Sullivan would work miracles. The exquisite humour of that last chorus of the *Bunundrum*, where the hero becomes Chief Conjurer in the land of Og-a-gog after all that trouble with the wicked emperor, the sense of satire and kindly irony that runs through the whole play, the clean wit not unworthy of the pages of *Punch*, and the perfect poetry of some of the serious bits which show that Gilbert could write serious stuff as well, make the *Bunundrum* one of the best of the Savoy operas. Of course, like them all, it has been repeated daily ever since eighteen-eighty-eight; but it does not lose by repetition. No great works of art do, do they?

The clouds were lying low, but not unpleasantly, over the peat bog and a traveller might have descried, sandwiched between the clouds and the brown earth, little figures delving and hurrying. Were he to have approached closer he would have seen that the figures were of people obviously clever. Some wore spectacles and little used cricket shirts, others had bought their ties in Paris.

The road to Mount Prospect was being repaired. The funds of the Society, replenished by the Gilbert and Sullivan performance, had paid for a thoroughly successful dinner for obscure peers which was held in the Shelborne Hotel in Dublin. The speeches were rather long.

With the money left over we were able to hire implements and horses. Like Ruskin we set to work to build a road. The track climbed a slight hill after many miles along the flat bog and lying below it we saw a black pool whose water was strangely still. The silence was intensified by a sound as of distant applause too half-hearted for Gilbert and Sullivan. It was water lapping and licking the granite on the hill-side shore of the pool. This edge was white with the powder of the ground stone, ground by ages of black water. The remaining shores were of reeds and meadow-sweet which disappeared into a blue and distant hill.

Mount Prospect at last in view! Eagerly we stumbled down the declivity of the shore of the lake and there it was that a surprise unnerved us. This nether shore was littered with paper so that it might well have been a Surrey beauty spot, and only when we examined the paper closely did we discover that it was not. Thousands of unopened envelopes and parcels lay everywhere. Upon them 'Viscount Mount Prospect' was written in the fading hands of many generations. Someone discovered a package less sodden than most others and battered by but one year's Christmas storms. It was just possible to read the word Harringay on the postmark, while within, the dye had not yet come off six cheap pocket handkerchiefs.

As we were discussing how to cross the lake and the marsh beyond it to where the blue hill swam, a Zion, before our eyes, a postman, black against the skyline, emptied a solitary letter down the slope.

For over a week the sound of hammers and axes resounded on the shore of the black lake. A flat-bottomed boat was built, slim yet not ungainly, and a happy band paddled away in it down the stream that led out of all that black water.

For many hours the weeds and rushes were too high to give a view of the landscape. The dark water writhed with tentacles of water-weed undisturbed for, probably, more than a century. The stream twisted so abruptly enclosing us in tall prisons of reed, black water and grey sky, that conversation was awed into silence broken by the bravado of community singing.

Now and then we went up backwaters and had to turn, and once we were confronted with a broken bridge in a style formerly Indian, now decayed beyond repair. Here and there, swans, more wild than the wildest of song and story, rushed hissing and flapping on our little party from the dark deep bends of the stream, possibly angered by the community singing. The lights were long among some tattered beech trees when we moored our boat beside the Taj Mahal.

But is the Taj Mahal covered with pink stucco? And are there curious Gothic pinnacles behind it? Has the central dome collapsed so that it looks like a diseased onion? Is there grass along the avenues? and if there are beech trees and box hedges around the Taj Mahal, are they overgrown and straggling?

So long as the lingering day lasted we trod among the deserted courtyards and sparsely furnished rooms – incongruously Adam and Chippendale within – whose fittings and mildewed portraits, whose hangings and crumbling walls, whose awful silence was stirred only by the hum of a late fly, the squeak of bat or the little ticking noises of hurrying beetles. Nowhere was there sign of living person or lifeless corpse. This was Ireland indeed. This was a romantic and poetical finale to a beautiful story. Lord Mount Prospect did not exist. He had been caught up in a bodily resurrection to sit for ever with other Ember Day Bryanites.

Such were our thoughts and such they would have remained had we not entered what we had taken to be the back of the house but which turned out to be but another front. Genius of optical illusions, you eighteenth-century builder! What appeared to be the Taj Mahal on one side was like a very rough sketch of the West Front of Peterborough Cathedral on the other. It, too, was pink in order that the sun might always appear to be setting across pinnacle and crocket.

A vast door showed us the way into a bare chapel with walls of dark Pompeian red. The building was lit by frosted glass fixed into windows boldly representing the pointed style. Never was there so much dust. Yet the eyes involuntarily turned to the pulpit, placed, as in all chapels, where the altar rests in a papistical church.

In the dim light we could see that this plain wooden pulpit, raised above the rows of empty pews, was a welter of papers, piled up to the very sounding board and encumbering the winding staircase. Then –

oh! horror! – a black-gowned figure, whose head was a skull off which all but the spectacles had withered, whose arm rested on a pile of papers, and whose fleshless finger kept a place – a dumb, still, black-gowned figure was propped upright against the papers.

Some time passed of clicking silence before anyone ventured near the sight. When the bravest did so, it was only to see that the papers were all a discourse, and that the fingers rested at the phrase 'and three thousand, two hundred and thirty-secondly. . . .' Lord Mount Prospect has preached his longest sermon and the mourners go about the streets.

The London Mercury

The Death of Modernism

A serious comment on architecture must always be in the nature of a sermon. Today it is impossible to get away from buildings. Their importance increases with the disappearance of rural scenery. Rapidly every inhabitable part of the world is becoming industrialised, and communities which formerly possessed a creative art of their own, by coming into contact with the rest of the world, imbibe another culture – the culture of industrialisation. Nor should we despair that there is no longer a city which is unexplored, no longer a country replete with eighteenth-century towns of mellow houses and spacious streets, nor even an island of medieval towers and fortresses that is not strung across with wires and scarred with tarmac roads. Only the swamps and thick tropical forests remain and on them it is impossible to build. We have prepared and planned the world beyond recognition, and can hardly be blamed for not turning our attention to the rubbish heap.

In England, with a brave pathos, many, though not all, of the older architects and speculative builders have followed only the mannerisms instead of the spirit of tradition and created an architecture like stage scenery. In the middle of this country of pylons, telegraph poles, factories and water towers, of moving vehicles whose shapes, never devised before, play as important a part in civic life as the stationary objects, they have deluded themselves that the link with tradition is the reproduction of the mere façade of the past. Hardly a villa rises without its half-timber, hardly a front door without its stained glass to hide the world. Hardly a monumental building is erected which is not masking some honest English face behind. On the ground floor the show is given away, for the feet of the honest person peep through. Palpably it would be impossible for that large acreage of shop window thinly divided by pilasters to support the weight of so many storeys of cosmopolitan masonry above, if the building were indeed the stone palace it pretends to be. No amount of skill will disguise the fact that it is a man in fancy dress; no bronze or mahogany devices increase the solidity of that ground floor and the thin pilasters. The truth will out, even when rustications are suspicious. This is a needless break with traditional architecture, as unnatural as it is pedantic, as superficial as the plaster work on Strawberry Hill. These architects and builders have bravely tried to keep to forms of the past, although their plans and materials demanded other proportions.

The revolting phrase 'The Battle of the Styles,' wherein architecture is now considered a fighting ground between old gentlemen who imitate the Parthenon and brilliant young men who create abstract designs, can only have been coined by the stupid extremists of either side. There is no battle for the intelligent artist. The older men gradually discard superfluties. The younger men do not ignore the necessary devices of the past. Both sides find their way slowly to the middle of the maze, whose magic centre is tradition.

What conflict there is, exists only between the principles of Gothic architecture and of the Renaissance. In the former the design is influenced by the construction: in the latter, the façade is designed and the rooms are fitted in behind it. It is therefore a Gothic revival to which the more sensible are tending.

In an extraordinary article which appeared in the October issue of the *Architectural Review* Mr C. F. A. Voysey, one of the oldest of living architects, used an old-fashioned word 'Gothic.' He has probably been misunderstood by those whose minds are not yet rid of 'period' taste. They will have taken him to mean by 'Gothic,' machicolations, and crockets, pierced hearts and artiness, which are but the trappings of medievalism.

Voysey means by Gothic the architecture of necessity. The Crystal Palace is Gothic, far more Gothic than the St Pancras Hotel. 'We must remember,' he writes, 'that this revolt against styleism and pursuit of utilitarianism was in the womb years before, and was the child of Science and the Prince Consort.' The influence of Voysey has been felt all over the Continent and is just being noticed in England, while the more prolific Gilbert Scott has faded out of existence.

Gothic, in the sense that Voysey used it, was even put into practice in the early days of Strawberry Hill Gothic. Those silent country boxes, with their decent fittings and well-planned interiors, expressed the needs of the aristocratic eighteenth century. Inside and out they had become traditional, shorn of the gaudier eccentricities of contemporary architecture abroad. Later, when the pseudo-Gothic of the late nineteenth century was reasoned out of existence, traditional English domestic architecture, by Voysey, and, in a lesser degree, Lutyens, Dawber, and Baillie Scott, again emerged. From the present sightless mass of Greek, Roman, Tudor and Cubist, we are waiting for some monumental architecture to appear that will be fit to house our numberless offices and flats. It is an architecture for artists and not for scholars. There are new materials, a new social order, new proportions to be commanded, and the possibility of creating a new beauty which this generation must not be too stultified to see.

The word 'modern' is becoming old-fashioned. It is used by one writer to describe the latest effort of the oldest old stager, by another, some building of Corbusier. Perhaps it were better to do away with it altogether and to discriminate traditional from what poses as such. And traditional architecture, while conscious of the claims of humanism, draws its vitality from the needs inherent in construction. This is the Gothic characteristic, and it is leading to the true Gothic Revival.

Architectural Review

'Upper School'

For this incident of my early youth I will probably be accused of disloyalty to my old school. If such a true account is disloyalty, then I am guilty. But I ought in justice to Marlborough, to say that the custom I have here described has now been abolished. Although 'Upper School,' with its many inhabitants still exists, I believe that its autocracy is altogether altered for the better. This account may seem to my contemporaries highly coloured. I merely describe it as it struck *me*. But then I was an unpleasant little boy, morbidly sensitive in some matters and 'highly strung.'

I never liked Crossman and I am sure I should not like him if I were to meet him now. He oiled up to the Bishop, who was the school 'Visitor.' He did his prep without the aid of a translation. He was a great pet with some of the masters. When he left school and went to Cambridge he was a great lad at the Palais de Danse, and had a topping little two-stroke motor-bike. The money that was supposed to be training him for Holy Orders he spent on morning coffee at a dashing Cambridge Café. Somehow his was always the jolly face that greeted me when first I returned from the holidays. 'Bad luck, Betjeman, you're still in Boggins's form.' And he, knowing Boggins, knew what awful bad luck it was, and grinned. Characteristically he was the first person to bring me the most terrifying piece of news I have ever had in my life. 'They're going to put you in the basket to-night, Betjeman.'

For those who have not been through 'in-college' life at Marlborough shortly after the war, I must explain what 'putting in the basket' means. There are six senior in-college houses, and thirty-five boys from each, the toughest and the youngest, live during the day, in an enormous barn-like structure called 'Upper School.' It is about as large as the Horticultural Hall. It smells of old biscuits and bat oil, and is lined with desks, save at one end, where there is a clearing so that the bloods may play indoor hockey. The bloods have double desks, chaps like me have small ones. If your desk is 'unflush' during prep, that is to say, so full of books that it will not close down properly, you are publicly beaten by a boy, known as a 'captain,' when prep is over.

Marlborough is a cold place, hundreds of feet above sea-level and in beautiful downland country. In Upper School there are two fires. One is known as 'Big Fire.' Four captains, chosen entirely because they are good at games, are allowed to sit here and the four captains choose about a dozen other boys, also good at games, to sit with them. The other one hundred and seventy boys crowd around the other fire, known as 'Little Fire,' or sit on hotwater pipes in those parts of the school to which they are allowed access.

'Big Fire' rules Upper School. It is true that a master comes in twice a day to take prep, but otherwise no person in authority enters the place. 'By the boys for the boys' – that's the rule and with it all the advantages of communal life. Sometimes one house is not represented at 'Big Fire,' and suffers accordingly. My house was bad at work, bad at games and not keen on the OTC. It was not represented at 'Big Fire,' and not very keen on it.

The most fearful disgrace which Marlborough can thrust you into is the basket. Your friends desert you. It only happens a few times a year, but it is as bad as expulsion. In after-life Marlburians chatting about old times in the bars of local golf clubs will say: 'Oh – Betjeman! – not much of a chap. He was put in the basket, wasn't he?' It is in the power of that tough autocracy, 'Big Fire,' to put you in the basket.

This is the process. There are two large wastepaper baskets in the Upper School. During the half hour after 6.30 tea, before 'prep' begins, 'Big Fire' (with the captains watching at the door) comes in and seizes the victim. His clothes are taken off save his shirt, and he is thrust into one of the baskets, filled with apple cores and wastepaper, by the fags. Sometimes ink, sometimes paper and sometimes only obloquy is poured on his head. He is allowed to remain on exhibition until just before prep begins, when he is allowed to go and 'stamped out' of the building. When he returns to prep, the master in charge asks why he is late. 'Put in the basket, sir.' The master nods. It does a fellow good. He has probably been suspected of thieving or worn coloured socks before he had been in Upper School three times or . . . never mind. Boys know each other best. There is nothing like the moral indignation of someone who is fifteen or sixteen. Besides the fellow was unpopular.

I disliked Upper School so much that I used to keep my books in a basement where they cleaned the boots. When Crossman told me that I was to be put in the basket, I felt too sick to make a gay retort. I can see his smug figure now, as he went off to morning work, his preparation done, his clothes shiny and patched by some loving mother in a rectory. All that day I could do no work. Put in the basket. I tried to think of what I had done wrong and remembered too much. I tried to be cheerful. I distinctly saw two boys in my house standing talking and looking at me. When I passed a group I thought I heard my name mentioned. In the hall I could eat nothing. The afternoon came and evening prep was nearer. Then came 6.30 hall. No one ate much. There was a lot of talking. 'Someone's going to be basketed. . . . I say, Betjeman, someone's going to be put in the basket.' When the master in charge of the hall let us go, there was a rush to the doors and across the court to Upper School. Even the greediest left his eating. There was no escape. If 'Big Fire' did not catch me today, it would tomorrow. I got up and walked slowly across the dark gravel to Upper School. The same smell of old biscuits and bat oil was there. The gas lights were on. But there was a listlessness and excitement everywhere.

Inside, boys were walking down the alley-way between the desks. At one of them someone was sitting and pretending to read *The Autocar*. People passed by, as if by accident, just to catch a glimpse of his face. But no one came near him.

'It's Pringle.' So it wasn't me after all. I felt I had better wait to see if the glorious news were true. They might be going to put two of us in. At five to seven, 'Big Fire' came in. Popington, an enormous fellow, as red as beef with a tiny head, and Spewett, a boy like a cod, and a 'cert' for a forty-cap next year, whom I never wish to see again, were followed by six or eight satellites. They walked straight up to Pringle and took hold of him. He offered feeble resistance. They took off nearly all his clothes. Then a pot was fetched, and he was smeared all over with red paint. We stood on desks and in clearings craning over each other's shoulders, watching in silence. An infant prodigy near me who was always a good little boy, gave a skip of self-righteous delight because he was not being put in himself. There was no noise now except the creak of the basket. 'Big Fire' hoisted it with Pringle in it on to a table that had been placed on a desk. We could just see Pringle's brown eyes through the slats. 'Big Fire' stood around, smiling knowingly or looking official, ready to give the basket a stir if it were needed. Just before prep started, and the captains came in beating their canes on the desks for the fags to start cleaning up the floor, Pringle emerged. We stamped as he walked out, a bedraggled figure, carrying his trousers on one arm, and in his hand a pair of very pointed black shoes.

From *Little Innocents*

Museums Should Be More Attractive

I wonder how many people went to have a look at the magnified flea yesterday? Or how many have pressed the button of Stephenson's 'Rocket'? Or have you been standing rapt in front of a seventeenth-century font cover?

Three sorts of people go to museums. Donors: Students: People-who-don't-generally-go-to-museums.

Donors or lenders go to museums because they like to feel a certain pride of possession. I am a donor myself, so I know. Once a year I used to put a horse chestnut in an empty case in an obscure part of the Geological Museum in Piccadilly. I had the pleasure of writing the label myself: 'Betjeman Bequest: Horse chestnut picked up in Ireland, 1933. Do not touch.' For three years they remained undisturbed. Now the Geological is moving to South Kensington and I hope the authorities will at last discover my horse chestnuts and move them to South Kensington, too.

Museums start with a decided disadvantage. However much you may like an object, be it a Chippendale chair or an assegai, you know that it can never be yours, however rich you may become. It belongs vaguely to the State and to those suspicious keepers who are watching you. It also belongs to the museum officials.

So long as the Englishman's home is his castle and he likes owning things, museums as they are at present will remain only fairly popular. In Russia, where the State is the castle, every village has its museum just as inevitably as every English village has its public house.

Then the museums follow up the disadvantage by adding to themselves another one. They are housed, and I am thinking of the Victoria and Albert Museum in particular, in buildings that would be more suitable as a political club or a training college for Government officials.

It is infuriating to be looking at an Adam chimney-piece and to find one's attention diverted by an elaborate and tasteless archway that is part of the building itself. It is equally annoying to glimpse through the skeleton of a mammoth a terracotta imitation of part of Salisbury

Cathedral, as one does at the Natural History Museum. And when there is a certain similarity between the architecture and the exhibit the effect is even more confusing.

One must be fair to the museums. They can't help their buildings now. And, after all, the British Museum and the London Museum are lovely structures.

But with such decided disadvantages it is hardly surprising that English museums, unlike those in Germany and France, which are better arranged, are popularly regarded as mausoleums or convenient places for an assignation. So the English museums are the haunt of students. Pale young interior decorators looking for colour schemes; cunning furniture manufacturers copying Jacobean designs; bearded clergymen examining credences; etymologists, entomologists, eschatologists, geologists, Egyptologists, anthropologists; Coptic critics, cryptic Coptics, Indians, Bloomsburians, Hampsteadians and Welwyners; all of whom are interested in dates and classification and who want to see everything in the world reduced to one great catalogue.

This is a quite justifiable idea. But it is not popular. My contention is that museums should be popular.

They should therefore be divided into two sorts. One sort for specialists, the other sort for people who don't generally go to museums.

The Geological, the Natural History, the Hunterian Museum of Anatomy (from which people are taken away fainting with horror), Wesley's Museum, and several other places should remain as they are at present. Everyone has his hobby and he likes to see its headquarters, where he can get expert information on his particular subject.

I do not, however, see how you are going to get people who are interested in nothing in particular to be interested in something in particular with museums as they are at present.

Speaking personally, I would not be converted to ethnology by the present crowded and gloomy array of objects in the Horniman Museum, nor would I be likely to go all out for Roman History on the strength of the sad little exhibits in the Guildhall Museum. Hardly any rooms in the British Museum entice me except as pleasant places for hide and seek when the keeper isn't looking.

I suggest, therefore, two reforms. Exhibits should be arranged in an attractive manner. There should be a little less red rope and a little less 'Do not touch,' and a little less, 'Now, then, keep your fingers off the glass!'

The other reform is that museums of furniture and allied craftsmanship should be far smaller and far more like real life. A Georgian staircase means nothing if it is not in the house it was designed for. A pulpit, however finely carved, looks out of place except in a church.

Day after day we learn of beautiful old London houses that are being destroyed. They would, most of them, make excellent museums just as they are and with the addition of appropriate furniture.

People like standing in rooms, not in museums. They prefer life to death. It is a significant fact that one of the most popular exhibits at the London Museum is the reconstructed cell from Newgate, with the ravaged figure of a debtor sitting by a dimly-lit lantern, among the straw.

The charm of the Soane Museum, that little visited and marvellous house in Lincoln's Inn Fields, is that the spirit of Sir John Soane still hovers over it. It is a personal collection. You feel you are calling on someone who will be down directly.

In fact, when the museum is shut, which it often is, you have to leave cards on the Curator. Then you are looked at by an old retainer and reluctantly admitted. 'That is Sir John's chair,' the retainer continues, speaking as though Sir John Soane had died in 1934, not in 1837.

You will be taken through room after room, through a folding picture gallery, past Chippendale chairs, designs for a new London, Vulliamy clocks, plaster casts, a monkish cell, until finally you come to the breakfast parlour, which must be the most beautiful small room in the world.

It is all just as Sir John left it. As you step out into the well-mannered calm of Lincoln's Inn Fields, you feel inclined to say to the retainer: 'Thank you very much. Please tell Sir John I am sorry he was out. I will call again another day.'

I am sure of this – until museums become more like private houses people will remain at home. They will continue to base their standard of values on what have been England's museums for the last hundred years – the shops.

Evening Standard

Launceston

Travellers coming out of Devon by road from Lifton lift up their hearts at the sight of Launceston. Over Polson Bridge, the Tamar is crossed and here at last is the Duchy. Dark on its steep green hill against the sky are the uneven outlines of the Norman castle and the roofs of the houses at its feet. Even more romantic is the view of Launceston from the road from the north from Holsworthy or Bude. The suburb of St Stephen, with neat late Georgian houses of local dark slate stands on a hill nearly level with the castle. It was the original Launceston. Its church, once collegiate, has a noble fifteenth-century tower but the inside of the church was scraped of all antiquity in 1883 by the Plymouth architect Hine. St Stephen is the mother church of Launceston and was the ecclesiastical gateway to Cornwall before the Normans built Dunheved Castle on the neighbouring hill. The view of Launceston from St Stephen has attracted landscape artists since the picturesque came into fashion in the late eighteenth century. It was one of the most romantic studies in outline in the kingdom. The steep hill descended southwards to the Kensey river. Along it, as there still are, were the old slate-hung cottages of the delicious rotten borough of Newport which sent two members to Parliament until 1832. (Launceston itself sent two more making a total of four for the twin boroughs in the glorious days before Reform.) On the near banks of the river was the market cross of Newport rebuilt, as it still stands, in a charming Gothic umbrello in 1829 by the Duke of Northumberland. Here the two members were proposed and seconded. An old packhorse bridge of stone and a ford cross the brown Kensey stream to the little church of St Thomas. The church has been so severely 'restored' in the 1880s as to retain little beside two fragmentary wall paintings under glass, one of St Roche to whom a dog brings bread; some ironwork on the south door and a Norman font so enormous that it makes the humble little church with its granite arcade seem smaller than ever. A few yards downstream an eighteenth-century bridge brings the road east of St Thomas's church. Beyond the church stood the ruined walls of an Augustinian priory and high above this the ruined walls of the old town of Dunheved with the fragments of the north gate with its pointed entrance arch outlined against the sky and topping this the castle itself and the church tower of St Mary Magdalene to the west of it.

Today this view lacks the Priory ruins (which are now very fragmentary and near St Thomas's churchyard) and it lacks the north gate which was demolished in 1834. The line of the town walls can still be seen in the curve of the houses. The outline of the castle and St Mary's church remain and between them the excellent spire by Mr Hine, who ruined St Stephen's church, of the Wesleyan church (1870). It is still an unforgettable though slightly different view from that which charmed the Georgian landscape artists.

Before climbing up to the town itself, the parishes of St Stephen and St Thomas should be mentioned. The former has on the hill into Newport, a little Roman Catholic church (1912) in local stone in a Byzantine style where are relics (as at Lanherne in St Mawgan) of the Blessed Cuthbert Mayne who was the first seminary priest to be executed in 1577 under Elizabeth I. The parish of St Thomas extends up the gentle wooded valley of the Kensey where is the little hamlet of *Tregadillet*.

The town of Launceston is the most rewarding inland town of Cornwall. The Norman castle of Dunheved consists today of a walled enclosure with two gates which give on to the bailey now defaced by army huts housing civil servants. Out of this rises a steep hill which is surrounded by the circular stone keep. All the walls are either twelfth or thirteenth century. Much mowing, tree-clearing and de-picturesquing has been done lately by the Ministry of Works. But it enables one to view the growth of Launceston from the keep. The old Launceston on the hill crowned by St Stephen's church moved for protection into the neighbourhood of the castle in the thirteenth and fourteenth centuries. The town under the castle was enclosed by walls of which the south gate survives with a twin entrance and a room above it which is now owned by the local Historical Society.

A market place grew up east of the castle walls and it is still there – the market square edged today by seventeenth- and eighteenth-century houses some of them slate hung. The fourteenth-century chapel of the town had a tower which survives. This is what later became St Mary Magdalene church, east of the Market Square.

Between the two hills of the Kensey valley were St Thomas's church and the Augustinian Priory. The latter was dissolved and a Norman arch from it was removed into the White Hart Inn in the Market Square of the new town below the castle. As this town grew houses descended the hill and joined the riverside town of Newport which started to grow a little, but never very much, in the later middle ages.

The great sight of Launceston, besides its position, is the Parish Church of St Mary Magdalene originally the chapel of the castle town. The building attached to the fourteenth-century dark elvan tower which has a painted early Georgian clock face was built from 1511–24, out of moorland granite at the expense of Sir Henry Trecarel, the ruins of whose manor house are noticed under Lezant. Trecarel had lost his son and his wife and so turned his attention to the church and never completed his manor house. What he has given posterity is a most amazing range of carved granite which looks, at first glance, almost like a Hindu temple in the elaboration of its decoration.

When one considers the hardness of the moorland stone from which these walls were carved, the skill of the masons when the use of granite as building stone had only started a century before, St Mary Magdalene's church becomes a medieval triumph of Cornwall. It is also very Cornish in that it is craftsmanship more than architecture. All along the freize under the battlements of the building is carved a series of Latin prayers opening with *Ave Maria, gratia plena*. Not one square inch of the south, east and north sides of the walls is without carving – shields of quatre foils and fleur de lys and coats of arms. Below the east window of the chancel is a carved figure of St Mary Magdalene surrounded by minstrels. The inside of the church is an anticlimax. The long granite arcades of the aisles and the carved wooden pulpit from Trecarel's day survive but there are Victorian roofs, glazing, pews; floor and a screen of 1903. The Piper monuments 1677 and 1731 are grand.

Looking over the churchyard is a handsome eighteenth-century stone house and east of it is the very attractive Pannier Market of 1842.

Up here on the hill top below the castle, there are between houses views in all directions, except the south, of steep little fields and hedges on hills on the other sides of valleys so that one realises Launceston is still what it has long been, primarily an agricultural town. Until 1835 it was also the County town of Cornwall before yielding that honour to Bodmin. For this reason there are eighteenth-century houses worthy of a county town. The most solid of these are the eighteenth-century mansions on either side of Castle Hill. They are built of what was then a precious rarity in Cornwall, red brick. This little street, which was cobbled until 1856, is the most perfect collection of eighteenth-century town houses in Cornwall. The fertile gardens slope sharply down and the house windows look across to the steep hills opposite. Their street fronts are protected by ironwork gates and low walls.

In the mid nineteenth century several seemly stucco mansions were built facing Devon and Dartmoor in the Italian and Gothic styles.

The Great Western branch railway from Plymouth was opened in 1864 and the London and South Western came from Okehampton ten years later and continued to Wadebridge and Padstow in 1886–89. Neither seem much to have altered the look of the town. The inevitable Passmore Edwards Library designed by S. Trevail of Truro appeared in 1900. The Town Hall (1887), and Guildhall (1881) are by Otho Peter of Launceston and Hine of Plymouth.

The motor age has been Launceston's chief trouble. The way into Cornwall by Okehampton has necessitated a bypass and along this there are some disastrous lines of modern and sub-Frank Lloyd Wright villas. These are, however, preferable to the intrusion into the old town of through traffic.

From *Shell Guide to Cornwall*

Film Clips (1)

Film reviews written for the Evening Standard

Dr Goebbels has just made an impassioned appeal to the German film industry for ugly stars. He says that films with beautiful women in them and handsome young men cause all the unhappiness in the world.

We, in England, can afford to laugh. We do not take things as literally as the German people. Shots are rarely fired at the screen. And we do not idolise handsome stars only.

Acton is a case in point. Cicely Courtneidge and Jack Hulbert, Mary Brough and Tom Walls are, I am assured, the most popular people there. Ealing idolises George Arliss, nor does it think Gordon Harker handsome.

> 'I'm not so cracked on
> Acton,
> But I've a kind of feeling
> That I'd like to live in Ealing'

wrote the poet Wordsworth when he visited Acton's oldest inhabitant in 1834. One hundred years from then and it is now. What a change!

*

This week the gorgeous East is held in fee – a very considerable fee – by Cecil B. de Mille, Walter Forde and Sam Wood. The highest fee was undoubtedly paid by Cecil B. for the cast and sets of *Cleopatra*.

Cleopatra is glorious fun. It is not a film for pedants or for critics. It is a film to see when your mind is mellowed.

It is all very well to scoff at the ridiculous lack of history in a Cecil B. de Mille spectacle. The lack is intentional. Shakespeare – I am not comparing Cecil B. with Shakespeare – did not bother about accuracy in either *Julius Caesar* or *Antony and Cleopatra*. He wrote them in modern Elizabethan English, and his scenery was modern Elizabethan.

Why should not Cecil B. de Mille, in combining the plots of both these plays, have his words and scenery in modern American. Anyhow, the effect is probably as accurate as any professor's reconstruction, for are we not told that the Egyptians were the Americans of the Ancient World?

The story opens (after we have walked through a cardboard Egyptian entrance to the Carlton, have been ushered by blonde *Egyptiennes* into our seats and watched an Egypto-Graeco-Brazilian ballet) with the seduction of Julius Caesar by Cleopatra (Claudette Colbert).

We then switch over to a party given by Caesar's wife Calpurnia in Rome. Although this Rome looked like the Ritz before luncheon and the RAC swimming-bath before dinner, although palms were placed about beside the pillars and although a guest says to Caesar's wife, 'the loveliest party you've ever given, dear,' I am sure it is like what ancient Rome really was – vulgar, noisy and luxurious.

The rest of the story shows the murder of Caesar and the subsequent seduction by Cleopatra of Mark Antony (Henry Wilcoxon).

This Mark Antony is certainly not the small, pleasure-loving, polite and rhetorical character of history. Henry Wilcoxon is more like a rowing blue who has suddenly come out of training.

This gives additional poignance to the final scene when both he and Cleopatra commit suicide and defy the unattractive Octavius Caesar and the puritanical Enobarbus (C. Aubrey Smith).

Despite the unparalleled luxuriousness of the settings, the thread of the story is not lost. . . .

I think Cecil B. de Mille in this film and in *The Sign of the Cross* has really shown us what the cinema can do. It is not what we always want it to do.

But it shows that, as regards spectacle, it has got the theatre 'cold'.

The best thing about *Cleopatra* is the cutting. Sequence follows sequence, chariots, ballets, drunkenness, flashing swords, rolling drums, crumbling ramparts, wind-blown sand in a neat and logical way until when the brazen doors of Egypt's capital burst open under the mighty battering ram, so, too, burst the mighty hearts of Antony and Cleopatra.

Cast, sets, music are swallowed up in the personality of the director. It is all, perhaps, a little too much of a good thing. But there is a certain noble madness about it like there is about a vast historical canvas by Benjamin Robert Haydon.

There was a sound at Shepherd's Bush all night
Of Victor Savile working after ten
All Beauty and all Chivalry, and bright
The lamps shone o'er fair extras and bored men;
A make-up man worked doggedly; and when
Arliss appeared, an unvoluptuous swell,
'Silence!' was called and no one spake again
Though all were waiting for the supper bell.

To revert from Byron, I trod the field of Waterloo the other day, at Shepherd's Bush.

It was a scene from *The Iron Duke*, now being made. George Arliss had just come down from a horse on which he had been sitting motionless for three hours.

The field was deserted except for here and there an assistant director picking his way among the model cottages dotted about on the imitation hills.

I think this was the most convincing set I have ever seen in a film studio. It was made more convincing by the importation of real mud for the field of battle. It was pleasantly refreshing to come into the studio and smell, instead of the usual grease paint and synthetic air, wet earth and crushed grass like Hampstead Heath after a shower of rain.

*

The Man Who Knew Too Much (at the New Gallery on Sunday) is unquestionably the best film this week; it is the best film there has been for many weeks; it is the best English film I have seen.

One of the chief reasons for its success is that it is really true to English life. The jokes are English, and the settings are in typically English surroundings.

To my mind the best American films are those quick-moving gangster stories with the actions hotted up by the intrusion of bumptious and attractive blondes.

The best German films are those sombre affairs with fierce propaganda and agonising photographs of suffering, all superbly directed.

The best French films are light, lace-covered things, with singing and satire.

The best British films are – what?

There have been very few films which you can call typically British.

They are mostly imitations of American ones, often just as efficiently done, but that does not mean that they are British. Costume films hardly count, for they represent only a phase in the film fashions.

*

British films were first seriously established by Alfred Hitchcock, who made *Blackmail*, and a good many excellent thrillers. His knowledge of London types, his observation of detail and his particular little tricks which enabled connoisseurs to pick out a Hitchcock film in five minutes made him the most famous English director.

Because he was famous, he was put on to do things to which he was not suited but which were regarded as sure 'box office draws.' Then they made him direct musicals, which require few of the qualities which Hitchcock possesses as a director.

Waltzes from Vienna was a result. It was competent, but not very interesting.

Hitchcock has been successful because he has made truly British films. I am always being told that cinemas are places where people go to see some kind of life they are not used to, so as to take them out of their everyday surroundings. I do not believe these are always so gloomy that they cannot be filmed.

Refugee, a German propaganda film, and *The World Moves On*, an American one, show scenes infinitely more gloomy than those in which most people live.

If the big British companies are going on doing spectacular stuff, then amateurs and people outside the trade will start making unspectacular films of English life.

In Glasgow it has already started with *Brighton Cross*, a story of the unemployed in the worst district of the city. Five earnest men have made it, including the Professor of Industrial Psychology from Glasgow University.

In Sheffield the municipal council are seriously considering the erection of a city film studio.

The Man Who Knew Too Much, Alfred Hitchcock's new film, is an honest-to-God thriller.

But I feel it has to do with what I have been talking about because it really is a film with an English quality about it that is missing from the more elaborate productions of our studios.

*

Sometimes, but not often, the heart of the film critic rejoices. Seeing

film after film, day after day, listening to the bray of the saxophone or
the synthetic hoot of a studio owl, I might have had all emotion
dragged out of me.

And now, this week, I have seen two new films which have stirred
me up as only good films can. They are both British films, and they
have borrowed nothing from America.

The Thirty-Nine Steps was once a story by John Buchan. I remember
the dirty much-read book in my school library. Now it is also a film (at
the New Gallery) by Alfred Hitchcock. Both are masterpieces in spy
stories, but that is all they have in common.

Alfred Hitchcock, with his usual intelligence, has realised that a
good book does not necessarily make a good film.

A young man called Hannay, from Canada (Robert Donat) is
accidentally involved in a spy plot. Someone has stolen an important
official secret. All this young man knows is that at an address in a
lonely part of Scotland there is someone who must be informed of the
theft.

A spy is killed in the young man's flat by villains. So he flies to
Scotland hotly pursued by the villains who killed the spy and by the
police who want him for murder. Then follows a sequence of fights
and escapes in 'The Flying Scotsman,' of desperate running across
misty moors. When he reaches the address in Scotland the young man
finds he has walked straight into the enemy's camp.

He escapes and is captured by the spies along with a young woman
(Madeleine Carroll). He is handcuffed to the young woman and so
remains for the rest of his breathless adventures. At the end, of course,
the spies are caught in a totally unexpected way.

Throughout the film your flesh tingles with what Leigh Hunt called
'agreeable terror.' Then there is the suspense which never slackens.
Who is the villain? What are 'The Thirty-Nine Steps?' And just when
you think you are in for a good cry you find instead a big laugh.

Hitchcock is a master of the unexpected. There may be a lot of tag
ends in this mystery which need explanation, but that does not matter.
Hitchcock set out to make you jump and scream and chuckle. He has
succeeded.

Now look at the film in detail. Here are a few exquisite touches
which I noticed. You may see many more. In the opening scene of a
low music-hall notice the noise the audience makes. Not the usual
discreet and unlikely silence followed by clapping. No – shouts, the
cracking of peanuts, the cry of a baby in arms.

Notice, too, the effect of letting a telephone bell ring unanswered.

See that neat character study of 'commercials' talking business in the train and relapsing inevitably into dirty stories.

And perhaps the finest satire of all is that on a political meeting. Donat is mistaken for the principal speaker. The last man has talked too long. The chairman is characteristically inaudible in his introductory speech. Donat, hiding a manacled hand in his pocket, spouts glorious claptrap. The audience cheers and stamps.

These are only a few of the brilliantly original touches which make this far the best thriller, so far, of the year. Then see what Hitchcock has done with Madeleine Carroll. He has turned her from a stately beauty into an attractive and untidy English girl. I have never seen her better in a film.

*

Mothers of England! I am glad to have an opportunity of addressing you tonight. There has been a widespread search by the casting director of British International Pictures to find a suitable girl of fourteen to take the part of Little Nell in Dickens's *Old Curiosity Shop*.

London girls are too sophisticated. South Kensington girls are too refined. Bonnie country lasses start 'acting' as soon as they are put before the camera for a test. Before you send up your daughter be sure they are demure, petite and indeed capable of being that little maid-of-all-work-for-all-the-world 'Little Nell.' It is a difficult part, though a good one, and a fine chance for native British talent.

Be warned, however, by the sad case of the little Bootle lassie.

> She travell'd all the way from Bootle
>   Where her parents wished her well;
> Till she came by train to Elstree
>   For the part of 'Little Nell.'
> It wasn't that she over-acted,
>   She didn't squint or flinch or squawl;
> She wasn't shy nor too self-conscious;
>   She merely couldn't act at all.

Move with the Times

'Now 'oo was the ole boy as used to be with Consolidated Dried Fruits before Lemon come on? Grogson was it?'

'No, not Grogson – let me think – it must have been Gregory.'

'No, not Gregory – shorter name than that – a little bald feller 'e was, with bright eyes.'

'Yers, I know 'oo you mean.'

By this time the rest of the table was interested. Macpherson of Autopolishes put down his cup of tea. Before helping himself to some more beetroot with his corned beef, he put in: 'Died, didn't he? I remember there was talk of giving him something out of the Benevolent, but he had passed on before we passed the order.'

'Ah, yes, we must all pass on.'

'That's it – come today and gone tomorrow, as the lodger said owin' two months' rent.'

A laugh went up at Crossman's remark. Crossman could always be counted on for a laugh. D'you remember his one about the schoolmistress and house-painter? Clever chap, Crossman. Go-ahead, too. Knew a good thing when he was on one. Doubled the orders for Youneedawear Slumber Suits in Barnstaple alone. 'I oughta recollek the name – be forgettin' me own next – perhaps Our Friend at the top of the table can inform us?'

Our Friend at the top of the table had been paying no apparent attention to the conversation. He had got through a cut off the roast, well soaked in HP Sauce, passed on to apple tart, and was contemplating bread and marmalade with some of the cream for which Mrs Yeo's hotel was famous. After that he would have cheese.

All the table waited on Our Friend's words. Anything to do with the past and Our Friend knew it. Forty-five years in business and still going strong. There had been an attempt to nickname him Johnnie Walker, but the name hadn't stuck. It was undignified. For years now Our Friend had been called the Admiral, and the Admiral he remained, for indeed there was something at once nautical and commanding about his neat appearance.

Our Friend deliberately took up his third cup of tea. Before drinking he cleared his throat. All attention was riveted. Even Gutteridge and Verschoyle paused in discussing the merits of Morris and Ford.

'Grigson was the name. Gregory Grigson.'

'That's right, Grigson.'

'Grigson.'

''Course. Can't think 'ow I forgot it.'

Tension relaxed. There was a renewed noise of knives and forks scraping on plates and of suction something like a vacuum cleaner imbibing water as the gentlemen ate and drank.

In groups they left the table, some to gaslit bedrooms, some to various sitting-rooms, all to sit with pen, paper, and a little attaché-case writing off to the firm, reporting progress, arranging for a room in another town next week.

Our Friend the Admiral was the last to leave as he had been the last to enter the room. He was a gentleman, and liked to make his meal approach as nearly the time of a gentleman's dinner without inconveniencing Mrs Yeo.

'Your table in the back room is cleared, Mr Battersby, as soon as you are ready for it.'

'Thank you, Mrs Yeo. I shall be proceeding thence so soon as I have finished this delicious lemon-curd tartlet.'

'Ah, now, they're my sister's. She knew you liked them. There was a time when I could put a plate of those lemon-curd tartlets as high as the centre vase on the table and it would be cleared before the meal was over. But the gentlemen don't seem to eat nowadays like they used to . . .'

'No, it's not like it used to be. *Eheu fugaces*, Mrs Yeo, *eheu fugaces*! Nervous excitement. They're on the move too much. Too anxious to get away. They haven't their hearts in their work. Now I am rarely finished before a Saturday morning. But these young fellows scramble through their orders to be off on a Thursday evening. Hurry – hurry – hurry. It ruins the digestion.'

'That's so, Mr Battersby, just as you say. But we must keep up with the times, mustn't we? I'm trying to get the Council to let me turn the backyard into a garage.'

'Ah, you study your guests *too* much, Mrs Yeo. Why can't they be content with the railways instead of having these motors? The South, the Great, and the Midland. They've always been good enough for me – though, of course, we keep a car at home for joy-riding.'

What harm was there in a little white lie like the last? One must keep up appearances if one is to keep up with the times.

Nice woman, Mrs Yeo. Quite a lady, and had worked Godolphin's up from next to nothing. Twenty-eight years she'd been here, and he'd been once a month almost every year since then – except the time, three years ago, when he underwent that eye operation. Funny how the old trouble seemed to be coming back again. After a long day naturally your eyes get tired at sixty-eight. Perhaps it was just anno Domini.

Nice of them to let him have this room to himself.

Don't feel like work this evening. Turn in and get a good sleep. Probably be all right in the morning. Deal with correspondence then. No, there was that eight forty-five post to catch. Some pressing matters to attend to. And he must drop a line to Kate.

Mr Battersby opened a letter.

WILLIAMSON & SON
The Quality Shop

High Street,   JEWELLERY
Exchester,   NOVELTY GOODS
Devon.   SILVERWARE

                                                  ART STONEWORK

                                                  REPAIRS EXECUTED

Dear Sir,

I beg to state that my father, Mr Joseph Williamson, Senior, passed peacefully away in his sleep last Tuesday.

It was a tranquil end of an esteemed parent. He had been ailing for some months.

Why do these young people use the typewriter? So difficult to read. Why not a good copperplate hand like his own? Or was this a circular letter to the trade? He hoped not. It would have been civil of young Williamson to have written personally to an old friend of his father's. He brought his eyes into focus once again.

I take this opportunity of also intimating to you with reference to the decease of the above, that the negotiations pending the illness of Mr Williamson, Senior, *re* the amalgamation of this firm with a larger concern are now almost completed. We are, under the circumstances, not renewing our stock just at present, and are anxious to save you an unnecessary call.

Yours faithfully,
Jos. WILLIAMSON.

Ah! Incorporated Art Gifts, Ltd, buying them up, of course. *Eheu fugaces*! Not a very civil letter, and there was another good customer gone. He'd heard enough of the Incorporated. They'd bought up Puxley's in the High Street here. It had been a sound little concern on the old lines, and now they'd taken down the old premises, put in one of their great blazing shop fronts, and filled the windows with flashy, cheap trinkets not worth the price of carriage.

Mr Battersby was senior West Country representative of Messrs Netherton and Goldberg, fancy goods manufacturers and silversmiths, Dalston Lane, E. He used to look almost lovingly at the bag of stock on a chair near him. At least he could offer his clients a quality article. He would never forget the time he had gone into one of the Incorporated shops in an effort to get a little extra business. 'Traveller? Not today, thank you. We've got enough to see to as it is. Quite enough stock, and up-to-date, too. Netherton and Goldberg? Never heard of them. Ah, they may be old established. I'm not saying they aren't. A damn sight too old established. Try the Tower of London, old man.'

A gratuitous insult. And from a young fellow who was obviously no gentleman. In his day, a gentlemanly bearing had been an essential of good business. Hullo, 7.45! Post goes in an hour.

With aching eyes Mr Battersby plied on in his neat copperplate, checking his order book and writing letters.

The gas seemed to be burning less brightly. Funny how gas can't be relied upon for light nowadays. Or was it his sight?

Well, he must drop that line to Kate. Thank goodness he had a good wife at home. He was not a man to go carrying on with the chambermaids at every house on the road like Crossman and the rest of them. Kate wouldn't mind a few words left out here and there and a little illegibility. She knew about his eyes. And hadn't she had her troubles, too? When she had that cancer in the throat they all said she would never recover.

He'd lost a lot of business then worrying about her at home and him miles away on the road. Anything might have happened. Thank the dear Lord he'd always been a good churchman. The Lord provides in his own good time and the Lord had provided for him.

By denying them children, He had enabled them to save enough money to pay the best doctors and surgeons, and Kate was with him still. The old trouble hadn't returned, though she'd never picked up her strength somehow. But the rent of the house was not much – an advantage of living in the provinces. A nice little place built just before the war and therefore sound. Outside Devizes. As Kate had said: 'In the town, yet not in it. A regular camellia.' And he had laughed and replied: 'Chameleon, my dear, chameleon.' How they had laughed! Always a little joke.

It would have surprised Spender and the rest of them if they had known what a jolly old boy the Admiral was at home. The Admiral in the messroom, eh? Well, here goes.

GODOLPHIN'S COMMERCIAL HOTEL,
FORE STREET, BIDWORTHY,
NORTH DEVON.

MY DEAR KATE,

Only a line. I enclose p.o. for 5s. 4d. (five shillings and fourpence) towards the car. Put it away carefully. Business is not picking up yet, but times are bad. The eyes are none too good. Back by the late on Sat.

Yours affectionately,
ALFRED.

N.B. – Poor old Williamson of Exchester is dead. You will remember I took you to look him up that time we were at Sidmouth.

The gas was full on in the commercial room. Price was packing up. He'd get off tonight. A row of coat-hangers in his Essex saloon showed you he was in the robes and mantles line. The Admiral came out with his letters.

'Drop you at the PO?'

'Thank you no, sir. A little air will do me good.'

'The old Admiral's showing his age a bit,' said Crossman, who was having a last pipe in the hotel doorway.

'D'you notice 'e doesn't seem to see straight. Look at 'im goin' down the street there. Quite unsteady. Yet he's TT as Pussyfoot himself.'

'Yes, the old boy's cracking up. 'Bout time 'e retired. I'll bet he's feathered 'is nest all right.'

'Too damn superior fer me,' said Huggins of Esivacs, who had joined the group at the door. 'Oi've no use fer a feller as lords it over yer when yer know 'e's got about as much business as could be put in a kangaroo's pocket.'

'I 'ear the Incorporated is buying up Netherton's,' said Crossman. 'Wonder if the ole boy knows?' Crossman knew everything, other people's business as well as his own.

When the Admiral returned, he popped into the commercial room, as was his custom, to say good night. Collins of International Pearl Collar Studs sang out: 'Seen the letter from Williamson's, Mr Battersby? That'll be a blow to your business. The Incorporated's taking them over.'

'Yes, Young Williamson wrote me,' but he noticed that Collins' letter was identical with his own, and he knew for a fact that Collins didn't go to Williamson's more than once a year. 'Good night, gentlemen.'

Mr Battersby once more tonight consoled himself with the thought that he at least had a quality article to offer to his clients. He turned down the bedroom gas. *Eheu fugaces*! Home soon now.

The car arrived from the Motor Supplies Co. Kate was delighted. The young man accompanying it, quite a gentleman, offered to give her a lesson. 'I shall be able to learn while you are away, Alfred,' she said. 'No carrying on now,' said Mr Battersby, with a jolly twinkle at the young man. But somehow, as the weeks passed, Kate hadn't picked up enough strength to get about and learn to drive the car.

In early March a surprise awaited Mr Battersby at Godolphin's. 'Yes, we've had the electric light put in,' said Mrs Yeo. 'We've got a lovely new fixture in your sitting-room.' He beheld a pink glass shade which deflected the light in a glaring circle from the ceiling to the table. He did not say that he had refused to have the electric light at home because it hurt his eyes. Mrs Yeo took him on a tour of inspection of all the switches and fixtures, an honour meet for him as senior hotel guest. But all Mr Battersby could bring himself to say was '*Eheu fugaces*!' 'Yes, Mr Battersby, just as you say. We must move with the times, that's what I say.' She understood Latin even less than Mr Battersby.

At the end of that week he received a further surprise, in the form of a letter from Netherton's head office in London. This was out of order. Their letters generally arrived at the beginning of the week.

DEAR MR BATTERSBY,

You will no doubt be surprised to hear that we have amalgamated with Incorporated Art Gifts, Ltd. Naturally for the good of the firm we must move with the times, and although the decision was not unexpected it was more sudden than many anticipated.

The Incorporated Art Gifts Company is a big firm, and of course they expect to reorganise our own concern. I am therefore taking this opportunity of thanking you very sincerely for your long and loyal service to the old firm. It is largely due to the loyal support of such servants as yourself that our high reputation has been maintained.

As I am retiring myself I am not in a position to do anything but advise. I shall naturally advise the reorganised company – if my advice is worth anything – to endeavour to retain your services. Although on consulting the books I see that your order list has somewhat decreased lately, I well understand that this is possibly due to the keen competition of Art Gifts, Ltd, themselves, a position that will now be obviated by amalgamation.

I wish I could hold out some hopes for you, but I understand that the system of representatives employed by the amalgamators is different from our own. Again believe me when I say that your long and loyal services have been deeply appreciated by Mr Goldberg and myself.

Yours sincerely,

JAS. NETHERTON,

Sales and General Manager.

A very civil letter and in his own handwriting too. Of course he'd heard rumours, but this was obviously the sack. A very gentlemanly way of putting it. Let's see, £1000 in the bank, and take off another fifty for the car. Not enough to last long with the possibility of more doctor's bills. His sight didn't seem to be improving either. A guffaw echoed from the commercial room. Put himself on the Benevolent like poor old Gregory Grigson? Have his private affairs discussed? Not he! The old Admiral reduced to the ranks. Some joke that would be. Impossible! He would say he was retiring to that feathered nest which they all supposed he'd got. Meanwhile business as usual and get on with the week's work. What was that they used to sing in the trenches? 'Old soldiers never die.' He wished he'd been young enough to go.

It was a wet Saturday when Mr Battersby returned to Devizes after that eventful week. He must save money now. Not take the bus, but walk to the station.

There was no light in the front room. Funny. Not like Kate to be out on a Saturday. Flo, the daily, answered the door.

'Oh, sir, I waited behind to tell yew, sir – they've taken Mrs Battersby to 'orspital. She'd been poorly all the week. It's the old trouble, they say, sir.'

Father Bengs, Father Wilkinson, and Father Lewis were having a hurried fish lunch in Saint Aidan's Clergy House, Crawley Street, E. 14.

'There's a gentleman to see you, Father,' said Herbert, the young servant.

'Who is he and what does he want?'

'He won't give no name, Father, and says it's an important personal matter.'

'The usual, I suppose,' said Father Simpson. 'Who's going to see him? It's your turn, Father.'

Father Lewis went to the clergy house door which was also the door to the church.

'I am a gentleman, sir, and a good churchman. Through no fault of my own, sir, I am temporarily out of employment. Rather I should put it down to "*eheu fugaces*" – if one may say so. I should be obliged to you, sir, if you would inform me whether you are in need of someone to do clerical work.'

'I am afraid not. I advise you to try your local employment exchange. You should have read the notice in the church porch, you know.'

Father Lewis was not an unkind man. But one must be practical. In the church especially it is essential to move with the times. The notice in the church porch ran: 'The Vicar regrets that he is unable to offer financial assistance to any but parishioners.' Luckily Mr Battersby's sight did not permit of his reading that notice.

'I always mistrust the ones that try to put over the gentlemanly act.' Father Lewis returned to his cooling fish-cake.

From *Under Thirty*

Film Clips (2)

Film reviews written for the Evening Standard

Man of Aran, with the sea for actor and people mere pebbles on the beach, contrasts with *It Happened One Night*, in which Nature is pretty well subjugated.

We are so used to the second that we may not like the first. But without much strain we can like both; and I don't see why cinema goers shouldn't be treated to a fresh kind of emotion for a change.

No one, on this island, at any rate, is tired of looking at the sea. *Man of Aran* consists of looking at the sea all the time, of rescuing nets from its clutches, of waiting for the tide to go down. After a few minutes one almost smells the sea and feels the spray on one's face, there in the scented atmosphere of a West End cinema.

Its waters become so familiar that the audience can spy quite a mile out the fin of a basking shark, black on the still surface. Then the fun begins: the island wakes to a new sort of life: figures rush to and fro, a small open boat is launched, the islanders set out with harpoons, and, after a long fight, the enormous fish is caught.

Most awe-inspiring of all in this film is the moment at the end when a storm comes up and there, in an open boat and a sea mountains high, the islanders are rowing for dear life, hidden every few seconds in a valley of the rollers. I suspect John Goldman's cutting had much to do with the successful effect of that storm on the screen.

There is one thing definite about *Man of Aran*. It could not possibly have been done on the stage. It could not even be adapted for the stage, because the islanders, superb natural actors as they are, play only a small part. Their struggle seems infinitesimal beside the fury of the waves.

Man of Aran is one up for Gaumont-British for having the courage to launch a story with no beginning and no end and no love interest.

*

I have just seen a film in which there were no professional actors, and no studio arts. In this film the producer and the director are the same man, while his only assistants are a cameraman and a cutter – and a cast of eight million.

I am prepared to stake what little of my reputation I have left on this film. It shows London as it really is.

The actors are all sorts of people who never thought of acting in their lives – a man selling live eels, assistants in a suburban emporium, Mr and Mrs Newlywed, of 'Cozineuk,' Colindale, a few down-and-outs with terribly unhappy faces on the Embankment, *The Daily Express* at work, an old dear having a quick one in a pub in Camden Town, a meat porter, and the whole staff of a big London factory.

The producer-director is Michael Dillon, and his cast are the citizens of Greater London. When Bob Flaherty made *Man of Aran* he tried to show us the life of that hard, wind-swept island, with its tiny population, in little over an hour. Mr Dillon has compressed the life of London into an hour.

He has done it with skill. I think he has the late Gustav Holst to thank for much of it. He has taken his music from *The Planets* and made a film of London.

[Michael Dillon] has hitherto been one of the only directors to get his musical background first and put the photography in afterwards. *The Planets* has acted as an inspiration to Mr Dillon from the moment when a tug goes under Tower Bridge into the dawn over the city to those last moments when one light after another switches out in an immense block of flats.

I know that all you good people who write to me, signing yourselves 'Picture Mad,' 'Film Crazy,' 'Your Loving Emily,' and all the rest of you will think this is a highbrow film because there is no star in it, because Janet Gaynor is not the little working girl heroine and Charles Farrell is not the big business man.

But you, Miss Picture Mad and you, Mrs Picture Crazy and you, Dear Emily, are the heroines of this film.

Why should a film be highbrow because it shows life as it really is? Is a sitting-room incomplete because there is not a cocktail bar in it?

Eight Million is the name of this London film, which you will not see until September at the earliest. It is just a story of London's life with thousands of incidents that occur daily and hardly ever get reported.

It is held together by clever photography, clever cutting and the music. 'Cutting' is what makes the cinema different from the stage. In a stage play let us suppose you are going to show Ralph Lynn hiding under a bed when Yvonne Arnaud comes into the room. Obviously the laughter depends on one joke only – the situation – and a joke can only make you laugh for two minutes at the most.

It occurred to Mr John Grierson, as it has often occurred to me, and even more frequently, I expect, to you, that there is nothing more irritating than the sickening commentaries provided for short films. Let me improvise an example.

> Here is the old world village of Rime Intrinsica, right in the heart of dear old Dorset. My! it is old-world, isn't it? Look at that funny old farmer! He lives in this funny old house with the roofs nearly on the ground. (Laughter.) But then he has a lot to do with the ground, hasn't he? (More laughter.) So I suppose it comes quite naturally to him to live in such a place.
>
> What a wonderful old boy! There he goes, driving his old sheep. See, they're trying to get over a stile.
>
> No wonder they look sheepish. (Laughter.) There he is, going into the wonderful olde hostelrye where mine host is giving him right right good ale to quaff yo! ho! ho! (Music off.)

Well, we have all had to put up with pretty silly nonsense from lantern lecturers, but nothing quite equal to the stupidity of many commentators whose words accompany much magnificent photography today.

That is the tragedy of it. The photographs are so good and the scenery they depict is so interesting that it is a pity our enjoyment should be ruined listening to futile jokes and obvious comments.

'This is an old house – do you see how the stones are all crumbling?' 'Of course I do, you fool.' I always want to reply, 'Why bother to tell me what I can see for myself?'

The General Post Office Film Unit is among the first to get rid of needless commentary.

*

I have just been seeing *Granton Trawler*, a short film showing a fishing smack and the hauling in of its catch. I forgot I was watching a film of a subject I had seen filmed many times before.

This was because instead of the usual maddening commentary I was allowed to hear the real noises of life abroad a fishing smack, the skipper shouting orders, the creaking of the rigging, the noise of water splashing over the deck, the wail of seagulls and finally, when we were in smooth waters, the almost inaudible comments of the crew on local football prospects as they sorted out the fish.

And this was only an experiment. There were other films equally exciting. *Spring on the Farm*, which has already appeared at the Tatler Theatre, showed a series of unbelievably beautiful views of English spring landscape. The only commentary was spasmodic and by a little girl of eight. The rest of the accompaniment was made on a spinet and by the singing of a small village choir.

I am not particularly poetic, but it seemed to me that this beautiful series of photographs and sounds was something like a lovely childhood experience that had come to me all over again – in a cinema of all places.

That is why I like good short films so much. They are the lyric poetry of the cinema.

I do not see why the principle of recording individual sounds, instead of mere conversations, should not be taken up by feature films.

There is a film made by the GPO about *Weather Forecasts*, for instance, which is just as thrilling as a gangster film. We see the storm approaching, we watch people getting ready for it, and we see the weather forecaster himself (he looks like an elderly William Powell and acts extremely well) sending out the news of the storm's approach.

You will soon be seeing these films yourselves. I am sure you will not be bored by them. They are in no sense highbrow. They are sensible.

I am afraid I may have caused you to think that the GPO shorts are the only ones made in England.

On the contrary, many people are making them. While you are reading this a handful of street musicians are making a short film of London's hawkers. They are providing musical accompaniment, while the stars of the film are London's pavement artists and street acrobats who perform opposite theatre queues.

Another fine film has been made of the Shrimp Fishing Industry of Gravesend.

I have not finished about short films yet.

Gaumont-British *Miniatures* are an enterprising series of short films showing different parts of Europe, ranging from Chipping Campden in the Cotswolds to Monte Carlo.

When this admirably edited series launches out on the industrial towns as well as the show-places, it will be doubly interesting. There are all sorts of places we should like to see: Leeds, the Docks, Greenwich, Manchester, Bristol, Liverpool.

Bath – said to be the most beautiful town in the world – has never been properly filmed, with its crescents, squares, pumproom and retired colonels pulled about in Bath-chairs.

Then this series may show us all that is ugly in England – the Great Worst Road and several other places. It can reveal the slums.

Perhaps the most exciting of the Gaumont-British films are the series called *Secrets of India*. Many of the shots were taken by the heroic cameraman S. V. Bennett, who nearly lost his life on the Everest Expedition.

The Fair City of Adaipur has for its 'star' the Maharajah of Adaipur, the direct descendant of the sun god and hereditary leader of all Hindu Princes.

Magnificent processions through gleaming marble streets and buildings are accompanied by strange Indian music.

Best of all is *Katmandu*, a film of Nepal, the hidden kingdom in the Himalayas, into which no white man is admitted without special permission.

This film was taken before the earthquake destroyed many of the old temples of this lonely kingdom.

We see the King of Nepal himself, who takes no active part in the Government of the country. He turns his face away as the camera approaches him, not wishing to take an active part in the film. Then the hereditary Prime Minister appears, who rules Nepal; he is not bothered by the camera.

The theory that short films are rather tedious instructional lectures (except, of course, for the news films) between the 'big pictures,' will, I hope, soon be done away with. They can be genuinely interesting and important.

*

A little while ago, when I was writing about short films, I had the inclination but not the space to mention the new 'three-minute films' which are being shown at some of the cinemas. Unfortunately they are regarded as highbrow. I cannot think why, because they are nothing of the sort.

The 'three-minute films' show, in the time specified, political problems by means of moving diagrams. They show what has happened to change the map of Europe since the war and the coming struggle for the mastery of the Pacific. I admit they are rather alarming, but they could not be clearer and easier to understand. They show in a few seconds by pictures what it takes columns of verbiage to explain.

I have been talking to one of the Entertainment chiefs and he ought to know what's what. Especially as he has acted in a film.

I mean Val Gielgud, play producer of the BBC, brother of the actor John Gielgud, and an actor himself. He is the star in an unpretentious film of his own story, *Murder at Broadcasting House*.

I asked him today – in his unofficial capacity – what he would like to see happen to the films if ever, in the far distant future, they came to be used for television.

'I would like to see special films made by the BBC in co-operation with some film company,' he replied.

'Of course, at Broadcasting House, we wouldn't have any sex. But I don't think we would have much difficulty in making such films entertaining.'

Talking of films without sex in them, let me introduce to you Arthur Elton, a director of sexless films. He is a peculiar figure in Wardour Street.

He has a yellow beard, dresses in rustic style, and lives in Bloomsbury. I remember that at school he always used to carry a peculiar umbrella in which he kept his books. It must have been made of some extra strong material.

Now he carries films in huge tins slung across his back in some string contrivance. He always was an ingenious man.

Arthur Elton has a peculiar position. He is film director to the Ministry of Labour. He has just made a really thrilling picture of Poplar Labour Exchange with a cast of thirty men who have never acted in a film before.

The cast contained two or three officials and the rest were unemployed.

The film was such a success – *Workers and Jobs* it is called – that now old Arthur Elton (he was always 'old' Arthur Elton even when he was at school) is off on a tour of distressed areas.

He will make films of South Wales and those parts of the North where unemployment is terrible.

Then, sitting back in our comfortable seats we shall see other people's sufferings.

Only this time the sufferings will be genuine, not studio-made.

*

Do you ever shut your eyes when you go into a cinema and keep awake? I did the other day, on purpose, in my local cinema.

I wanted to find out whether the film was worth hearing as well as seeing. It wasn't.

I won't tell you what the film was, but this was the impression I got.

Organ solo (Gounod) . . . Cessation of music . . . 'It's not just you, darling . . . it's the you of you.' . . . 'Yeah! . . .'

More music a little more cheerful. . . .

The noise of a motor car. . . . etc, etc.

It sounded like a lunatic's ravings as conceived by an Art Repertory company.

On the other hand, a well-directed film can make you laugh if you hear it almost as much as if you see it.

John Grierson, the wild-eyed director of the Post Office Film Unit, is experimenting in 'heroes'. He has long made what are acknowledged to be the best documentary films to be found anywhere.

Basil Dean has taken them up, and you will soon be able to see them at your local cinema.

John Grierson's latest experiment is to employ a poet to write a poem to a series of shots of collieries, most of them at a standstill. The poet is a tall, thin friend of mine, called Wystan Auden. He produces tall, thin volumes of verse that actually bring him in money. He is one of the few poets to achieve this.

The poem for the film is recited on the sound track, and a choir sings specially composed music by Mr Britten, a young composer.

The next thing to do, obviously, is to have the soundtrack of this short film put into a wireless programme. No other film, not even *One Night of Love*, could, I think, stand up to so severe a test.

*

It was a hot day and at that time in the afternoon when people are sparse and lethargic.

I had been watching in the cool of the Carlton an ordinary public showing of *BBC – The Voice of Britain*. At the end of the film there was violent applause.

Proportionately it was more applause than is given a good film on its first night. This evidence should be enough to convince you that a 'documentary' film can be as interesting and exciting as any drama of misunderstood wives and debonair villains.

BBC lasts for nearly an hour. It has no recognised film stars, no story, in the ordinary sense of the word, threading its way among the shots. How clever, then, of Messrs John Grierson and Stuart Legg, who made it, to make what sounds like a short film into one of feature length!

I cannot possibly give you a list of the various sidelights on the BBC and the many characters, public and private, who are introduced.

I cannot express in words the beauty of the sequences, the humour poked at the staff and at listeners, the satire and the brilliant sound accompaniment. That this is the most important documentary film yet made in England I have no doubt.

I can just ask you to notice the little details. Listen to the spoken words and see how the directors show on the screen at the same time not generally the speaker but the objects he is talking about, or what you are probably thinking about while he is speaking.

Notice how the shots of Nina Mae Mackinney cut, dissolve and sway with the rhythm of her singing.

A good many prominent characters ranging from Bernard Shaw, with his rich Irish voice, to Clapham and Dwyer appear and talk in the film. I think the finest face of them is that of the ascetic Gerald Heard, as dolichocephalic and haunting as Conrad Veidt.

A good humorist is my colleague, Low. He says in the film: 'We cartoonists draw cock eyes and splay feet to give the waxworks life.'

The directors of *BBC* have done more than show mere waxworks; they have so shown our 'civilisation' by this film, that it is sometimes terrifying.

Jacob Epstein

Ever since he first made his public appearance in 1907, Jacob Epstein has been accused of blasphemy, immorality, obscenity, sensationalism, perversion, delighting in ugliness, breaking the Ten Commandments, breaking the conventions, incompetence, decadence, adultery, treachery, lack of patriotism, and many others of the major crimes which it is possible to commit in the present state of society. Though these accusations may not have increased in volume, they have not decreased in vociferousness, so that now the man-in-the-street, if he does not, like Lord Darling, confuse Epstein with Einstein, considers him to be the sort of person it is not safe to leave children alone with nor even to go near himself. You may be sure of one thing, Epstein is rarely considered as a sculptor. This is largely due to the fact that people are not interested in sculpture. They find it as uninteresting as its sister art, architecture. The art critics and the collectors and the intellectuals have made it a sort of hidden professional secret. You have to 'understand' it. But there is no 'understanding' about it. If you have eyes you can see it. It merely depends on how you look at it. So I imagine that an article on Epstein in a book of this sort, which contains characters so diverse, will be most useful if it merely suggests an outlook on the artist's work, and thereby his life and character.

Primarily Epstein is a Jew and proud of it. But unlike so many Jews who assimilate the customs and aesthetic standards of the country of their adoption, Epstein has chosen to get his inspiration from Jewry. The word 'Jewish' when used in connection with art, and particularly architecture, suggests a certain flamboyance and garishness with which we associate the interiors of cheap restaurants, an exaggeration of the mannerisms of the age in clothes, colour and decoration. Epstein, however, has not been imitative; his Jewish blood has stood him in good stead, for his sculpture has an Old Testament quality that is a change from the Graeco-Roman efforts of Royal Academicians. This Biblical quality is, moreover, indigenous to him and his race, a more genuine source of inspiration than could be Greek or Roman sculpture to an Englishman. Yet we were told by the popular press that Epstein was blasphemous when he made Christ a beardless Jew. Certainly

Epstein has been influenced by Rodin, African sculpture and Cubism; but they have been a means to an end: they have given the finish to his amazingly accomplished technique. They have not been his inspiration. Jewry has made him a poet.

To the casual observer, you may take it that he is a normal man, with an impressive appearance, unaffected manners, a delightful gift of conversation, and an utter indifference to public opinion or to the opinion of art critics. He is far too busy to bother about either.

That is an unusual thing about Epstein's life and character: he is a sculptor and he is busy. Despite the strong wave of public feeling against him, Epstein has his loyal supporters, and he has executed busts of characters so far apart as Lady Gregory and Admiral Lord Fisher. We have all heard of sculptors who were so poor that they had to steal stone from quarries and run away with it in a wheelbarrow by night. But Epstein, though he has not had an affluent career, has had the support of the few people in this country who are interested in sculpture. And so the abuse that has been showered on him has only gone to strengthen the loyalty of those who support him. Perhaps, you, reader, will be interested in sculpture if you go to look at the work of Epstein in the right frame of mind. So let my opening words be the advice of Epstein's greatest and earliest champion, the late T. E. Hulme: 'I make this very hurried protest in the hope that I may induce those people who have perhaps been prejudiced by ignorant and biased criticisms to go and judge for themselves.' That advice was given about Epstein's first Exhibition at the 21 Gallery in 1913. Today much more of his work is on public exhibition. Some of his earliest work is to be seen high up on what were once the British Medical Association's buildings in the Strand (1908). His other carvings include: the Oscar Wilde Memorial at Père Lachaise Cemetery, Paris (1912); 'Rima,' Hyde Park (1925); 'Day' and 'Night,' on the Underground Building, Broadway, Westminster (1929); and his bronzes are to be found in the Tate Gallery, the National Gallery, Dublin, the Imperial War Museum, the Dundee Municipal Gallery, the Metropolitan Museum, NY, Chicago Art Institute, the Leicester Art Gallery, the Brooklyn Museum, the Vancouver Art Gallery, the Aberdeen Art Gallery, the Baltimore Art Institute, the Edinburgh Art Gallery, the Glasgow Art Gallery, the Manchester Art Gallery, while he has frequent Exhibitions at the Leicester Galleries in London. I give this long list of names simply in order that my readers cannot say what is nearly always said by somebody in a conversation about Epstein: 'Well, I have seen photographs of such and such and I do not like it.' A photograph will give you no idea of a piece of sculpture. Enough of Epstein's work is publicly exhibited at present to allow almost anyone to visit it and judge for himself. But before he judges, let him have an impartial mind.

I will deal with Epstein's symbolic carvings first of all. I suppose that nearly everyone who goes to see a carving entitled, let us say, 'Night,' will have a preconceived picture of Night in his mind. If he is the average man and subscribes to *Punch*, he will be influenced by the cartoons of Sir Bernard Partridge and picture Night to himself as a tall woman, not unlike Britannia, in a black cloak, holding in her hands a new lamp-post or some floodlights or whatever happens to be the subject of the cartoon. Or perhaps his idea of Night will be influenced by an illustration in some book he had as a child, and he will expect to see it rendered into sculpture in the form of a relief, showing heavy trees flattened out in a semi-modernistic realistic manner, while five-pointed stars and a moon peep out above them, and quaint little owls, naughty little bats, and wicked little foxes adorn the lower half of the relief. Or perhaps you, reader, are more advanced, and think of Night in abstract terms. In that case I am not going to try to compete with you. But I do not see why you should approach Epstein's carving of 'Night' on the Underground Building in London with the ideas of Sir Bernard Partridge, or Edmund Dulac, or Max Ernst already in your mind. When I look at the Nurse Cavell Monument, by the late Sir Reginald Frampton, I do not expect to find in it the qualities that grace a painting by Sir Godfrey Kneller, much as I might welcome the change. Sir Reginald Frampton is as much entitled to his idea of a Nurse Cavell Memorial as anyone else, and certainly the public should not look for qualities in sculpture that are to be found in the utterly different art of painting; the only objection to the Nurse Cavell Memorial that you can have is that it is not your idea of what such a memorial should be. I will readily admit that it is not mine. But then the late Sir Reginald Frampton was not my idea of an artist. Sir Reginald thought the same about Epstein: 'He does not know the A B C of sculpture,' he said in a criticism of 'Night.'

Now sweep all this controversy aside, and, if you are in London, go and look at 'Night' for yourself. The first thing that will strike you is that the carving subordinates itself to the simplicity of the building. In fact, it looks as though it had been cut out of the building itself, instead of appearing as a messy appendage like the carving on the County Hall, Unilever House, South Africa House, and almost any recent large English building you like to mention. And now for the sculpture itself. A large impersonal being, with a Mongolian face, enormous arms suggesting latent power, is sitting in a composed position with its legs apart. The figure is swathed in heavy drapery, whose few deep-cut folds add to the general strength and impersonal calm of its appearance. Stretched across the knees is the beautifully executed figure of a corpse with arms folded on the breast and legs swinging helplessly out underneath, the foot dangling pathetically inert. The limp weakness of the corpse gives greater strength and majesty to the impersonal being. On the other side of the building, the same impersonal figure is holding up the arms of a little child. That represents 'Day.' To Epstein Day represents youth and Night death, a reasonable conception, while the impersonal figure, a successful interpretation of the Supreme Being, holds everything in its hands. I would hardly call this work blasphemous. In fact, it seems to me a conception worthy of a poet, executed with consummate skill and paying due regard to its architectural surroundings.

'Night' and 'Day,' however, are examples of Epstein's carving which will have a more universal appeal than his 'Rima.' Anyone in his senses can see what they are. With 'Rima' the case is more difficult. Rima is the 'Bird Goddess' of W. H. Hudson, the writer on natural history, to whom Epstein's sculpture is a memorial in the Bird Sanctuary in Hyde Park. In the first place the carving had to be visible from a path thirty yards away, which ruled out any question of doing a purely illustrative panel in light relief; and in the second place, the area of his design had been predetermined by a committee. Mr Arnold L. Haskell, in his book *The Sculptor Speaks* (Heinemann, 8s. 6d.), gives us Epstein's opinion of the work. In parenthesis I should say that this book, free from the horrors of art jargon, is the best detailed account of Epstein's work and theories one could hope to read; it is convincing and interesting, being a lively record of Epstein's conversation.

I was only walking across Hyde Park the other day, and went to see 'Rima.' I tried to view it as impersonally as possible. The wind was blowing and the leaves falling. It seemed just right. I really cannot understand what all the fuss was about. While I was doing the work in Epping Forest, my wife said, 'They will never be able to make a fuss this time.' [Smiling.] I shall never forget Mr Baldwin's expression, though, when he pulled the strings and the work was unveiled.

Later, he goes on to quote the actual passage describing Rima's death, from Hudson's book, which he had in mind when carving the memorial:

> What a distance to fall, through burning leaves and smoke, like a white bird shot dead with a poisoned arrow, swift and straight into that sea of flame below.

Now go and look at 'Rima.' It is not a bad walk from the Underground Building. On your way you will pass that curious mass of contorted marble in front of Buckingham Palace, the memorial to Queen Victoria. The smooth academic slickness of the sculpture is much to be expected; up Constitution Hill you will see the Quadriga on the top of the arch; it looks like an unseemly scuffle going on in a public place. Then there is the Machine-gun Memorial at Hyde Park Corner. I have heard this described as 'modern but effective.' It represents soldiers, heavily modelled in bronze, standing with their backs to a block of Portland stone, bearing a machine gun. After this slow crescendo to a finale, you come back to nature with a start as you cross the Park towards 'Rima.' Even from a distance, 'Rima' among its trees compels your attention. That is just what a work of art should do. It should give you a shock, make you think and feel, and it should dominate the landscape. For all its domination, Nelson's statue in Trafalgar Square has never, to my knowledge, been even discussed as a work of art. And as for the other statues, except for Charles I and Chantrey's George IV, I doubt whether one person in a thousand knows what they look like.

'Rima' is, at least, not undistinguished. Almost everyone knows what it looks like – that struggling creature with its arms pressing the sky, sinking between an upward rising eagle and a dove, through the stone panel down into the earth beneath. The natural reaction is, 'No, I don't like it. It makes me look at it, but there is something terrible about it.' And then as you continue to look at it, the harmonious design, the play of light and shade, the movement in 'Rima's' body, and the diagonal slope of the composition fix themselves on your mind. And, possibly, after a time you will realise how much deeper and finer is such a memorial as this, when compared with the little bunny rabbits and fairies of the 'Peter Pan' statue in Kensington Gardens. The two works are as different as are Blake and Alfred Noyes, or El Greco and Sir Luke Fildes: the first appeals to your feelings by means of form, the second uses the intercession of associations. To me the first seems the purer and the abler thing to do, and its effect is more lasting on the mind.

Of course, it is likely that 'Rima,' no matter how one argues, will displease many people just because they have read Hudson, and do not feel as Epstein does about his work. To me 'Rima' captures the spirit of Hudson's writing in a marvellous manner. I can think of no other living sculptor who could interpret an author's meaning in stone. I will take a favourite author of mine, Tennyson, and imagine an ambitious sculptural memorial of him by any Royal Academicians. The obvious combination of the May Queen, the Lady of Shalott, and Guinevere standing on a craggy bit of Cornish cliff, comes to the mind, while Sir Lancelot, holding a neat replica of Somersby Rectory, kneels in some bronze rushes below the grass at their feet. Of course this is an exaggeration – though the Cavalry Memorial and the new one to Queen Alexandra, and the RAF Memorial lead one to expect the worst from Academicians – but clearly, the effect conveyed by such a group would not suggest Tennyson, even if one read the inscription underneath. I doubt, too, whether it would arrest the attention, there is so much of that sort of thing about. But wherein lies the true beauty of Tennyson? His description of landscape, his lyrical qualities, his observation of the minutest forms of nature, and a sense of sky and space engendered in the fens. I do not know how to put that into stone, but I know of only four sculptors in England who would be capable of doing it, and Epstein is one of them.

Thus it is obviously wrong to approach Epstein's 'Rima,' after what you see of academic effort on the walk from the Underground Building, expecting a literal interpretation of some passage out of Hudson's books. 'Yes,' you will say, 'of course, I don't expect that, but damn it all, when a man is carving a memorial to someone who wrote about nature, he might at least interpret nature accurately instead of *distorting* it.'

That's where the public criticism of Epstein always thinks it is in the right. Epstein *distorts* nature. That must be wrong. And that brings us back to the inevitable argument: 'Well, if you want an exact replica of nature, have a photograph taken, or if it is sculpture you want, make a plaster cast or a wax model.' And somehow that silences further discussion, for by this argument it is impossible even to justify Marcus Stone. Time and again I have heard people say of 'Rima': 'It is so distorted; the hands are too big; I can see no need for doing that sort of thing.' But Epstein, like Michelangelo before him, deliberately accentuates a detail in order to get a desired effect. In the case of

'Rima,' the large hands complete the balance and rhythm of the design and at the same time give a sense of being in space to the figure, so that it seems only momentarily to be captured in stone, so full of life is it, as it struggles free from the confined area of the panel. And Michelangelo himself, against whom not the most Academic of Academicians will breathe a word, has frequently deliberately accentuated the muscles of his figures in order to give an effect of power. In painting distortion is an accepted necessity. No one has ever claimed that the work, say, of the Italian primitives, El Greco, or the French impressionists has ever successfully portrayed the human figure photographically. Whether in sculpture or in painting, the lines of the human figure, or of anything else, are not to be seen immediately on the surface; an artist finds new lines for us. That is his function – to give pigment or stone a life of its own conceived in his own brain. It is hard to explain why one shape pleases one man and not another. But it takes an artist to make a pleasing shape. I will borrow from Mr Haskell again and quote Epstein's account of an amusing occurrence, illustrating this point.

A. L. Haskell. What is art?

Epstein. I was once asked very much the same question by a judge in a New York Court. A Mr Steichen had bought Brancusi's well-known abstract work, 'The Bird.' The United States refused to admit it as a work of art, and charged 40 per cent duty on it as a 'manufacture of metal.' Steichen protested, and I was called in as an expert witness. This is what happened, after a long inquiry as to my qualifications:

District Attorney. Are you prepared to call this a bird?
Epstein. If the sculptor calls it a bird, I am quite satisfied.
Judge. If you saw it in the forest, would you shoot it?
Epstein. That is not the only way to identify a bird.
Judge. Why is this a work of art?
Epstein. Because it satisfies my sense of beauty. I find it a beautiful object.
Judge. So a highly polished, harmoniously curved brass rail could also be a work of art?
Epstein. Yes, it could become so.
Customs Officer. Then a mechanic could have done this thing?
Epstein. No, he could have polished it, but he could never have conceived it.

We finally won the case.

A. L. Haskell. Then you could not give a more comprehensive definition of art?

Epstein. No, not one that would be of the slightest use. All I can say is what I told the judge, my own personal reaction: 'This is a work of art because it satisfies my sense of beauty.' No one can say much more.

This incident helps, more than any theorising, to an interpretation of Epstein's carvings. The best thing to do is to approach his work without prejudices and previous mental pictures of what it ought to look like. No one liking poetry, and reading Shelley's 'Moon' for the first time, would think of saying, 'He *ought* to have written this or that, as Wordsworth or Shenstone would have done.' Why, therefore, *ought* Epstein to acquire the mind of Watts, Leighton, Frampton, Reynolds-Stephens, Chantrey or Jagger? If English people had the perception of the visual arts that they have of literature, there would be more hope for English sculpture.

Poor Epstein, his trouble is that he is a three-dimensional artist in a country which judges by two-dimensional standards. This is only a recent development. The grand age which made Westminster Abbey a repository of the works of such men of genius as Roubiliac, Flaxman, Wilton, Rysnack, Nollekens, the Bacons, Smith and Chantrey, is not far removed from the present generation of arty deans and chapters who want to clear their works away. Yes, the very deans and chapters who want to remove such statues and decorate the empty spaces with Pre-Raphaelite hangings come from that generation which has let every decent English churchyard be filled with glaring Italian marble crosses, sentimental angels, and Aberdeen granite obelisks, and has stuck the walls of village churches with tawdry brasses and vulgar or 'refeened' memorials – a generation bred on romantic literature, grounded in the Royal Academy, and finally plunging into a Celtic twilight, never to emerge. Salutary as were the sour grapes in other respects, the children's teeth are set on edge. One thing at least the romantic generation has acquired, and that is, a blind veneration for the past. Many deans and many chapters would give the aesthetic and unbiased consideration to some piece of grotesque carving in one of their cathedral churches that they would not think of giving to Epstein. Yet their Gothic carvings of evil spirits or good, as gargoyles or in bench-ends, rood-screens and misereres, are surely as much and more a distortion of nature than the public carvings of Epstein? Let me press home the argument in favour of *life* in sculpture as opposed to mere photography, by one more instance.

From my earliest childhood I have owned an old Teddy Bear called Archibald. His head is the shape of a large inverted pear; his eyes are brown wool with white wool in the middle; his body is egg-shaped, and he has tubular arms much longer than his legs. His paws are padded with some sort of cambric, and his expression is that of one who contemplates infinity from very near to. So deeply written upon my mind is the shape and expression of old Archibald, that when the word 'bear' occurs in conversation and someone is talking, perhaps about Polar Bears in Greenland, I think of lots of animals looking like Archie, rolling about on the Polar ice. Yet I went to the Dublin Zoo the other day and saw a Polar Bear at close quarters. It bore no resemblance to Archie at all. The eyes were small and wicked, the head was diminutive and cunning, and only in the shape of the body was there a suggestion that Archie came from the same species. Yet there is no denying that while being so different from a Polar Bear, Archie is undoubtedly a bear, although in detail he differs from all bears. Archie is to me a work of art as much as was Brancusi's Bird to Epstein. He satisfies my sense of beauty, as once he comforted my childish sorrow. I chose such a homely example of the sculptor's art – Archie, by the way, was made in a toy factory – because it is when he is at the stage of liking dolls and bears and other stuffed animals that the average Englishman is nearest appreciating sculpture. Thereafter the literary quality, that I have mentioned, comes into his appreciation, and it may be said, without reserve, that stuffed animals and dolls are the only examples of pure form appreciated for its own sake in England. It takes a lot of sophistication and conscious effort to shift the burden of literary association and meet pure form face to face again.

I have hitherto dealt entirely with Epstein's carvings – that is to say, his work in stone – largely because it is more for the public eye, metaphorically and otherwise, than is his work in bronze, and also because it is so stupidly ridiculed. When Sir Reginald Blomfield, the late Sir George Frampton, and the late Sir Frank Dicksee have said a thing is bad, you may be sure it is good. These three and a postman and a policeman (reported in the *Evening Standard*) started a newspaper outburst about 'Night' and 'Day,' to which I have already alluded. They were opposed, however, by Mr H. G. Wells, Mr Bernard Shaw, Mr C. F. A. Voysey, Sir William Orpen, Sir James Barrie, Edgar Wallace, Wilenski, and many others, including Mr

Hugh Walpole, who wrote in a letter to the *Manchester Guardian*: 'It is difficult to judge Mr Epstein's sculptured figures from photographs, but even in the photographs they are extremely interesting. Taking the photographs in conjunction with the names and expressed views of those who condemn Mr Epstein's work, I should suppose the figures to be masterpieces.'

But it is no use my continuing a sermon on how to look at Epstein's carving. If you like the shapes he carves, after you have received the first shock at seeing something you don't expect, then Epstein will have justified himself. But do not say he is incompetent or echo the sentiment of the late Sir Reginald Frampton, that he does not know the A B C of sculpture. He is a most accomplished craftsman, and his bronzes, which anyone can appreciate, since they are 'like' the people they represent, will dispel any public impression that he is incompetent.

His bronzes I have left to the last. There are more of them, as it seems to be his favourite material, but they speak for themselves, since they are, in almost all cases, portraits. But whereas a portrait in oils shows only one aspect of a figure from a certain angle, a bust has to be a portrait from countless angles, and no photograph can do it justice. Epstein works in the same bold poetical way over an intricate piece of portraiture as he does over a piece of monumental carving. He avoids any effect of mathematical correctness, which we can see in most Edwardian and late Victorian sculpture dotted about our towns. Such sculpture hardly ranks as portraiture, and the sublime insipidity into which the faces have been changed of these once famous people makes it impossible today to distinguish between General Havelock or General Napier, Councillor Robinson or Alderman Cleeves. Epstein realises that the two sides of a face are never alike, and he exaggerates this dissimilarity. His bust of Ramsay MacDonald is a particular instance; one eye is a fraction lower than the other, so is the brow, and the horizontal cleft in the chin is not quite parallel with the lips. It is not until one has looked at the bust for some time that these details become apparent. Then, when they have all been absorbed, the portrait is not merely a likeness – but a speaking likeness.

Probably no artist, save Rembrandt, has been such a master of light as Epstein. By means of the rough texture of his portrait busts, he is able to create shadows and heights in the face so that the bronze becomes flesh. It is possible to see this rough texture imitated by more prolific sculptors, and it at once becomes apparent that they do not know what they are at. They make the features jagged in an uncomprehending effort to be 'modern.' The subtle exaggeration of a remarkable feature in a face and the use of texture to convey light are never better displayed than where Epstein is modelling a bust from someone of his own choice. For this reason the bust of Iris Tree and of his daughter Peggy Jean are, for me, the most satisfying.

Epstein's bronzes speak for themselves. For the unprejudiced, so do his carvings. But when Epstein creates a work of art he does not want it to be judged by the reader of *Punch* whose taste has long ago been weaned to the gentle academics of Academicians, nor by the newspaper reporter out for a scoop, nor by the Bloomsbury monarch seeking the abstract and ever escaping it. He creates a work of art to please himself, just as any other artist does. And that brings us back to the beginning of the dissertation – what is Epstein, after all, when he has been exonerated from blasphemy, worshipping ugliness, lack of patriotism, etc., etc.? He is a Jew, and like all Jews subject to influences. During his career he has run the whole gamut of sculpture, admiring and being helped by, but never copying, styles so varied as the Egyptian, Japanese, Negroid, and the abstract Greek. The sculpture that appeals to him most is, I believe, the African, and it seems to have appealed to him for a long time. Mr Haskell quotes him as saying that negro sculpture is governed by the same considerations that govern all sculpture.

> In every good school of sculpture there are certain values quite apart from any interest in the object represented. The *Venus de Milo* is very much more than just a beautiful woman. The person who will not look or feel beyond the representation itself, cannot comprehend the very essence of sculpture, though he will persuade himself that he understands the Greek ideal, and that the work of the primitive negro is unworthy of study.

And what Epstein appreciates in negro sculpture is its blending of abstract forms – that is to say, pleasing shapes – with an underlying naturalism, a likeness to the human figure. It suggests new ways, outside the inevitable classical one, of interpreting nature.

Epstein is not primitive nor is he 'modern.' He is an artist who, by some freak of chance, has gained a reputation in a country which has somewhat stereotyped sculptural conventions. The 'moderns' are those who are typical of their generation's theories of what sculpture should be. Epstein is too important to belong to any period at all.

From *Twelve Jews*

Goodbye to Films

Yesterday I wrote my last article as film critic in this paper. When I started off, a pale green bogus-intellectual, a year and a half ago, what a different man was I.

A visit or two to some Continental films, a sarcastic sneer to any people who told me they were in love with Greta Garbo, and that was the sum of my cinematic experience. The word 'montage' was on my lips, 'art' was written in poker work across my heart, 'prose style' was embroidered with raffia on the reverse side of it.

I was as typical a middlebrow as ever thought he was highbrow and tried to write poetry in Hampstead.

And now what would you see, were these lines of type to fly about and form themselves into a portrait of the author as on some French surrealist short film? You would see a bald elderly man, still pale green, but with a tough expression, grim business-like lips and a pair of unscrupulous eyes gleaming behind recently acquired horn-rimmed spectacles. In fact, you would see a typical member of the film business.

For the film business does not want any rot about art. Those garish offices in Wardour street are not temples of the drama, they are shops with very clever men behind the counter who sell the products of Hollywood, Elstree and other film factories to exhibitors.

Every product of the factory is advertised as 'colossal', 'stupendous', 'poignant', 'the sensation of the century', just as fruit on a street stall is labelled 'choice', 'grand-eating', 'luscious', too often regardless of its merit.

Into this world of false values I came and like some chartered accountant, I had to go over the books every week and tell you what the real figures were, whether this film was bad or that good.

This was not so difficult at first. Stars did not mean much to me, so I was able to judge a picture impartially. And then the awkward thing happened. I found I really enjoyed all sorts of Hollywood films.

A murder story held me spellbound, a fast moving comedy in almost incomprehensible American made me hit the critic sitting next to me on the head with excitement.

Then I wondered why I was entertained, and I couldn't find out. I only knew that if a film was pretentious I was bored. Historical films, singing in old Vienna, crooners against a picture postcard background of Monte Carlo or Haiti bored me to distraction.

Then I thought 'Well, this film may entertain me, but it may not entertain my readers.' So I did what I was told to do, wrote the story of the film first and then said what I thought of it afterwards. And that was all I could do and all anyone else has done yet.

'Criticism' is perhaps hardly the word to apply to the work. 'Information' would be more appropriate. But you can't learn all you want to know from the story of a film.

The story is merely an excuse for the kissing. The film that has the biggest popular success, according to an American producer, is the film with the most kissing in it which yet pleases the censors.

But cutting and timing, not kissing and hugging, in my opinion, make a film entertaining. I hope this is not too intellectual of me. Whatever its plot, a cleverly cut film is a good one. Cutting and timing are largely the director's job.

They make a film run smoothly, they do not prolong nor foreshorten the jokes and the dialogue, they are responsible for the swift change of the scenes on the screen. Not even three dimensions and colour will save a film if it is badly cut. At the moment the best cut fictional films are American comedies and thrillers.

Yet it is impossible to write about cutting and timing three times a week. It is dull enough once a year. Indeed, cutting and timing are only noticeable after you have been to see about a hundred films. And even then they are as subconscious as scansion is when a poem is being read.

So instead of all this theoretical stuff, stars have been invented for me to write about and for you to read about. When I became a film informer I was determined not to mention stars more than necessary.

I considered them as 'pandering to the box-office and to the lowest elements in a cinema audience.' But now if I were to meet Greta Garbo in the street I would faint right away with excitement.

First reluctantly, and later willingly, I wrote about stars. There wasn't much else to write about. I have always thought that the various company changes, bankruptcies and amalgamations are only of interest to stockbrokers.

I was writing for their wives, so I wrote sweet nothings about Clark Gable, Garbo, Chaplin, Montgomery, Hepburn, Arliss, and all the rest.

I had always been told that the stars in person were disillusioning. A good many of them are. They are ordinary shy people who don't want to be bothered by a lot of fatuous questions.

Of those I have met some stand out in my memory as really good company. Jean Parker, Helen Vinson, Gracie Fields, George Arliss, Robert Montgomery, Loretta Young, Paul Graetz, and Dolly Haas I remember in particular.

I thank heaven for the stars I have met. I also thank heaven for those I have not met. They have still all the glamour for me that they had for my readers. And now goodbye to them all.

Films were gradually turning me dotty. I used to come out of a Press showing and caress the bricks in the street, grateful that they were three-dimensional. If I saw a thuggish-looking man with his hat pulled down over his face, I expected to be shot in the back.

Worse still, I was becoming unable to think. Thinking was being done for me on the screen and not very hard thinking, either. I was beginning to become historical in my style. 'Jean Arthur, whom you will remember in *Passport To Fame*, and who before that was in so-and-so, and so-and-so, is now in so-and-so.' Paralysis was creeping over me.

Only now and then was I woken up. The last great awakening came with *BBC – The Voice of Britain*, John Grierson's documentary film now showing at the Carlton. Here is a form of film which makes you think and which really is the good old 'art' that I was looking for in my early days.

I do not think this sort of film, nor indeed the thrilling sort of news-film promised us in 'The March of Time' series, will ever supersede the fictional films with stars in them. But they will become vastly more important.

Meanwhile, so long as kissing is popular, fictional films will be made. And so long as they are entertaining, we will go to see them. The old, old story seven times a week is, however, more than enough for the most willing ears after a year. The times may not change, but film writers ought to.

Evening Standard

Two:

1936 to 1939

Two
1936–1939

The face of Britain was changing fast between the wars. JB became increasingly aware of this and distressed not only by the major redevelopment of parts of London such as Grosvenor and Berkeley Squares but also by the gradual erosion of rural England. The Council for the Preservation of Rural England had been born in the mid twenties and the architect Clough Williams-Ellis' book *England's Octopus* was its virtual manifesto. The great boom in arterial roads and bypasses was just beginning, and with it endless swathes of ribbon development, stretching deep into the country. The 'family car' was a new phenomenon and vans and lorries were multiplying by the minute. Suburbs were growing in rhythm with rail and road transport, and the slum clearance programme begun in the 1890s (which was later called 'urban renewal') involved moving the denizens out to new estates on city edges.

Although high ideals for planning were being put into practice in some places such as Letchworth and even crystallised in small pockets like Welwyn Garden City, elsewhere there was less general chaos. Some 'planning legislation' was in place, but it was still optional for local authorities and extremely expensive for them to act upon because they had to compensate thwarted developers. Georgian buildings were being pulled down left, right and centre, which so incensed JB and many of his contemporaries that it resulted in the forming of the Georgian Group, pledged to conserving the best of what was left.

Having been sacked from the *Evening Standard* in 1935 for refusing to kowtow to advertisers, JB, whose foot was already firmly in the door of the BBC, began to work for them in earnest. He saw the Home Service as a brilliant soapbox from which to expound his views on the despoliation of Britain and the need for careful planning. His scripts were often so libellous that they ended by being heavily cut by his producers.

'People who do not live in Swindon consider it a blot on the earth. . . . Instead of trusting to good workmanship and a plain exterior and broad streets, the speculators have thought of their money before other people's health and happiness: they have crowded the houses onto the sites and they have spent money on outward show instead of internal good arrangement. They have thought of themselves before the town as a whole – as speculative builders do . . . As it is, Swindon still gnaws its way along country lanes eating up villages . . . The town plan has come too late to Swindon, as it has come to most towns. Now it flounders about like a helpless octopus, spreading its horrid tentacles into quiet untroubled places, waiting no doubt till one long and loathsome tentacle shall twine with that of the vile octopus London and Bristol will stretch out a tentacle to meet it from the West . . .'[1] JB's invective against the inertia of local government and the greed of speculators was counteracted by positive messages to his growing public. He told them to plant trees, to employ a qualified architect from the RIBA, and to 'fight against flashy rubbish that the speculator inflicts upon you – you will help to leave England fit for your children to live in. It's a hard fight, but my goodness, it's worth fighting.'

JB also broadcast a series of talks on west country seaside resorts called 'Seaview' and west country towns and cities called 'Built to Last'. His crusade was woven in and out of them.

Travelling around the country, preferably in trains, occasionally in an old Ford Prefect, gave him fodder for a steady flow of articles in the *Daily Express*, the *New Statesman and Nation* and the *Architectural Review*. He reflected for instance on his companions in a station waiting room or on fellow drivers on the 'Great Worst Road': 'Now is the time when imperious chauffeurs, like disappointed eagles, come flying by go buzzing past, a golliwog hanging in a back window, father, mother and youngsters huddled together inside. A loudly dressed man comes hooting past everything in a long low loudly-painted open car. Like the persistent whir of a dentist's drill, the motorcycles thread in and out. . . .'[2]

JB seldom, if ever, said no to journalistic jobs. He wrote on 'Venus and Champagne' for *Harpers*, 'the Curse of the Cottagey Cottage' for *Decoration*, on the Bressey Report for *The Criterion*, on Baillie Scott for *The Studio*, on 'Funny Books' for the *New Statesman and Nation*, and on Dickens' character Samuel Weller for *A Pickwick Portrait Gallery*. '*The Pickwick Papers* and Sam Weller are alone in my category of humour. There are three sorts of literary humour which I enjoy: satire, represented by Dryden, Swift, Thackeray, *The New Yorker*, and some of its imitators, and Evelyn Waugh; parody, represented by Horace and James Smith, Hilton, J. K. Stephen, Calverley, and Max Beerbohm; pure humour – Shakespeare, Hood, Edward Lear, Thurber, P. G. Wodehouse . . .'[3]

JB was thirty when war broke out. In a typically eccentric way, he applied to join both the RAF and the Royal Marines, both of whom turned him down on medical grounds: he ended by joining the Film Publicity Division of the Ministry of Information, for which he was well-suited from his experience of films and working for Shell in their publicity department.

If for many writers the late thirties were dominated by foreign affairs, by the march of Fascism through Europe and the Spanish Civil War, by the sharpening of class feeling and the birth of a new left-wing movement, his own life was dominated by his fight against the desecration of England. He was a 'parlour pink' and in his book *An Oxford University Chest* he wrote a suitably long essay on the Cowley motor factory to balance that on the university and to demonstrate his egalitarianism. His long diatribe in the Hogarth sixpenny pamphlet entitled *Antiquarian Prejudice* let off clouds of steam. 'What'll give us the opportunity to act? A Ministry of Fine Arts? a change of government? or a change of heart?'[4]

1. Swindon – Part of the *Town Tour* series broadcast on the BBC Home Service, 8 May 1937.
2. 'Teas', *Evening Standard*, 21 June 1935.
3. Contribution to *A Pickwick Portrait Gallery* (Chapman & Hall, 1936).
4. Hogarth Press, 1939.

How to Look at a Church

There's something much kinder about a house which has been lived in
for generations than a brand new one. Apart from the fact that ten to
one an old house is better built than a new one, it's part of England,
not a bright red pimple freshly arisen on its surface. An old house
reflects the generations that have lived in it. Your mother's taste for
frills and silk lampshades, your grandmother's passion for framed
watercolours, your great-grandmother's needlework and heavy well-
made furniture. It may be a bit inconvenient and muddled, but it is
human.

But of all the old houses of England, the oldest and the most
interesting are the Houses of God – the Churches. Better still, they
are open to the public, or they ought to be. Each generation has
contributed to the adornment of an old church, and the result isn't a
museum of showpieces, but a living thing, still in use. Old glass still
diffuses the daylight on the latest hats as softly as it did on the wigs of
the eighteenth century or the woollen hose of the people of the
Middle Ages. Elizabethan silver is still used for the sacrament. And
from the tower a bell, cast soon after the Wars of the Roses, lends its
note to the peal that ripples over the meadows and threads its way
under the drone of aeroplanes. The magniloquent epitaph and well-
carved bust of some dead squire looks down in breathing marble from
the walls, and the churchyard is a criss-cross of slanting old stones.
Here lies the England we are all beginning to wish we knew, as the
roar of the machine gets louder and the suburbs creep from London to
Land's End.

Supposing your great-great-grandfather were to come back to the
village of his birth. So great has been the change in the face of
England since the War that probably the only place he would
recognise would be the old church. And even that would be sadly
altered. Nine out of every ten churches in England have been terribly
mutilated by the Victorians. And I'm afraid that it's no good expecting
to find much merit in Victorian work, sticky pitch pine pews, church
furnishers' horrors in the way of reading desks and stalls, cumbrous
altar frontals, anaemic stained glass and sharp unyielding newcut

stone. Nor has the present generation improved things – 'refained' unstained oak, powder blue hangings, untidy little children's corners, gimcrack devotional objects, theatrical floodlighting, fearful stained glass, colour schemes thought out by 'artistic' religious people. The Victorians were downright ugly and had the courage of their ugliness, the present generation is timid and 'refained', tinkering and harmful.

Yet under this mere surface decoration, the old church struggles on. Your great-great-grandfather would recognise it. The proportions are probably the same, some windows, some carving, some tombs, some woodwork would remind him of the place he knew before he closed his eyes in the big box pew and slumbered away the parson's elevating sermon.

Looking at churches is really learning to look beyond the Victorians. Church architecture has been made incredibly boring by the antiquarians. In their anxiety to find a Norman window, or to open up an Early English piscina, in their insistence on the difference between the varying modes of Gothic architecture, they've omitted to see the church as a whole. They've turned what should be the enjoyment of part of England's beauty into a wretched wrangle over medieval dates. Forget that old bore who lectured to you at school on Norman fonts, forget those long hours trying to distinguish between Early English and Decorated. I'll give you a rough and ready rule for all this. There's not enough Saxon architecture for you to bother about. Norman architecture which went on till about 1100 consisted of round-headed arches and round stubby columns and thick walls. It was a brave attempt to copy the architecture of the ancients. 'Gothic' architecture which came along after the Norman, cannot be divided accurately into styles. You may take it that the more pointed an arch is the nearer it is to the earliest Gothic. It gradually grew wider and flatter until by Henry VII's reign the arches of windows and arcades had become almost flat. And anyhow much of the Gothic you see will be Victorian. Don't imagine, as all the guide books do, that churches ceased to be worth looking at after the reign of Henry VII. Some of the most beautiful were built by Wren and the Dances and local Renaissance architects in the seventeenth and eighteenth and early nineteenth centuries. In those days, too, our greatest sculptors and artists did most of their work for memorials in churches. Now that sort of thing is generally left to commercial-minded monumental masons. They, in turn, find it cheaper to buy tombstones already carved from Italy to which they add a name in hideous lettering than to use good local stone. Because of this there's hardly a churchyard in

England which hasn't, during the last fifty years, been defaced by staring white monuments in Italian marble.

Let us visit the church of Hagworthy St Philip. There isn't such a church nor such a place, but we'll invent one that stands for the typical English village church.

The guide book says: *Hagworthy St Philip: Norm. with Perp. additions. Note interesting EE pisc.* This gives you no idea of what Hagworthy church is like. You'll have to use your eyes and your common sense.

The country round Hagworthy is limestone of that grey, yellowy quality that is quarried in the Cotswolds and in parts of the Midlands. What few old cottages have been allowed to survive by progressive local councils are built in it. So is the church. No one but a fool visits a church without looking carefully at the exterior. Hagworthy church is all of a yellowy-grey limestone, but the chancel, at the East end, seems to be cleaner cut and sharper than the rest. The windows in it are full of elaborate tracery, but the stonework is shallow and less delicately finished than that in the windows of the nave or body of the church. In fact, it looks a little too good to be true. You may therefore conclude that the chancel is Victorian, especially since the roof is covered with bright red tiles and steeply pitched. This roof contrasts with that of the nave which is almost flat and covered with lead.

The tower has some tiny windows with round heads to them – mere slits, and survivals of the days when glass was difficult to procure. These windows are Norman. Then take a look at the windows of the nave. Do you see that in the upper portions of some of them there are pieces of glass which have a feathery silver quality on the outside? These are bits of medieval stained glass. Now look at the stained glass on those Victorian chancel windows. They have no silver featheriness. The colour shows through on the outside. This spells Victorian or modern glass. You've only to go inside to see how right you were. The little bits of medieval glass glow like jewels. They diffuse the light, but they don't throw coloured lights. The Victorian glass is thinner and more garish. It doesn't diffuse the light but blocks it out altogether – medieval glass usually had a lot of white in it; Victorian glass usually has none. Only in the brightest sunlight does the Victorian stained glass let in any light and then the light falls in colours on to the floor, not diffused with the even silver glow of broken daylight.

One more thing to notice before you go into Hagworthy church. All the best old tombstones covered with cherubs and urns are on the south side of the church. On the north side the entrance door is blocked and there are only a few hideous new white marble tombs.

This is because a legend grew up in medieval times that the devil lived on the north side of a church. The north door was blocked so that he couldn't get in and, generally, only disgraced people were buried in the shadow of the church.

Let us go in by the South door. There's some Norman zigzag carving over its round arch. When the door is open the familiar smell of wet earth, hassocks and old hymn books reaches one. Hagworthy is fortunate in having only its chancel spoiled by the Victorians.

The first things you notice when you enter an old church are the walls. At their best they are plastered and covered with a limewash beneath which, here and there, are the remains of medieval wall painting, the wing of an angel, the halo of a saint or the fearsome form of a devil carrying off a shrieking soul to hell. The Victorians liked to pull the plaster off the walls inside churches, and thereby destroyed hundreds of hidden wall paintings. You'll notice this has been done in the chancel at Hagworthy. How dark, dull and characterless that chancel appears contrasted with the white, light-reflecting walls of the nave.

Next you'll notice the arches and the windows and the sculptured heads called corbels from which the arches seem to spring. The same rough rules that I gave you earlier on apply to the distinguishing of architectural styles inside as well as outside a church.

Now notice the woodwork. Hagworthy is lucky. There is an old West Gallery where the choir used to climb up with its instruments of fiddles, serpent and flute. The old choir has been replaced by a wheezy organ played sincerely, if not accurately, by the vicar's wife. But the old gallery's still there. The new choir sits in the hideous chancel – a Victorian innovation. And then in odd corners there are still some of the old box pews, with doors and even a fireplace and baize lining to the seat backs and watered silk cushions. Box pews are generally of pine and sometimes painted. Earlier pews are usually of oak and are no more than benches, often elaborately carved.

Then the pulpit may be a fine piece of Elizabethan woodwork, with a sounding board above it and carved panels. All such woodwork exists at Hagworthy – in the nave. But in the Victorian chancel there are pitch pine stalls for the choir and an oak reading desk for the Rector, and it's hard to say which is uglier, the sticky pitch pine of the stalls or the church furnisher's Gothic of the reading desk.

Then have a look at the monuments on the walls – all of them excellent up till the date of 1840 when they tail off and the lettering becomes ugly and the designs heavy. On the walls you'll be able to trace the rise and fall of the big family of Hagworthy, first the simple brass let into the floor, then the kneeling figures gaily painted of the Jacobean monument, then that disconsolate widow of Queen Anne's reign weeping among cherubs, then that chaste female of the reign of George III leaning elegantly on a half-draped urn, then the Victorian tablet to the squire's son who died in the Crimea, and then the chancel, a hideous memorial to the good squire himself, and finally the ugly little brass tablet on the wall to the last of the squire's race to live in Hagworthy.

And here we'll leave Hagworthy and return to a general rule. If there's a slight smell of incense and the English Hymnal is used and the church is open and easy to get into; if the altar has many candles on it and a carved and painted wood at the back called a reredos, and a glowing frontal, then the church is 'High'. If there are only two candles and a brass cross on the altar and a couple of vases of flowers and a non-committal frontal, then the church is 'Broad' or what is termed 'ordinary'. If there is a bare table at the East end with an alms dish on it and a chair at the north side and a little reading stand on the table, then the church is 'Low'. Low churches are often locked.

I have not mentioned many other things to be found in a church, the well-carved or painted Royal Arms, symbols of the union of church and state; the commandments-boards and paintings of Moses and Aaron; the old organ cases; scratch dials, records of the medieval time system; ringers' rhymes; epitaphs; hour glasses; roofs; clerestories; and old brasses.

The old churches of England are the story of England. They alone remain islands of calm in the seething roar of what we now call civilisation. They are not backwaters – or they shouldn't be, if the clergy and people love them – but strongholds. I only hope I've shown you, in this talk, that a church isn't just an old building which interests pedantic brass rubbers; but a living building with history written all over it and history that, with very little practice, becomes easy and fascinating reading.

The Listener

Gentlemen's Follies

A year or two ago, Lord Berners wanted to build a tower on a tree-clad eminence, known as Faringdon Folly, in Berkshire. The local council, which was responsible for hideous council houses and the clumsy arrangement of electric light poles and the destruction of plenty of sound ancient cottages, objected to the erection of the tower, on aesthetic grounds. Of course, when the case reached the Ministry of Health, which for some mysterious reason is the arbiter of public taste in these matters, the objections of the local council were overruled and Lord Berners was allowed to build his tower. Today its Gothic pinnacles gleam white above the dark trees and suggest that there is possibly a mouldering abbey screened by the foliage below. The view from the tower is extensive – the very view described by the laureate Pye in his poem, 'Faringdon Hill' – and Faringdon is proud of the tower, and pays an entrance fee to climb up to admire the prospect and the money thus paid goes to charity.

But that is beside the point. The interesting part of this story is an analysis of the emotions of the local council when it objected to the tower. The ostensible objection was that a tower would ruin the look of the country. This is understandable, for almost all English building this century has succeeded in ruining the landscape, and even local councils are nervous about what private individuals may do. But this objection was only half-hearted. The local council was plainly bewildered. Since local councils were founded, the idea of a private individual erecting a building for no other purpose than the improvement of the landscape had never occurred. No wonder Faringdon was bewildered. Here was a man actually building a tower for the sake of building a tower. He was known to be an artist and a musician and a writer, which made him suspect at once. And this tower he was going to build was not even a water-tower. It was just a tower. The local council was shocked at anyone spending his money in such a purely decorative way – this was the real objection which the local council made, though it never expressed itself so honestly.

I think the attitude of the local council and of Lord Berners to the English country may be taken as representative of the twentieth and the eighteenth centuries. The twentieth century, for which the local council stands, sees England not as landscape, but as material for drainage schemes, slum clearance, rating, road improvements, and site valuations: the eighteenth century, for which Lord Berners stands, in this instance, sees England in terms of parks, landscape, trees, prospects, and noble buildings. It is the difference between a sense of money and a sense of spaciousness. The local council cannot believe that anything short of a direct material benefit to the community can be of any use.

Most 'follies' are the products of the eighteenth century. They were built to improve the landscape. True, they were primarily to improve the landscape as seen from the houses of the builders of them. The Belvederes of Devon, Ralph Allen's Sham Castle at Bath, memorial columns here and there, the eye catcher at Rousham, Dinton Castle, the 'ruins' at Virginia Water, and the temples, pavilions, bridges, castles, and columns in the gardens of such places as Stowe, Blenheim, Kenwood, Up Park, Goodwood, Wrest Park and Alton Towers. Sometimes, indeed, these 'follies' were fanciful in the extreme. The west walls of Castle Howard, County Wicklow, are painted pink in order that the sun may seem always to be setting on them. The entrance porch to the castle is arranged as a false perspective of a cloister.

All this is landscape delight. The word 'folly' as a term of patronising abuse seems to have been a later development. Perhaps it started in a rather sinister way at West Wycombe. Here the church tower is surmounted by a gilt ball in which several people can sit. The church itself is beautiful and secular. Psychic people are afraid to enter it and ghosts have been seen flitting among the junipers on the slope of the church hill. The ghosts and the oppressive atmosphere may be due to the unlaid presences of the 'Monks of St Francis', eighteenth-century wits who dabbled in black magic at West Wycombe. Some of them are buried in the mausoleum below the church, another sinister and stupendous folly in flint and stone.

The monkish atmosphere has long been associated with follies. Fonthill Abbey is chief of the monkish follies, though now nothing remains of it but a magnificent site, a few rare bushes and a small Gothic wing. But the monkish follies were, for the most part, designed to improve the landscape.

More personal follies are fairly prevalent, and the stories about them reach fine heights of fancy. The more extraordinary seem to have been erected in Queen Victoria's reign, when individualism could still sometimes afford to indulge its whims, when whims were more extraordinary than in previous ages. Mr Oswell Blakeston, who had made a thorough study of follies, says that Major Peter Labellière was buried on the top of Box Hill in a deep well-like cavity, 100 feet down. The coffin was let down head foremost with the feet upright. 'The eccentric major was firmly convinced that at the Resurrection the world will be turned topsy-turvy, and he took this precaution in order that he might find himself on his feet.' Another religious eccentricity is the concrete building outside Gillingham in Kent, called 'Jezreel's Tower'. This is a temple designed for the followers of the beliefs of Captain Jezreel, who wrote *The Flying Roll*, a prophetic book about the end of the world. The Jezreelites were to stand in it and resist the conflagration at that dread time. There are still some followers of the Captain. I remember attending one of their services in a little house called 'The New and Latter House of Israel', in the Camden Road, London. Another concrete folly is Petersen's Tower at Sway, in Hants. This building stands about 200 feet high and was an early experiment in concrete construction. At Woolstone, in Berkshire, is a folly which is typical of many in England. It represents someone's revenge on a neighbour. It consists of a red-brick house, four storeys high, one room thick, and without a staircase. It was never finished, for the builder ran out of money. He was determined to overlook the squire's garden, because he had some idea that if his house was higher than the squire's, he would be squire himself. Family feuds are another cause of follies. On the shores of Lough Ennel, in County Westmeath, are two houses, Belvedere and Tudenham. The families quarrelled and a sham ruin of immense height was erected between the two demesnes, so that neither house should get a view of the other. It takes the Anglo-Irish, that noble race, to outdo even the English in eccentricity. Adolphus Cooke, of Cookesborough, County Westmeath, bought some balloon-backed chairs which greatly delighted him. So he had the square windows of his Georgian house made into balloon shapes. As these were Victorian times and the windows were plate glass with sashes working vertically, they would neither open nor shut once they were constructed, by reason of the balloon shape.

In 1937 the Shell petrol people started a series of lorry-bills, painted by eminent artists, of the various follies of England, Scotland and Wales. They did good service, for this was the first time that any public record was made of the subject. Follies are what most guide books, with characteristic antiquarian bias, would call 'modern'. The motor car has brought 'follies' into their own. It is hard enough to see anything from a modern motor, but even motorists can hardly fail to notice things like Fish Hill Tower at Broadway, Bishop Copleston's Tower at Honiton, Haldon Belvedere and the countless water-towers and columns and obelisks which more spacious ages erected. Perhaps the time is coming when these things will be fully chronicled, though information of them is hard to find since they are not 'ancient' monuments. The most ridiculous of them will remain as inconsequent reminders of the delightful eccentricity of a great nation; the more beautiful will serve to show that there was once a time when England was a huge landscape garden diversified by the seats of the great. Today, landscape for most of us has shrunk into a back garden, and the most daring folly is a stone dwarf or an earthenware rabbit at the end of the crazy paving. Give me the most Byzantine water-tower in its stead!

Country Life

Bristol: An Unspoiled City

Bristol is still the most beautiful big city of England: far finer than London which must, a hundred years ago, have been the loveliest city in Europe. But London has pulled down its best domestic buildings, and has erected instead huge blocks of unwanted flats in a commercial Renaissance style. Bristol has been spared much of this sort of 'progress'. London has not solved its traffic problem, but instead is continually hacking chunks out of the centre of itself, building huge bridges – such as the new Waterloo Bridge – where they are not wanted, in a feeble attempt to stave off the increasing flood of motors on the road. And all the time London goes on building blocks of flats and offices where the traffic is thickest and where there should be open spaces – so the traffic gets worse and worse. Bristol has not such a difficult traffic problem as London. What problem there is will be partially solved by the four ring roads which I am told are being built round the city. One of them, the inner one, runs right across Queen Square. This is unfortunate, but unavoidable. If we have many motor cars, we must pay the price not only in tax and the cost of the car but also in the scenery which motors are intended to take us to see. The road through Queen Square is part of a circle round the inner part of Bristol, which, it is intended, will divert that most unpleasant rush of traffic on to Bristol Bridge. This circular road will have very few houses or offices actually on it, and will be a really useful through road instead of a main street with a succession of traffic blocks.

London once had the most beautiful Georgian estates laid out in the days when people really knew about vistas, proportion and handsome living-rooms. London has destroyed or is destroying all of these. But Bristol is still in possession of Clifton, a place of quiet terraces where perhaps this very evening retired colonels and admirals are putting down the newspapers to look for a moment across the trees and garden beds, lit up by lamplight, now that evening has closed in, and watching the Avon Gorge, perhaps, with the Clifton Suspension Bridge floating across it. Terrace after terrace, crescent and square – stately houses, some of them turned into flats, but still preserving their outward beauty: Clifton is as impressive in its way as Bath. Bristol,

then, has a suburb which is better than anything which has been
spared to London, unless it be those fine terraces round the Regent's
Park.

But I have never heard of anyone – recently, at any rate – coming to
Bristol to see it. They come for business with bowler hats on their
heads in small saloon cars, and they hurry away. Or they come to die
among the ilex and plane-shaded terraces of Clifton, but they do not
think Bristol is a show place. People go to Canterbury to see the
Cathedral, they go to Stratford-on-Avon and see so much half-timber
that they don't know what is Elizabethan and what is 1925, but they
never go to Bristol to see the most unspoiled large city left in England.
I should think Bristol Cathedral is one of the least known in England.
Yet it is, now that it has been cleaned up and painted inside, one of the
most beautiful. I should think Clifton, with that amazingly delicate
Suspension Bridge, is *almost* – I say almost for it isn't quite – as lovely
as Bath. The main streets of Bristol certainly are none too lovely, but
once you get out of them you come across row after row of exquisite
Georgian houses. You climb up hills by steps and look back on a forest
of towers, spires and the masts of vessels which have threaded up the
Avon Gorge to reach the port of Bristol. From this port they set out to
find America.

Bristol certainly keeps itself to itself. You can travel up in a bus from
the Tramways Centre to Clifton Suspension Bridge and find yourself
feeling very out of it. Everybody knows everybody else even in this
enormous town. 'Come and play roulette, this evening, Harry'. 'Sorry,
I can't, Jack, the guv'nor doesn't allow it'. 'Nice weather it's been,
hasn't it?' Oh! Bristol, dear Bristol, how at home you make us feel
after the haggard angry faces in London; after the crowds in the
underground, what a change is the family party in the Clifton bus;
after the rush and noise, how sedately the trams screech through your
streets and whirr up your almost perpendicular hills!

I am getting carried away. I meant to talk about the lovely streets of
Bristol. Here is a list of some of the chief ones – Royal Colonnade; the
Arcades (so much better now than the Burlington Arcade of London
which has been vulgarised); Brunswick Square, with its Ionic Chapel
on one side and the Doric Cemetery gates and Dr Dymoke's Gothic
house further along: Portland Square with the exquisitely proportioned tower of St Paul's Church rising tier on tier, out of all that
stateliness; King Square, with its eighteenth-century houses with fine
front doors – King Square forming an even, bright foreground for the
heights of Kingsdown where Georgian terraces command blue vistas;

the Theatre Royal – its front has been spoiled, but inside it still has the quality of a playhouse where Mrs Siddons might have acted; Royal York Crescent, as fine as anything in Bath; the Paragon; Caledonia Place; the West Mall and the Mall; that little half-crescent under Clifton Suspension Bridge near where the trams to Hotwells come to an inconsequent end; the climb up Zion Hill; and further back, best of all the streets of Clifton – Vyvyan Terrace. Those are some of the places which, if they are allowed to survive, will bring crowds to Bristol in ten or twelve years – for Bristol and Bath will be the only places to retain Georgian architecture.

Georgian houses are plain – there is no half-timber or fake half-timber about them. The windows on the ground floor are long and thin. Those on the next floor are shorter but of the same width. Those above are shorter still and almost square. The roof – if it is visible – is laid with tiles which are neatly graded – those nearest the eaves are largest and get smaller row by row till they reach the ridge. All these little tricks lend proportion – the secret of pleasing buildings. Now look at the details of Georgian houses. Notice the ironwork along the areas – Portland Square, Bristol, has lovely ironwork. Notice the doors, front and drawing room and bedroom – well made, with delicate moulding and well spaced panels. Notice the ceilings – pretty cornice, and then that absence of decoration which is decoration itself. Georgian architecture is not obtrusive: it is polite and gracious, like the nicest of our grandfathers. Bristol is full of it.

You will have noticed that I have declined to mention the few famous buildings of Bristol – and by that I mean famous to the outside world – such things as the Cabot Tower, the University Tower, St Mary Redcliffe, Wesley's simple Meeting House and various ye olde things. They do not need noticing as everybody notices them. What do need noticing are the squares and streets I have mentioned and many more whose unpretentiousness makes Bristol the best big town left in England.

The Bristol Corporation, I believe, really understands Bristol. It has established a panel of architects who pass every new design, and that panel, I hope, refuses to pass vulgar villas and shops in the fake half-timber style. The engineers and architects work together in an enlightened policy to keep Bristol intact and to spare, as far as possible, the agricultural country around it. Landowners are helping them by agreeing to keep spaces on their estates open. It is the duty of Bristolians to back the Corporation up.

This evening I drove round my favourite parts of Bristol with a friend. Bristol was looking its best. Sunset behind the Avon Gorge; quiet little squares; the new Sea Mills Estate with schoolchildren showing off in the evening sunlight and vistas of trees and fields and pleasant cottages that that magic estate has managed to create – and then I plunged back to Bristol. I had better not say by what road. But I saw villas which were as ugly, as out of keeping, as silly, as pretentious, as be-timbered, as be-stained-glassed, as be-rockeried as any of the worst outside London. They were built by private speculators, not by the Corporation. They were as bad, even worse, as to plan and appearance, than any in London. This was tragic. The beauty of Bristol lies in its individuality. It is one of the only towns in England to remain untouched by the tentacles of London. These estates were as bad as London itself. Bristol must keep away from London. No 'moving with the times' which means nothing. Keep away from London: keep away from London.

The Listener

The Country Town

I've been asked to conclude this gloomy series of talks with a reference to the devastation and preservation of the towns of Cornwall, because I haven't mentioned that county in this series. Thousands of us know those charming fishing ports, tumbling down steep hillsides to the fake antique shops on the quay. Thousands of us have regretted the odd-shaped bungalows which ruin the skyline on the cliffs above, and the little pink villas which seem to have escaped from Swindon or Wolverhampton, suddenly wedged in between feathery-grey slate cottages. The least spoiled towns of Cornwall are Bodmin, Liskeard and Helston. Nearly all the sea coast towns are spoiled by so called 'development'. So instead of throwing stones at glass verandahs, I'm going to tell you about an imaginary town and what has happened to make it hideous. I mean, we're all agreed, aren't we, that every English town has changed for the worse since the last war, in appearance. I'm sure that the drains are better, the road are wider and more slippery, the shops have brighter lights, the 'slums' have been cleared. I'm sure all sorts of progress has occurred. I only wish I knew what progress was. Some people think it means money, others electric light, others think it means large windows and unadulterated milk. But I'm discussing appearance, so let's imagine a fictitious town, and I'll lay a hundred to one that almost every progressive bit of development I mention has occurred in the town in which you live, much as it has occurred in what I'll call Mudminster.

Mudminster, despite its name, was a charming town of about 10,000 inhabitants before the war. The old minster rose grey among elms and willows which grew beside the sinuous river Mud. Narrow streets, survival of the haphazard days of medieval building, clustered round the minster. Broad tree-lined streets entered the town and standing behind high walls were the trim brick Georgian mansions – windows long at the ground floor, getting smaller, at each storey above – inhabited by doctors and solicitors. Old bow-windowed shop fronts with square panes in them and one or two pretty Victorian shops were in the High Street. Above the shop fronts noble merchants' houses appeared. A delicate bridge of the eighteenth century swept over the river in a single span: it was made of limestone and had a balustrade, rather like Henley or Maidenhead bridges, if you know those places.

If you stood on the hill above Mudminster, you'd see a few red roofs below you among the elms and clustering around the grey minster tower; the silver sweep of the Mud and the track of the branch railway winding into its little buff-coloured station. If you stood in the town you'd get an impression of horse's hoofs on cobbles, stable smells, the minster bells striking the quarter and lilac hanging over a garden wall.

Transport yourself to Mudminster today. If you stand on that same hill, you'll see pink roofs and few elms, for the elms have got elm disease and the Council is too keen on money to plant any more trees; the large pink roof of a cinema against the Minster, and the town will have seemed to stretch for two or three miles in each direction along the main roads. Houses like pieces of cake, like toothpaste, spread out in ribbons along the roads. Stand in the middle of the town and you'll get an impression of throbbing motor cars, a blue mist of petrol, a shindy of hooters drowning the minster bells and the loudspeaker from a wireless shop blaring across the tarmac.

Mudminster has moved with the times. The old bridge has gone and a fearful thing in a Municipal Renaissance style in concrete by the Borough Surveyor has taken its place – for the convenience of motorists: the elms and limes in the approaches have been cut down, for the convenience of motorists: the narrow streets have been widened, for the convenience of motorists: the Georgian houses have been pulled down for a car park, for the convenience of motorists: the branch line is disused, owing to motorists; the old houses above the shops have been pulled down or defaced, for the convenience of multiple stores: the old square-paned shop fronts have been replaced by slimy stretches of opaque glass scrawled with neon-lettering, for the convenience of multiple stores: a cinema has gone up right against the old Minister – as at Malmesbury in Wiltshire: Mudminster sky is strung with wires, its streets stink and roar, its old houses have gone – except for one ancient building of the fourteenth century, 'Ye Olde Ghoste House', which has been so carefully preserved that it's now so old that you can't believe it's true. The thirty-mile speed limit extends for two miles down every main road, because new villas have been built on either side. These villas are in various so-called Tudor style and one is called 'modern'. They bear no relation to the landscape in either material, colour or proportion. They aren't even well built. Electric light poles march with telegraph poles down either side of each road.

Mudminster has moved with the times. This is progress. Why, all the 'slums' have been 'cleared'. The people who lived in those airless courts off the high street are now housed some two or three miles off down the London Road. It's true that they have to walk three or four miles to work, that their rents are higher and the bus service is infrequent and expensive: it's true that the children have to cross a couple of main roads on their walk to school: it's true that the nearest shops are a mile away, and the cinema is two miles, but have they not a bathroom and a garden (on clay soil) and a lovely recreation ground only half a mile away which the Council hopes one day to be able to plant with trees? And then if you ask a Councillor what he has done to preserve Mudminster, he'll proudly show you 'Ye Olde Ghoste House' I mentioned – as though that sort of 'preservation' was anything more than archaeological humbug to appease some elderly museum curator and to make copy for the newspapers.

But don't let me condemn our present glorious age. There is a lot to be said for it. If, for instance, a bypass had been built round Mudminster, the approaches and the old bridge could have been saved. But various interested parties on the Council were getting a bit out of the contract for the new bridge, and others owned property along the main roads. If the Town Planning Act had been brought into force, much villadom might have been diverted from the edges of the main roads into districts nearer the town. But interested parties on the Council had bought land on the main roads, so the Town Planning Act was deliberately held up – this actually happened at a certain well-known old West Country town, until the land was sold for building sites. Then you'll say, why don't the Council control the shop fronts of the Multiple Stores, preserve the Georgian buildings as well as the 'Ye olde' ones, forbid the erection of inharmonious, ill-proportioned villas?

And now we can leave Mudminster and ascend or descend to Plymouth, Exeter, Salisbury, Bath and Bristol, the towns we have been discussing in the earlier talks of this series. From what I've just said, you might imagine that *all* local councils were sinks of corruption. There is evidence, plenty of it, to support this theory. I know a caterer in a big town in the Midlands, who said, 'Yes, I used to be on the Council, but it never brought any business to my firm, so I resigned.' This attitude is quite usual. It's not so much corrupt as ignorant. People join a council with the honest intention of getting a bit of business out of it. It doesn't occur to them that this is dishonest, or that a council is unpaid public duty. But local councils are often

maligned. All the towns I've visited lately and about which I have had
talks with members of the Council and with residents, show what a lot
of good local councils can do, and how they are restricted from doing
good.

You must remember, to begin with, that if you serve on your local
council as a Councillor, you aren't paid. You may have as many as two
or three committees to attend a week – all for nothing, but the curses
of the ratepayers. Consequently most Councillors are retired trades-
people, or retired civil servants, or retired military or naval people.
Others haven't time for the job.

It often happens, therefore, that a Councillor is quite ignorant of
local government. He can't understand acts of Parliament and legal
and technical language. He can't read an architect's plan or imagine a
so-called 'improvement'. So he records his vote on the same side as his
friends and leaves it at that. As a result of his vote a whole town may be
ruined. In the last fortnight, for instance, the streets of Salisbury have
suddenly sprouted with concrete lamp standards which have turned
the town hideous and driven all character from its streets. Possibly
that's a result of ignorant voting. In the hands of an unscrupulous
Town Clerk or some other servant of the Council even worse may
happen to a town than ugly lamp standards. Its green spaces may be
built on, its best buildings destroyed, its views blocked. And the rates
may leap to fever height.

That many councils have goodwill is evidenced from the wonderful
support I have had in this series of talks from local authorities.
Architects, Councillors and a Mayor have given their help and joined
in discussions and explained the position. Councils where they have
the goodwill haven't the powers: officials of Bristol, Salisbury, Exeter
and Plymouth have shown that the local council has no control over
designs of new villas, the preservation of Georgian street façades, the
protection of any buildings later than 1714. The only powers they
have are advisory, and few people are willing to take advice over their
own property. Bath is the only city which has powers for protecting its
eighteenth-century buildings and controlling new materials and
elevations. As a result, Bath is the most beautiful city in England, and
making money out of its beauty. Bath obtained these powers as a result
of special Acts of Parliament. Bristol hopes to do so soon. But neither
Plymouth, Salisbury nor Exeter, nor any other towns in the West have
such powers. This is a ridiculous position. If good things disappear at
the rate they are going now, there will be little decent left in any of
these once lovely cities. As I talk, the Royal Hotel, Plymouth, is cut in

half, the Higher Market at Exeter is coming down, Bristol is spoiling some of its fine Georgian work, Salisbury is strong with concrete lamp standards: fearful villas are going up in inaccessible suburbs of every large town. The same Acts of Parliament as have been granted to Bath should be given to and compulsorily adopted by every old town in England, if England is to remain worth seeing. This isn't preservation for preservation's sake, it's the self-preservation of our country.

But there's no use in a local council having these powers if it has neither the intelligence nor wish to use them. The Mayor of Exeter among his many wise remarks said, 'I should like to think that the average citizen was genuinely concerned with the preservation of our ancient buildings and the design of the new ones. But I'm afraid he doesn't usually give it a second thought.' This is only too true. Mr Barnes, a Salisbury resident, said 'In all my nine years as a ratepayer, I've never voted in a municipal election because there has never been more than one candidate in any ward in which I have been living.' So there is another handicap to local councils – a complete lack of public interest in local government. Disinterested and keen people are left to fight with ignorance, apathy and, sometimes, corruption. It is you who are listening tonight who will have to pay for this inefficiency. You'll pay not only in high rates, but in your national heritage. Get on the local council, force an election, if you have the time for the work. Save England from bad local government; save our old towns, our stately Georgian streets, build worthy new towns in the right place. You take care about your plants in the garden, the house is important too. The whole town looks at a building, only a percentage looks over the fence at the garden. Think in terms of streets, not single buildings and little bits of ancient stone. Compel those who develop large estates to assign a certain area to open spaces – this was Councillor Gordon of Salisbury's suggestion. Councillor Gordon also remarked that 'in the end every community gets the buildings and the environment it deserves.' I don't like to think that Plymouth is so unworthy of itself, that it pulls down its magnificent Regency buildings, or Exeter so unworthy of its ilex-shaded terraces and elm close that it must destroy the Higher Market and permit such hideous treeless suburbs, or Salisbury so regardless of its beauty that it can't control the design of its lamp standards and modern shop fronts. The criticism given by residents, the sympathy displayed by such men as the City Architect of Bristol and of Plymouth, the Mayor of Exeter, Councillor Gordon of Salisbury is equal to that of those who talked from Bath in the first talk in this series. Such men need public backing. If you really love English scenery and old English towns with their Georgian stateliness and ancient texture, you'll support such people. There are hundreds of smaller towns – and larger ones – which need waking up.

Wherever I went on my tour, I found discontent with the local council. The main criticism was needless destruction, ugly and inconveniently situated suburbs, noisy streets; one person remarked that when a council wasn't corrupt it was so torn apart by political issues that it paralysed itself. This is especially true of some large towns. Local Government should be above politics.

The alternative to Local Government was envisaged by Mr Oliver Stonor of Exeter. 'The conclusion of the whole matter seems to me to be that there is none, or no adequate, machinery for dealing with the preservation of good buildings which are neither medieval nor "ye olde": and there ought to be, and that it ought to be a machine made up of people with specialised knowledge and not of town councillors who, though honourable men, are often, of necessity, lacking in special knowledge or even in special taste.' I would carry this a step further and advocate a Ministry of Fine Arts or of National Planning, or whatever you like to call it, which could override local councils and fine people heavily for putting up ugly houses – a more permanent form of litter than that which you now get fined £5 for. I'd send people to gaol who stole our heritage of decent houses and streets by destroying them. This is all rather against the spirit of democracy, for which we are supposed to stand. But Government control will have to come in soon, unless you join the local council and oust the ignorant and incompetent. It will be hard work, but it will be worth it. You'll have helped to convert England to its former beauty before it's too late – you'll have helped to make the England you knew as children worth living in for your own children. The alternative is Government control.

In conclusion let me quote Councillor Gordon again. 'In the end every community gets the buildings and environment it deserves.' Is Government control what we deserve?

BBC broadcast

How to Look at Books

What the roulette table is to the gambler, the second-hand bookshop is to me. It has a fatal lure. I like the dusty shelves, the gas-jet popping in the inner room, the learned proprietor who only produces his treasures when you show him that you too love books, the worthless odd volumes ranged at a penny each in a tray outside the shop, the odd mixture of the interesting and the unreadable ranged in rows of brown leather, red board, green board and paper jacket all round the walls.

I started collecting books when I was twelve. Now, my room at home is like a second-hand bookshop and books have overflowed into other rooms in the house: they are piled up on the floor, ranged round the walls of bedrooms, littered over the table in the hall. I ought to tell any intending burglars that I have nothing really worth his coming to get. I've only been able to afford shillings. I'm not like Dr Rosenbach, the American buyer, who thought nothing of paying three or four thousand pounds for a single small volume. That kind of book buying doesn't interest me. Still, I always hope that one day, when I'm turning over the junk outside a shop which also deals in doorknobs, rags, oil lamps and broken fire-screens – I always hope that I may find, lying between a dirty copy of *Eric, or Little by Little* and an odd volume of Macaulay's *History of England*, that little pamphlet Shelley was sent down from Oxford for writing 'The Necessity of Atheism', with perhaps an inscription from Shelley to the Master of the College which sent him down. I should sell it at once, buy a car and a vacuum cleaner for my wife to clean the books in our house at present and invest the rest in more books of the kind I like – ones about architecture and topography and poetry books. But the days of picking up bargains like that are nearly over. Once a London bookseller went down to see the books at Lamport Hall, an old country house in Northamptonshire. Accidentally, he came into an old lumber room where there were piles of books among the furniture, covered in dust and eaten by mice. In among them he found a rare edition (1599) of Shakespeare's *Venus and Adonis*. In 1919 this book fetched £15,100.

The nearest approach to a bargain I ever made myself was in Exeter. There was an old bookshop selling up and in an upper room I came across a pile of paper covered children's books; they had been printed about one hundred and thirty years ago, and coloured by hand. Now people generally throw away nursery books, so old books for children are comparatively rare. I bought the lot for half-a-crown. Some years later, when I was terribly hard up, I sold the best of them to a Bond Street dealer for £10.

But I have always regretted it. I can't bear to part with a single volume and I'd like to take this opportunity of asking my friends to post back to me immediately the many books they have 'borrowed'. Richard Heber, the greatest book collector who ever lived, said you should have three copies of every book: one to look at, one to read and one to lend. I can't afford this. When Heber died in 1833 – he was, by the way, a brother of Bishop Heber who wrote 'From Greenland's icy mountains' – he had eight houses, each full of books and 158,000 books altogether.

But I'm telling you about buying books, and I've been asked to tell you about how to look at books. First of all you should know how to treat them. It turns me sick to see some great brute lick his thumb and turn over the pages, even of a ledger, with his sticky finger. You should turn over the pages of a book with the right hand and at the top right hand corner. If you turn the pages over in any other way, you crease the paper. Then you should never turn down the corner of a page. It's sacrilege. Every book is somebody's friend, even if it isn't yours.

Don't strain the binding of a book by bending it back. Hold a book only half or three-quarters open – especially if it's an old book. If the cover works loose of an old book, its value is reduced by half, and, what's more, its beauty is gone.

And here's a message to the wives of book collectors. Don't dust old books with a duster. It scratches the binding and flips the leather labels off the backs. Use a feather broom.

I can't possibly tell you all the secrets of book collecting in a few minutes. I don't know a quarter of them myself and the bookseller's trade takes a lifetime to learn and is, even then, more than one brain can carry. You have to know all about cancel title pages, errata, bindings, pirated editions, proof states of plates, large paper copies, suppressed passages and the hundreds of forgeries which still are practised. And talking of forgeries, beware of those 'old coloured local views' you see some unprincipled booksellers selling. They're often grey steel engravings torn out of books and coloured up last week with watercolours in the back of the shop. Today, hundreds of lovely steel-engraved books of local views are torn up and the plates cut out and coloured and stuck on to lampshades or waste-paper baskets, or framed and sold at 10/- when they cost the villain who did the work about 2d apiece. I once remonstrated with a bookseller who was cutting up an old book of the 1830s in that manner. I told him the author's ghost would rise up and haunt him. But he wasn't alarmed and said, 'I've got to live, haven't I?' I said I didn't see why. No one who loves a book cuts out the illustrations. Besides, many old coloured plates fade when they're exposed for long to the light.

The condition of a book is one of the most important things about it. A first edition of Milton's *Paradise Lost*, for instance, may be worth a hundred or two, but if its margins have been cut a quarter of an inch, or if it has a page missing, even one of those blank fly-leaves at the beginning or end, or if it's been rebound, may be only worth a few pounds. To attract the collector, a book must be in what is sometimes called, in the trade, 'Jennings' condition' – this phrase comes from a collector called Mr Jennings who likes his books to look as they did when they were published, without a scratch on the binding, or a stain on any of the pages.

But I don't expect many listeners have a first edition of *Paradise Lost* or a first folio of Shakespeare to sell. And I would here issue a warning. Don't suppose that any old book is valuable, just because it's been in your family for years. We have a family Bible dated seventeen something, but it's only worth a few pence. And please don't write and tell me you have an old book which may be valuable; take it to the nearest second-hand bookseller or to the biggest public library and find out there. I'm not an authority and I couldn't afford it, if it were valuable – which it probably wouldn't be. The things that determine the value of a book are condition and rarity, not age. There are many valuable books not ten years old. There are many valueless ones, two hundred years old.

There are, however, various things you can find out about a book, whatever its value, which are of interest. You sometimes see after the title of a book in an advertisement – Crown 8vo. This is a usual size for a book. It means Crown Octavo. And that means that a sheet of crown sized paper has been printed on both sides ready for folding into pages. Octavo means that the sheet is folded eight times, making sixteen pages in all. If you look at the bottom of the page of many books you'll find here and there that a capital letter or some other distinguishing mark has been printed. When you find this mark count the pages until you come to the next letter in the bottom margin. If there are sixteen pages, your book will be octavo. If there are only four pages, your book will be a very big one, called a folio, in which the sheet has only been folded once, like a piece of writing paper. If there are eight pages, that will be a quarto and means four folds, or rather a process involving one vertical and one horizontal fold across it. A quarto volume is generally half-way between a big folio and the octavo, the usual size for a novel. There are, of course, smaller sizes. Prayer books are generally duodecimo – twelve-folded. These marks at the bottom of the page are to guide the binder, so that he knows in what order to bind the folded sheets without having to read through each book to get the pages in the right order. Sometimes binders trim the pages with a machine which works like a guillotine, sometimes they leave them uncut. Uncut editions are supposed, by some, to be more valuable than cut ones. Goodness knows why.

I've been talking far too much about the cash value of books. I'd like to end by talking about their real value and that depends entirely on how you look at them. I love books and collect books, because I like to look at them.

Books are, to me, the last link with the beautiful in England. English books are still the best printed and bound in the world. English literature is still the greatest reading.

In the old days they took such care about the production of a book. I took one down from my shelves shortly before I came here. A little-known poem called *The Favourite Village* by a Sussex clergyman called James Hurdis who lived about a hundred and fifty years ago. My copy is a gilt-edged octavo in a sumptuous leather binding. The binding is tooled with a beautiful design in the Adam style, all wreaths and borders. Even the gilded edge has tooling on it. The pages have faded to a soft cream colour and the type on the pages – by the way, it's always called 'type' never 'print' – is a brownish black. The date of this book is 1810, nine years after the poet's death. The margins of the page are browned and there's room to read. The sober blank verse is widely spaced and, though the type isn't large, it's easy to the eye, because it's so spaciously arranged on the page. The whole book is as delicately proportioned as a Greek temple.

And then as I smell its pages, I smell the England that has gone: a slightly musty smell which all old books have and which makes me think of the golden leather backs of the rows of shelves in a country-house library, of the deep silence of the fields outsides, of the looped curtains fluttering in a withdrawing-room window, of globe-shaped elms and spreading cedars, of the sudden ping-pong of the stable clock; and then as I read this gentle descriptive verse, I forget that the page is lit by electric light, the type, the colour, the faint smell of the book, the feel, the shape of it, take me back to autumn evenings at the poet's house, to neighbours coming in, to mulled claret and coaches going away and uneven roads and the wind roaring over the downs and the sea splashing along unbungalowed cliffs. I can forget aeroplanes, motors, wires strung over the village, motor bicycles, road houses and the daily newspaper and its advertisements; I can forget them all because here, enclosed in this handsome leather, are gentle poems, delicately printed, on handsome leisurely pages. Because I'm holding in my hands something that Mr Newport Charlett (whose crested bookplate is pasted on the fly-leaf) took out and read when it came in the case of books by coach from London. And as he read it in his country house – wherever it may have been – for he was a rich man to have his books bound so well – as he read it, that England which we all love was going on its silent spacious way around him. And here am I reading this very book, with Air Raid Precautions and other delights going on around me.

Jack can start up his motorbike and Bertha can put on the crooner record, but here in leather I have England enclosed for ever. And not their most hideous noises can take it away from me. And round my walls are more and more leather volumes, all England in a room.

So that even when I'm in prison for refusing to let the local council pull down my house or for obstructing the electric light company in erecting a transformer in my garden, even when I've lost all I love, I'll still have one consolation – the feel, the look, the smell, the content of an old book. And when I'm let out of prison, I'll spend my first and last sixpence in a second-hand bookshop.

BBC broadcast

Three:

1940 to 1945

Three
1940–1945

By now JB had established his own peculiar niche in the literary world. John Murray had published more of his poems – *Continual Dew* in 1937 and *Old Lights for New Chancels* in 1940. His literary peers were wary of him but the general public loved him and his familiar voice on the BBC Home Service was a comforting one. His love affair with England was used to positive advantage by his producers at the BBC who commissioned him to dwell on calming and homely topics while the threat of Invasion lingered on.

In January 1941, JB was seconded by the government to become Press Attaché in Dublin to the British Ambassador, Sir John Maffey. Ireland had become virtually independent less than twenty years before and JB's job was to improve Anglo-Irish relations – many of the Irish were pro-German. Although on the surface JB joked as ever, his understanding for and love of Ireland ran deeper than that of most of his English counterparts. He had spent long sojourns there in the early thirties, staying with friends and had developed an instant liking for its people. JB became quickly immersed in cultural activities, wrote reviews for the *Dublin* magazine and made a pioneer study of the architect Francis Johnstone, rescuing his papers from decay and disorder. He was immediately co-opted onto the Committee for the Recording of Irish Architecture and was asked to give an address on the fabrics of the Church of Ireland to a large gathering of its clergy.

JB's time in Ireland gave him a broader view of life and a greater feeling of responsibility. He made friends with the president, Eamon de Valera and admired him greatly and wrote astute and far-sighted confidential reports about the situation in Ireland for the British government and, always in later years, wrote about that country with understanding and tenderness. When writing about England he wore his heart, as ever, on his sleeve: 'Not until you have been away from it, as has the author of this book, for more than a year, do you realise how friendly, how beautiful, is the meanest English town. Not the most magnificent scenery, misty mountains, raging seas, desert sunsets, or groves of orange can compensate for the loss of the Corn Exchange, the doctor's house, tennis in suburban gardens, the bank and the bank manager's house, the rural garages, the arid municipal park, the church clock and the jubilee drinking fountain. Even a town like Wolverhampton looks splendid through Memory's telescope. While tears of homesickness blur the focus of Blandford's market square and the grey, shut-in climb of Bodmin's main street. Sitting here, remembering the provincial towns of England, I wonder why it is that they hold me, as they do thousands of my countrymen, with a spell that not all their obvious faults can break. . . .'[1]

On returning to England, in 1943 JB resumed his work in the Ministry of Information Films Division, making documentaries about Britain's war effort which were used to boost morale. He was in charge of a series of positive documentaries called 'The Pattern of Britain.' In 1944, he was moved to the P branch of the Admiralty in Bath where he was in charge of two publications which were circulated to various Admiralty strongholds throughout the country and supplied information about the latest bomb damage and source of supplies.

At this time JB began writing book reviews for the *Daily Herald* which was run by the Odhams Press. It was *the* Labour paper of the day and had the largest circulation in Britain second only to the *Daily Express*, which was owned by Beaverbrook. Percy Cudlip, who had been JB's boss on the *Standard*, was now editor of the *Herald*, and agreed to pay JB 14 guineas a week which rose in the end to 18 guineas during his stint. He reviewed over a thousand books for the *Herald* and looked through many more besides, sometimes, in those early days, employing his colleagues in the Admiralty to do the latter for him. He was writing for the ordinary punter about T. S. Eliot and Albert Camus – a different art to writing for some of the more highbrow magazines like *The New Statesman and Nation* and *Horizon*. His manner was direct and straightforward and wherever he could he added local colour and personal reminiscences. 'Eric Gill was a sculptor and carver: he designed lettering (you will see it over the bookshops of W. H. Smith and Son and on the Underground posters). He was a Pacifist, a sort of Socialist, and a devout Roman Catholic. He used to wear curious clothes of his own design. I remember how stimulatingly inappropriate he seemed one day when I was talking to him on the moving stairway at Paddington . . . He was wearing his usual open khaki shirt that continued on down his thighs as a sort of skirt, thick stockings and stout shoes (or were they sandals?) . . .'[2] Or of Hugh Walpole, 'I was dim, he was famous, I had plenty of time, he had little. . . . I remember his breezy manner rather like a hearty clergyman, his clear unprejudiced criticism . . .'[3]

JB became increasingly aware of his popularity with the public and hence his responsibility at this time – to keep their spirits up and to keep the home fires burning.

1. *English Cities and Small Towns* (William Collins, 1943).
2. *Daily Herald*, 6 July 1944.
3. *Daily Herald*, 11 May 1944.

Some Comments in Wartime

The title of this talk might lead you to think that I was going to make some sort of political comments. But I'm afraid you will be disappointed. I don't know anything about politics. Instead I am going to talk about some of the pleasant things I have discovered as a result of this war, and observations about things, scenery and people in these islands. For instance . . . I have become grateful for small things which I had not time to notice in that hurried turmoil we called civilisation before the war.

It's because I hope I may perhaps waken an answering feeling in you that I'm giving this talk, which is really just pointing things out to you which you may not have noticed already; things we now have time to see, possibly for the first time. For instance, the country, which people who don't live in it call 'the countryside'. It used to be the thing to say 'Oh, the country's all right in the summer, but I should go mad if I had to live in it all the year round'. By now, many thousands of town people will have spent a winter in the country for the first time. They will have seen that the country in winter is as full of life as in the summer. They will have noticed how willows burn red in the meadows before they bud and how oaks turn gold with early leaf. They will have known the pleasure of feeling rain on the face and retreating to a warm cottage and the comfortable feeling of listening to the storm outside.

The country has ceased to be a great park to which towns people could come in their motor coaches and drop paper about the lanes. Country people have ceased to be 'rustics' and 'yokels', they have become flesh and blood, foster parents of the towns. To many children who have been evacuated to country districts now for some months, the country is a great farm instead of a great park and I don't think any child who has migrated from the towns to the country, will ever again despise country life. I know of many who would like to be farmers when they grow up. Evacuation may have brought about what is so badly needed, the return to the land.

For those of us who live in the country, the war has increased our love for it. I used for ever to be on the rush, even in the country.

Hedges and fields swirled by from the windows of cars and trains. Then when my activity was slowed down, I started to see again and to feel. I noticed how sycamores turn silver when the wind presses against them, how elms are full of shadow, how ash trees are feathery, how many different sorts of willows there are. I noticed how golden lichen mellows red brick. I stood on bridges and watched water beetles and water boatmen scudding about on the surface, mud coloured fish lurking in the depths below. One garden wall, one stream, one tree, one tiny little bed of earth became something to watch and enjoy, whereas before I had taken them for granted and hurried on in pursuit of that fussy grab for money called 'business'.

And then duties in the Observer Corps got me up sometimes at appallingly early hours. The hours ceased to be appalling when one was actually alive in them. There were the night noises, the sharp scream of some animal done to death, the crack of a twig and rustle of grass and then the deep, deep silence of night. Suddenly and especially at this time of the year there is that burst of sound before the dawn breaks, when all the birds start singing. Then a silence. Then the first light of dawn and then, less suddenly, the birds break into song again.

The country seems to have gone back to the peace of the last century. It's a relief to see the hideous tin signs of place-names removed from the walls of cottages, to hear the comfortable plod of horses and rumble of iron-rimmed cartwheels instead of the endless gear changing of motors. I have never disliked the noise of aeroplanes – not even of enemy ones – because at least they do not change gear in the air and except for a few types of machine, the roar is rather heartening. One sound alone we will miss in the country – the church bells. The mellow lin-lan-lone across the hay. And here I would like to put in a word of advice. If any country air raid warden thinks he is going to be able to ring the church bells as a warning of a raid, let him be sure he knows how to handle a bell. I picture to myself an excited warden running up the belfry stairs, giving a colossal pull at a bell-rope and finding himself either hauled up to the belfry roof and crashing down unconscious on the floor with his skull cracked open, or else I see him with the skin ripped off his hands as the bell rope slides through them, or else I see him hanged by the neck as the rope end coils itself round him. Bell-ringing is an art and I wonder how many country wardens have learnt it? As this is not a talk on bell-ringing, and I have not the time to tell you how to ring a church bell, I beg all wardens who contemplate ringing to consult a ringer immediately,

The time came for me to leave my family in the country and take up

work in a big town. And the town instead of being the roaring hell of
the past, that I dreaded visiting, had submitted itself to a decent
discipline with comparatively few motors on the roads. Now the
buildings stand out and I have time to see them – decent Georgian
terraces built of brick with windows neatly graded in height; fanciful
and often beautiful Victorian churches with their tall spires and
towers, towering office blocks in all sorts of fancy styles made more
fanciful still by strips of paper pasted across the windows. Luxuriant
plane trees hanging over squares, that healthy smell of tar melting in
the sun instead of the blue petrol vapours of the past.

Best of all is the evening's pleasure of bicycling in the suburbs.
Before the war I used sometimes to give talks on architecture and on
town planning, I remember referring to Swindon as a great octopus or
starfish or something stretching out its tentacles of jerry built houses
into the quiet country (Swindon forgives me). But now I am so
forgiving I *like* suburbs: nothing is ugly.

Bicycling in the suburbs of a great city, I see a strange beauty in
those quiet deserted evenings with the few remaining children
showing off in the evening sunlight, laburnums and lilac weeping over
the front gate; father smoking his pipe and rolling the lawn; mother
knitting at the open window; the little arcade of local shops, the great
outline of the cinema, the new bricks pinker than ever in the sunset,
the sham Tudor beams, the standard roses, the stained glass in the
front doors, the pram in the hall, the drainpipes running zigzag down
to the side door. Now the hedges are growing up and the trees are
giving a greenness to it all. I see a beauty in it. I mean, there they are,
those houses: they are part of England; I've got to put up with them.
Then I will try to see the best in everything, even in the half-baked
Tudor dreams of the man who designed that deserted roadhouse. And
in the moonlight, when the colours disappear, not the maddest,
flashiest modern factory looks anything but beautiful. I have bicycled
by stucco terraces of George IV's time and seen the great Corinthian
columns and uneven chimney pots bathed in silver moonlight and I've
almost fallen off my bicycle with genuine emotion. I thank heaven for
the blackout, for without it I would never have known how beautiful a
city can look in moonlight. I know of a soldier who was left on a rather
deserted beach in South Africa during the Boer War and there he
started to collect the sea-water snail shells he found in the sand. He
classified these shells and started to take an interest in the subject.
Soon he was collecting snail shells all over the place – and now he is a
great malkologist and has a room in the Natural History Museum and

has written standard books on the subject. Malkology, I should say, is the study of snail shells. I wonder how many people will find themselves specialists, as a result of this war, in subjects which the war has drawn to their attention – fresh water fishes, astronomy, cow parsley, lichens, architecture, planning, geology, building materials, patent manures, marsh plants, refuse, trees, cloud formations, winds, tides, seaweed, rhododendrons – all subjects which we never bothered about when we had not the time, but which have now, one or other of them, forced themselves on our attention. War has a splendid effect in making you aware of your surroundings and the best way to get to like them is to find out all about them; why villages are where they are, why the roads wind, why certain fields are of such peculiar shapes, how old the church is. It does not, by the way, take more than a week or two to tell the date of a building from its appearance. You can soon learn by comparing it with others whose date you know and seeing how it differs.

Yes, the war has wakened my wits a bit and showed me the beauty of England, in all sorts of places where I did not expect to find it. It has done something else. It has made me see that possessions don't matter and that what really does matter is people, not their possessions. As a result of billeting and various war occupations I have had to meet all sorts of strangers and as a result, I like to think I have made a new lot of friends. Neighbours whom I hardly knew in the past, I now consider friends. War brings out the best in people; dithery old fusspots suddenly cease to fuss: the most unexpected people show great courage and pessimists become cheerful. War divides us into where we really belong. Class nonsense and incomes and possessions become of no importance. The cake is cut at right angles to the way it was cut before. The potential fifth columnists of this country are not only those who hold divergent political opinions from the majority, and have gone to jug for it, but those who are still out for themselves only. People who are so afraid of losing their job, that they will stop at no dirty trick to retain it; self-made men willing to sell their country in order not to lose any more of their incomes; rats who repeat and invent evil gossip about their neighbours in order to appear more loyal than they know themselves to be. They are the people who are determined that nothing matters so long as things remain as they used to be for them – the narrow man who has worked his way up, betraying his friends in the process, the man who thinks only in terms of money, the man who isn't sure of himself and hasn't the guts to see his own defects. War sorts us all out and the process is sad and painful,

very sad and very painful for some of us. But also it teaches us to look
at the world about us and gives us new interests. Better still, it teaches
us to consider other people and to value a man not according to his
income but according to his heart.

BBC broadcast

Back to the Railway Carriage

I want you to imagine yourself in the waiting-room of a railway station on a wet evening. You know the sort of room: let me recall it – a wind whistling down the platform, a walk battling against the breeze to the door marked General Waiting Room, the vast interior, the black horse-hair benches and chairs, the mahogany table, the grate with its winking fire, the large frame of yellowing photographs of crowded esplanades and ivy-mantled ruins, the framed advertisement for the company's hotel at Strathmacgregor – electric light, exquisite cuisine, lift to all floors, within five minutes of sea and pier – the gaslight roaring a friendly bass to restless conversation of other people also awaiting trains.

Just such a scene as this, which may be witnessed any evening at a hundred junctions, lost among the suburbs of industrial towns or far away in the country where branch line meets main line – just such a scene as this was witnessed sixty, seventy, eighty years ago. I shall have the railways complaining that I am calling them Victorian. Let them complain. They *are* Victorian, that is their beauty. But they are not only Victorian, they are Edwardian and modern as well.

Think yourself back into that waiting-room and learn with me the first lesson the railway teaches us – to pay a proper respect to the past. Railways were built to last. None of your discarding last year's model and buying this year's. That horse-hair seat has supported the Victorian bustle, the frock coat of the merchant going city-wards first-class, your father in his best sailor suit when he was being taken to the seaside, and now it is supporting you; and it's far from worn out. That platform has seen the last farewells of sons and parents, has watched the city man returning home to break the news to his wife that he's bankrupt, has watched his neighbour come in a new suit one morning and with a first-class, instead of a third-class, ticket. Turn from the human history to the history of stone and steam and iron. The railway station in the old days was a monument to science. Euston, whose fine Doric portico – one of London's noblest buildings – was the new gateway to the North; King's Cross whose simple outlines are a foretaste of all that is good in modern architecture; Temple Meads,

Bristol, in the Tudor style, far from gimcrack, but cut out of local
stone; Newcastle Central station, a lovely classical building, and many
a lesser station. I know little stations among the Shropshire hills built
in a solid but picturesque Gothic style to tone in with the romantic
scenery. I know of huge suburban stations which are dusty from disuse
and full of top-hatted ghosts in the corners of echoing gas-lit booking
halls. Best of all I know that station in Cornwall I loved as a boy, the
oil lights, the smell of seaweed floating up the estuary, the rain-washed
platform and the sparkling granite, and the hedges along the valleys
around, soon to be heavy with blackberries. I think of Edward
Thomas' lovely poem on Adlestrop, a station in the Cotswolds:

> Yes. I remember Adlestrop –
> The name, because one afternoon
> Of heat the express-train drew up there
> Unwontedly. It was late June.
>
> The steam hissed. Someone cleared his throat.
> No one left and no one came
> On the bare platform. What I saw
> Was Adlestrop – only the name.

That verse recalls one of the deeper pleasures of a country railway
station – its silence broken only by the crunching of a porter's feet on
the gravel, the soft country accent of the station-master, and the crash-
bang of a milk-can somewhere at the back of the platform. The train,
once in the centre of a noisy town, has drifted into the deep heart of
English country, with country noises brushing the surface of a deeper
silence. Edward Thomas expressed this in the last stanza of his poem
on Adlestrop station:

> And for that minute a blackbird sang
> Close by, and round him, mistier,
> Farther and farther, all the birds
> Of Oxfordshire and Gloucestershire.

You need never be bored in a train. You can always read a book, and
an even more interesting book to read than that on your knee is the
faces and habits of your fellow passengers. I know the types so well:
the fussy type – the old person who wraps a travelling rug round his
knees and gets up to lean out of the window at every station and ask if

this is the right train for Evercreech, receiving the answer 'yes' every time. He continues to look out, as though his anxious face will cause the guard to blow his whistle sooner. The vacant fool who taps with his toes on the floor and whistles to hide his embarrassment when the train comes to an unexpected halt between stations. The talkative person who tries to get into conversation – the war has brought on a big increase in this type. You know the sort of thing. I enjoy seeing how long I can answer 'yes' and 'oh' without getting involved in conversation.

'Colder today, isn't it?'
'Yes'.
'But the days'll be getting longer soon'.
'Yes'.
'Does this train stop at Chippenham?'
'Yes'.
'Stops on the way first, I suppose?'
'Yes'.
'Got a married sister at Chippenham'.
'Oh'.
'But my Mother's family comes from Wootton Bassett'.
'Oh'.
'Come from Stoke Newington myself'.
'Oh'.

Then there's the lady who gets in with a friend. She gossips the whole way upon the advantages, or the disadvantages, of permanent waving, on whether to go back on the 5.18 or the 6.24, on the other hand if she catches the 6.24 she'll miss the 8.50 bus to Pinehurst turn and have to wait for the 9.40 unless the 8.50 hasn't gone or the train comes in earlier than schedule. But if she catches the 5.18, then there may not be time to get the stuff for the curtains, and then there's the wait for the 7.34 bus the other end, so it's hardly worth it really.

The only type of passenger whom I find it rather hard to stomach is the man who pares his nails with a penknife.

But the greatest gift the railways give to us is the proper treatment of time. Of course there are expresses that will hurtle you from place to place in no time. And there used to be cars volleying along a tarmac road at sixty miles an hour. But I prefer a leisurely journey in a stopping train, seeing the country, getting to the place much sooner and much more comfortably in the long run. And if the train is a bit late, what matter? There are one's fellow-passengers to study, the unfamiliar view of a place one knows well from the road seen at an odd angle from the railway, the photographs below the rack to look at, the railway noises to listen to. And for me there's the pleasure of a railway time-table. It's one of the ironies of this war that the centenary of Bradshaw, which occurred last November, should have been obscured by the war. The original Bradshaw was a Quaker and a great worker for peace. How I enjoy his pages – particularly those at the end which deal with the Great Southern Railway in Eire! 'Stops to take up at Inny Junction Halt on Thursdays and Saturdays'. Inny Junction Halt is hidden away among the footnotes of Bradshaw. What romance there is in the name! For Inny Junction is a station lost in an Irish bog in the middle of Westmeath: there's no road to it, nothing but miles of meadowsweet and bog myrtle and here and there the green patch and white speck of a distant Irish smallholding, and the silence is livened only by rumblings of distant turf carts and the hiss of a waiting Great Southern engine on Thursdays and Saturdays.

Trains were made for meditation. And I advise slow trains on branch lines, half empty trains that go through meadows in the evening and stop at each once oil-lit halt. Time and war slip away and you are lost in the heart of England.

BBC broadcast

Francis Johnston

To understand Irish architecture, to derive a melancholy enjoyment from the crumbling magnificence of its country houses, you must have a faint idea of Irish history. That ecstatic pleasure you feel returning to Ireland, which comes from the sensation of walking about in an aquatint – blue hills, very green and very little fields, white cottages, islanded lakes, brown stretches of bog with fissures of black water, silver light that drifts over grey-blue granite of castles and mansions – a light so hopeless for the photographer – those noble clumps of beech trees through which wind grassy avenues to who knows what ruined splendour – oh it's all marvellous! The meanest town has a terrace or two of houses which would call forth a pamphlet from the Georgian Group if the terrace were in England and a letter to *The Times* from Lord Derwent himself if its existence was imperilled. But here in Ireland, we are so rich in such terraces, that they are pulled down without comment. What a wonderful country, says the smart Baroqueteer – what was it George Moore said? Something about Ireland having gone straight from the eighteenth century to the twentieth without any industrial age in between?

Yet if you live in Ireland for a year or two, you begin to see the cracks. The decayed Irish family with the maid pouring a little hot water into the soup when the unexpected guests arrive, the tarnished silver (thought to be three times as valuable as it is), the damp library and the enormous, empty stables – it is amusing enough seen on the stage in electric London. But if you know Ireland well, it is only sad and not at all funny. Then it will surprise you to find how little the Irish – the 'mere Irish' as they used to be called – rate the Georgian splendour which surrounds them. 'Merely British' they say, and prefer, the more prosperous of them in the newly-established middle class, to live in a villa whose outside looks like anything on the Great West Road from jazz to Tudor. And for their artistic inspiration the Irish go back to the Book of Kells and Celtic knots and Romanesque, to the age before the British invaded them. And you, too, will begin to see that much Georgian which looked so splendid at first, is perhaps mere façade. Scottish architecture is three-dimensional, as well built in front as at the back and the string courses go round all four sides. Irish architecture is often front only, as if the people who put it up couldn't pay for any more. Often it is not Irish but Imperial architecture, built to impress, like New Delhi.

I repeat that to understand Irish architecture you must have a faint idea of Irish history. Nor is it necessary to become a Broadbent in the process. Ireland as a nation is older than England and brought Christianity to Britain. Much of that early Christian Ireland survives. Its appeal, so far as stones are concerned, is more archaeological than aesthetic, yet no one can see the little unmortared oratory of Gallerus unmoved nor fail to be impressed by the round stone cells of the Celtic monastery on Skellig or the seven ruined churches at Glendalough.

But from Norman times in Britain to Hanoverian, Ireland has been subjected to invasion. There is hardly any medieval architecture when you compare Ireland with Britain and houses continued to be fortified well into the seventeenth century. The brute Cromwell was possibly the greatest destroyer of all. Ireland was in a state of tribal warfare, both intertribal and against British invaders, for centuries. So there is very little medieval architecture left intact. Only hundreds of not very interesting ruins which look romantic enough rising jagged against the sunset on a mound in the bog, but which are not often worth closer inspection: – a bit of a church with a burial ground round it of Victorian and modern Celtic crosses, and those smooth, dark green yews; a round tower, a chieftain's castle, perhaps an Englishman's, like Spenser's miserable ruin at Kilcolman. Architectural excitement, as opposed to archaeological, does not begin until the eighteenth century.

For the last fifty years of the eighteenth century, Ireland really looked like becoming a nation once again. Then the great houses were built for the landowners and to this day they remain. One of the first architects, as opposed to castle builders, was Richard Cassels (1690–1751) of German origin. To him are ascribed Leinster House, the Rotunda Hospital in Dublin, and the great country houses of Powerscourt, Carton, and Bessborough and probably Lord Langford's ruined palace of Summerhill. His houses followed a plan which became usual for the large Irish country house – a central block flanked by pavilions either side of the main front, and connected with the main block by ornamental walls or colonnades. The earliest of these houses are baroque. Internally they are adorned with elaborate plasterwork on walls and ceilings, the finest examples of which are in the Rotunda Hospital Chapel at Dublin and the two houses now used as hostels of the National University on Stephen's Green, Dublin, and in Florence Court, County Fermanagh. Marble chimney-pieces, too, were wonderfully elaborate.

The easiest decorative plaster and marble work in Ireland was the work of Italians who instructed native craftsmen so that by the end of the eighteenth century there was an Irish school of stuccadores and stonecarvers as accomplished as any in Europe. There is hardly a large house in Ireland whether it be Baroque, Adam-style, Roman, Greek or 'Gothick', whether it be deep in the country or one of the noble squares and terraces of Dublin, Limerick, Cork, Waterford or Kilkenny, which has not at least one room with delicate plaster ceilings and a marble chimney-piece, and possibly, under a few layers of colour, hand-blocked wallpaper. The pages of those rare grey volumes of the Georgian Society which form an incomplete if impressive catalogue of Irish houses are full of such rooms. These and Mr C. P. Curran's valuable illustrated pamphlet *Dublin Plaster Work* are the only *detailed* studies on eighteenth-century Irish architecture of which I am aware.

So imagine Ireland of the years immediately preceding the Act of Union. A country of peasants and peers with room in the larger cities for genteel districts of houses for the professional and merchant classes. So it remained until 1916. And this pattern of life still informs the country landscape. There are no villages clustering round a Tudor manor, few middle-sized houses. Instead, there are smallholders scattered far and wide, and among them, walled-in and aloof, down long avenues planted with beech, the big houses. Two or three hundreds yard away, walled-in once more, is the kitchen garden. Many of these big houses are now convents or monasteries: others are farms: still more have been demolished or stand burnt out and sightless among the stumps of oak and beech which once graced their pleasure grounds and demesnes.

When the Act of Union was passed in 1800, when Ireland ceased to have her own Parliament in Dublin, when Grattan's hopes were frustrated and the dupes and lackeys of Castlereagh sold Ireland to England, a civilisation passed. Dublin ceased to be a capital and became a provincial city. Not until the Easter Rising of 1916 was she a capital again. Landlords, who had hitherto had a town house in Dublin, moved to London to attend Parliament at Westminster. The Irish Parliament House became a Bank and the splendours of the Royal Court at Dublin Castle, symbol of an honourable Union of two

equal countries, Britain and Ireland, each with its own Parliament but
with one King – these splendours became a sham. Many of the
landlords had crossed to England and became absentees. They lived
on rents collected from Irish tenantry by hardheaded bailiffs. Many
landlords, it is true, remained, but their class which, had it not been
for the Act of Union, might have been part of the Irish nation, was
identified by the Irish with England. And not many years after the
Easter Rebellion of 1916, England herself betrayed these landlords.

So the Irish Georgian architecture which is now so much admired
by English visitors is really the architectural memorial of that twice-
betrayed race the Protestant Anglo-Irish. It is a race which has
produced the great Rebels for Irish Nationalism from Wolfe Tone to
Erskine Childers, great admirals from Eyre Coote to the Cunning-
hams, great generals from Wellington to Alexander, poets like
Goldsmith, Allingham and Yeats, novelists like Maria Edgeworth,
Lever, and George Moore, Somerville and Ross. We know of the
lovely work of aliens in Ireland such as Sir William Chambers' Casino
at Clontarf, James Wyatt's Castle Coole, Cooley's Royal Exchange,
Dublin, John Nash's work at Rockingham and Caledon. Most Irish
houses have, locked away in a press or framed and fading in an upstairs
passage, signed elevations and plans of the house. Often these reveal
that work hitherto vaguely ascribed to Cassels, Wyatt or one of the
Adams is really the work of an Irishman – Grace, Henry, or
Robertson. They were probably articled to English or Scottish
architects by whose name their own was eclipsed.

The first man to be famous as an Irishman and an architect was
Francis Johnston. He was inevitably at that time a Protestant, for I
doubt whether a Roman Catholic would have been admitted to the
posts and to the patronage which Johnston enjoyed. But he was an
Irishman and Dublin-printed topographical books of the early
nineteenth century were loud in his praises. Sore from their betrayal
by the Act of Union, the writers of these books were delighted to be
able to praise an Irishman. Nor was their praise without justification.
Johnston was as inventive as he was industrious. He was a pioneer of
the Gothic Revival. His ornate and beautiful Chapel Royal in Dublin
Castle is quite as 'correct' as Savage's Chelsea New Church, London,
which was erected more than a decade later and is generally hailed as
the first 'correct' building of the Gothic Revival. He was equally at
home in the classic manner, in its severest phase whose beauty
depends on simple vaulting and relation of window to wall space. I
have seen many Irish houses but I know none at once so dignified, so

restrained and so original as Francis Johnston's Townley Hall, near Drogheda. Study of the detailed drawings by Johnston and the few facts that can be gathered about his personal interests show that he was interested in structure and mechanics and carpentry and music. His mind was practical and mathematical. He collected clocks, delighted in furniture which had sliding doors and secret panels, was interested in change-ringing and had a miniature church tower with bells, erected in his back garden at Eccles Street, Dublin. He was also possessed of much public spirit and founded the Royal Hibernian Academy which he endowed by his will. That institution still flourishes, but the grave of its founder is neglected and almost indecipherable in the cemetery of his beautiful Dublin church of St George.

Material for the detailed study of Johnston was available in the form of a large collection of drawings from his office which was left to the Architectural Association of Ireland by William Murray the third, architect and descendant of Johnston. The earliest drawings in the collection are by James Wyatt: then come a few by Thomas Cooley to whom Johnston was articled. The drawings of Ballymakenny Church are so like a Cooley drawing, if one compares them with those in the Armagh Free Library by that architect, as possibly to be by Cooley and not by Johnston, were they not dated after Cooley's death. The last drawings are clearly the work of the first of the three William Murrays who inherited Johnston's practice. Mixed with these later drawings are more by Daniel Robertson, Sir Richard Morrison and other architects of nineteenth-century Ireland. The whole collection is now loaned to the National Library of Ireland in Dublin. It was classified and catalogued for the first time by Messrs H. G. Leask, T. L. Cullimore, Miss Eleanor Butler and the author of this essay.

Johnston evolved classic and Gothic styles which were distinctly Irish and which are a change from the façadism of much earlier and later work by his contemporaries and successors. His Gothic manner influenced Sir Richard Morrison and his son, those ubiquitous Irish castle builders and, more interesting still, the nameless architects of many a small Swiss or Gothic shooting box among the hills, and many a seaside villa or lakeside cottage ornée. His classic manner can be traced in the works of that scholarly Greek and Egyptian Revivalist Mulvany, architect of the Broadstone Station and the buildings on the Dublin to Kingstown line. That most original Irish architect, John Semple, of the bridge-building family, and designer of an amazing

Gothic structure, the 'Black Church' Dublin, with its parabolic-vaulted interior, alone seems to have been unaffected by his style.

Not until the advent of Benjamin Woodward, Lynn and Thomas Drew later in the century, do any architects so Irish and so distinguished as Francis Johnston reappear. Until these Gothicists, Irish architecture continued in the Georgian Gothic and Georgian Classic traditions for far longer than it did in Britain. In the squares of almost every Irish city and town, and amid the trees of cultivated land – Irish landlords usually adorned their pleasure grounds and neighbouring hills with tree plantations, since few could afford to build temples and eyecatchers – you will find buildings which you would swear were built in 1820. If records of them remain, very often they are so late as 1860 or 1870. From 1850 onwards buildings went slightly off-colour, as it were South Kensington compared with Belgravia. William Allingham describes one in *Laurence Bloomfield in Ireland* (1864) –

> Window and door in city-villa taste,
> With stucco ornaments and columns graced,
> Square spacious rooms, fill'd full of splendid things
> Bright rosewood tables, gilded curtain rings; ...
> Harsh lights upon discordant colours fall,
> Large, costly, dull engravings deck the wall;
> Chair, ottoman, by some unlucky doom
> Door, window, fire, stand wrong in every room ...
> Best thing the farmyard, practical and neat
> With swine, calves, poultry, stacks of hay and wheat; ...

This essay is but a preliminary sketch of the life of an Irish architect of the best period. A person with patience and a nose for finding drawings in houses and libraries will be able to gather material for many more lives of almost-forgotten eighteenth- and nineteenth-century Irish architects. The Irish Architectural Records Society is already starting on this too-long neglected work.

From *The Pavilion: A Contemporary Collection of British Art and Architecture*

Cooke of Cookesborough

Ireland is the breeding ground of eccentrics. And the finest, grandest, most lovable eccentrics are to be found among that fast dying race, the Anglo-Irish. Transport yourselves, dear listeners, to that green island of white cottages, peat smoke, mountains, lakes, little fields, quiet lanes unspoiled by the motor car, wide skies uninvaded by the aeroplane; to those peaceful counties with their crumbling Georgian houses, the tall beech plantations around them, the mouldering garden walls, the grass-grown avenues. Think of the last century there, when amid mortgages and occasional discontent, the peers, the baronets, the squires and squireens hunted, laughed, joked and drank away their time in an expansive, hospitable manner in what is still the most hospitable country in Europe, where every inhabitant is a wit and every other inhabitant a poet.

And transport yourselves into the very middle of Ireland, to its quietest and loneliest part – the county of Westmeath. The year is 1876, and the time summer, and the town is Mullingar. We are here to witness the great dispute over the will of Adolphus Cooke, to be heard in the granite assize court beside that enormous railway station, even bigger than the imposing court, and with a refreshment room which seems to be out of all proportion to the size of the station.

The court, and, for all I know, the station refreshment room, is crowded with people of every sort. What has happened is this: Adolphus Cooke, a Westmeath squire lately deceased, has left his money to the younger son of a neighbouring peer. The will is contested by the plaintiffs, partly on the ground that Adolphus Cooke was off his head and not in a position to make a will. That is the part of the trial that will concern us. Legends about Adolphus Cooke are rushing about. The two half-wits are remembered whom he called his guides, philosophers, and friends. One, of military bearing, was said to have drilled the geese at Cookesborough, Mr Cooke's estate. When he met Mr Cooke, they would exchange military salutes. The other half-wit was far less military. He was more for conciliation.

Mr Cooke would consult these two men when his neighbours asked him questions – to show, some said, his opinion of the intelligence of the surrounding gentry.

Then, there were the rumours of poor old Mr Cooke's theories of the soul. Mad with learning he seemed, to Christian Ireland. He believed in the transmigration of the soul. Was he not supposed to have employed a man specially to look after an aged turkey cock, and was not this turkey cock said to contain the spirit of his grandfather? Then there was the strangest rumour of all, a sort of ghost story. Mr Cooke was supposed to have thought he might turn into a fox in the next life. 'Very useful', he said in his slow, precise way, 'for I know this district well'. And shortly after his death there had been a meet of the Westmeath and a fox was killed in the kitchen of Cookesborough. 'The right place to find a Cooke', said a local wit. But the story is more sad than witty, for Mr Cooke disapproved of fox-hunting and the killing of animals of any sort.

Those were the rumours. Now for the facts. Mr Cooke's family had been settled in Westmeath after one of the English invasions of Ireland. Their house was like many other big houses in that country – a large Georgian structure, plain without and decorated within with many pieces of delicate Chippendale furniture, glistening silver, and ceilings and fireplaces adorned with exquisite plasterwork and carving. Round the house was a large beech- and oak-planted park and a walled garden some way off from the house. A winding drive, called an avenue in Ireland, led to the lodge gates.

Adolphus Cooke had never liked his father, who had been a great sporting gentleman, famous for his dogs, horses and fighting cocks. Adolphus had inherited from him a knowledge of livestock, but he had been forced as a boy into the army, and this was hardly congenial to him. He had fought in the Peninsular War under Wellington – this is rather remarkable when you reflect that there must still be many people alive who remember Adolphus Cooke – and later he was sent out on some mysterious military expedition into Africa. Here he was court-martialled for his humanitarian views. He was by no means a coward – indeed he was a very brave man, but he refused to shoot the natives. I have before me a photograph of the old man. It shows a beautiful old face with bright eyes, a high forehead, a mane of hair. A beard hides the chin. The figure is clothed in shapeless wrappings – a sort of exaggerated cloak. He certainly looks eccentric as he sits at a table, leaning on a stick.

Now for the trial. The occasion seems to have been one of public holiday. Even the Judge enjoyed himself. He seems to have had a gay opinion of Mullingar:

'Is this town of Mullingar a very literary neighbourhood?' he said.

'I cannot tell, my lord'.

'There are fifty-two public houses in it – how many booksellers are there in it?'

'I don't know, my lord. There are not many'.

One witness says, referring to Adolphus Cooke: 'He was showing me the improvements he was making about the place at this time'.

COUNSEL: 'What were the improvements?'

'He showed me where he had collected a lot of brambles for the use of the crows, as they were losing their time'.

'Say what he said to you'.

'If you will allow me, I will. "Nulty", he says, "there's an improvement. I am getting the brambles cut down for the use of the crows, they are losing their time building their nests, striving to gather them up themselves. Don't you think that an advantage to them?" I said: "I think it is, if they will take them"; but I question whether they did'.

Another curious improvement to Cookesborough was made by Adolphus, and it came out in this trial. He had some chairs with balloon-shaped backs – like half an hour-glass – which he greatly admired. So he had the windows of his house made like them. They were sash windows, and those who are of a practical turn of mind will realise that from being this shape, they would neither open nor shut.

He had another idea, to be buried in a cellar dug in the lawn sitting up in a chair, and surrounded by his books. The idea fell through, but this evidence of a builder, who produced a sketch of a marble chair, is worth quoting:

'Tell us what Mr Cooke desired you to do with reference to that sketch.'

'He desired me to get one of the best white marble chairs that could be got; but when he heard the price of it, he said he was not worthy sitting in it'.

'For what purpose did he say he wanted it?'

'To sit in it'.

'Where was the chair to be put?'

'In the tomb'.

'Where was the tomb?'
'In the lawn'.
'Where was the lawn?'
'Before the hall door'.
'He was to sit in the marble chair?'
'Yes'.
'When he was dead?'
'When he was dead'.
'What else did he tell you?'
'He told me he would sooner stand'.

I could go on quoting from this trial, but you will be wanting to hear the result. Well, it transpired that Adolphus Cooke was a good landlord, infinitely kind to his tenants. Indeed at one time some men had attacked his house in order that he might think it was his servants, sack them and give their jobs to the attackers. He saw through this. He was a shrewd man of business. True he had strange views about animals. A cow fell in a ditch and he told his men to leave it there, that it might serve as a warning to the other cows. He had odd views, too, on sanitation. He wanted to install a water closet at Cookesborough, but it was to be two fields away from the house. His personal opinions were very decided. He disliked missionaries; admired the Koran; did not dislike the Roman Catholics – odd in an Irish Protestant at that date. He wore strange clothes, all witnesses agreed to that. He was extremely learned and on his death-bed he read Sophocles in the original Greek to his doctor, who did not remember any Greek. He had beautiful manners and his last words were addressed to his butler: 'Give the doctor a chair'. His servants adored him. The Judge in summing up, said the whole story was very sad. Here was this poor old man, frightened of death, with all sorts of theories about his soul and anxiety about his estate and tenantry and servants and no direct heirs. So he left his property to a son of the man he thought the best landlord in the district. The jury agreed that Adolphus Cooke was right in the head. But when the seven-day trial was all over there could not have been much money left.

I have visited Adolphus Cooke's tomb and I have visited Cookesborough. The tomb in Reynella Churchyard is built in the shape of a stone beehive. As for Cookesborough, it is no more than the name for some ruined stables and small fields dotted with white cabins. The avenue is there, all grass grown. I drove up it a year or two ago. A sham Gothic gateway marked the entrance to the estate; the oak trees, which Adolphus loved and refused to cut down, were all gone: a row of beeches, too old to be of any value, hung along the approach to the stables. The stables all had square openings. As for the house, only a grass platform marked the site of that odd building with its balloon-shaped windows. All that anxiety, all that money, all that kindness had been wasted and lost in the deep silence of Westmeath.

At one time Adolphus Cooke was said to have thought his spirit would enter the body of a screech owl. It was dark before I left Cookesborough. For all I know, it may have been the spirit of poor Mr Cooke which screeched in such a sad and terrifying way, as an owl swooped over the ruined stables and disappeared into the tree-less expanse of what once was the property of Mr Adolphus Cooke of Cookesborough.

BBC broadcast

Fabrics of the Church of Ireland

*An address given to the
clergymen of the Church of Ireland*

It is so easy and so wrong for a member of the Church of England to appear patronising when talking of the fabrics of your churches here. Indeed I think with pride of my own Church's cathedrals, abbeys, village towers, and I think with some justification, that nowhere in Europe is there a Gothic style lovelier than Perpendicular, no village in the world so graceful as one above whose thatch and elm trees rises the silver lacework of a Somerset belfry.

And I think of poor Ireland's history – those little ruined churches (nearly all, by the way, exceptional as architecture) among the yews and crosses, the absenteeism, the pluralism, the 'troubles', and finally that last great betrayal when your Church was disestablished. He must be cold indeed who can read unmoved Bishop Magee's great speech, 'What a magnanimous sight. The first thing that this magnanimous British nation does in the performance of this act of justice and penitence is to put into her pocket the annual sum she had been in the habit of paying to Maynooth, and to compensate Maynooth out of the funds of the Irish Church.' If this evening some of my words seem critical of the Church's architectural policy since disestablishment, do not, please, think that the criticism is levelled with any motive but that of affection. I address you, I hope, in all humility.

I chose for my subject the fabrics of the Church of Ireland because I think them, many of them, more beautiful than you do yourselves and because I hope to kindle in you some of that enthusiasm, which I have already found awaking among some of your clergy, for those decent churches 'that top the neighbouring hill', those despised 'neat edifices' whose towers and spires are so restrained, often so graceful, rising like some over-simplified drawing of an English country church, from their surrounding beeches: they are peculiar to this country and they are unmistakably Church of Ireland.

First the importance of a fabric as an aid to worship. Probably, you have forgotten, because it is so long since you sat in one, what the view of the East end of a church looks like to a layman in the congregation or to a child. You are always doing something, reading from a book or performing some of the sacred offices. But to us who are not always as devotional as we should be, whose eyes stray, a badly proportioned altar, a glaring window in 'Cathedral glass' (that odious invention in green and pink), a bad brass, chipped plaster, a wriggling text, a fearful stained glass window from the ecclesiastical department of a London store, a silly 'arty' one from Dublin, a candle bracket which has not been cleaned for months, a broom which has not been put away, dusty armistice poppies, a damp stain on the wall, a loose encaustic tile, a cumbrous lectern or reading desk from some brute of a church furnisher – one or all of these can eat into our souls.

The fabric of the church is very much concerned with worship. The decoration of a church can lead the eye to God or away from Him. The Roman Catholics know this. We may not like those bleeding bullock's hearts on the statues, those Munich windows, those organ-grinder paintings of S Patrick and S ?Fruchtna: we may not like the brass and white marble, the sticky staring Stations of the Cross, those gaudy banners and the sky blue grotto but remember that to the unsophisticated and to the uncritical they lead the straying mind to prayer and worship and they help to hold those immense, devout congregations to whom liturgical worship probably means less than it does to us.

Such objects as these, gaudy though they be, are preferable to a restricted view of the top of a harmonium and all its pigglery of fretwork and baluster, or the snake-like coils of the heating apparatus. And it is because the fabric of a church, especially its interior, is important to us laymen that I venture to suggest a return to Georgian furnishings and internal arrangement which, without offending the Canons, will not yet err on the side of the over-elaborate nor turn what should be the House of God into a Lecture Hall. My reason for suggesting this style is dictated by its prevalence in your fabrics.

First let us survey, in a very general way, the buildings we possess. Such a survey must be very superficial. No one in the Church of Ireland has yet turned his attention to an architectural list of all her fabrics. Most of what little information I have been able to obtain, I have found in Diocesan clergy lists written by Canon Leslie, Dean Webster, Reminson, Atkinson, Healy and Seymour. But none of these authors is concerned primarily with architecture and one merely has to be grateful for what crumbs of information they let fall. I can only find particulars, of anything approaching contemporary date, on thirteen dioceses and eighteen dioceses are still unchronicled as to fabrics. I would respectfully suggest that at the earliest opportunity machinery be devised for obtaining full information of date of building; architect, interior furnishings, plate, woodwork, hangings, frontals, galleries, organs, glass and condition of every church in this island which still has a roof on it, and that this information be available for architectural students if not in printed form at least in one single manuscript volume. Such a source would lead to a work on the Churches of the Church of Ireland as a companion volume to the Cathedrals of the Church of Ireland and help to awaken a pride in fabrics which could not but be helpful to the Church.

There are, I suppose, about 1400 Church of Ireland places of worship here. Of these I have only had time to get at the history of 656 – in Meath, Cashel, Emly, Waterford, Lismore, Ferns, Raphoe, Derry, Ossory, Ross, Dromore, Armagh, Clogher, Cork. And even here I am for the most part only able to discover the date of building – in 42 cases I am unable even to discover that – so that leaves me with 614 fabrics to classify. But I think the area covered by the dioceses mentioned may be taken as fairly representative from Armagh and its 103 fabrics in the North to Emly with its 9 fabrics (Seymour mentions 11 in 1908) in the South.

I have divided the fabrics into four sections: (1) Ancient and seventeenth-century (2) eighteenth-century (3) 1800–45 (4) 1846 and later. Section 3: 1800–45, contains far the largest group, 315 churches, and I propose to dwell chiefly on these, since this number is more than double the next largest section. I will take each section in chronological order.

There are thirty-one ancient structures and nine seventeenth-century ones among those of which I read. From the amount of writing there has been on ancient architecture in Ireland and the amount of archaeological survey and conjecture, you would think the subject were exhausted. And I think we can safely assume that every wall in any Church of Ireland church which contains a single Romanesque arch or Gothic opening has been exposed to the light of day and restored out of recognition. Admittedly no comprehensive book has yet been published on Irish medieval ecclesiastical architecture, most of the best of which is in ruins. And many Church of Ireland churches which contain ancient parts in the fabric are scarcely recognisable from late Victorian churches. Dromore Cathedral for instance may have some ancient stones in it, but it takes a Sherlock Holmes to discover where they are. Armagh is as good as rebuilt and its exquisite early Victorian stone screen by Cottingham has been removed by some brutal breakers of Cathedral tradition so that the building loses its effect of length, its mystery of vista opening on vista, and much of its proportion. Waringstown is said to be the most complete seventeenth-century interior in Ireland, but it has been ruined by a Victorian chancel purporting to be in the same style, by Victorian tracery and texts. S Patrick's Nave is Victorian, Christ Church is mostly new stonework by Street. Both are ancient all right but the Victorian is what you see the most of. Kilkenny Cathedral is ruined by internal scraping.

There is a strong tendency among clergy to confuse old with beautiful – all sedilia are 'fine', all box pews are 'unsightly', all piscinae are 'interesting', all three-deckers are 'cumbrous'. The Tractarians, the Camden Society, Pugin, and a religious reverence for the ancient, probably combine to breed this attitude. It has done untold harm in England and Ireland. It has educated people into the belief that old things are, per se, lovely. How many crowds we have all seen gaping in bored bondage of duty while a verger points at some crumbling, scraped piece of ancient stonework and tells them how many hundreds of years old it is while at his back, maybe, is some eighteenth-century sculptured monument which he passes by unnoticed, though it stands a far greater chance of appealing to his listeners' aesthetic sensibilities.

Archaeology is the death of architecture and in the interests of pedantic antiquarianism nearly every ancient church in England or in Ireland has been given undue prominence and too much 'restoration' while finer structures of later centuries have been allowed to decay, to be destroyed, or to be improved to look like Victorian mission chapels in an industrial slum.

There are 117 eighteenth-century churches on my lists. This is an amazing proportion. We are always told of the wicked Bishop of the eighteenth century, the starved curate, and the pluralist rector. Even in so recent and excellent a book as Mr Chavasse's *Publick Worship according to the Use of the Church of Ireland* (1938) we read of the 'unspiritual depths of the Hanoverian period'. Yet these low people erected three-quarters of our churches. It is true that the average date is about 1780 and that in the earlier half of the century little was done. A pioneer of church building was Primate Robinson who ruled Armagh with princely despotism from 1765 to 1795 and from whose liberal will many learned members of the public still benefit. He it was who appointed Thomas Cooley (1740–84) his architect and the exquisite watercolour elevations of many of the churches this talented young man built for the Primate are to be found in the Public Library at Armagh. On Cooley's death Robinson employed the great Francis Johnston. Another church builder was the notorious Lord Bristol, Bishop of Derry (1768–1803), nor does Bishop Maxwell of Meath (1766–98) seem to have neglected his duty. These three dioceses have a total of sixty-two eighteenth-century churches, mostly built by these Bishops.

I have been at some pains to discover the type of churchmanship prevalent in the Church of Ireland at this time and I think I may fairly safely conclude that it was generally old-fashioned 'high'. Bishop Dopping of Meath (d. 1697) received Roman Catholics into the fold with this formula 'And I, his minister, by the authority committed unto me, do absolve thee from all ecclesiastical censures which thou hast or mayest have incurred by reason of thy former errors, schisms and heresies, and I restore thee to the full Communion of the Catholic Church. In the name of the Father, and of the Son, and of the Holy Ghost. Amen.'

We know that it was customary to bow to the altar; we find that people were at pains to rail in the communion space and pave it with black and white marble even before they paved the nave. We find in the old Canons that a decent covering of silk was required for the Table, as well as the fair linen cloth, and that there was no specific injuction that Tables should be of wood – about half a dozen are of stone and at least two have Latin inscriptions – nor was there any canon forbidding lights or pictures. At Grange (Armagh), built by Cooley in 1773, from the time the Church was built it was required that the men should sit on one side and the women on the other side of the church. At Kilbixy (Meath) 1798, the seats are arranged like a College Chapel facing North and South, with the pulpit at the West end: a rather similar seating system I have seen at Glenealy (Glendalough) and there are probably other examples of this Little Gidding-like pewing. Sermons were doctrinal, but there does not seem to have been the fundamental disagreement over doctrine with Roman Catholics that came in the next century. (Indeed Bishop O'Berin of Meath who overlaps into 1823, the greatest church builder of all Irish Bishops, submitted a memorandum to Lord Castlereagh on a union of the Churches of Rome and Canterbury.)

These eighteenth-century churches are often gems of a great period of architecture – the Rotunda Hospital Chapel whose plaster ceiling must be among the finest of its size and date in Europe, S Mary's Dublin, S Peter's Drogheda, Waterford Cathedral, the many little country examples Gothick or Classic; notice the excellence of the joinery – the Irish were by race always great craftsmen – the delicacy of mouldings on doors, panels, pulpit, canopy, cornice. The clear glass window shining on to well carved oak or cedar or pine: the red and gold silk carpet thrown over the holy table, the two silver candlesticks on the Table, the Commandment board in black and gold and portraits of Moses and Aaron on either side, the well turned balusters of the rails, the Tuscan columns supporting the little gallery at the West, the crimson pulpit cushions and crimson hangings from the clerk's desk, the black and white marble floor, the brass spider suspended in the nave; picture the surpliced incumbent in his wig reciting the offices. He may have given Communion but three times a year, but all communicated and knew their Cathechism.

And a word here on box pews. In an eighteenth-century church they are part of the architectural composition and when they are removed the church loses its proportion, that dependence on wainscot and wall space which makes a building good or bad to look at is essential to the satisfactory shape of the interior. Nor are the pews purely architectural decorations. They exclude draughts and keep the congregation warm more handsomely and reliably than a heating apparatus. Moreover they can be adapted for present day worship by raising the level of their internal floor.

It is tragic to think that in every diocese I have considered at least one eighteenth-century church has been demolished within living memory and almost every other has been despoiled of its fittings ie 'improved' also within living memory. In England today people are just beginning to take pride in eighteenth-century churches – generally too late because of 'improvements' – but they have not the number of them that you have here.

Now we come to the greatest period of church building in this country, 1800–45. It is the time of which everyone complains, especially those with a bias towards the study of antiquity. These little churches, generally in a Gothic style, are described contemptuously, if graphically, by Allingham in *Laurence Bloomfield in Ireland* (1864) when he is contrasting the Church of Ireland and Rome in the town of 'Lisnamoy'.

> With churches that on rival mounts encamp,
> One praised for neatness, one admired for pomp;
> *This*, which combines the gaudy and the mean,
> (Alas! the white old chapel on its green)
> With misplaced ornament that leads your eye

To note the baldness, like a wig awry;
That, less prodigious, odious not the less,
All prim and trim in tidy ugliness,
A square box with a tall box at the end,
While through the wall a stove pipe's arms extend.

They were built by the Ecclesiastical Commissioners on money borrowed from the Board of First Fruits. Here and there I have found them undisturbed by later generations – at Ballymaglassan for instance, near Dunboyne – and not all but most of them have the same excellent joinery as did the eighteenth-century churches, the same dignified internal proportions, box pews, three-deckers – generally in the middle of the South Wall, – and the pews always face the chancel which is shallow. If one might say the eighteenth-century churches were built for reciting the offices of the Catholic Church of Ireland in a family chapel, one would say the early nineteenth-century ones, in the country, were built for the same reason but with a projecting chancel and the pews facing east for the most part, that the sacramental nature of the church might be stressed and that they were designed not for one or two families, but for several families to hear the offices and receive the Sacrament.

But since they were generally built as cheaply as possible, the walls are thin, – wooden tracery in a Walter Scott Gothic style in the windows – within were deal woodwork painted buff and grained, thin wooden supports for the gallery painted grey and mottled to look like granite, white or cream walls, the same altar carpet and pulpit hangings and cushions as before, a mellow red tiled floor, a ceiling to keep out the cold as in the eighteenth century, some excellent engraved glass depicting the arms of the local landlord (by Baily of Dublin) in the East window among some other coloured panes in amber, crimson, and emerald in the upper lights, to take the glare of the sun from the congregation's eyes. The choir sat in the gallery and had either instruments, a tuning fork, or a barrel organ.

The blue sky shone in on this humble, clean, cheerful conventicle, through pretty little diamond panes set in wooden glazing bars and the prevailing colours of the place were white and yellow and darker shades of red. Hardy conjures it up well in his poem 'In Mellstock Churchyard' on a similar Dorset church:

On afternoons of drowsy calm
We stood in the panelled pew

Singing one-voiced, a Tate and Brady psalm
  To the tune of 'Cambridge New'.
We watched the elms, we watched the rooks
  The clouds upon the breeze,
Between the whiles of glancing at our books
  And swaying like the trees
So mindless were those outpourings
  Though I am not aware
That I have gained by subtle thought on things
  Since we stood palming there.

Nor am I aware that I have.

Let us look into one of these churches again today. An enthusiastic Vestry, some of whose members have been on a tour of English churches, decided in 1910 to 'improve' the church. The box-pews were removed and a heating apparatus had to be installed – radiators which send a gray patch of dirt above them up the plaster of the wall. The choir was taken down from the gallery and the gallery was removed so that the church looked out of proportion at once. The old red cottage tiles were taken up and fearful encaustics from London or Dublin replaced them, slippery and yellow and blue and red and black. The East window was taken down and one in the best Decorated Gothic obtainable at £30 was erected. This East window was filled with cathedral glass and the old enamelled glass destroyed. The Georgian communion table was removed into the Vestry and a Gothic one from a church furnishers shaped like a box bed put in its place. Greatly daring the incumbent's wife added a frontal in pale green to the table and 'dangerously high' the local peeress added a retable on which bunches of flowers are placed in brass vases in all seasons of the year – so that the effect is of a cottage mantelpiece, or Popery without its symbols.

Some brass rails (with rather an awkward catch where they slide together at the communion service) walled off the chancel in place of the old Georgian leaden woods or simple wooden ones. Between the chancel facing North and South were placed choir stalls and a harmonium. Here it is possible for the ladies in the choir to demonstrate turning or not turning East in the Creed for the congregation to study the latest model from Switzer's on the head of the organist. The three-decker has been taken down and a marble pulpit (I regret to say from an interdenominational monumental masons) rather dwarfs the chancel arch while the new lectern is in the

most flamboyant Perpendicular and purest unstained oak and effectively screens a view of the Table.

To crown everything the ceiling was taken off and a pitch pine roof
substituted (to match the new pews) so that the church was twice as
cold as it had been. The walls have been painted olive green and a
dado of brown Lincrusta runs round head high. The chancel has been
papered orange. The Georgian wood tracery has been removed from
all the windows. Stained glass or cathedral glass (according to the taste
of the Vestry) has replaced it. But since the original church, the
original dignity, has disappeared, it doesn't matter much what happens
next.

This may be an extreme example, but one or more of these
'improvements' have wrecked nearly every church in Ireland of the
dates we are considering. All you can do is to stop it happening any
more. And if people say that the date was mere churchwarden Gothic
and produced nothing remarkable refer them to Francis Johnston's
Castle Chapel (1806–11), the Cathedral of Commissioners' Gothic
and the pioneer of the Gothic revival in Europe – refer them to
Downpatrick Cathedral that exquisite blend of woodwork and white
walls like a Dutch Church interior marred only by an inappropriate
Victorian altar, to Hillsborough Church, recently barbarously treated,
but still worth seeing, Lismore Cathedral and its 1827 spire, to Collon
which has also been despoiled of its three-decker and barrel organ.

Antiquarians with no feeling for Georgian things will say that this
Gothic is incorrect. What do they mean by incorrect? Not medieval?
Certainly not. It is Georgian. It is contemporary architecture. In some
instances, as in the architecture of Semple (c. 1830) in the Dublin and
Kildare diocese, most bold and original architecture was being
produced – the Black Church, whose magnificent interior is spanned
by the first parabolic arch in stone erected between the Saracens and
these days of concrete: Tallaght with its romantic outline of pinnacles
(recently restored without their spearheads – but still restored):
Monkstown Church laughed at today, a source of wonder and
admiration tomorrow, for its originality and romantic outline. It is
only when they are 'improved' to look like semi-Tractarian churches
that they become ugly and uninspiring.

And here, before I conclude with the last period for consideration, I
must point out that while in country places First Fruits Churches were
generally in the old High Tradition, in the towns there were being
built churches which were little more than preaching houses – this
marked the entry of Methodism into Ireland and that preference for

eloquence rather than doctrine which was to appear and the consequent insistence on 'conversion' and Evangelicalism. I see from the old plans that the Round Church, Dublin (S Andrew's) had the pulpit at the North side and the communion table below it in the middle of the church. S George's had an arrangement such as now exists only in the Free Church, Dublin, and I dare say there are other examples.

From 1845 onwards is a time of considerable building in Northern Ireland and in the towns. Ireland gave William Burges, one of the greatest architects of the Gothic Revival, his chance at S Finbar's, Cork, and Burges took it. Drew excelled himself at S Anne's, Belfast, and I think we can safely say that the Church of Ireland has two modern cathedrals (Nicholson, by the way, has scarcely done justice to Drew's beginning) which are the best modern cathedrals in these islands, far better than Liverpool, both of them, and only equalled by the Catholic Apostolic Cathedral in Gordon Square, with Truro as a close runner up.

Among the parish churches there is Burges' Templebrady (which I have only seen in drawings); there are also four fine buildings surely built as Tractarian fanes, Christchurch, Bray by Carpenter & Slater, S Andrew's, Dublin, by Lynn, and Ardragh Church by Slater, and Butterfield's Chapel at S Columba's. An interesting experiment in Decorative church art is to be found at Clare. I think that it needed the Tractarian persecutions to fire the Gothic Revivalists in England of the Victorian period. There was little hope for Tractarianism here after the disestablishment – at least of such as could express itself in the architecture of revived Gothic.

One hundred and forty-two churches come into this period, but there seems to be less to say about them than about the other periods. Two architects stand out for me as church builders – Sir Thomas Drew and Lynn. Sir Thomas Drew had a wonderful sense of mouldings, like his English contemporary Bodley, and what his churches lack in texture – he was prone to cathedral glass and red sandstone dressings – they made up in the boldness of their mouldings and their proportion. Lynn was even more interesting. I only know one work, S Andrew's, Dublin, and that is to me the noblest Gothic Revival interior in Dublin, but I understand he built other churches and I shall be glad to hear of them.

I have come to the end of a long carping disquisition and it may seem that I have suggested nothing constructive as I originally set out to do. But if I were to presume to give advice on the Georgian or

Laudian Table, the correct position of the choir (in the West gallery), the pointing of walls, the painting of plasterwork, the painting of woodwork, the restoration to their original simplicity and charm of eighteenth-century and First Fruits Churches, I would be giving general rules where only particular apply, and raising in your minds battles with angry parishioners who love their brass flower vases and harmonium and think the church has always looked as nice as it does now except before they came when it didn't look so good.

So I would suggest that if you are fortunate enough to be incumbent of an unspoiled church to fight to keep it as it is, and if you are the incumbent of an 'improved' one, to see if anywhere in vestry or Glebe House the original Table and silk cover and woodwork and fittings are lying about. Should the initial step be taken of making an inventory in one volume or series of volumes of Irish Parish Churches and should a book on the many worthy buildings that remain be produced – then, when the interest in Church of Ireland churches is revived, leave a notice on the door of where the key can be found, if you must keep the church locked.

I feel now, having come to the end of it, that what I have been saying is very unimportant, very secondary here in Ireland. I am sure the fabric does not matter so much as I may have implied. After more than two years' residence here I shall return, when I do return to England, with the profoundest gratitude to Ireland. Neutrality, politics, IRA, Unionist – anything put aside it is very wonderful to have lived in a country where everyone – Roman, Anglican, Nonconformist, believes in another world and where everyone goes to Church so that one feels after all that whatever one may feel about the fabrics, the Church of God itself is sure.

Coming Home

First, for the benefit of those who have not done it lately – on leaving home. The boat slides away from the quay. There is a moment's pain. Those lucky people waving from the shore: they can go back to change their books at the library, read the evening paper, fix the black-out curtain, put the kettle on, let the dog out, or go to a lecture on the Home Guard. But for you and me it is diminishing cliffs, then sea, then a landscape which is not England. We buoy ourselves up with thoughts of adventure before us, we think of soul-stirring articles about democracy, freedom of speech and thought, how awful the Nazis are. Or we may even think that we are helping to build a new world. Or we may turn in and have a drink: or be seasick. But deep down in our innermost selves, or rather in my innermost self, I think we put ourselves to this inconvenience of leaving our homes not because of all these advertised abstracts, but because we want to see England again.

It is something really terrible, this longing for England we get when we are away. The other month I found my eyes getting wet (fortunately there was no one about) at the sight of moonlight on a willow stump covered with ivy. It reminded me of a willowy brook in the Berkshire village where we used to live before the war. And then I looked at the stars and even envied them in their icy remoteness, because they were also shining on my home village. We have all been taught in my generation to avoid the sloppy and sentimental. Exile from England has uncorked the bottle of sentiment for me and I could go on gushing for hours, indulging myself at your expense. I remember the most trivial things about home. The trouble about the cow parsley, for instance. Someone had decorated the altar of the parish church with cow parsley. One side said that cow parsley was an unworthy flower for so prominent a place, the other side said that cow parsley looked very nice on the altar, much better than garden flowers and it was always put on the altar at that time of year, anyway. I have forgotten what happened. Then I think of a story someone told me during the Battle of Britain, before I left England. She had to go and judge a Women's Institute competition for the best decorated table

centre in a village in Kent. Bombs and aeroplanes were falling out of
the sky; guns thundered and fragments of shell whizzed about. 'I am
afraid we have not *everybody* here', said the head of the Institute. 'You
see, several of our members had to be up all night, but we have quite a
little show all the same': and there they were, the raffia mats, the bowls
of bulbs, the trailing ends of smilax writhing round mustard and
pepper pots. God be praised for such dogged calm.

My eyes, my nose, my ears all strain for England when I am away:
oil lamps on bold Gothic mouldings at evensong in a country church;
tattered copies of *Hymns Ancient and Modern*; the crackle of the slow
combustion stove; the pleasantly acrid smell of flowering currant
bushes on the platform of a local station; the cat in our backyard
'licking the sunshine off its paws' on a still summer day; shopping in a
big town and for me, the gambling den which will one day bring my
wife and children to starvation – the second-hand bookshops, the stalls
in Farringdon Street, London; remote haunts in Highbury and
Islington. There used to be a form of funny illustrated joke. It showed
Englishmen in the tropics dressing for dinner. I don't think that joke
funny any more. I believe these Englishmen did it because they
wanted to pretend they were home again, not because they were
highly conventional.

Really, this self-pity must stop! I am not half so badly off as
thousand of others. I don't dress for dinner. I have a job which enables
me to return to England quite often. I am not some luckless prisoner
or a wounded man, sweating in a hospital in the East. I shall
see England every three months or so. But there are certain things
about England I have noticed on my more recent visits which you
in England ought to know about. First, English people – persons who
in the old days would get into the railway carriage with you on a cold
day and leave the door open. They shut the door now. People in
public buses and trains are much pleasanter. Heaven protect us from
the railway carriage military strategist. But if you have luggage, people
will help you to lift it in, even if you are a civilian as I am. Why, the
other day in the train, a party got in with a luncheon basket and
insisted on sharing out their sandwiches and drink with the rest of us
in the carriage. Twice in a week I was given a free cup of tea in
country public houses. Everywhere I went I found people much nicer
to one another than I ever remembered them before the war. From
only one stranger did I receive a rebuff, a formidable spinster in some
uniform or other. We were passing through a village I knew and I
enquired whether Mrs So-and-So still lived there. She said 'Yes'.

Then she looked at me and I saw behind her cold grey eyes an argument going on. 'This unhealthly looking Bruce is trying to get military information from me'. So she suddenly added, 'No, she doesn't'. I cannot say I minded, for her attitude showed the trained, cautious behaviour of my countrymen, still on the watch for paratroops.

And if strangers are pleasanter, my friends I find kinder still. They uncorked the last bottle of wine, they shared their sugar ration with me, they were delighted to see me although they were all intensely busy. I was warm, comfortable and well fed during the whole of my visit. Indeed I would go so far as to say that a certain chain of hotels, one of whose houses I patronised, has improved since the war. The food is no longer so pretentious and you can see what you are eating. The prices are lower too. But the two most noticeable things of all about English people since the war are these – the breakdown of class distinctions and the new standard of values. It seemed to me as though people now take you for what you are like personally, not for how you stand in the social scale. Then there seemed to me to be less materialism about, less bother with money. I noticed people reading books on philosophy and religion, sitting next to me in trains. I could swear that those people, before the war, would have been reading the financial news or filling in competition crosswords. Of course, all this sudden revelation which has led me to make what may seem sweeping statements may be due to absence from England. Possibly everyone was simply delightful before the war and I didn't realise it.

I did realise, however, and I realise more strongly than ever today, how exquisitely beautiful are the villages and old towns of England. There are the obvious things: Ludlow's great sweep of old houses up the hill from the rich Shropshire valley; the flint towers of Norfolk and Suffolk, where roads wind like streams among the elms; the bulging barrows of the chalk downs where thatched houses cluster among elm trees in hollows and white roads wind up from them to the sheepfolds; Salisbury Close with its ancient houses, stone walls, wide sweeps of grass, and cloud shadows chasing over the silver-grey magnificence of the cathedral; hundreds and hundreds of place names of hundreds and hundreds of unspoiled places with stone churches, heavily ticking church clocks, modest post offices, creeper-clad wardens' cottages, rusty croquet hoops on rectory lawns, swinging inn signs and well-stocked gardens where brick paths lead through thyme and vegetables. To think of the names is to feel better: Huish Champflower, Whitchurch Canonicorum, Willingale Spain, Bourton-on-the-Hill, Iwerne Minster, Piddletrenthide, South Molton, Wotton, Norton, Evenlode, Fairford, Canon's Ashby, Bag Enderby, Kingston Bagpuize. The broad sweep of England's beauty is obvious enough, the immense variety of building stone and sorts of landscape to be found in a single county. But this is so easily destroyed, not by bombs but by witless local councillors, people on the lookout for building land, electric light companies, county councils with new road schemes, the wrong sort of 'planner'.

Planning is very much in the English air now. And that is a good thing if by planning we also mean preserving. But let the planners be careful. It would not be worth our being away from England, those of us who live in the country, if we had to come back to find our villages transformed into single blocks of flats towering out of unfenced fields, with an inter-denominational religious room at the top of each tower for services conducted by wireless (voluntary attendance). And those of us who live in old towns do not want to see everything swept away to open vistas where vistas were never intended. Hitler has opened up a few good ones. Let us leave it at that. Of course we do not want slums to remain, nor to live in cottages in the country where there is no water and where the roof leaks. But slums can be rebuilt into habitable places – not always as flats – and cottages can be repaired. Perhaps we shall be allowed to live in the sort of England recommended by the Scott Committee, where country shall still be country and town shall still be town and where we who wish to keep the country worth looking at will not all be thought cranks and reactionaries.

Think of a single old brick or piece of stone in an English house or garden wall; centuries of sun and rain have mellowed it and overgrown it with lichens and moss and shaved off its sharp angles; think of the slopes and swags of an old tiled roof seen from the top of a country bus; think of the lay-out of an old town or village, the winding roads to it, the Georgian merchants' houses in the middle, the L-shaped farms on the outskirts, the church tower gathering the hours round it like a hen her chicks. In a single week of our planning, centuries of texture can be brushed away. Is all to be re-planned, are we only to bask on our own flat roofs and swim in municipal pools and feel half-naked at home because our outside walls are all of glass? Are all roads to be straight and all wild-rose hedges to be swept away? All trees except quick-growing conifers to be cut down? All this for the rather doubtful advantage of running hot water in everybody's bedroom and aeroplanes for all?

I do not believe we are fighting for the privilege of living in a highly developed community of ants. That is what the Nazis want. For me, at any rate, England stands for the Church of England, eccentric incumbents, oil-lit churches, Women's Institutes, modest village inns, arguments about cow parsley on the altar, the noise of mowing machines on Saturday afternoons, local newspapers, local auctions, the poetry of Tennyson, Crabbe, Hardy and Matthew Arnold, local talent, local concerts, a visit to the cinema, branch-line trains, light railways, leaning on gates and looking across fields; for you it may stand for something else, equally eccentric to me as I may appear to you, something to do with Wolverhampton or dear old Swindon or wherever you happen to live. But just as important. But I know the England *I* want to come home to is not very different from that in which you want to live. It it were some efficient ant-heap which the glass and steel, flat-roof, straight-road boys want to make it, then how could we love it as we do?

When people talk to me about 'the British', as though they were all the same, I give up. They have never lived in England and I know how useless it is to explain to them about cow parsley on the altar, villages, Women's Institutes, life in English towns. One cannot explain anything at once so kind and so complicated. If I could explain England, if it really were a planned ants' nest which we could all generalise about, I, like thousands of others, would have no home to which to return.

BBC broadcast

Daily Herald Book Reviews (1)

The small things are the happy things I am sure of it. Two autobiographies this week explain just what I mean.

One, *My Candle at Both Ends*, by John Carveth Wells (*Jarrolds*, 12s 6d) is indescribably sad.

Not that its young author – now paralysed and having to pick up again for the umpteenth time a means of living – is unhappy. But his vigorous, angry, moving, and prejudiced book reveals tragedy beneath the fantastic adventures he has had all over the world in thirty-two years of life.

He was brought up away from his parents; he ran away from school; now he made money, now he sold matches; always his energy was boundless.

He is the victim of what will, I hope, be the lowest ebb of our country's history – the inter-war period. It was a period when we lacked faith and sought a sensation in great names, long journeys, daring escapades; we found them unlasting and lost our tempers.

It was a rootless time of too much work for some and none for others, of uncertainty and impending doom.

Those of us born in it had no settled time to look back to, and we were apprehensive of the 'sack' next week. Consciously and unconsciously, this book expresses all the horror of those days.

*

Before the war, in the serious thirties, young writers used to talk about Marx over their morning coffee.

Politics were all the thing and the lefter the righter.

Since the French Revolution I doubt whether any movement on the Continent has had such an influence on English writing as the Spanish Civil War. I cannot help noticing how the younger writers today are less political.

Instead of Franco, the State is the villain, and they are keen in their defence of the individual; they have more respect for the past, less hope for the future. They feel menaced by too much State control of private lives.

I glean all this from *Penguin New Writing No.* 19 (9d) and *Modern Reading No.* 9 (*Wells Gardener, Darton*, 9d).

People who like to read literature as opposed to thrillers – not that thrillers are always illiterate – should buy these publications. They contain the scrappy bits of youth's writing, typed on private paper in Government time at some ARP post, scribbled down on OHMS paper in a camp; they are stolen minutes of creation after fatigue or boredom.

They are too often like the best chapter of a novel which their author can't finish, or they are unduly miserable, full of backyards and chicken dung, or almost over-detailed accounts of daily life in one of the Services.

But they are nearly always good and they show which way the wind is going to blow and who, if he survive, will produce a book worth reading one day.

I commend John Ward's story of a Civil servant visiting a very poor family about a pension in *Penguin New Writing*. Ward is twenty-eight.

Michael McLaverty has a touching story about a woman drunkard in *Modern Reading*, interesting because it describes life among those least-described people, the Roman Catholic third of the population of Northern Ireland.

But when Henry Miller, in the same booklet, a mature writer and excellent critic, likens D. H. Lawrence to Our Lord and St Francis of Assisi ('Jesus was killed off; Lawrence was obliged to commit suicide – that's the difference') he exposes himself to ridicule and destroys his own case by overstatement, to put it mildly.

*

There is a shortage of English authors.

Every week about a quarter of the books I receive for review are by Americans.

Another quarter are by journalists who have been out on some war front, and who seem to race one another to see who can get out a book on the very latest phase of the war first. This does not make for good reading.

Another quarter consists of essays and pamphlets. The remaining quarter are the more usual English books.

The explanation is quite simple. Every English writer of note who is not over-age or physically disabled is doing some sort of war work and has no time to write at length.

So I advise you unless you see a new book warmly recommended, to content yourself with an old book or a reprint of an old one.

*

If you want to feel the waves wash over you in the hottest weather . . . If you want to be transported to the depths of winter or away into a sinister calm on the Indian Ocean . . .

If you want to smell tar and scrubbed wood and to hear the creaking of masts or to grope through a sea fog and if you want a rattling good story to accompany all this . . .

Read Conrad.

Tales of Hearsay and Last Essays, by Joseph Conrad (*Penguin*, 9d) has just been reprinted.

The reprint sent me back to other books on my shelves by this great writer of sea stories – *Lord Jim*, *Typhoon*, and *Almayer's Folly*, to name a few.

And I advise you to buy any old copies of Conrad you can see in second-hand shops – he is still fairly plentiful – or to get him out of the library; he is sure to be there.

Conrad was a Pole who ran away to sea. He loved everything English, and early in life started writing sea-stories (he always wrote them in longhand with a lot of crossings-out) in the very perfect English of someone who had learned a difficult language thoroughly.

I remember 'Bartimeus,' another fine sea-story writer, telling me that Conrad always retained a faint foreign accent, but that he had a most wonderful choice of words in his conversation. So he had in his seemingly effortless prose.

'The Last Tale,' in *Tales of Hearsay* is considered to be his best bit of writing, but my own preference is for 'The Black Mate.'

Conrad's Polishness comes out, not in his language, but in his love of heroism. The point of his stories is almost always something to do with a heroic deed whose true nature does not come out until you have reflected on the tale afterwards. Although he likes heroics, his stories are never horrible.

Now Conrad is a great writer of novels and stories. He never overloads the balance between plot and descriptive writing.

Most novels you read have either a very good plot and poor description, or good description and no power of telling a story.

A great writer is one who can convey all his plot, atmosphere and characters at once, so that you could not possibly cut a sentence out without spoiling the effect.

Above all, a great book is a readable book which can be read again and again. I must think of that last sentence before I go in off the deep end about a novel.

*

There can be no one alive who does not sometimes get overwhelmed with gloom at the mess we live in.

I don't just mean the war, but the muddles and injustices and waste that seem to have been going on ever since we were alive.

But there are very few people who can analyse the trouble clearly, and there are fewer still who offer a solution which does not reduce human society to an ant-heap.

One who did see things clearly offered a solution – and expressed his mind forcibly so that a child might understand – was Eric Gill, who died recently.

I showed this last (and best) little book of essays by him to an economist who said, 'The man's a European Gandhi,' and to a statistician who said that the book made him want to preach a sermon.

*

If I were asked which two authors had made the greatest impression on the English language since the last war, I would answer P. G. Wodehouse and James Joyce.

The first has altered the language. Bertie Wooster's expressions are on everybody's lips or at any rate expressions in the manner of Bertie.

When there was that dust-up about Mr Wodehouse broadcasting from Germany and outraged librarians burned his books, they could not burn the effect of his books.

I wonder, too, whether admirers of his writing really noticed the rumpus. I remember Dr Joad telling me that at the time somebody on the Brains Trust mentioned him as a favourite author – I think it was Lady Asquith or Lady Astor, I'm not sure which – and said, 'G. P. Wodehouse.'

The BBC waited in shocked silence for a storm of angry letters for mentioning a traitor's name. There was a storm of letters all right, but they one and all corrected 'G. P. Wodehouse' to 'P. G. Wodehouse' and did not mention his 'treachery' at all.

Literature knows no barriers, what? By Jove, no, old boy.

If Wodehouse has altered the language, Joyce has altered the manner of writing it. But just as Spenser is called 'The Poet's Poet,' so Joyce is 'The Prose Writer's Prose Writer.'

He used to go about with a little notebook and take down what people said when they were off their guard. I mean how people really speak, not how they speak in books.

And then he filled in the gaps with what they thought.

As is the case with most of us, he showed that what we think is much longer and more complicated and personal than what eventually comes out of our mouths.

Take this bit from *Ulysses*, a book which was burned for being 'dirty reading matter' soon after it was first published in 1922. (I smuggled my copy out of France through the Customs in the seat of my trousers.) You must imagine a bored schoolmaster and bored boys at the end of a lesson:

'You, Armstrong,' Stephen said, 'What was the end of Pyrrhus?'

'End of Pyrrhus, sir?'

'I know, sir. Ask me, sir,' Comyn said.

'Wait. You. Armstrong. Do you know anything about Pyrrhus?'

A bag of figrolls lay snugly in Armstrong's satchel. He curled them between his palms at whiles and swallowed them softly. Crumbs adhered to the tissues of his lips. A sweetened boy's breath. Well-off people, proud that their eldest son was in the Navy. Vico Road, Dalkey.

'Pyrrhus, sir? Pyrrhus, a pier.'

All laughed. Mirthless, high malicious laughter. Armstrong looked round at his class-mates, silly glee in profile, in a moment they will laugh more loudly, aware of my lack of rule and of the fees their papas pay.

Twenty years ago this sort of writing was considered modern and incomprehensible. Now it is part of the technique of most novelists.

Lots of people have written long and turgidly about Joyce and they have not made him easier to understand.

Indeed, to understand him fully you need a knowledge of Dublin in the nineties, and there are not many who can therefore get all his meanings.

Even in the passage I have quoted you need to know that Dalkey is a suburb of Dublin and the Vico Road a rich part of it.

Stephen Hero, by James Joyce (*Cape*, 9s 6d) is a part of a first draft for one of his earlier books, *A Portrait of the Artist as a Young Man*.

It is interesting, but by no means very interesting unless you know Dublin and Joyce already. But in that case you must have it.

If you want to read a book by Joyce that is easy and understandable, get *Dubliners* out of the library. It is a marvellous picture of Irish middle-class life.

*

Don't try to be a poet or a writer or an artist or a musician today. At least, not unless you've got a private income – and a good thick one.

The last person to make his living by poetry was Tennyson. The rest of them starved or had incomes from private or other sources, or if they lived in the eighteenth century they had patrons, which comes to the same thing.

If you want to be a writer it's just the same, unless you are willing to give to writing money-making rot the precious hours that you might have given to writing a book worth reading. And as for art, you'll find yourself a 'commercial artist,' which often isn't an artist at all. I don't know about musicians, but I expect there's some similar dreary fate for them.

And if you *must* be one of these things, and some of us must be, because we can't help it, let your ordinary slavery to bring in money be in a job which has nothing to do with what you want to do.

Thus you will not ruin your taste and love for what you know you were born to do. Be a ploughman like Burns or a Post Office official like Trollope. You may be famous in your lifetime (unlikely); you may make enough money to devote yourself entirely to your art (very unlikely); you may, after years of obscurity and poverty, be given a Civil List pension by the State (announced in *The Times*, so that people will know you are badly off) of about £150 a year as a result of wire-pulling by influential friends.

I am not being cynical. Those are the facts about artists in the twentieth century. And yet artists go on cropping up, and despite the lack of the right sort of encouragement and too much of the wrong sort of encouragement from schools and colleges.

In fact, I've come to believe that part of the process of being any good as an artist or writer is having the faith and the guts to overcome the terrific obstacles your fellow countrymen put in your way before you can start.

These thoughts are borne out after reading *The Horse's Mouth*, by Joyce Cary (*Michael Joseph*, 10s 6d).

So far as one can extract a story from this glorious welter of words, it is this:

Mr Gulley Jimson, aged sixty-seven, is an eccentric artist who lives in a boathouse on the Thames at somewhere like Wapping. He has just come out after doing a month in the clink for pestering one of his former patrons.

About the first thing he does is to telephone to this patron again and say he is the Home Secretary or the National Gallery, and try to get hold of some of the pictures which his patron bought from him.

For Mr Jimson is a genius, and his earlier pictures are admired and bought for hundreds of pounds by the cognoscenti. That money circulates among dealers and millionaires while Jimson starves. He can't get canvas, can't buy paint, drinks, is turned out of his boathouse, lives in a doss, goes to jail again for stealing, sponges, borrows, and starts huge pictures in his new and most advanced manner which no one can understand, except a boy of the neighbourhood called Nosey.

Eventually the local council decides to pull down the building where he is doing a mural (like most local councils, it hates art) and he bursts a blood vessel and is clearly going to die in hospital.

The story is unimportant. In fact, it rather looks as though the book had been written from a scrap album. Mr Cary has pasted bits of writing he was proud of into his story. This, though it helps out the character of Mr Jimson as an irrepressible believer in himself and William Blake getting more cheerful as circumstances get worse, strains probability to breaking point and defeats all connected narrative.

But Mr Joyce Cary is an important and exciting writer, there's no doubt about that. To use Tennyson's phrase, he is a Lord of Language. He talks about the night getting 'as dark as the inside of a Cabinet Minister.' And here are rich people.

> 'Sir William had a bald head and monkey fur on the back of his hands. Voice like a Liverpool dray on a rumbling bridge. Charming manners. He really deserved to have his name handed up, or down, to posterity.'

And here is Jimson talking in the bus:

> 'A government can't be too strong. I hope your government is a lot of devils. Or they won't have much chance against devils like you and me, ma'am . . . . For of all the ungrateful, spiteful, cruel savages in the world, when it comes to dealing with governments, give me a Free and Sovereign people.'
>
> 'Speak for yourself,' said the egg woman.

'I can't speak for anyone else,' I said, 'I don't know the language.'

If you like rich writing full of gusto and accurate original character drawing, you will get it from *The Horse's Mouth*. Mr Cary is the right horse.

*

A bunch of Irish books has been waiting my attention for some time.

Two fundamental facts everybody who reads about Eire must know in order to understand what they read and, indeed, to understand Ireland at all:

1   Eire is a country with a very strong sense of the presence of God. I don't say this makes the Irish better than other people, more reliable or hardworking or kind. It doesn't, but you can't help noticing as soon as you land the feeling that the Catholic Church is everywhere.

I remember taking Dr Joad to High Mass at Maynooth, that huge training college for priests rising grey out of the wide green levels of Kildare, and as the great roll of the *Kyrie* rose up from eight hundred throats through the ornate chapel where we were sitting, he leaned over to me and said, 'This is formidable.' That sums it up well.

2   The Irish are not mad and spooky and vague and dreamy, as some of them would have us think, but extremely logical. It is *we* who are the other things.

We are poets, they are realists.

They hate compromise (they regard the Belfast situation as one of our compromises) and we love it.

If you remember this and read the story of *Eamon de Valera*, by M. J. MacManus (*Gollancz*, 8s 6d) you will be starting on the right foot.

De Valera's father was a Spaniard and his mother was from Limerick, and he was born in New York but brought up in Ireland.

His hobbies are higher mathematics, his religion is Catholic; he is not a great orator; he has much personal charm.

That is the private side of him. The story of his life is the story of an astute politician whose aim is to make the whole island of Ireland an independent republic, and he makes no concealment of this aim. Neither world wars, economic wars, nor even the sentence of death that we once imposed on him, have deterred him.

Inevitably, Mr MacManus' book is concerned with what will seem parochial matters to those outside Ireland, but when 'Dev' emerges as President of the League of Nations we get a glimpse of his greatness.

The book is adulatory, as any biography must be which is written while its subject is living by one of his supporters. But it will dispel many illusions.

You will see that de Valera is no Nazi, no sympathiser with Germany, no bomb-thrower and I suspect that he regrets the old hatred of England which once made doubly difficult our negotiations for a working basis with Ireland – a basis which de Valera, on his terms, still earnestly desires.

The history of the English in Ireland does not make elevating reading . . . There is reason for this hate. Irish history is full of 'If only England had . . .'

*

'The Germans, advancing from Chipping Norton, have captured the key point of Little Rollright.'

When listening to the news I have always substituted the names of towns and villages I know. I even do it now, when it is the Allies who are advancing.

It helps to realise what 'occupation' and 'liberation' must mean to the people who live in battlefields.

And as I do so, I hope that the buildings remain. No amount of re-planning will compensate for the loss of familiar views and buildings. To the economist, historian, general, politician, these places are maps and figures. To the planner they are so much cubic space.

But when you think of them as homes with families in them, then the poets and novelists step in and the impersonal ones step out.

I think the full significance of war is best described by poets and novelists of the land where the war is being fought. Poets don't always translate. Novelists do.

That is why *Children and the Dagger* (*Allen and Unwin*, 7s 6d), by Frantisek Langer, is an important book – to me, at any rate.

Podoli, in Czechoslovakia, might be Little Rollright, Oxon. Think of it as that.

The Germans occupy it. Their guards watch every house. Sabotage occurs. They suspect that a dynamite dump is hidden in the district and that the village children know where it is.

The schoolmaster, a decent old German who has been imposed on the Czech school, is asked to interrogate the children. He gives up because they put him to shame and he is sent to a concentration camp.

A young officer from Nazi HQ takes his place. He will outwit these miserable urchins of an inferior race.

He is good at games, handsome and sporting. The guards are relaxed. He plays football with the children. He teaches them scouting – such thrilling scouting games where they have to bring back to him information about the movements of all the villagers, just like real war.

Only one boy suspects him and he was the old ringleader of the school before the Nazi came. And watching one night through the Nazi schoolmaster's window, he sees him making a report from all the scouting notes – a report which will condemn the whole village. He must get it and the boy struggles with the schoolmaster and knifes him.

Then wrath breaks out, lorries roar, the Nazi colonel himself arrives. The children are threatened with torture. A mock trial occurs, but at it the colonel is obliged to accept an old Czech patriot as the criminal. The patriot is hanged on the village green.

Furious at having taken the wrong step, the colonel drives away. He vows never to show even a semblance of justice again. He looks out of the window of his car as he passes through another village just like Podoli. He notices the name on the signboard. It is LIDICE.

The story is well told and not overdramatic. It has the naive simplicity of good translation. It is as though Hans Andersen were writing about devils. But the Jews of Europe have not even a village. Do you remember Browning's 'Holy-Cross Day'?

> By the torture, prolonged from age to age,
> By the Infamy, Israel's heritage,
> By the Ghetto's plague, by the garb's disgrace,
> By the badge of shame, by the felon's place,
> By the branding tool, the bloody whip,
> And the summons to Christian fellowship.

*

Robert Neumann's *By the Waters of Babylon* (*Hutchinson*, 6s) is certainly not Jewish propaganda. Yet I would quote this from it about Jews in our own day, and you can compare it with Browning who was writing of 1600; and see how little the human race changes:

'Concentration camp, fled over the frontier, disappeared, gone mad, imprisoned, shot while trying to escape, died of sun-stroke whilst scrubbing the pavement, died of heart-attack while waiting for a visa, died of a stroke during domiciliary search, fallen out of the train, fallen out of the bedroom window, fallen off a bridge, found in the gutter with a smashed skull, found drowned in a well shaft, found hanged in a lavatory, kicked to death in a barrack cellar, dead, dead, dead.'

The book, which is a reissue, is really ten stories, each the biography of one of a busload of Jews travelling to Palestine for a variety of reasons ... the [mystic] marching to the promised land, the engineer, the Austrian [financier], the defeated boxer, the king's mistress, the writer, the lawyer who is ashamed of being a Jew, and so on.

The book has humour. It is also shocking and merciless. To have read it is to feel very much older, and there is a timelessness in the telling which makes seven centuries of pogroms seem but a blink in the eye of Eternity.

Evelyn Waugh is about the only living writer whose novels I can read a second time with pleasure. This is because he hates writing and does not suffer from verbal diarrhoea, as do many lengthier novelists.

Each word and every sentence is the product of much cerebration, no word is unnecessary, nothing is careless or inappropriate.

There are several good novelists with impeccable prose style, but none living that I know of who combines such style and narrative power as Evelyn Waugh. His new novel is, I think, his best yet and that is saying a lot.

Since the theme of *Brideshead Revisited* (*Chapman and Hall*, 10s 6d) falls in line with the new novel of Mr Francis Williams, late editor of the *Daily Herald*, and a new pamphlet by Mr Victor Gollancz – both reviewed here – I feel no compunction in devoting more space than usual to a single book.

The message of Mr Waugh's book which may escape those who are looking merely for wit (and they will find plenty) is that worldly values are not worth having. Mr Waugh gives the Christian argument against the world. Mr Gollancz gives a Judaeo-Christian one and Mr Williams feels an ethical urge against worldly standards.

Brideshead Revisited is the autobiography of Charles Ryder, an infantry officer.

His unit is suddenly shifted from an arid suburb outside Glasgow to the South of England. Dawn next day reveals the park of a great country house, Brideshead. Ryder had been there before and most of the book is about his relations with the Catholic family of Lord Marchmain, which inhabited the house before the war.

The characters of the Marchmain family are first introduced scandalously by a clever aesthete, and one's interest is kept up by the discovery of what they are really like as Ryder meets them.

Sebastian, the younger son, takes to drink because his family will not leave him alone and ends by living in squalid happiness in Morocco, still drinking like a fish. Through all his drink we see him as a human being whose very weakness is lovable.

In fact, this is a great study of a drunkard. And then we meet Rex Mottram, the go-ahead MP always in the smart set and of course a little in with Ribbentrop and Co. before the war and violently anti-German when war is declared. 'It's a bluff. Where's their tungsten? Where's their nfanganese? Where's their chrome?' (Don't you remember those businessmen's arguments?)

And when we meet Rex, with his 'flavour of Max and F. E. and the Prince of Wales of the big table at the Sporting Club, the second magnum and the fourth cigar, of the chauffeur kept waiting hour after hour without compunction,' we realise the Sebastian is *someone* and poor Rex Mottram is an undeveloped child.

And so we go through the whole family – Lord Marchmain, the old reprobate living in Venice with his comfortable mistress: Lady Marchmain, so good and saintly yet so unattractive as a character: Julia, the lovely eldest daughter whom Ryder nearly marries, and Cordelia, the nun-type: Brideshead, the heir who sees things whole and so surprisingly.

This book is as rich in characters as a Dickens novel but they are never caricature.

In *What Buchenwald Really Means* (*Gollancz*, 3d), Victor Gollancz points out that you and I are as much responsible for these Nazi torture camps as the Germans.

We knew about them before the war. They consisted largely of German Christians, German Jews, German Communists and German Trade Unionists.

But whereas you and I could have protested without getting into trouble, Germans could not have done so without going to one of the camps themselves for speaking against the Nazi Government.

It was easier for us to protest and now we blame the Germans for what the Nazis did to those of them who did not agree with them.

All the three writers I have noticed today have one theme in common – the importance of the individual, his rights and sanctity as someone with an immortal soul which no slave State must ever be allowed to crush or 'educate' out of him.

Winter at Home

Now comes the time when gardeners have given up trying to sweep away leaves. We have taken the honesty out of the top shelf in the linen cupboard and stuck it in the brass altar vases of the village church. Last Sunday the last of the Michaelmas daisies were too frost-bitten to be conducive to public worship. Now England, having got rid of tourists and those who feel they must seek sunlight, settles down to be herself. With any luck there will be fogs in November and December so that the sky will not be poisoned with aeroplanes and a quiet of eternity will be about us, just the drip drip from wet branches and smells of woodsmoke and fungus in the lanes. The Women's Institute will take on new life with a revival of basket making; more leather-work purses will be made than there is money to put into them, and even Mrs Hutchinson's talk on her visit to Rhodesia will seem interesting, although the magic lantern is certain to fail.

Ah! the sweet prelude to an English winter! For me it is so infinitely a more beautiful season than any other, which is just as well since it goes on for most of the year. It is a time when there is more colour in the country than there was ever before. Ploughed fields take on a look like a farming scene in the initial letter of a medieval manuscript. Bricks are an intenser red and Cotswold stone is more golden, the limestone and granite of the north is more silver, bare branches are like pressed seaweed against the pale blue sky. Whatever remains green is more deeply, richly green than it was before. This waiting, intense stillness is generally a prelude to a storm. The smallest sound is easily heard. Cocks are continually crowing, ducks quacking as though they were happy, and even across three miles of still, misty fields, it is possible to distinguish all six of the church bells as men practise method ringing in the oil-lit evening tower. But this night there is not one of those gigantic winter sunsets and the house is more than usually full of spiders, huge hairy ones which cast a shadow twice their own size on the drawing-room carpet. And then, in the night the storm begins. Will the trees stand it, this gale which makes them roar and creak and roar again? Will the earth ever be able to soak in these torrents which beat the house, brim the water-butts and swish on grass and gravel? And has anyone remembered to shut the upstairs window?

Winter is the one time when I feel I can indulge myself in reading what I like instead of what I ought to read. Time stretches out a little more and I stretch myself with it. Slow books come back and I try to forget our jerky modern novels. While the storm shakes the shutters, I re-read Scott, generally starting with *The Heart of Midlothian*. And as the great rumbling periods, as surely and steadily as a stage-coach, carry me back to Edinburgh, the most beautiful city in these islands, I feel an *embarras de richesse*. There is too much I want to read, too many memories I wish to experience.

Winter is the time for reading poetry and often I discover for myself some minor English poet, a country parson who on just such a night, must have sat in his study and blown sand off lines like these, written in ink made of oak-gall:

> 'Soon as eve closes, the loud hooting owl
> That loves the turbulent and frosty night
> Perches aloft upon the rocking elm
> And halloes to the moon.'

And here they are, these lines, widely spaced upon the printed page and hundreds more, by the Reverend James Hurdis, DD, Incumbent of Bishopstone, Sussex, printed a century and a half ago, some of the most perfect descriptions of an English winter that were ever written in English. And you and I are probably the only people in England who are reading Hurdis. The smell of the old book is like a country church when first you open its door, the look of the pages is spacious like the age in which it was written and the broad margins isolate the poetry as Bishopstone must then have been isolated among windy miles of sheep-nibbled downs.

There is no need only to escape into the civilised past, which is more easily done in winter than in any other time of the year. Even modern barbarism becomes almost human, especially in places which make their money out of summer visitors. Am I wrong in thinking that the blonde with a handkerchief wound round her head and a cigarette in her mouth, is a little politer now when she refuses to sell me the cigarettes I know she has in hundreds under the counter? Do I perceive a mood less casual in the bar-attendant at the grand hotel? Is it possible that when I ask for a room at the reception desk I will actually be accommodated instead of being sent away with a scornful refusal? Maybe this is all imagination. But of this I am quite certain, when I receive my fee for describing to you these joys of winter, I shall indulge in the greatest winter joy I know. I shall take the train to the coast and spend a night by the sea.

The train from London will be fairly empty. By the time evening has set in there will be hardly anyone in it at all, for the larger towns on the way to the sea will have taken off most of the passengers. What started as an express, will have turned into a local train, stopping at oil-lit stations while the gale whistles in the ventilators of empty carriages. Standing out white on a blue glass ground, will appear the names of wayside stations and reflected in a puddle, the light of a farmer's car in the yard will sparkle beyond the platform fence.

Then we will go into the windy dark until at last there is a station slightly more important than those we have passed, lit with gas instead of oil and that is mine. I will hear the soft local accent, smell the salt in the wet and warmer air and descry through the lines of rain that lace the taxi's windscreen, bulks of houses that were full and formidable in summer and now have not a light in any of their windows.

And then I will see the village of my youth and of my holidays. There will be cigarettes in the post office, no one about but the old friends who are permanent residents. And before I see friends or buy cigarettes, I will run down the lane to the sea, feathery tamarisk weighed down with rain drops and black against the night sky, noise of lapping waves and smell of seaweed, soft crunch of sand under my shoes and there, all to myself, faintly visible under a watery moon, the cold and spreading beach. No vestige of picnics now, no cars in the car park, no lovers on the cliff path, no bathers, golfers, sports girls or sand castles, nothing but shadowy cliffs and the ever faithful sea.

Thump-umph! I will hear the breakers sucked and shot away from the blowhole and in the little moonlight, the rollers will be, to my imagination, more mountainous than ever they have been before. And safe in bed, I shall listen to the gale beating the window and hear, above the wind, the plunge and roar of the breakers against the cliff.

> 'They come – they mount – they charge in vain,
> Thus far, incalculable main!
> No more! thine hosts have not o'erthrown
> The lichen on the barrier-stone.'

With Parson Hawker's poem *The Storm* in my head, I shall switch the light out for one of the long, deep country sleeps of winter.

Four:

1945 to 1949

Four
1945–1949

'Not even a *popular* poet if there is one could possibly live by his poetry,' replied JB when asked by Cyril Connolly for his magazine *Horizon*, whether a poet could earn enough money to live on. '. . . If someone is born to be a writer, nothing will prevent his writing. Perhaps the bitter tests of today are a good thing, but you need great strength of character. At all costs avoid an advertising agency, where you will either have to write lies or embellish facts in which you are not interested; such work is of the devil. Journalism is a better way out for weak characters such as I am who are slaves to nicotine and drink. It teaches you to write shortly and clearly. It allows you to say what you think – at least reputable journalism does. It forbids you to be a bore.'[1]

JB's journalistic work accrued. His interest, which was growing when he was a schoolboy, in nineteenth-century literature and poetry, and particularly in that of the 1890s poets, made him the obvious candidate to help edit anthologies, to write prefaces, articles and reviews on these and related subjects. Parcels of review books arrived almost daily. Sometimes he would find reward – a new edition of Kilvert's Diary or of Thomas Bewick's wood engravings, or a novel like *Prater Violet* by the 'flawless writer' Christopher Isherwood. 'It is a pitying, affectionate view,' he wrote, 'of a parable with a film studio as its setting. . . . And its author looks on, fearing death and wondering why we were all born.'[2] He singled out Albert Camus' *The Outsider* as being so well written that it was in a class by itself. But if JB erred towards disturbingly depressing books he also favoured humorous ones and was constantly being asked to review books on many light-hearted topics.

His work often took him on two or three-day forays into the country and, whatever his particular mission – an expedition to Alexandra Palace to appear on television or a journey to Aberdeen to write a radio broadcast he would take in everything along the way and store it up in the enormous architectural encyclopedia inside his head. From his first bicycling explorations in North Cornwall, through his *Architectural Review* days when for three years he was paid to look at buildings, JB had built up an almost unsurpassed knowledge of England. He had no equivalent. There were antiquarian scholars of England on the one hand, whom JB decried for having no sense of place, and specialist-enthusiasts on the other. He began to be seen as an all round public defender of the English character. When a row of thatched cottages in the village of Letcombe Bassett near Wantage was threatened with demolition because of inadequate drainage, JB wrote a long case against the planners, which was published in the *Architectural Review* and which he discussed with a planner on the radio, bringing the story to national prominence.

Letcombe Bassett's battle with the planners and the health authorities was mirrored in many English villages. The Ministry of Town and Country Planning had been created in 1943 and soon afterwards the new Minister was empowered to prepare lists of buildings of special architectural or historic interest which could act as a guidance to local authorities but it would be years before these lists became in any way representative of what merited safeguarding. Appalled by the rising tide of demolition and wholesale redevelopment, JB felt the only hope was to continue to eulogise his surroundings to the public whenever he could, so that it might dawn on them how valuable they were.

His long-standing friendship and affinity with the artist John Piper, who shared his passion for topography and architecture, had resulted in their inspired collaboration on many ventures. At this time they included the *Shell Guide to Shropshire* (1951) and *Murray's Guides to Buckinghamshire* (1948) and *Berkshire* (1949). Their observations – Piper's through his photographs and drawings, and JB through his writing – cast a new light onto hitherto unregarded barns, Baptist chapels, gravestones, farmhouses and all manner of hidden places. They had strong and unconventional views and, luckily, were given a free rein by their editors. They remained unperturbed by their peers' slavish following of fashion. 'I am convinced he will continue to disregard changes in contemporary taste,' wrote JB of Piper in the *Penguin Book of Modern Painters* in 1947. 'It is his mission to weld closer together his deep, learned and poetic love of England with his clearly-formed principles of what a picture should be.' JB's principles were like Piper's, deeply felt, and the pictures he conjured through his radio broadcasts, as in the series 'Coast and County', were clear and singular.

In post-war Britain his contemporaries were beginning to land powerful literary jobs – his old friend Alan Pryce-Jones now edited the *Times Literary Supplement*, while Cyril Connolly continued to edit *Horizon* – and JB was receiving more and more commissions to write about subjects which appealed to him, such as provincial newspapers, golf, or church-crawling.

1. *Horizon*, September 1946, reprinted in *Ideas and Places*, ed. Cyril Connolly (Weidenfeld and Nicolson, 1953).
2. *Daily Herald*, 6 June 1946.

Sabine Baring-Gould

S. Baring Gould. Sabine Baring-Gould, spelled Sabine and pronounced Saybin – the name appears on novels and volumes of history,
anecdote and description, mostly about the West Country, France and
Germany. And there is the name again in the index of authors in most
hymn books – he wrote the words of 'Onward Christian Soldiers' and
of 'Daily, Daily sing the praises': he wrote the words *and* composed
the music of 'Now the day is over'. With his friends Bussell and
Sheppard and others, he hunted out the folk songs of the West and
published them before even Cecil Sharp was on the scene. To Baring-
Gould the world outside Devon is first indebted for the song
'Widdecombe Fair' which appeared in his book *Songs of the West*.

I might as well give you here a description of how he used to collect
these folk songs. You must imagine the tall, young clergyman Baring-
Gould, ascetic-looking, with a largish nose driving up in a dog cart to a
Dartmoor cottage in the eighties. No progress then; places really *were*
remote; white witches, the evil eye, ghosts and strange customs
survived in these lonely, unvisited West Devon hamlets.

Over cider of an evening in lonely inns or at open hearths, old men
would sing songs centuries old: the words were broad as the Devon
they were singing, the airs were often descended from plainsong. Up
drives Baring-Gould one day, then, in his dog cart and with him the
elegant clergyman F. W. Bussell, Vice-Principal of Brasenose College,
Oxford: Bachelor of Music. The friend of Pater that exquisite prose-
writer: Bussell himself is so exquisite that Baring-Gould tells the story
of how he specially had orchids sent from London to match his
clothes. (Bussell lived with his mother in a house Baring-Gould built,
and sung falsetto at village concerts to the amusement of the village
and the distress of his mother.) 'We visited Huccaby', says Baring-
Gould, 'to interview old Sally Satterly, who knew a number of songs.
But she was busy, she had to do her washing. Mr Bussell seated
himself, inconsiderately, on the copper for the boiling, till she lighted
the fire under it and drove him off. I had to run after her as she went
about her work, dotting down her words, while Bussell followed,
pencil and music book in hand, transcribing her notes.'

The energy which Baring-Gould threw into collecting folk songs, he threw into everything else he did through the eighty-nine years of his life – from 1834 when he was born in Exeter until 1924 when he died in Lew Trenchard, a few weeks short of his ninetieth birthday. It has been the custom for the last twenty years to decry Baring-Gould as hopelessly inaccurate and amateur. That immense work of his *The Lives of the Saints* is mentioned by hagiologists with a superior smile: modern archaeologists with their horn-rimmed intensity and arid laboratory-like methods of research, blench at the thought of Baring-Gould with a shovel and a few men off the estate opening up an ancient earthwork: historians despair of his facts. All the same, inaccurate though they may be, all his works are eminently readable from the three-decker novels he wrote as a young man to the rather prolix reminiscences of his old age. And not only are they readable but they must have been the inspiration of many children and nourished the first love and pride in Devon and Cornwall which those children remember. I was one such child. I suppose *In the Roar of the Sea*, that tale of the smuggling on the north coast of Cornwall, was the first grown-up novel I ever read. Cruel Coppinger haunts me today. And as for *Strange Survivals* and his other books of antiquarian lore, they first stirred me to marvel at rough pieces of granite, hewn centuries ago, seen lying in tamarisk-sheltered churchyards or lonely crossroads on Bodmin Moor. Baring-Gould brought to life for me the strange-named saints of little holy wells, he peopled high Cornish lanes with ghosts and hinted at curses and tragedy round some sheltered, feathery-grey slate manor-house of Elizabeth's time, now a decrepit-looking farm. And I suspect that many of those archaeologists and historians who despise him today took up their careers on account of Baring-Gould's pioneering enthusiasm. So, even if the words of his hymns are known all over the world, his enthusiasm for Devon and Cornwall is why we love him in the West.

But I am going to try to make you see him as a man, although I never met him I will try to give you a sketch of him from what I have gathered by talking to those who knew him and by reading his books. The Baring-Goulds are an old Devon Family, with land-owning, military, naval and clerical branches as have all such families. Baring-Gould's father, after a short career in the East India Company's army, came into his estate as a squire, but preferred travelling in Europe to staying at home in Devon. He dragged his intelligent wife and little children round with him. Thus did Sabine learn languages and enjoy continually being on the move; even when he restricted his orbit to

Lew he was ever exploring within and beyond its boundaries. Baring-Gould senior had strong views on education. He thought children's minds were blank pages on which the parents' wishes could be written. 'I was educated to be a mathematician', says his son. 'At the present day I cannot do a compound addition sum'. The father disapproved of learning by heart 'The only date, as a consequence, I can remember is 1066' adds the son. He admits too that he was never particular about accuracy, but had the gift of rapidly getting a general impression of the main purport of a mass of facts. Finally the father believed in repressing the imagination and refused to allow fairy stories to be told his children. The result on the son we know.

If there is one thing Baring-Gould will willingly credit and write down in one of his books as the stark truth, it is a good ghost story or some unlikely, but highly entertaining anecdote. And he has a marvellous gift of telling such a story.

I do not need to trouble you with the early career as a master at Hurstpierpoint; how much against his father's wishes he became a clergyman, was ordained curate at Horbury near Wakefield, found a wife there: went to Dalton in the same county of Yorkshire in 1867 and made great friends with Yorkshire millworkers. Then there were two years at Mersea on the Essex marshes where he did not like the place nor people.

Baring-Gould the man, so-to-speak completed himself when he had ejected an unsatisfactory tenant from Lew House in 1876 and with his wife and growing family – there were fourteen children when the family was complete – entered the village of Lew Trenchard as squire and parson in one – that is to say as squarson. Lew Trenchard is a wooded kingdom on the western edge of Dartmoor. Motorists rushing over Lew Down on the road from Okehampton to Launceston would not suspect that the Baring-Gould kingdom lay within a few yards of them. It is sunk below the main road, out of sight. A meadow with a moorland mill-stream and a Dower House, slate building with granite mullions; unfenced roads running half-way up the valley slopes, on one side to farms on the other to the Manor House and church. It is a valley of luxuriant growths, huge blackberries, ropes of birdwood, thick woods of fir and larch and beech and right in the middle of it deep, blue-black and terrifying, a huge pond, cliff-surrounded, tree-shadowed – known as the Quarry pool.

But the loveliest thing in the village is the church of St Petroc. Small wonder that Baring-Gould never sought church-preferment, said what he liked to Bishops and fellow clergy, avoided local clerical meetings – except to meet friends at them. He had come into an earthly kingdom that he loved. 'I felt I had a work to do, not like that of Newman in England at large, but at Lew Trenchard the small'. And at Lew he gave himself three objects – 'one the moral and spiritual improvement of Lew Parish, two the restoration of the church, three making habitable and comfortable the houses on the estate, including my own.' He achieved the last object for the Manor House – at the moment let outside the family – the few cottages, and the Rector's house bear the mark of Baring-Gould. They are slate buildings with Rhenish features, the sort of thing you would expect of someone imbued with the Scottish and German craze of Queen Victoria's later years. They harmonise well with the firs and that yawning Quarry pool.

As for the church it is almost overwhelming in its beauty. It is a small building, just a nave and north aisle and low tower on the woody hillslope. But when you open the door the full glory of a great rich Devonshire screen bursts upon you. Encrusted with saints and vines and leaves, it cuts across the whole church and through it you may glimpse the altar and monuments. A lovely chandelier from Malines that shines from the chancel like gold through the screen's elaborate tracery. The church is filled with carved benches, new and old, in the Devon manner. If, afterwards, you visit neighbouring Devon churches, where the screens and benches have gone, they will seem empty and incomplete. This screen and the benches were put in by Baring-Gould. He fulfilled his second object, the restoration of the church.

It is not for me, a stranger twenty-one years after the squarson's death, to say what he may have done towards his greatest object in coming to Lew 'the moral and spiritual improvement of the parish.' We only know that he was welcome in all cottages, that people said what they liked to him and he to them, as equals. Here he describes himself having a glass of metheglin with a gossiping old woman, Marianne. 'I reproved her once for never coming to church. "Oh" said she, "I've got my Bible here" pointing to one on a side table. I looked at it, the cover was thick with dust, so with my finger I scribbled on it *Marianne's Bible*. "You may have a Bible" said I, "but it is never opened. If you read it you would find therein, 'Thou shalt not bear false witness against they neighbour.'" "Oh!" she said, "I am so short of amusements. Men have horse races, fox-hunting, shooting and cock-fighting. What are we poor women to do for a little entertainment? To get a lot of women by the ears is rare sport!"' Such an equality as shown in this and hundreds more conversations he records in books and reminiscences, is a true equality of humans. The fact that he was squire and parson was accepted without resentment as part of the divine order of things by both parties. Life was easier to live in those days.

There was no pomposity about him, he dearly loved jokes and stories in talks with parishioners. His friends were his neighbours and he was unknown in any 'literary' set. There he stood, every day, at a high desk writing his books for love of Devon and Cornwall and to make money to improve Lew Trenchard and to educate his family. He worked and lived for Lew Parish and House, and snapped his fingers at the world. Bitterly would he have resented the form-filling life the State has imposed on us today. I can imagine he would have gone to prison rather than submit to the inquiries that the State now makes into our affairs. He was an intense individualist, and did not mind what he said or wrote about those with whom he disagreed – particularly Roman Catholics and Protestants – for Baring-Gould was a thorough Tractarian, an old-fashioned High Churchman. For instance, I find him writing this about a fellow undergraduate at Cambridge named Maclagan. 'He was a canny Scot, and a Scot, like a fox, sweeps his tail over his traces, lest in any way he might compromise his future prospects by anything he had said, or by association. MacLagan buttered his bread well with ecclesiastical margarine. He became eventually Archbishop of York.' And this tale, told me by his former curate, the present Rector of Lew, is characteristic of his humour and outspokenness. A Protestant Bishop objected to the last two lines of the chorus of 'Onward Christian Soldiers' 'With the Cross of Jesus, Going on before'.

He objected to a cross as Papistical. So Baring-Gould suggested altering it to 'With the Cross of Jesus, Left behind the door.'

Sabine Baring-Gould died on 2 January, 1924, aged eighty-nine. He lies under a granite cross in Lew churchyard. After his death, a volume of his sermons was published called *My Few Last Words*. Like all his work they are simple and direct such as would appeal to those who prefer deep things to smart and clever things, as children and old people do. His sermons were short and dramatic – his record short one, the present Rector tells me, two and a half minutes at Easter. He also recalled how he banged the pulpit with his fist for the final words of one sermon which were 'The thing is – do you want to be a cabbage or not?'

BBC broadcast

Seeking Whom He May Devour

Last month I and my friend John, who's an artist, were church-crawling in a county which, for safety's sake, I shall call Northants, since that was not the county. It had rained all day and we had struck a bad patch. Nearly all the churches seen had been ruthlessly restored, and we had reached the last on our list. At the risk of boring you, I will read out what the Directory says about this particular church and parish: 'PAULBY 3½ miles south-west of Bywinkle. The church of St Peter (now disused) is an ancient structure in the mixed styles comprising chancel, nave, south porch and embattled tower containing a clock and two bells. It was formerly the private chapel of the Paulby family whose mansion, long demolished, stood on a site near the church. Attached to the east end of the chancel is the curious Paulby mausoleum erected in 1773 and containing the embalmed bodies of the family in open coffins . . .'; nothing else of importance save that 'The population (in 1901) was nine'. A remote spot, as you might expect, and the mausoleum seems to have stirred even the brief, though informative, Directory to an adjective or two. As for the church, it clearly cannot have been damaged by so-called 'restoration', floodlighting and the like.

The place was not easy of approach. John drove and I was obliged to open gate after gate along a rough unmetalled track. As though to fulfil the promise of a lovely church at the end, the late afternoon sun burst through rain clouds and shone gold and sharp on leafless trees and on brown grass and black hedges spangled with crystal drops. The scenery was the mild, undulating pastoral country of the Midlands.

After three miles of gates, we arrived at two heavy stone piers, with a farm gate incongruously propped between them. Beyond was a straight and noble avenue of limes, part of what once had been a park. Clear in the long shadows of the late sunlight rose a grassy platform on which had stood the long-demolished mansion. And there we saw, sharp in this lovely light, a gem of a small church, its brown ironstone tower spotted with golden lichen, its lead roofs all uneven, its windows mostly broken but where glass remained unevenly reflecting the sunset from diamond quarries. Tacked on to the chancel was a thing like a toy fort – the Paulby mausoleum.

Now let me get nothing wrong, in view of what happened. There was a sort of lodge by the gates.

'The church is certain to be locked', said John. 'Let's ask there for the key'. An old woman came to the door. She looked as though she had never washed in her life. 'Have you the key of the church?' we asked. She chewed to herself a bit before answering, then grinned.

'You can go down there. But don't'ee let'im catch'ee. 'Ee don't loike visitors.'

'Mad', I thought, as we walked along the avenue.

The church was, of course, locked. But we found a window so broken that we were able to climb in. A success or a disappointment? I hardly know. Umber-coloured walls whose markings, in the poor light, might have been either wall paintings or damp: a plaster ceiling with holes in it: the pews removed: the floor spotted with droppings of bats. But what struck us both was a sense of impending evil. If you believe in God, you can believe also in the Devil. There was a devil somewhere in the failing light of that dismantled church.

Not quite dismantled. The altar in the chancel was apparently still in use, for there were two candles on it, but no covering. As I neared it, I had a sense of stronger evil still, as though this once-Christian sanctuary had been defiled.

Imagine the altar in that darkening church. A bare table against the east wall. And beneath it, in the floor, a black hole. I could just discern a flight of steps descending to a room like a wine cellar, lined with stone bins. This was the Paulby mausoleum. From the nearest bin the head of a coffin, brass-studded and baize-covered, was projecting about a foot.

At that moment there was a clatter at the other end of the church, a key turned and there in the light of the south door stood a tall, elderly man in a black MA gown such as is worn by university dons and some schoolmasters. He stood still, his hands at his sides. We stood still, caught like schoolboys. Then John walked down the nave to speak to him. I followed. The man spoke first:

'What are you doing here?'

'Looking at the church'.

'Did anyone give you permission?'

Before we could reply, he had said, 'Please leave at once, this is a private chapel'. He stood on one side to let us pass, rather as a host lets his guests precede him from a room, polite but inexorable. Then he turned the key and locked himself in.

Out in the open, our courage returned. 'I'm sure he's up to no good', John remarked. 'He's probably going to say a Black Mass'. Remember the altar was right over the entrance to that mausoleum and the bodies are embalmed. The idea did not seem to me so fantastic in that fading light, walking down the avenue of dripping limes, as it does here in a broadcasting studio.

'I'd rather like to go back and see', I said. As I turned round I saw the man watching us from the broken window through which we had climbed. So I suggested returning to the motor, driving out of sight and coming back to the church from another direction.

I wish I had never made such a suggestion. I wish I had never seen that mild pastoral country, those limes black against the evening, the brown, wet grass round the church, the toy fort with its pinnacles so deadly still in the gathering dusk.

I wonder if you know what a low-sided window is? It is one at eye-level in the chancel wall, from which persons in the churchyard can see the altar. There was such a window at Paulby, and we crept towards it and looked through. Do not ask me how or why I know that the gowned figure gesticulating at the altar was saying a Black Mass. Enough that I do know. We were so preoccupied with watching him; he, with his back to us, was so preoccupied with his unholy service, that a disturbance in the open vault below the altar must have been going on a full minute, before I realised where it was. On a still autumn evening in the country there are always noises, someone chopping wood, or mending a chicken house, or the rustle of a live thing in a hedge.

One takes them for granted. And this shove and slide, shove and slide, an inch at a time, seemed unconnected with what we were witnessing. Seemed unconnected, until I saw – we both saw – a thing come up from the vault under the bare altar table. It did not walk, or crawl or float. It seemed to ooze on to the floor of the darkening chancel and it looked like a cream-coloured worm, as big as a human being. But the life in it could not have been human life. And as we ran for our lives towards the car we heard a shriek from the church, which carried far across the wet and glistening fields. It was like the squeal of a hare in the grip of a stoat, but more terrible, for it was long, high and hoarse, the death cry of a man in the grip of his final adversary.

John has just sent me a cutting from the local paper which sheds some light on our adventure. It is headed: 'PAULBY'S LOSS'. It goes on 'A link with bygone times is severed by the death of Robert Paulby, aged 65, bachelor, whose body was found on November 20 last in the chancel of Paulby church, the cause of death being established at the Coroner's inquest as heart failure. Deceased, who was the last of the family (formerly chief landowners in the district), resided in a small house near the church and was of retiring disposition. Mr Paulby, who was educated at Oxford University, was keenly interested in occult and antiquarian matters and was supposed, at the time of his unfortunate demise, to be making notes in the church of an historical nature relative to his ancestors. The funeral took place . . .' But I will not read on.

Pray for the soul of Robert Paulby. In his greed for power he tried to learn more than man is meant to know. In dark paths of his exploration, he came face to face with an Evil One and then it was too late to remember I Peter, v. 8. 'Brethren, be sober, be vigilant; because your adversary the devil, as a roaring lion, walketh about, SEEKING WHOM HE MAY DEVOUR'.

BBC broadcast

Aberdeen Granite

Most of us know successful Lowland Scots. Products of the manse and emancipation, they come to England and work their way up to the high administrative posts in Government Offices and universities. Where organising ability, knowledge of finance, hard work and disinterested 'service' to the 'community' are required – to be rewarded with a not extravagant salary but eventually a pension and a decoration – where such careers are open, there you will find the Lowland Scots. Hard, logical, calmly energetic, they are the reverse of flibbertigibbets. Naturally such an abstract-minded people excels in architecture, the severest – I had almost said the most abstract – of the visual arts. Compare the average Italian church of the eighteenth century with a public building of the same time in Edinburgh. A rich façade greets your eye in Italy, a rich façade, alas stuck on to the front of the church as though it were nothing to do with the building behind it. Now gaze at a Scottish bank or kirk or hall of the same date. The architecture goes all round the four sides, the decoration is sparse. What there is in the form of simple mouldings or low relief, is essential only to emphasise the lines of construction. Scottish architecture is the hard logic of the theological Scot in the hard stone of Scotland. It is the energy of the organising, thorough and patient lowlander translated into a visual style. You will see it even in medieval work. St Mungo's Cathedral, Glasgow is severer even than the severe Cistercian buildings of England like Fountains Abbey. Moulding, proportion, construction, no flowing carving, no fal-diddles – because of its thoughtful simplicity I find Glasgow Cathedral the most satisfying medieval cathedral in these islands, its severe serenity is alarming.

Then suddenly, as though he said to himself, 'I can't stand this restraint any more', the Scottish architect goes mad and produces something more wildly exuberant, more ornate and peculiar than anything to be found in England. Roslyn chapel, for instance, is a late medieval building which so flowers with carving, pendants and unbelievable riches of decoration that you might almost consider it to be a Burmese temple, were you not certain you had come out in a bus

on a short journey from Edinburgh. Even in the Presbyterian kirks,
the Victorian Scots sometimes let themselves go. All may be plain
within, covenant-keeping fittings, bare table, towering pulpit, plain
glass, grim walls and rising rows of sermon-centred pews, but suddenly
the architect has said 'You may restrain me inside the kirk, but you
wait till I get outside' and all the marbles of the cliffs of Scotland will
be jammed on to the front and a steeple will be built of such fantastic
richness that, except for an absence of Christian symbolism in the
form of cross or statued saint, it might have been conceived by the
Pope of Rome himself. I think particularly of the steeple of a
Presbyterian kirk at Queen's Cross, Aberdeen. I never saw such a
thing. I cannot describe its style or changing shapes as it descends in
lengthening stages of silver-grey granite from the pale blue sky to the
solid prosperity of its leafy suburban setting. I only know that when I
tried to draw this late Victorian steeple, I gave it up at the seventh
attempt. It is this mixture of the romantic and the severe that makes
Scottish architecture to me the most exciting in Europe. It was this
anticipation of treats for the eye that drew me to Aberdeen. For even
in lowland Edinburgh there are contrasts enough, Edinburgh, that
most beautiful of all the capitals of Europe, no, not excepting Rome –
Edinburgh, though it produced John Stuart Mill, also, thank God,
gave birth to Sir Walter Scott. If Edinburgh can thrill with contrasts,
what, I thought, may I not expect to find in Aberdeen? I did not know
whether the lowland Scottish genius for an institution had a Highland
counterpart.

James Gibbs, the Adam Brothers, Colin Campbell, James Stuart,
'Capability Brown', Sir William Tite, Thompson, Gibson – these are
only some of the names of Classic architects who have come from
Scotland to embellish England with their buildings. Inevitably many
Scots became civil engineers when that science divorced itself from
architecture, and the famous names of Nimmo, the Stevensons and
the Rennies are among the first. For, naturally, engineering made a
strong appeal to the Scottish mind, so attracted by fundamental
structural principles in building.

'Aberdeen Granite' – the title is, of course, absurd. Decided on over
the telephone and like all such decisions made on that horrible
instrument, repented of afterwards. For I intend to talk about the
architecture of Aberdeen and I thought so straightforward and
uninviting a title as 'The Architecture of Aberdeen' would be too
much even for so cultivated an audience as that of the Third
Programme. But we in the south think of Aberdeen Granite as that

highly polished pink stuff which flushes the white cheeks of Metropolitan cemeteries and forms glistening shafts to Gothic Revival façades. But the granite which comes from the immediate neighbourhood of Aberdeen is grey and silver, a lovely stone, immensely durable and worked with consummate skill in the deep shadowy quarries. The pink granite comes chiefly from Peterhead, thirty miles north of the city and from the Island of Mull on the other side of Scotland.

Yet, on second thoughts, perhaps the title is not so absurd. For I don't see how anyone can go to Aberdeen and not become interested in granite. I shall not forget my amazement, taking the tramcar one windy day, down to the Sea Beach for the first time, and standing on a lonely shore below the tufted links which separate Aberdeen from the sea. All around me was the veined and glittering produce of the cliffs of Scotland pounded into rounds and ovals by resistless breakers. So beautiful, so varied were the stones on the beach, grey, silver, pink, red, crimson, white, green, purple, pink, red and silver again, that, for a moment, it was like standing in a dream of avarice surrounded by precious stones. And then, on the tide line where the waves had washed the pebbles so that they were still wet, they glowed with an intenser colour just as the city of Aberdeen glows a deeper, richer silver after rain. I collected fifteen different sorts of granite in as many minutes and packed them in a box to send to my daughter of four-years-old. She, as yet uninfluenced by worldly values of what is a jewel and what is not, thought of these sparkling pebbles as precious stones. And so they are. It was the desire to see the stone that first took me to Aberdeen. Granite is the strongest building stone in these islands, the hardest to shatter and the hardest to work. So hard is it that joints are hardly perceptible and a great column in such granite can be made to appear as a solid unjointed block.

The granite called me to Aberdeen, the fact that it was highland and I know only lowlands also called me, and so did the thought that the City was the birthplace of James Gibbs, the great architect of the eighteenth century, and J. N. Comper, the great church architect of today. But there was a third reason for going – the excitement of seeing a place I had never visited before. I bought guides of all dates in one of the many marvellous second-hand bookshops of Edinburgh, for old books about Aberdeen are cheap in Edinburgh and vice versa. Finally I bought a modern one so as to see what the city looked like today. There were the usual photographs of crowded commercial streets, draughty promenades, bandstands and putting-greens.

From Waverley station north and north for hours. I had not realised there was so much Scotland. The train ran on, over wide brown moors with bluely distant inland mountains and then along the edges of cliffs whose grass was a deep Pre-Raphaelite green. And down steep crevices I saw rocks and fishermen's cottages above them, but still no Aberdeen. Could there be such a thing as a great city with tramcars, electric lights, hotels, and cathedrals so far away among empty fields, so near the North Pole as we were going? In England spring had brought the leaves out on the trees, but here the wind-swept beechwoods were bare and daffodils and primroses were freshly yellow on brown woody banks that sloped to browner, tumbling streams.

And then the line curved and objects familiar to me from my guide book illustrations came to view. Here was I, a filthy Saxon, alone at last in Aberdeen. My hotel had a plain grey granite front contrasting with the brown jazz-modern of its interior. I was in Aberdeen, but in this slick lounge with its leatherette and walls of empire wood and sub-Brangwyn decorations, I might just as well have been in Manchester, in Leeds or Salt Lake City. This is progress. This is internationalism.

You can never enjoy the beauty of a Western city in its shopping streets. The multiple stores which affront the dignity of Aberdeen are no less offensive than their brothers shouting out along the now unlovely buildings in Princes Street of Edinburgh. My hotel, where old-fashioned cleanliness and comfort contrasted unexpectedly with its jazzy decorations, was in the shopping area. I would have to turn down side-streets to see the real Aberdeen.

And now, rather than bore you with street names and long lists of buildings, I will select a few from three periods of Aberdeen's building – the medieval, the early nineteenth century and the modern, for oddly enough modern architecture of Aberdeen has its high spots. And if any Aberdonians are listening who think I have left out some of their best buildings, I must ask them to forgive me. There is so much that is fine in Aberdeen, that I *must* select.

Away down the tramlines to the north, surrounded by new granite housing estates at a decent distance, and on a rise above the beech-bordered meadowland of a river, stands Old Aberdeen, which is a Cathedral, a University and some Georgian houses, built of huge blocks of granite, a strange textured place with an atmosphere of medieval and Jacobite grandeur about it, a place that really makes you feel you are in the Northernmost seat of learning, so remote, so wind-swept and of such a solid, grey strangeness. Here is the old King's College of Aberdeen University and here is its chapel with a low tower from which spring ribs that support a Renaissance style crown.

St Giles', Edinburgh and St Nicholas, Newcastle and St Dunstans in East London have similar spired adornments. But none of these are so satisfactory as that of Aberdeen. This chapel inside is remarkable for its canopied stalls in dark oak, the only medieval church woodwork surviving complete in Scotland after the ravages of Knox. It is not at all like the lace-like soaring of the East Anglian woodwork, it is squat and square and rich with inventive designs through which trail wooden thistles. And to the solid architecture, designed for resisting storms and simple because of the hardness of the granite from which it is made, the elaboration of this woodwork is a perfect contrast. Finally there are windows like the rest of the chapel, very early sixteenth-century, of a style so curious and original as to be unlike any Gothic outside Scotland. The buttresses run up through the middle of the tracery and the arches of all the windows have depressed rounds to them. Not far from King's Chapel is St Machar's strange Cathedral. The West end is the thing to see, seven tall lancets of equal height flanked by square towers with no openings. And on top of each tower a dumpy spire in a style half-Gothic, half-Renaissance. The interior has, alas, been stripped of its plaster and ancient furnishings, except a wooden roof of some richness though too high and dark to be visible, so that the effect of the building inside is merely one of size.

You cannot walk back and down the main streets of Aberdeen proper, as opposed to old Aberdeen, without being aware of the noble planning of late Georgian times. Wide streets, such as Union Street, stately groups of grey granite buildings in a Grecian style, crescents on hill tops and squares behind them. These are largely the work of two architects, friendly rivals, John Smith the City Architect and Archibald Simpson – the centenary of whose death in 1847 was celebrated in Aberdeen a week or two ago. Smith was, I think, the less interesting of the two. He built in correct classic and fifteenth-century style and with granite, close-picked and single-axed, so that it was tamed to carry almost as much carving of capitals and mouldings as a softer building stone. A lovely screen in Union Street, rather like that at Hyde Park Corner, is his, and many a handsome classic and English Perpendicular style public building. But the original genius is Archibald Simpson. At the start of my visit my attention was held by a huge wall of granite, so bold, so simple in design, so colossal in its proportions that I stood puzzled. I had seen nothing like it before or since. Egyptian? Greek? Eighteenth-century? Modern? No, it can't be modern, for see the granite is weathered. This was the New Market built by Archibald Simpson in 1842. The magnificence of the entrance is designed to

show the strength and quality of grey granite, the architect realised
that there was no point in carving this hard unyielding material into
delicate detail. Let the stone speak for itself and then emphasise its
scale and texture by a few strong mouldings and broad pilasters
projecting only an inch or two from the face of the building. The
inside of this covered market is worthy of its outside, colossal, simple,
constructional. I seemed to be stepping into one of those many-vista'd
engravings by Piranesi. It was a great oblong hall with curved ends and
all around a row plain circular-headed arches rising to the glass and
timber roof. Half-way down the wall height ran a gallery of shops.
Shafts of sunlight slanted through the arches on to wooden shops and
stalls of the central space and the surrounding gallery. Archibald
Simpson. Here was an architect of genius, a Soane, a Hawksmoor,
someone head and shoulders above the men of his time. Simpson's
work is almost always of the sort that depends on proportion for its
ornament. For instance these very plain two-storey houses in crescents
as at Bon-Accord and Marine Terraces, where all the subtlety was in
glazing bars in the windows now alas too often destroyed in favour of
plate glass. But his greatest work is a brick tower and spire opposite
the Art Gallery. The fact that it is in red brick makes it stand out, but
not glaringly, among the grey granite of the rest of the city. It must
have looked more wonderful still when the lead spires for which
Aberdeen was famous were making further contrast. How can I tell
you why this tall, plain spire is so marvellous that only Salisbury is in
my opinion its rival? I think it is because of the way it grows out of the
high thin-buttressed tower below it, because of the pinnacles and tall
gables at its base, because its very plainness is so carefully considered.
It was designed in 1844, long before any architect had succeeded in
creating in the Gothic style on Gothic principles of construction – all
other architects were only *imitating* at that time.

No one can dismiss Marischal College, Aberdeen, when looking at
the work of the present century. Wedged behind a huge town hall in
an expensive and attractive mid-Victorian baronial style, I saw a cluster
of silver-white pinnacles. I turned down a lane towards them, the front
broadened out. Oh! Bigger than any cathedral, tower on tower, forests of pinnacles, a group of palatial buildings rivalled only by the
Houses of Parliament at Westminster. This was the famous Marischal
College. Imagine the Victoria tower with a spire on top, and all that
well-grouped architecture below of lesser towers, and lines of
pinnacles executed in the hardest white Kemnay granite and looking
out over the grey-green North Sea and you have some idea of the first

impression this gigantic building creates. It rises on top of a simple Gothic one designed by Simpson in 1840. But all these spires and towers and pinnacles are the work of this century and were designed by Sir Alexander Marshall Mackenzie. You have to see them to believe them. True they do not bear close inspection. The hollow central tower reveals a brick core within to support its spire, the inside seems small after all this outward magnificence – but as a piece of architectural showmanship, Marischal College is fine, an equivalent of Sir George Oatley's soaring University Tower at Bristol.

Aberdeen's best modern building I have left to the last. It is the addition to St Andrew's Episcopal Cathedral by J. N. Comper, an Aberdonian who has already done much distinguished work in the city. You go in by a rather dingy entrance in a flat Perpendicular-style building designed by Simpson in 1816 when he was a man of twenty-six. You push open the door and your heart gives a leap – there stretching away as in an old Dutch oil-painting, is Comper's superb renovation of the interior. White arcades by Simpson in a simple style with big mouldings lead to a great double-aisled East end which Comper had added in a style perfectly blending with the older building. White plaster vaulting diminishes away in perspective adorned with baroque gold and coloured shields. And there, far at the east end, is a great baldachin over the altar in burnished gold with a gold spire rising from its canopy in a manner reminiscent of the spire on King's Chapel. And beyond the gold of this baldachin, intensely gold in this blazing whiteness, you see the deep blue tints, the green and the red of Comper's large East window.

I have only briefly sketched some of the glories of Aberdeen. I must leave it there in those miles of Highland where the Dee comes falling from the conifer forests of John Smith's castle at Balmoral. I leave it sadly with the words of a little known Victorian poet:

Farewell Aberdeen 'twixt the Donside and Deeside
   How oft have I strayed through the long summer day
On the fringe of the links o'er thy wide-spreading seaside
   To see the pink pebbles caressed by the spray.
How gay as a student by King's rugged steeple
   I loitered in archways and meadowpaths green
To my Jacobite sympathies kind were the people
   Though deep in Balmoral dwelt Hanover's Queen.

From windows of dreamland I see thy grey granite
   All sparkling with diamonds after the rain,
The Dee and the arch and suspensions that span it
   And fir-covered forests that rise from the plain.
Down Union Street with majestical motion
   Electrical tramcars go painted in green,
The ships to thy quaysides come in from the ocean
   But I leave for ever my loved Aberdeen.

BBC broadcast

Evelyn Waugh

Far be it from a cautious critic to say *this* man will last, *that* one will be forgotten. But here in the felted impersonality of a broadcasting studio, let me fling caution to the winds and say that Evelyn Waugh is the one English novelist of my own generation – that is to say of us who are in the forties – who is certain to be remembered while English novels are read. Each of whose books is, to me at any rate, as a full glass of dry, still champagne-wine – delicate, invigorating, uplifting and healthily purging.

I do not think it is just because Evelyn Waugh is of my own world and age that he appeals to me. We have both known Oxford of the twenties, schoolmastering, country house life in England and Ireland, chattering parties with the Bright Young Things in chromium flats and then piling into open cars to drive through midnight London and bathe by the moon in a Middlesex pond.

No. That's not the reason. I think Evelyn Waugh will last and will always appeal to those who like the English language, because he is a consummate user of it, an accurate and learned observer, a born storyteller and possessed of a faultless ear for dialogue, finally because he is a whole person with a complete philosophy of life.

Consider him as a craftsman. He dislikes writing, because ... writing is to him severe self-discipline. He will never use two words where one is enough. He is the reverse of gushing. So his books are short, and full. Indeed he is so *ungushing* that he is difficult to quote, for the effect of one paragraph usually depends on the one that precedes it. A good example of this comes in *Vile Bodies*. Lord Balcairn, the gossip writer, had been refused admittance to Lady Metroland's party. He gate-crashed in a false beard and was turned out. So he put his head in a gas oven. He arranged a sheet of newspaper on the tray but noticed it was the gossip-page written by his rival. Contrast the sordidness of this paragraph I am going to read, with the splendour of that which follows:

He put in another sheet. (There were crumbs on the floor). Then he turned on the gas, it came surprisingly with a loud roar; the wind of it stirred his hair and the remaining particles of his beard. At first he held his breath. Then he thought that was silly and gave a sniff. The sniff made him cough, and coughing made him breathe, and breathing made him feel very ill; but soon he fell into a coma and presently died.

So the last Earl of Balcairn went, as they say, to his fathers (who had fallen in many lands and for many causes as the eccentricities of British Foreign Policy and their own wandering natures had directed them; at Acre and Agincourt and Killiecrankie, in Egypt and America. One had been picked white by fishes as the tides rolled him among the treetops of a submarine forest; some had grown black and unfit for consideration under tropical suns; while many of them lay in marble tombs of extravagant design.

Every novel of Evelyn Waugh's is packed with significant description, almost feminine in its catty observation of detail, but never, as one finds in so much sensitive writing by women, too long.

Listen to this account, from *Scoop*, of the interior of a daily newspaper office and one's approach to the sanctum of its full-blooded and alarming proprietor, Lord Copper,

> The carpets were thicker here, the lights softer, the expressions of the inhabitants more careworn. The typewriters were of a special kind; their keys made no more sound than the drumming of a Bishop's finger-tips on an upholstered prie-dieu.... At last they came to massive double doors, encased in New Zealand rosewood which by their weight, polish and depravity of design, proclaimed unmistakeably. 'Nothing but Us stands between you and Lord Copper'.

Notice the use of that word 'depravity' at just the right moment. I have been hard put to it to choose which of about nine extracts I have made from his books will best illustrate Evelyn Waugh. He has this gift of story-telling, of holding your attention so that every word sparkles in its setting, and greedy, you reach forward for the next.

I have left to the conclusion of this talk, the most important part of Evelyn Waugh's work, his mental and spiritual growth, his outlook on human life. Some critics, particularly those who are materialists or who think that there is such a thing as 'progress' and that everything is getting better and better, conclude that Evelyn Waugh is getting worse and worse. They reckon his latest novel *Brideshead Revisited* his greatest failure, while I regard it as his greatest achievement. They see all those gifts of story-telling, dialogue, observation and brief wit still there – there in even greater abundance than before – they are infuriated to find them used to support a *theme* which they regard as either reactionary or mad. For there is no doubt that Evelyn Waugh's writing has remained on the surface, as witty as ever, but his books have a seriousness underlying them now which is too strong for those who prefer the bubbles to the wine.

Consider for a moment, Evelyn Waugh as a person. His father, Arthur Waugh, was a scholar and writer. His elder brother, Alec, is a novelist. He, the youngest, is deeply read in the prose and art of the last century. In 1926 when all the smart were mad about Cézanne and significant form, Evelyn Waugh was interested in the then despised Pre-Raphaelites and published a short book on them. He went to an Art school and in 1928 published an authoritative life of Rossetti. Through the brambles and dark forests of Pre-Raphaelite detail he plunged towards the lilypond of the nineties with its writhing roots. From here it was a short step to the works of Ronald Firbank, the one writer whose style may be said to have coloured Evelyn Waugh's prose. Firbank who has never been fully appreciated, specialised in allusive dialogue. But the world of his marvellous conversations was one of pure fancy, set in Ruritanian baroque. Both *Decline and Fall* and *Vile Bodies*, Evelyn's earliest novels, have much Firbankian fantasy. But there is in them what there is not in Firbank – a detestation of twentieth-century life, stimulated no doubt by his love of the century before. But he shared with Firbank a preoccupation with style. But he was also preoccupied with people.

Vile Bodies brought him success and with the money, he set out to travel, especially to countries where there were people comparatively untouched by so-called 'civilisation' – South American jungle, Spain, Mexico, Abyssinia. His return to England made urban life seem more detestable still. *A Handful of Dust*, the most perfect of his books within the limits he prescribed for it, is a heart-rending condemnation of twentieth-century England. It is the story of Tony Last, a country landowner – the surname 'Last' is in itself significant – and of the intrusion of amoral London life into his peaceful marriage to his attractive Brenda. Brenda is led away by lust and the twittering thrill of a flat in London among people who gossip about one another on the telephone from bed every morning. She deserts her husband, her son and her village for a rootless life of electric bells, daily papers and chic restaurants. The final chapter is a series of unbearably touching contrasts between Tony, lost up the Amazon and Brenda, betrayed by her lover and lost among her smart friends in London. As one may expect, Tony's native South American Indians seem hardly less human than Brenda's jazzy hangers-on. If this is the last word in mortal misery, it is also Evelyn Waugh's last word on the unhappiness one individual can inflict upon another.

In the year that *A Handful of Dust* was published – 1934 – its author was received into the Roman Catholic Church. Clergy and religious denominations had always been a prominent feature of his books. There was reason behind the decision. His interest in people is not merely in their income groups, age-groups, their economic status. Had it been, he would, like Roger Simmons in *Work Suspended*, have 'married an heiress, joined the Communist Party and become generally respectable'. He is interested in why they were born and where they are going after death. I speak as an Anglican not as a Roman Catholic myself, but to his logical mind, the Roman Catholic Church, once he had accepted its premises, provided a fully worked-out philosophical system. Never a lover of this age, he is now chiefly interested in how people prepare for the next. His last novel *Brideshead Revisited* (1945) is an astonishing achievement. For here all the skill of the novelist has gone to elaborating the theme.

He has managed to convey the complete *poverty* of success that is purely worldly, and the *deep riches* of poverty that is only in this world's goods. The young careerist Canadian, a British MP, who races through the pages is no more than a clever ape though he is doing well in the world of big business and knows all the latest news. The drunken Sebastian, without stamina or ambition, a prey to the bottle and the flesh, is a fully-grown person because he has a sense of sin and guilt and a fine natural sense of a Divine order of created things. I will always remember a remark Evelyn Waugh made when someone said to him that she did not like Lady Marchmain, Sebastian's mother in that book, a sincere, rather humourless Roman Catholic all high principles and good works, '*You* may not like her. But God loves her'.

The latest work of Evelyn Waugh differs wholly from that of almost all other modern novelists. For whereas they are generally concerned with the relations of one human being to another, or one set of human beings to another set, he is also concerned with the human mind and soul as part of the Divine creation.

As he himself said in his only autobiographical article I have ever read, one which appeared in an American Magazine, *Life*, 'So in my future books there will be two things to make them unpopular: a preoccupation with style and the attempt to represent man more fully, which, to me, means only one thing, man in his relation to God.'

BBC broadcast

Hawker of Morwenstowe

Stormy nights, and a sea mountains high, and the thunder on the shore, heard three miles inland – those are the times when I like to think of Parson Hawker, the Cornish mystic and poet. These are the outward details of his life. He was born at Plymouth in 1803, he went to the Grammar School, Cheltenham, and as a boy he was given to practical jokes. There was, for instance, the time when he dressed himself up in seaweed and little else and sat singing on the rocks at Bude and combing his hair. Some of the people of the place thought he was a mermaid. He went to Oxford and at the age of nineteen he married a lady of forty-one. He loved her very much indeed all her life. She died in 1863 aged eighty. 'It will be long before I shall sleep,' he wrote, 'Nearly forty years and never five nights away from her. And now I start up to desolation.' But a year later, at the age of sixty, he married a Polish girl of twenty and had two daughters. He died in 1875. For forty years he had been Vicar of Morwenstowe.

These outward details of a man's life don't tell you what he was like. Walk with me down the lane to meet him. The parish has not changed much. High stone hedges stuffed with rock plants, thin fields, and suddenly in a dip of the hills, there is the church tower its pinnacles like hare's ears peering above the wind-slashed trees. There is no village near the church. There rarely is in Cornwall. All nature, trees, plants, bushes, lean longingly towards the land and away from the sea. All twigs and stones are covered with lichen, thick as moss, and bright orange or silvery-grey. And everywhere is slate; slate outcrops on the cliffs, slate and granite of the church, slate like rawbones, rising in the surface of the road, and down there below the shelving churchyard, in a little valley a short distance from the sea, is Morwenstowe Vicarage, built of slate too, by Parson Hawker.

Hawker would stand at his Vicarage door, hand outstretched to welcome. He was large, silver-haired, red-faced, excitable, and humorous, with blue eyes. He refused to wear black like a clergyman, so he had a plum-coloured tailcoat, a fisherman's dark blue Jersey with a red cross embroidered on the side where the centurion's spear pierced our Lord, breeches, and high seaboots made of Hessian. If he had a hat it would be a plum-coloured or brown beaver. He did not tolerate fools who came to see him. There is the story of a tourist who said, 'Mr Hawker, what are your views and opinions?' The Vicar took him to a window in the passage facing the sea. 'There is Hennacliffe, the highest cliff on this coast, on the right; the church on the left; the Atlantic Ocean in the middle. These are my views. My opinions I keep to myself.' But he dearly liked a talk with genuine people. Tennyson called once, with his long black hair, Spanish face and cloak. They walked out on to the cliffs, quoting Homer and re-translating him to the thunder of the rollers hundreds of feet below them.

But Hawker did not pine for literary company. His parish was enough for him and he hated leaving it. He was a keen farmer of his own land and a generous employer always giving away all the little money he had in tips and buying drink and food for his workers. He was a champion of the poor people – against the rich farmers. He resented state interfering with private life, specially the Workhouse system – then only just beginning – which was so hard on the poor and old:

> The poor have hands, and feet, and eyes – he wrote
> Flesh, and a feeling mind:
> They breathe the breath of mortal sighs
> They are of human kind.

But to see him at his most active, you must see him at a wreck. On this wild coast harbours are few and small. Smugglers abounded. They and everyone else still believe it unlucky to rescue a sailor from the sea and they buried the bodies on the shore above high water mark. Hawker was one of the first to give Christian burials to shipwrecked sailors. Here is his own account of the wreck of the 'Caledonia' in 1843.

At daybreak of an autumn day I was aroused by a knock at my bedroom door; it was followed by the agitated voice of a boy, and member of my household, 'O, sir, there are dead men on Vicarage Rocks.'

In a moment I was up, and in my cassock and slippers rushed out. There stood my lad, weeping bitterly, and holding out to me in his trembling hands a tortoise alive. I found afterwards that he had grasped it on the beach, and brought it in his hand as a strange and marvellous arrival from the waves ... I ran across my glebe, a quarter of a mile, to the cliffs and down a frightful descent of three hundred feet to the beach. On a ridge of rock, just left bare by the falling tide, stood a man, my own servant . . . with two dead sailors at his feet, whom he had just drawn out of the water, stiff and stark. The bay was tossing and seething with a tangled mass of rigging and broken fragments of a ship; the billows roll'd up yellow with corn for the cargo of the vessel had been foreign wheat; and ever and anon there came up out of the water, as though stretched out with life, a human hand and arm . . .

To this day you may see the wooden figurehead of the 'Caledonia' in Morwenstowe churchyard, over the grave of her crew. You can see too, that the really big things of life, birth and death, were ever-present with Hawker. And he lived in an atmosphere of eternity:

> Day melts into the West, another flake
> Of sweet blue Time into the Eternal Past.

His Church was his home. You might call him a High churchman, for he venerated Archbishop Law; but he thought himself back into the Eternal Past and lived in the old Celtic church of Cornwall, that Church which had Christianised the western parts of these islands long before St Augustine came to Canterbury. To Hawker, Morwen-stowe was the shrine of St Morwenna, the Celtic saint who founded her church there.

When anything troubled him he would go down to her church with its Norman arches and through the screen to the dark chancel, where the wind rattled the glass 'there to utter aloud my want. Almost invariably I perceive the reply. Words flow into my mind silently'. He wrote down these words in a book which, like his other works, has been edited by his son-in-law. Here are two of Hawker's thoughts in that chancel: 'HEAVEN – A tranquil Ocean of illimitable space, alive. FAITH – We stretch forth our hands to feel the air and to find out what the ethereal space around us contains. At the first there is nothing: our fingers close on our empty palms. By and by there is something soft and warm; we perceive that it is the touch of an angel. We discern the folds of his garment. We feel the pressure of his robe. Anon there shall be the gleam of his forehead and the shadow of his waves of hair. Gabriel shall beam forth and Lord Michael shine.'

Hawker's angels, his faith, and the ancient Celtic church of which he was a member are expressed in that magnificent poem of his about

the Holy Grail, the Cup which Our Lord used at the Last Supper and
which was said to have been brought to England by St Joseph of
Arimathea. This poem, the *Quest of the Sangraal*, is about King Arthur
and Tintagel, just like Tennyson's *Idylls of the King*. Much as I revere
Tennyson, I feel that on this theme Hawker was the finer poet – and
small wonder for Tennyson's theology was so Liberal that his Belief
was as vague as Hawker's was sacramental and defined.

> Forth gleamed the east and yet it was not day:
> A white and glowing horn outrode the dawn;
> A youthful rider ruled the bounding rein,
> And he in semblance of Sir Galahad shone;
> A vase he held on high; one molten gem,
> Like massive ruby or the chrysolite;
> Thence gush'd the light in flakes; and flowing, fell
> As though the pavement of the sky brake up,
> And stars were shed to sojourn on the hills
> From grey Morwenna's stone to Michael's tor,
> Until the rocky land was like a Heaven.
> Then saw they that the mighty quest was won:
> The Sangraal swooned along the golden air:
> The sea breath'd balsam, like Gennesaret
> The streams were touched with supernatural light
> And fonts of Saxon rock, stood full of God!

And the poem ends, as did every day of Hawker's life, with the boom
of the sea, this time calm and boding:

> There stood Dundagel throned, and the great sea
> Lay, a strong vassal at his master's gate,
> And, like a drunken giant, sobbed in sleep.

High on the cliffs at Morwenstowe is a little wooden hut which
Hawker built to watch the moods of the Atlantic, a whole silver stretch
of it from Padstow Point to Lundy Light. Hear him describe a storm:

> War, mid the ocean and the land!
> The battle-field, Morwenna's strand,
> Where rock and ridge the bulwark keep,
> The giant warders of the deep.
> They come – they mount – they charge in vain,

Thus far, incalculable main!
No more! thine hosts have not o'erthrown
The lichen on the barrier stone.

Have the rocks faith, that thus they stand,
Unmoved, a grim and stately band –

and then he goes on to describe 'The baffled army of the waves!' and
ends:

The way, O God, is in the sea,
Thy paths, where awful waters be;
Thy spirit thrills the conscious stone,
O Lord, Thy footsteps are not known!

And I shall leave you with the music of a church tower that Hawker
put into words:

Tintagel bells ring o'er the tide
The boy leans on his vesselside;
He hears that sound, and dreams of home
Soothe the wild orphan of the foam.
   'Come to thy God in time',
   Thus saith their pealing chime:
   Youth, manhood, old age past,
   'Come to thy God at last.'

That is I think a ring of six bells – the usual number in a country
church tower 'Come to thy God in time' – now soft, now loud like
bells heard over water. I shall not bother you with the whole poem
about the ship with the bells of Boscastle church on board and of how
she went down in the sight of the great grey cliffs of home. But here's
the last verse to haunt you with thoughts of church and Parson
Hawker and of Cornwall:

Still when the storm of Bothreau's waves,
Is wakening in his weedy caves:
Those bells, that sullen surges hide,

Peal their deep notes beneath the tide:
'Come to thy God in time!'
Thus saith the ocean chime:
Storm, billow, whirlwind past,
'Come to thy God at last.'

BBC broadcast

Daily Herald Book Reviews (2)

Artists and architects can give as much to the world as writers. Indeed, I think the fact that we see so many photographs today, still and moving, accounts for the renewed interest in art.

We begin to use our eyes, and find the artist is to the *average* photographer what the poet is to the reporter. The former interprets, prophesies, enriches: the latter states or *should* state plain facts.

Certainly, *War Through Artists' Eyes* (*Murray*, 12s), sumptuously produced, with plenty of good colour-reproductions, and an excellent explanatory preface by Eric Newton, is war as vivid, humorous or terrible as described in prose.

We see that sinister Dead Sea of twisted metal of German aeroplanes, by Paul Nash; the scorched drama of a freshly-fallen bomb by John Piper; that Brighton Pier in the hills of Abyssinia. Menelek's Palace, by Edward Bawden: the sleeping figures, still and terrible in the underground shelter by Henry Moore; the uproarious, full-throated humour of Sidney Smith's groups of soldiers in shirtsleeves singing; the humorous lively soldiers of Ardizzone.

Many of the artists in this book have been out with the forces, painting and sketching under fire. One of the best, Eric Ravillious, has been killed.

*

That ancient triad is quoted by Robert Graves in a preface to *Ha! Ha! Among the Trumpets*, by Alun Lewis (*Allen and Unwin*, 5s).

And there *are* modern poets besides the writers of song-lyrics. These poets are greater, because they do not depend for their full effect on the aid of an orchestra. The words themselves should be their own music.

Alun Lewis was a Welsh school-teacher – Wales, for the last thirty years has produced some of our best poets – and he was killed in India in March last year with the South Wales Borderers.

Sometimes he is like Wilfred Owen, a mighty poet who was killed in the last war, particularly when he describes the sadness of saying goodbye to his wife on the railway station:

'Some women know exactly what's implied,
Ten years, they saw behind their smiling eyes,
Thinking of children, pensions, looks that fade,'

or that sadder picture –

'Or maybe when he laughs and bends to make
Her laugh with him she sees that he must die
Because his eyes declare it plain as day.'

Just read those lines out loud and then ask yourself whether as
rhythmless prose, or as a song-lyric, they would so shortly and so
memorably be expressed.

*

It may seem odd in the *Daily Herald* to open up the book reviews this
week with *Rudyard Kipling* by Hilton Brown (*Hamish Hamilton*,
10s 6d).

The subject is generally considered unutterably Tory.

As Mr Frank Swinnerton says in a foreword, Kipling has been
critically unlucky – 'a sort of literary bounder who was somehow
responsible for the Boer War.'

At last Kipling has come in for some critical luck, for Mr Hilton
Brown's Appreciation (which is also partly a biography of a famous
writer whose desire for personal privacy was so great that next to
nothing is known about his private life) is balanced, readable and
thorough. It is the sort of book, were one a famous man, one would
wish written about oneself.

Having read Hilton Brown, you will be able to re-read Kipling with
a clear political conscience if politics have ever got in the way between
you and literature – as they certainly should *not* have done.

For Kipling, however much he may infuriate with his mannerisms
and prejudice and cock-sureness, is literature. He is a Lord of
Language as well as a great story-teller and verse-writer.

I say re-read Kipling because there can be no one reading this page
who has not read some of him at some time.

*

Shelter Sketch Book, by Henry Moore (*Editions Poetry*, London, 15s)
is mercifully without text.

There are hundreds of sketches, some of them in colours, of figures
sleeping, eating and snoring. Particularly moving, helpless and static-

looking seem his sketches of the human body when its owner is asleep.

Mr Moore is the artist who can fix forever in your mind the look of the gaping mouth, the outstretched arm, the crouched-up leg. He brings back those memories of smells of sweat, carbolic and damp earth and stone which we smelled in public shelters when we woke up in the middle of the night.

His figures are like sculpture but living sculpture of a game of statues.

*

Sean O'Casey spars like a bird on his own eloquence. He hardly minds what he says for the joy he has in saying it. And as he writes I feel I am listening to the magniloquent talk of a Dublin pub.

I see the velvet-brown porter and through the windows of the snug inn watch those green trams swish past the fine seedy Georgian façades of Guinness-coloured Dublin brick.

O'Casey brings with him a smell of peat smoke and that world of internal strife which only those who know Ireland know.

He has described it as no author has ever done before or since, in his two great plays, *Juno and the Paycock* and *The Plough and the Stars*.

These plays really are Dublin and they really portray the very poor of that 'slum-poisoned and square-pampered' city. English people think of Irish literature as all to do with Yeats and twilight and gold curtains at the Abbey Theatre.

Yeats was a great poet as all agree. But he was 'literary,' though he loved Ireland.

So the autobiography of Sean O'Casey – and this is the third volume which is called *Drums Under the Windows* (Macmillan, 15s) – is the voice of the Irish people or, at any rate, those who come from the poorer parts of Dublin. O'Casey describes the room of his sister and her five children:

> 'A fanciful bastion of rags, bones and bottles, the family heredita-
> ments, a few chairs, a table so rickety that it seemed anxious to
> dissolve itself out of the life it tried to live; one large iron bedstead,
> rusty with shame at the beggarly clothes that tried to cover it. They
> drank their tea from jam jars and raked out a fire with a lath broken
> from the bedstead.'

And what had these children and thousands more to brighten their lives but this sort of street scene, where:

'Someone in trouble, someone in sorrow, a fight between neighbours, a coffin carried from a house, were things that coloured their
lives and shook down fiery blossoms where they walked.'

On the family side he describes the death of his brother Tom and of
his sister, his own difficulties working as a navvy on the Great
Northern Railway of Ireland, his illness and departure to a hospital.
But O'Casey was a brand plucked from the burning.

He never shows self-pity and his mind is afire for a Gaelic-speaking
Ireland. This volume describes the journey of his enthusiasm through
the fiercely nationalistic world of the Irish speaker, through Yeats and
Shaw to Jim Larkin and James Connolly and the Irish Labour
movement.

O'Casey is a great playwright. We cannot see his plays done over
here by Irish actors. The next best way to get to know him is through
his autobiography.

*

'... never praise, praise dates you. In reviewing a book you like,
write for the author; in reviewing any other, write for the public.
Read the books you review.... Never touch novels written by your
friends.'

My friend Cyril Connolly has sent me his book, *The Condemned
Playground*, for Christmas – a good name, too, for Christmas Day and
Boxing Day – (*Routledge*, 10s 6d) and I *am* touching it.

It contains healthy New Year remarks for a reviewer like me:

'There are three kinds of reviewers; the cynical, who know they are
beaten, who turn out consistently adequate copy, and are completely reliable, having sacrificed the critical sense for a certain
knack of amiable appraisal or polite disappointment; those who are
still fighting, who are on the whole unsatisfactory, because they turn
and twist, go off the deep end ... ; and those who are not aware of
any problem, who go cheerily on for thirty or forty years and are
bitterly hurt to find that they have long been the dupes of
publishers and the laughing stock of the public.'

Which am I? At home I use newspaper for cleaning the chimneys of
our oil lamps, so that there was only about half my year's work for the
Daily Herald from which to judge.

Since, over Christmas, even publishing lets up, I thought I would use the breathing space for a few imaginary reviews.

They should help to keep you and me calm and balanced about forthcoming books.

For books have a way of dividing themselves into types – the international, the agricultural, the biographical, the slushy, the thriller, the old-world charming.

So I shall invent title and publisher and review some of them.

First comes *I was Eye-Witness*, by Courtenay Belvedere (*Sludge*, 22s 6d). This is an account, in diary form, of a visit to Europe with the Allied armies.

The writer banged it off on the typewriter at top speed and sent it in sections by all sorts of illegal methods to Messrs Sludge in the hope that it would be out before Christmas and the first book on the subject to appear.

So did Messrs Sludge, but there was a delay at the binders and the only thing that might have made the book interesting, its topicality, was gone.

So Sludge has raised the price a bit, chucked in some stock photographs of tanks and aeroplanes from the picture agencies and confidently placed it on the bookstalls rather late in the day. The text is egotistic, superficial, full of misprints and disconnected.

Dawn for Dvoynich, by Vladimir Icontych (*Glorious Freedom, Ltd.*, 18s). This novel weighs 15lb. It is about how the coming of electric light affects the people of a primitive village in the far east of Siberia (or near west to American readers).

High Pastures (*Manure and Silage*, 8s 6d). Two chartered accountants decided to take up farming. Readers will remember their previous book, *The Empty Cowshed*, which described in non-technical terms, how they reared their first heifers and how very interesting *they* found it. The new book is the same sort of thing, only about grass and just as long.

Nor must I forget pure fiction.

Vyvyan Weep has completed his or her trilogy, that chronicle of an upper-middle class family, without which no modern literary decade is complete.

His or her third volume, *But Not Withstanding* . . . (*Buy and Large*,

12s 6d), takes up the tale of the Rickmansworth family from 1918 until the present day.

The central figure is Robinia Rickmansworth ('Twinkles' to the family).

The book is full of what a reviewer might call 'minute observation' and an angry one 'padding.'

> Peter hesitated a moment and knocked at the door. Twinkles on the other side of it, ensconced on Mummy's comfiest sofa, half knew it was Peter and half thought it might be Florrie with the tea.
>
> In either event, if she were to say, 'Come on' in her Special voice, Florrie would not notice and Peter might think she was going to make it up with him. And she wasn't sure that she was. The Sevres clock that Daddy had bought for Mummy – oh! years and years ago, before Twinkles or Wendy or Binks had been thought of* – ticked quite twenty times before she said, 'Come on' in her Ordinary voice (etc., etc.).

Zoma Beebright's ninety-first novel *Tigerface* (*Pulpets*, 8s 6d) is up-to-date nonsense. Tiger Carruthers, an atomic research worker, loves Tonia Wainwright. Tiger wishes Tonia to help him in a dangerous atomic experiment. Does she trust him enough to put her life in his hands?

Realising that to do so is to help Tiger to Fame and to benefit Humanity still more, with the blessings of Science she does so. The experiment is successful.

*

On Friday Bernard Shaw will (D.V. – or perhaps I should say Life Force V.) be ninety. Looking at his birthday present, *G.B.S. 90*, edited by S. Winsten (*Hutchinson*, 21s), full of tributes from well-known people, I was interested, not so much in its contents as in thinking of Shaw himself and what he must be feeling.

I look at the pictures in the book. There he is, in the familiar Norfolk suit outside some sunny, emancipated house. There he is again, lying in the sea in a striped bathing dress. There he is, a beardless Dublin Protestant nearly eighty years ago. And here he is today at Ayot St Lawrence.

JB's footnote:

* See *Not Only But Also ...* (Vol. 1 of *Rickmansworth Chronicles*, by *Vyvvan Weep* (*Buy and Large*, 12s 6d); *10th edition printing*.

The last man to be self-satisfied, for all his life he has condemned smugness, he has more reason for satisfaction than any Irishman alive.

He can see the Victorian conventions he flouted alone, flouted now by the majority. The Socialism he advocated is now in the ascendant. His plays are performed all over the world. The adjective 'Shavian' is in the dictionary.

He is one of the last giants of English literature alive and I cannot but think he feels lonely. He who started a lonely revolutionary lives now a lonely victor.

For in this volume even Dean Inge must seem to him to be a new boy, James Bridie and Priestley right down in the infants' class, and even Lord Passfield, whose memory fails, is a younger contemporary by three years.

The sad part about this book is that the well-known writers write too shortly and the less well-known are too long and dull. But all are united in their affection for him as a man.

For Shaw is not just a great man, but also a good one. Thousands of humble people have received those famous postcards of individual advice; many have received kindnesses from him even more generous than advice.

Because the world lacks great and good men, I join the rest of us in wishing him his century with his faculties unimpaired.

An almost complete set of Shaw has appeared in the Penguins (1s per volume).

*

To each his private pleasure. Mine is looking at buildings, old, new, and middle-aged. So soon as I have delivered these reviews to the *Daily Herald* I go off for the afternoon on a tram.

Away in the suburbs I watch the sun redden behind high Victorian churches, children scamper over municipal asphalt, cats dash into speckled laurel bushes, and I think myself back into my childhood and see in any quiet street a new vista and in every small garden a new fancy.

I am perfectly happy Mr J. M. Richards clearly has the same pleasure. His book, *The Castles on the Ground (Architectural Press,* 8s 6d), is the first study of the modern suburb which looks at it from my own point of view that I have read.

He makes an effective plea for the fake half-timber, the leaded lights and bow windows of the Englishman's castle – the small homes on the outskirts of the big town.

In effect, Mr Richards says it's no good being superior about 'Jerrybethan' and 'suburbia' and making pleas for simplicity and restraint and 'good taste'. The truth is that ninety people out of hundred *like* modern half-timbered villas and suburban life. What we must do is to see why they like them and so become fond of the suburbs ourselves.

His theme is eloquently echoed by coloured pictures done by John Piper. Here we have a well-known topographical and romantic artist opening our eyes to a new beauty – the beauty of the despised, patronised suburb, the open heart of the nation.

Those who will use their eyes will find the new scene as live and lovely as the rurality which was there before.

*

Open a book, bury your nose in it and sniff. New books printed on rough paper smell like damp clothes; on smooth paper, they smell like custard made with bad milk; on shiny paper, they smell harshly of ink.

But old books! Ah, old books! They smell of leather and autumn woods and silent, forgotten libraries, locked churches and sun-soaked garden walls.

I bought a set of Ruskin last week, thirty-nine sumptuous volumes, for hardly the price of the fine paper and less than the price of the binding and pictures.

You can still buy Ruskin for a few shillings in second-hand shops. People are beginning to read that great Victorian again.

The old books are the best. Ruskin is one of the best of all. He wrote about art and architecture and life. Though you may not agree with him, you can always understand what he means.

And his prose is everything prose ought to be – beautiful, readable, connected.

Though he wouldn't like it to be said of him, Le Corbusier is really like Ruskin. His famous book *Towards a New Architecture* (*Architectural Press*, 15s) appeared first in 1927. Now it is re-issued, finely translated from the French by Frederick Etchells.

Le Corbusier is like Ruskin because you can understand what he means. But he is also like him because he is interested in the look of things. He likes the look of a building first, and invents the reasons for liking it afterwards.

The first half of his book looks at old buildings – Roman, Greek and

Renaissance – and deduces mathematical theories for any happy proportions they may have.

'Architecture can be found in the telephone and in the Parthenon,' he says. If a thing fulfils its function it is therefore beautiful. This is not true. A water-closet fulfils its function, but it is not beautiful.

Le Corbusier teaches us to use our eyes again and to see the beauty of sleek motor cars, aeroplane hangars and *some* flat-roofed houses.

He has also done untold harm. Silly people have designed square taps, octagonal sinks, rectangular baths because they have read too much into Le Corbusier.

But the less silly will like his book and its pictures, for opening their eyes to the beauty of the industrial age. They will leave it at that. Le Corbusier is an artist, not an engineer.

*

The sun is throwing green light on to the paper where I write, through the young leaves of a beech hedge. The air is full of wallflower and lilac smells. A cuckoo repeats itself in the limes on the other side of the house. My feet are wet because the dew is still on the grass and I have slight rheumatism as a result.

If it were not that there are so many books worth mentioning beside me on the table – their binding curling up in the rising heat – I would spend all this column in praise of Richard Jefferies (1848–87), the great nature writer who was born in the downland country above Swindon.

Henry Williamson's selection and notes on him have been reprinted – *Richard Jefferies* (*Faber and Faber*, 8s 6d) – on chemical green paper.

Despite a hectoring preface, 'If you don't like Jefferies, you are no good,' this is a learned, sensitive, enthralling selection. It shows the two sides of Jefferies – the portrayer of natural downland scenery and wild life, the speculator on eternity and man's purpose in creation.

Forget that unfortunate, arty word 'whilom' in this passage on the polished white skull of a hare, picked up on the downs. It will give you *some*, only a little, of his quality:

'Holding it in the hand the shadow falls into and darkens the cavities once filled by the wistful eyes which whilom glanced down from the summit here upon the sweet clover fields beneath.'

This is a book I shall hold on to even after I am sold up.

*

'. . . and the next moment she was in his arms and he was kissing her hungrily, as though he would never let her go.'

'He tilted her head back and silenced any further remarks as his mouth, hard and tender, came down on hers.'

'Viola clung to him, returning his kisses with ardour, radiant with happiness.'

'Simon smiled and looked down into her eyes, the smile dissolving into swift desire as, once again, his lips found hers.'

'Gently he pressed his lips to hers, as though he feared she would yet escape him.'

'He crushed her to him, kissed her again and again, wildly, passionately, with a fire which seemed to run through his veins like wine . . .'

Those quotations are from the last pages of each of the half-dozen novels mentioned below.

Same old jargon, same old story of boy meeting girl, same grey type on eye-straining paper and same old sales, no doubt colossal, when compared with any original writing.

Too often, I know, I write about what we *ought* to read and ignore what we *do* read. But don't despise them, these folk tales of modern Britain. The books are not so sexy as these quotations might lead you to think.

The ladies who write them believe in the importance of happy home life, that true love has no secrets from itself, that surface appearances are deceptive, and that doctors are better than any of these men.

Most of them, especially Helen Eastwood and Barbara Cartland, can tell a story. But because they make, presumably, much more money than better writers, they are inclined to praise riches and worldly success in their books. After a two-days' wallow, I almost came to believe in fairy tales myself.

The Church of St Protus and
St Hyacinth, at Blisland, Cornwall

I know no greater pleasure than church-crawling. It leads you to the remotest and quietest country. It introduces you to the history of England in stone and wood and glass which is always truer than what you read in books. You meet all sorts of people on your travels.

It was through looking at churches that I came to believe in the reason why, despite neglect and contempt, innovation and business bishops, they still survive and continue to grow and prosper, especially in our industrial towns.

You must have the instruments of a church-crawler. The first of these is a map. A one-inch ordnance map (no others will do) tells you whether the church has a tower or spire for it is marked with a cross and a black square if it is a tower, a cross or a black circle if it is a spire. You can generally assume that a country church is old, even if it has no tower or spire, if the map shows dotted lines of footpaths leading to it.

The next thing you need is an eye. Look at the church for what it is, a place of worship and a piece of architecture combined. Guide books will tell you that something is in the 'debased' style, meaning that it was built in the sixteenth, seventeenth or eighteenth centuries, but it does not matter when it was built or whether it is 'pure' or 'debased'. What does matter is, do you like the look of it yourself?

Instead of bothering about dates and what the guide books say, use your eyes. Something is not beautiful simply because it is old, but it is more likely to be than not, for most of what is modern, especially in the way of church furniture, is ugly.

Of all the country churches of the West I have seen, I think that Blisland is the most beautiful. I was a boy when I first saw it, thirty or more years ago. I shall never forget that first visit to the edge of Bodmin Moor, that sweet brown home of Celtic saints, the haunted, thrilling land so full of ghosts of ancient peoples whose hut circles, beehive dwellings and burial mounds jut out above the ling and heather.

Perched on the hill above the woods stands Blisland village. It has not one ugly building in it and, what is unusual in Cornwall, the houses are round a green. Between the lichen-crusted trunks of elm and ash that grow on the green, you can see everywhere the beautiful silver-grey moorland granite. It is used for windows, for chimney stacks, for walls.

The church is down a steep slope of graveyard, past slate headstones, and it looks over the tree-tops of a deep and elmy valley and away to the west where, like a silver shield the Atlantic sometimes shines in the sun. An opening in the churchyard wall shows a fuchsia hedge and the vicarage front door beyond. The church tower is square and weathered and made of enormous blocks of moorland granite. However did the old builders haul them to the topmost stages?

When I first saw it, the tower was stuffed with moss and with ferns which had roots here and there between the great stones, but lately it had been vilely re-pointed in hard straight lines with cement. The church itself, which seems to lean this way and that, throws out chapels and aisles in all directions. It hangs on the hillside, spotted with lichens which have softened the slates of its roof. Granite forms the tracery of its windows; a granite holy-water stoup is in the porch.

That great church architect, Sir Ninian Comper, said a church should bring you to your knees when you first enter it. Such a building is Blisland. For there, before me as I open the door, is the blue-grey granite arcade, that hardest of stone to carve. One column slopes outwards as though it were going to tumble down a hill and a carved wooden beam is fixed between it and the south wall to stop it falling.

The floor is of blue slate and pale stone. Old carved benches, of dark oak, and a few chairs are the seating. The walls are white, the sun streams in through a clear west window and there, glory of glories, right across the whole eastern end of the church are the richly painted screen and rood loft: all of wood.

The panels at the base of the screen are red and green. Wooden columns highly coloured, twisted like barley sugar burst into gilded tracery and fountain out to hold a panelled loft. There are steps to reach this loft, in the wall. Our Lord and his Mother and St John, who form the rood, are over the centre of the screen.

My eyes look up and there is the irregular old Cornish roof, shaped like the inside of an upturned ship, all its ribs richly carved, the carving shown up by white plaster panels.

These old roofs, beautifully restored, are to be seen throughout the whole church. Unevenly, they stretch away beyond the screens and down the aisles. I venture in a little further.

There, through this rich screen, I can mark the blazing gold of the altars and the medieval-style glass, some of the earliest work of Comper. Beside me in the nave is a pulpit shaped like a wineglass, in the Georgian style and encrusted with cherubs and fruit carved in wood.

The screen, the golden altars, the stained glass and the pulpit are comparatively new. They were given by the Collins family, and designed by F. C. Eden in 1897. Eden had a vision of this old Cornish church as it was in medieval times. He did not do all the medieval things he might have done. He did not paint the walls with pictures of angels, saints and devils in amber and red.

He left the western window clear so that people in this reading age might see their books; he put in a Georgian pulpit. He centred everything on the altar to which the screen is as a golden, red and green veil to the holiest mystery behind it.

In Blisland church is Norman work, there is fifteenth- and sixteenth-century work and there is sensitive and beautiful modern work, but chiefly it is a living church whose beauty makes you gasp, whose silent peace brings you to your knees, even if you kneel on the hard stone and slate of the floor.

St Protus and St Hyacinth, patron saints of Blisland church, pray for me! Often in a bus or train I call to mind your lovely church, the stillness of that Cornish valley and the first really beautiful work of man which my boyhood vividly remembers.

BBC broadcast

St Mark's, Swindon

The train draws into the outskirts of a big town. It is Swindon. One hundred and eight years ago, there was nothing here at all but a canal and a place where two newly built railways joined, the Cheltenham and Great West Union Railway (the Gloucestershire line) and the London to Bristol line, known as the Great Western.

On a hill above the meadow was the old market town of Swindon. Then New Swindon was built in the meadow by the Great Western. It was a convenient point between Bristol and London. It consisted of sheds and a few rows of model cottages with open fields round them. These cottages are of Bath stone taken from the excavations of Box Tunnel. They still exist and are called the Company's Houses. They must form one of the earliest planned industrial estates in Britain.

The parishioners of St Philip and St Jacob in Bristol entreated the Great Western to build a church for their workers; directors found the money, subscriptions were raised, land was presented and by 1845, St Mark's Church was built.

There it stands today close beside the line on the Bristol side of the station, a stone building, all spikes and prickles outside, designed by Gilbert Scott who was then a young man and who lived to build hundreds of rather dull copy-book churches all over Great Britain, and to build St Pancras Hotel, the Foreign Office in London and to 'restore' many cathedrals.

One cannot call it a convenient site. Whistles and passing trains disturb the services, diesel fumes blacken the leaves and tombstones and eat into the carved stonework of the steeple. No matter, it is a great church and though it isn't much to look at, it is for me the greatest church in England. For not carved stones nor screens and beautiful altars, nor lofty arcades, nor gilded canopies, but the priests who minister and the people who worship make a church great.

If ever I feel England is pagan, if ever I feel the poor old Church of England is tottering to its grave, I revisit St Mark's, Swindon. That corrects the impression at once. A simple and definite faith is taught; St Mark's and its daughter churches are crowded. Swindon, so ugly to look at, to the eyes of the architectural student, glows golden as the New Jerusalem to the eyes that look beyond the brick and stone.

Swindon *is* superficially ugly. That pretty model village of the eighteen-forties has developed a red-brick rash which stretches up to the hill to Old Swindon and strangles it, and beyond Old Swindon it runs tentacles to the downs and it spreads with monotony in all other directions. It is now the biggest town in Wiltshire, sixty times the size of the original market town. Swindon has few, if any slums; it is only just ugly architecturally: I would rather see a red-brick rash like Swindon enlivened with Victorian towers and steeples sticking out of it, than I would see a gleaming glass city of architect-designed flats with never a church but instead only the humped backs of super-cinemas, the grandstands of the greyhound tracks and the other shrines of the modern barbarism.

Swindon is largely a Christian town and much of the credit for that goes to the priests and people of St Mark's. It is not Sabbatarian and smug. It has its cinemas and theatres and art gallery and library and sports grounds and good old Swindon Town Football Club – but its churches are part of its life. That is the unusual thing about Swindon.

In the centenary book of St Mark's, there is a photograph of Canon Ponsonby wearing side whiskers and a beard that ran down his chin but not over it. This saintly Victorian priest (who died in 1945 aged nearly a hundred) caused St Mark's parish so to grow in faith that it built five other churches in New Swindon.

Two of them, St Paul's and St Augustine's, became separate parishes. He also caused the Wantage Sisters to open a mission house in Swindon.

The beautiful daughter church of St Mark's, St Luke's, was designed by W. A. Masters. Except for the railway works (which are awe-inspiring inside), St Luke's is the only fine interior, architecturally, in Swindon.

It is not about lovely St Luke's, nor about little St John's, nor about the missions which St Mark's supports abroad, nor about the many priests who have been Swindon men that I want to end this article. Up a steep hill going out of the New Town winds Old Swindon, there is a church built of wood and called St Saviour's. That was erected in 1889–90, in six months, by St Mark's men, mostly railway workers.

When you consider that they did this in their spare time and for nothing, that some of them sacrificed their holidays and that their working hours were from 6 am to 5.30 pm in those days, you can imagine the faith that inspired them to go out after a long day's work and build a church.

With foundations of faith like this, St Saviour's grew and in 1904 it had to be enlarged. Over one hundred once again set to work and the church was extended entirely by voluntary labour and in spare time.

I don't know why it is St Mark's parish hangs together and is a living community, full of life and spirit. Perhaps it is because Swindon is the right size for an industrial town, neither too big nor too small. Perhaps it is because the sort of work men do in a railways works – 'inside' as they called it in Swindon – perhaps it is because the men 'inside' do not do soul-destroying work such as one sees in motor factories where the ghastly chain-belt system persists.

Perhaps much of the work in a railway works is really worth doing and not beneath the dignity of man, but whatever it is, I know that the people of Swindon first taught me not to be so la-de-da and architectural, not to judge people by the houses they live in, nor churches only by their architecture.

I would sooner be on my knees within the wooden walls of St Saviour's than leaning elegantly forward in a cushioned pew in an Oxford college chapel – that is to say if I am to realise there is something beyond this world worth thinking about.

The church-crawler starts by liking old churches, but he ends by liking all churches and of all churches those that are most alive are often those hard-looking buildings founded by Victorian piety – churches like St Mark's, Swindon.

BBC broadcast

Bournemouth

Bournemouth is one of the few English towns one can safely call 'her'. With her head touching Christchurch and her toes turned towards the Dorset port of Poole she lies, a stately Victorian duchess, stretched along more than five miles of Hampshire coast. Her bed has sand for under-blanket and gravel for mattress and it is as uneven as a rough sea. What though this noble lady has lately disfigured her ample bosom with hideous pseudo-modern jewellery in the shape of glittering hotels in the Tel-Aviv style, her handsome form can stand such trashy adornment, for she is lovely still. Warm breezes caress her. She is heavy with the scent of *Pinus laricio*, *Pinus insignis*, the Scotch fir of orange-golden bark, the pinaster and black Austrian pine. She wears a large and wealthy coat of precious firs. Beneath it we may glimpse the flaming colours of her dress, the winding lengths of crimson rhododendron, the delicate embroidery of the flower beds of her numerous public gardens which change their colours with the seasons. The blue veins of her body are the asphalt paths meandering down her chines, among firs and sandy cliffs, her life-blood is the young and old who frequent them, the young running gaily up in beach shoes, the old wheeled steadily down in invalid chairs. Her voice is the twang of the tennis racket heard behind prunus in many a trim villa garden, the lap and roar of waves upon her sand and shingle, the strains of stringed instruments from the concert hall of her famous pavilion.

The sea is only one of the things about Bournemouth, and one of the least interesting. Bathing is safe. Sands are firm and sprinkled in places with shingle and in others with children. There are lines of bathing huts, bungalows and tents and deck chairs municipally owned, mostly above that long high water mark which hardly changes at all, for the tide at Bournemouth always seems to be high. Zig-zag paths, bordered by wind-slashed veronica, ascend those unspectacular slopes of sandy rock from Undercliffe to Overcliffe. From Undercliffe the lazy motorist may shout out of her motor car window to her children on the beach, from Overcliffe she may survey the sweep of bay from Purbeck to the Needles, and, sickened by so much beauty, drink spirits in the sun lounge of one of those big hotels or blocks of flats which rise like polished teeth along the cliff top. The sea to Bournemouth is incidental, like the bathroom leading out of a grand hotel suite: something which is there because it ought to be, and used for hygienic reasons. Deep in a chine with its scent of resin and tap of palm leaves and plash of streamlets and moan of overhanging pine, an occasional whiff of ozone reminds us of the sea. But Bournemouth is mainly a residential town by the sea, not a seaside town full in summer only.

The inland suburbs of Bournemouth are like any other suburbs, indistinguishable from Wembley or the Great West Road. And they stretch for miles into Hants and Dorset, leaving here and there a barren patch of pylon-bisected heath. The main shopping streets have the usual ugly lengths of flashy chromium, though a pretty, early-Victorian stucco thoroughfare survives called the Arcade. The public buildings are less blatant and alien looking than the latest blocks of flats and hotels. But the beauty of Bournemouth consists in three things, her layout, her larger villas and her churches. All of these are Victorian.

Earliest Bournemouth is on the western and Branksome side of the Bourne which runs into the sea by the Pavilion. It consists of a few villas built by Mr Lewis Tregonwell whose name survives in a terrace and a road and whose house was part of the Exeter Hotel. He started building in 1810. In 1836 a local landlord, Sir George Tapps of Westover and Hinton Admiral, built on the eastern bank of the stream. Adding Gervis to his name, he went on building and called in Benjamin Ferrey, the Gothic church architect and friend of Pugin, to lay out his estate. Thus Gervis Place arose with its stucco Tudor-style villas. Tudor or Italian, the villas were varied, well spaced in their setting, roads were broad and planted with trees, but everything had to wind. Nothing was to be regular. That is why there is no formal promenade in Bournemouth and why there have always been so many footpaths and curving roads in the older and finer parts of the town. The place was carefully planned from its beginnings on the principle that nature abhors a straight line, the picturesque school of Georgian gardening surviving into Victorian times. This sense that Bournemouth is a garden with houses in it survived the century. The name Tapps-Gervis increased to Tapps-Gervis-Meyrick, hence Meyrick Avenue, Meyrick Park, Meyrick Road. And if you are not sure of the owner of the road, you may often guess its date from its name – Adelaide, Alma, Gladstone. They are hidden behind trees and

flowering shrubs, down lengths of gravel bordered with rhododendron, these Victorian villas. Some are hotels, some are now government offices. They reflect every phase of leisured Victorian and
Edwardian life – here a hint of Madeira, there an Elizabethan cottage,
then an Italian villa like the Royal Bath Hotel. All these are in stucco
and not later than the seventies. Then brick came in and we have
'Flemish style' buildings, with gables and white wood balconies and
leaded panes, of which J. D. Sedding's Vicarage at St Clement's and
big house at the top of Boscombe Chine, called The Knole, are
beautiful, satisfying examples. They look stately and practical. Later, a
brilliant local architect, Sidney Tugwell, designed villas in the new art
style with tiny windows fluttering cheerful chintz, low-pitched roofs of
local stone and broad eaves – wholesome and simple buildings like
home-made cakes. He had his imitators. And each of these strongly
individual Victorian houses, not content with its garden-like road,
Knyveton Road, Manor Road, Alum Chine or further inland round
Meyrick Park, has, or once had, a beautiful garden of its own. So that
the real Bournemouth is all pines and pines and pines and flowering
shrubs, lawns, begonias, azaleas, bird-song, dance tunes, the plung of
the racket and creak of the basket chair.

Lastly the churches have the colour and clearness of the town. I
doubt if any place in Britain has finer modern churches than
Bournemouth and, what is more, they are all open and all alive. I
visited fourteen of them on one weekday and found them all clean and
cared for and in most of them people at prayer. Excluding Parkstone
with its beautiful St Peter's and the lovely Basilica of St Osmund I
thought the finest Bournemouth church was St Stephen's in the centre
of the town – designed by J. L. Pearson. It is worth travelling 200
miles and being sick in the coach to have seen the inside of this many-
vistaed church, all in clean cream-coloured stone, with arch cutting
arch, a lofty hall of stone vaulting providing view after view as you
walk round it, each lovelier than the next and worthy of a vast
cathedral. Away in the suburbs there is much that is beautiful, J. D.
Sedding's famous church of St Clement, scholarly and West-country
looking in stone; Sir Giles Gilbert Scott's little Roman Catholic
Church of the Annunciation, a brilliantly original design in brick, his
first work after Liverpool Cathedral; St Francis' church by J. Harold
Gibbons on a new building estate, white, Italianate and vast. As the
day drew to an end I entered a red-brick church in a hard red-brick
shopping street at the back of Boscombe. St Mary's, Boscombe, built
about 1920. Here, out of the noise of the street, was a white, cool and

spacious interior, friendly, beautiful, with golden screens and gold and blue east windows, gaily painted roofs and wide and high West-country arches. Clean and white and cheerful, the perfect seaside church. That last experience seemed to typify Bournemouth. You arrive tired from a long journey, you first see only the car parks, buses and jazzy blocks of flats and hotels. You turn into a side road and all is colour, light and life.

BBC broadcast

Christmas

I hope you have had plenty to eat and drink, I hope you are feeling uncritical and kind, with all those Christmas cards on the chimneypiece with the really well-intentioned messages from people you don't think about from one year's end to another. Today kindness and friendliness are still banging about in the tobacco smoke and in the firelight, in the still streets and behind the lit windows of houses. The slight indigestion we all feel from having eaten rather more than usual, has not yet induced ill-temper. Thoroughly sentimental. This is the time to be it. I wrap up my mind in artificial snow. I imagine a robin perched on my shoulder, and the announcer luridly disguised as Father Christmas to support the illusion and the new Directors of the BBC dressed as elves and sitting on wooden toadstools around this microphone as I am talking. And you can imagine any old nonsense you like, so long as you can put up with my being thoroughly egotistic and sentimental.

For this is Christmas and I'm going back, back to a small boy with projecting teeth and yellow skin and no brothers or sisters. Spirit of the past call up Mrs Wallis! Her address was her daughter's house, 103 Dongola Road, Philip Lane, Tottenham and she used to work for us. And dearly I loved her. Dearly and dependently. She must have been quite seventy then, so she would be well over a hundred now, if she were alive.

She was an old-fashioned person, small and dumpy and she wore a black bonnet when we used to take the train to Philip Lane Station and walk to see her daughter in Dongola Road. Mrs Wallis listened for hours while I read poetry to her. My mother recalls how once she came home and found me reading poetry aloud outside the lavatory door behind which the old girl had locked herself. She played draughts with me and always let me win. I teased her and she laughed. I exceeded the bounds of decency and decorum and she didn't mind. But when I came back of an evening from my day school she had mountains of hot, buttered toast waiting for me. And I never knew her angry or fussed. And then came that fatal Christmas day. I woke up early. Heavy on my feet were the presents of my relations, presents of sympathy for an only child. I don't remember what they were. But one of them I do remember. It was one of those pieces of frosted glass in a wooden frame and behind the glass a picture in outline which one was supposed to trace on the glass with a pencil. 'To Master John, with love from Hannah Wallis'. I stood up on my bed among the brown paper of the opened parcels. I stood up. I stepped a step. Crack! I had smashed the frosted glass of her present.

Hannah Wallis, you who are now undoubtedly in Heaven, you know now, don't you, that I did not do that on purpose? I remember thinking then that she might think I had smashed it because I did not think it a good enough present and that it looked too cheap among the more expensive ones of my relations. But, as a matter of fact, it was just what I wanted. And now I had smashed it. I remember putting it on a shelf over my bed between some books so as to hide the accident. Guiltily I went down to breakfast. 'Did you like the slate? It was just what you wanted, wasn't it? The biggest I could get!' Poor people were poor in those days and she must have saved up for it. 'Oh, yes and thank you very, very much. It was lovely.' Oh the guilt and the shame! I did not dare, for fear of hurting her feelings whom I loved so much – I did not dare to tell her I had smashed it. Yet that evening when my room had been tidied and the presents put away, I found the broken glass and frame put in my waste-paper basket. She must have found it out. But we neither of us ever mentioned it again. I think that cracked glass was the first crack in my heart, the first time I lost ignorance and the first time I realised the overwhelmingly unpleasant things of the world.

And as I look back I don't seem to remember subsequent childhood Christmasses. Other things get in the way. Gangs of boys who used to waylay me as I walked back from school and throw me into a holly bush on the edge of Highgate Cemetery. Intense home-sickness when I first went to boarding-school, where there was a smell of bat oil and stale biscuits and everyone shouting '*Quis?*' '*Ego*'. 'Anyone seen my ruler? Anyone seen my pencil-case?' 'Shut up!' 'Betjeman, you'll get unpopular if you go on like this.' Then I seem to have directed all my wits to making myself popular, siding with the majority, telling lies to get out of awkward situations. I remember one whopper. It's worth quoting as an example of how absolutely stinking small boys can be to one another. There was one immensely popular boy, good-looking, upright and, I suppose, rather self-righteous – he is now a prominent Labour MP and has, I expect, quite forgotten the incident. He accused me of bullying another boy.

'I'll fight you for that in the morning.' Fight me! Oh Lord, and he learned boxing. It would hurt and I wouldn't win. I should become more unpopular than ever. How could I get out of it? The next morning I hit on a brilliant lie. We received our letters at breakfast. I had one and pretended to blub. Very sober and weepy I went up to the champion of the right who was going to fight me. 'I'm awfully sorry, Per, I can't fight you this morning. I've just had a letter from home. My mater's frightfully ill.' 'Oh, I'm most awfully sorry. Of course we won't fight.' It makes one blush, doesn't it?

And after that the lies, the subterfuges and the indulgences increase and increase, so that I cannot possibly remember them all. They get between me and Christmas. Making money, increasing my possessions, lust, sloth, self-esteem – they stand between me and that innocence now lost, so that the small boy with projecting teeth and yellow skin is as different in spirit as he is in looks from this bald-headed man with *green* skin sitting here and talking at this moment.

Does this seem to have nothing to do with Christmas? It has everything to do with it. My birthday, which used to seem so important in childhood, is now of no importance and passes practically unnoticed. But Christmas is the one time which becomes more and more important to me. It is the one time when the world, at any rate in England, seems to get away from the world, when my struggle to get money, possessions, and to score off enemies stops.

Christmas is also the one time when I feel where my roots are, at home and among my friends and family. And the unwonted silence everywhere rubs it in, for once Time seems to merge into the Eternal and I do not think of the dead as gone for ever, but as waiting for me and watching me in this wintry silence when wheels no longer spin, nor hooters hoot, nor lorries thunder down main roads and aeroplane engines have ceased to rip the sky with noise.

I have now to speak so personally because I can think of no other way of saying why Christmas means much more to me than my birthday. The greatest reason of all will take some putting across – even to anyone who has listened so far. It is this.

I cannot believe that I am surrounded by a purposeless accident. On a clear night I look up at the stars and, remembering amateur astronomy, know that the Milky Way is the rest of this universe and that the light from some of the stars has taken years to reach this planet. When I consider that the light from the sun twenty million miles away takes eight and a half minutes, the consequent immensity of this universe seems intolerable. And thus I am told that some little clusters seen beyond the edge of the Milky Way on certain nights are other whole universes in outer space. It is too much, though believable. And then on any day about now, I can turn over a piece of decaying wood in our garden and see myriapods, insects and bugs, startled out of sluggish winter torpor by my motion. Each is perfectly formed and adapted to its life. From the immensity of the stars to the perfection of an insect – I cannot believe that I am surrounded by a purposeless accident.

But I can believe this most fantastic story of all, that the Maker of the stars and of the centipedes, became a Baby in Bethlehem not so long ago? No time ago at all, when you reckon the age of the earth. Well it's asking a lot. If I weren't such a highbrow it would be easier. No man of intelligence can believe such a thing. A child of Jewish parents the Creator of the Universe? Absurd.

But if it is not true, why was I born? And if it is true, nothing else is of so much importance. No date in time is so important as Christmas Day, the Birthday of God made man. And carol singers, and Salvation Army bands, and Christmas cards (yes, even Christmas cards from ardent unbelievers who always seem to observe Christmas) and cathedrals and saints and church bells, and hospitals and almshouses and towers and steeples and the silence and present-giving of Christmas Day all bear witness to its truth.

Beyond my reason, beyond my emotions, beyond my intellect I know that this peculiar story is true. Architecture brings it home to me. I suppose because architecture is, with poetry, my chief interest.

Last week I was in the most beautiful building in Britain – King's College Chapel, Cambridge. You know it. It is a forest glade of old coloured glass, and between the great windows columns of shafted stone shoot up and up to fountain out into a shower of exquisite elaborate fan vaulting. It is the swansong of Perpendicular architecture, so immense, so vast, so superbly proportioned, so mysterious, that no one can enter it without gasping. All the schoolchildren of Cambridge had filed into a carol service and there they were in the candle light of the dark oak stalls. We stood waiting for the choir to come in and as we stood there the first verse of the opening carol was sung beyond us, behind the screen, away in the mighty splendour of the nave. A treble solo fluted to the distant vaulting.

Once in Royal David's City . . .

It was clear, pure, distinct. And as I heard it, I knew once more – knew despite myself – that this story was the Truth. And knowing it I knew that because of the Birth of Christ the world could not touch me, and that between me and the time I smashed Mrs Wallis's Christmas present, the figure of God became man, crucified in the great East Window, hanging there.

BBC broadcast

Interlude

SS CENTIPEDA &

GIOMONSELLA

Martyrs

THE
CATHOLIC TRUTH SOCIETY
Price 1d

[written after Penelope Betjeman and Joan Leigh-Fermor (née Eyres-Monsell) holidayed in Rome together in 1949]

Saints Centipeda and Giomonsella both came of noble families. On her
mother's side the youthful Centipeda was related to Julius Caesar and on
her father's side the infant Giomonsella was descended from Sappho.
Thus they were both offered the best the world could give, delicacies,
riches, wines, olives, chalcedony and myrrh. But these dainties they both
steadfastly refused, preferring holiness.

Though they loved their parents, they were passionately devoted to one another. Many a time the Mother Superior of the convent to which they went found them in close embrace in the cloisters, legs and arms wound together in true Heavenly Union.

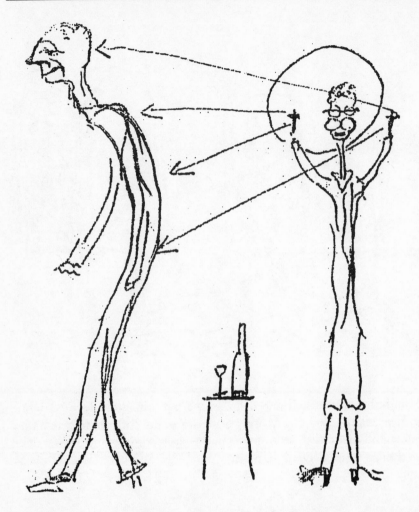

One of Saint Giomonsella's first miracles was the conversion of her brother (Saint Graham Hermaphrodite) by shaming him with crucifixes, a notorious drunkard and evil-liver who was subsequently martyred on the Harvard campus.

The continual supplication at the altar of Saint Centipeda brought about the conversion of her noble father Woad, a fierce Spartan General who subsequently became a Franciscan. Little is known of their subsequent lives, except that various chroniclers tell us of their unbridled attachment to one another.

They were both martyred in front of a beautiful Indian by rapacious Hindu priests. Where their blood was spilled, a well of water sprung up, known to this day as the Well of Saints Centipeda and Giomonsella. Even in death their hands were clasped.

Their heads were removed to Rome where they are exposed today in the beautiful reliquary of lapis lazuli, sardonyx and bronze, in the high altar of La Chiesa de Saint Centipeda.

    SS Centipeda and Giomonsella orate pro nobis.

Five:

1950 to 1955

Five

1950–1955

JB was becoming a worthy citizen. Having worked for the British Council and for the Oxford Preservation Trust in the late forties he now served on the Oxford Diocesan Committee as well as the London Diocesan Committee. The work involved many meetings, but also enriched his knowledge of ecclesiastical architecture. His *Collins Guide to Parish Churches*, commissioned years before was beginning to take shape and his network of contacts, to whom he could turn for local information – in far flung corners of Cumberland or Lincolnshire – was ever increasing. He had, after all, been looking at churches ever since he was eight or nine years old in an almost religious fashion but it was a physical impossibility for him to visit every single one in the country.

In 1949 he became literary adviser and editor of *Time and Tide*, a periodical edited by the formidable and unusual Lady Rhondda, which flew a liberal-to-leftish flag. At this time there were many weeklies which voiced educated opinion and were more widely read than they or their equivalents are today. JB now had the power to commission reviews from friends and figures he revered, like Siegfried Sassoon and Walter de la Mare. He was also able to write literary leaders himself in his section '*Men and Books*'. His predilections predominated – he devoted a whole page to 'Trivia Anglicana', for instance, which was a round-up of church pamphlets. His praise of *The Birmingham Post Book* and *Who's Who* was unbridled and given pride of place. '. . . In the train home I look through these thousand pages and find them more full than any novel . . . Eleven Cadburys (chocolate and Bourneville) are in the *Who's Who* and three of some cousins of mine, Collins (collar studs and army buttons) . . . the Non-conformist tradition comes percolating through . . . O new and polished motors parked in factory yards where a wall is painted "Directors' Cars Only"! O city of twenty-nine Dog Fanciers' Clubs, sixty-eight Boxing Associations and nearly a thousand Sports Clubs, three Mountaineering Clubs (where are the mountains?) O, what vigour and life are yours!'¹ The books section fluctuated in length depending on how much political writing Lady Rhondda wanted to include in each issue. Politics definitely came first, but JB lasted six years before he became exasperated at his expendability, voiced his annoyance at being thought flippant, and was sacked.

After reviewing for seven years for the *Daily Herald*, JB was offered a higher wage in 1951 by Michael Berry whose family owned the *Daily Telegraph*. With no let up at all, he began the weekly slog afresh for what turned out to be an even longer stint. However good the money, reading or skimming through several novels a week became a nightmare. He did not have time to take the care he would have liked. JB was a terrific stickler for proper English usage. He believed steadfastly that Latin should be compulsory in schools as a way of teaching the writing of good English. But depressed as he might be about his uninspiring but necessary journalistic work, he felt mildly proud when Myfanwy Piper chose a selection of his prose from magazines and broadcasts of the past twenty years which was published as *First and Last Loves* in 1952.

In 1954 he began a weekly column for *The Spectator* called 'City and Suburban' for which he got £8 a week. He used it as a sort of weekly notebook and wrote about pylons, threatened buildings, doomed canals and railways, the invasion of concrete lamp-posts, atomic power stations and indeed any issue about which he felt strongly. In 1943 the Abercrombie Plan for the County of London had been created as a basis for the rebuilding of the war-damaged city and private redevelopment had been strictly controlled. But in 1954 building licences were removed. Land prices then jumped, and huge blocks like New Zealand House began to rise from bomb and demolition sites.

JB's strong lobbying pieces which defended, attacked or praised, were interspersed with short light-hearted paragraphs on anything that came into his head or passed under his nose that week – Teddy boys, dentists or girls' summer frocks.

He used *Punch* as a place to wax satirical. In an article called 'Amenities' he wrote, 'In my position as Borough Engineer and Surveyor of this city I often find myself up against obstructions. . . . Trees in urban areas are a source of danger to the community. Their branches may break off and fall on the head of a ratepayer. Even if their branches do not fall (and intensive pruning can sometimes safeguard against this), their leaves fall on to the public highway, thereby causing untidy litter and adding to the skilled and expensive work of the public cleansing department. Trees in rural districts are bad enough, sapping as they do the good from agricultural soil and lending only primitive and partial shelter in return. . . . I have been accused of disregarding amenities when I demolish obsolescent property, whether Elizabethan, Georgian, or some other fancy style, in order to make the roads safe for kiddies, who must always come first, and for lorries, without which goods could not be delivered to the chain stores which are the greatest asset, commercially and artistically, to any city which wishes to move with the times and by means of mutual co-operation and economic planning donate its contribution to the municipal and national revenue, thereby speeding European recovery and global security in the midst of so much stress and strain. Have the objectors to the destruction of old houses, I wonder, ever lived in one? Are they aware that nearly all these properties, howsoever historic or culturally important, very often have windows well below the minimum standard size laid down by the Medical Officer of Health? Anyhow these buildings have all been listed and recorded by experts, so there is no further need to keep them standing. . . .'[2]

By the mid fifties, JB was a well known public figure. He had often taken part in 'The Brains Trust' on the radio and appeared with his friend Gilbert Harding on television. His prowess at acting cultivated at the Dragon School and University now stood him in good stead. He felt utterly relaxed on camera. He was such an old hand at radio, that his appearances on television were seemingly effortless, unlike those of most newcomers who sounded stilted and looked contorted with embarrassment. He was also well used to public speaking, whether at protest meetings or Women's Institutes. As a result of this profession-alism he was asked to take part in various commercial television ventures which were just beginning to blossom. He wrote the commentary for a series of twenty-six short films produced by Shell called 'Discovering Britain' and all he had learned from viewing those early documentaries in the thirties came into its own.

Coming fresh to the making of documentaries which were not government-briefed (as they had been when he worked in the Ministry of Information) but were his own creations, he found a new excitement. His passion to get things across came to the fare and he took inordinate trouble with his scripts, reading them through again and again over the images on the screen. He now saw a way of showing the

beauty of his surroundings to the public which might galvanise them
into realising how wonderful England was.

1. *Time and Tide*, 11 July 1953.
2. *Punch*, 11 March 1953.

Theo Marzials

BBC Home Service broadcast, Christmas Eve, 1950

Cast your mind back, if it will go back so far, to gaslight burning either side of the chimney-piece; a large coal fire is leaping in the grate, fans and watercolours are hung upon the walls, china is displayed on white enamel shelves rising tier above tier in one corner of the room. In another corner is a piano and beside it a silk screen – Louis Seize style. The folding doors of the sitting room have been thrown open into the dining room so as to make the place bigger. We are warm, well-fed and ready to be entertained. It is a suburban evening in the nineties and some friends have come in with their music. Mr and Mrs Pooter, Mr and Mrs Cummings, Gowing, Mr Padge, Eliza and her husband, and others. What harmonies we shall have, what arch looks will be cast between the palm leaves or above that vase of Cape gooseberries, and what are the songs that will be sung? I think it very likely that some of them will be by Theo Marzials, the most famous song-writer of the eighties and nineties. We shall have 'Twickenham Ferry'. Mr Pooter, will you sing that? It is suited to all tenor voices, and oh! the ripple of the air suggests the long lazy wave of brown Thames water down where the river is nearly tidal and rowing boats must take care.

[SONG: 'Twickenham Ferry']

And now that Mr Pooter has broken the ice, perhaps Carrie, his wife, will be brave enough to sing a duet with him – 'Go Pretty Rose'. I remember how well my father used to sing it in the bath.

[SONG: 'Go Pretty Rose']

And now what about one of the ladies on her own; this roguish little piece, since we are all warming up and enjoying ourselves – 'The Miller and the Maid'. I see that the words are by Mike Beverley and the music by Theo Marzials. But, as a matter of fact, Mike Beverley was a name Theo Marzials liked to assume when writing some of his lyrics – why, I have no idea.

[SONG: 'The Miller and the Maid']

And there is one piece of Marzials's which is still sung at school concerts and in village halls – 'Friendship'. The words really *are* by Sir Philip Sidney – Philip Sidney isn't another name for Marzials. The melody by Marzials is Elizabethan in flavour, for it was in Elizabethan lyrics and music that Marzials took the greatest delight. I expect that in somebody's drawing room, somebody listening tonight, there is a copy of that big, oblong book called *Pan-Pipes* with decorations by Walter Crane and music arranged by Marzials from Elizabethan and seventeenth-century lyrics. 1883, that was the date of the book. It looks like a stained glass window of that time as I open it before me.

[SONG: 'Friendship']

And now for the story of Marzials. Many years ago I went into a second-hand bookshop at the foot of Highgate Hill near Dick Whittington's stone and I bought for 1s 6d a book of poems called *The Gallery of Pigeons* by Theo Marzials. 1873 was the date but it was not the kind of poetry you would expect to read of that date. No, it was bold, strange, arty stuff, a foretaste of some of Swinburne's and William Morris's later work. Here are some characteristic lines that I remember:

> I chased her to a pippin-tree,
>   The waking birds all whist (*sic*),
> And oh! it was the sweetest kiss
>   That I have ever kiss'd.

> Marjorie (*sic*), mint, and violets
>   A-drying round us set,
> 'Twas all done in the faience-room
>   A-spicing marmalet;
> On one tile was a satyr,
>   On one a nymph at bay,
> Methinks the birds will scarce be home
>   To wake our wedding-day!

I imagine that last fantastic scene really means a room with William de Morgan tiles all round the walls and a table where some cherry-lipped maidens are putting spices into marmalade – a very daring fancy for 1873 or, indeed, for any age. Though I have quoted rather ridiculous lines of Marzials, he *was* a poet, there is no doubt about that. He was a stern critic of himself and I remember that my edition of his poems had comments which he had written in the margins – 'Naughty, naughty little Marzials', 'Pre-Lauberian period', 'Ridiculous, but I like it' and things like that. I started to look him up in books of reminiscences and I found tantalising information. For instance, there was this by Ford Madox Hueffer in a book he wrote called *Ancient Lights*, published in 1911:

> The mention of chocolate creams reminds me of another musician who was also a Pre-Raphaelite poet – Mr Theo Marzials. Mr Marzials was in his young days the handsomest, the wittiest, the most brilliant and the most charming of poets. He had a career tragic in the extreme and, as I believe, is now dead. But he shared with M the habit of keeping chocolate creams loose in his pocket, and on the last occasion when I happened to catch sight of him looking into a case of stuffed birds at South Kensington Museum, he had eaten five large chocolates in the space of two minutes.

Hueffer admired Marzials's poems and quotes one of his little tragedies in two verses:

> She was only a woman, famish'd for loving,
>   Mad with devotion, and such slight things;
> And he was a very great musician,
>   And used to finger his fiddle-strings.
>
> Her heart's sweet gamut is cracking and breaking
>   For a look, for a touch, – for such slight things;
> But he's such a very great musician,
>   Grimacing and fing'ring his fiddle-strings.

Then I remember in a book of reminiscences by H. de Vere Stacpoole – there were some references to Marzials's genius and to his having been led astray in Paris.

Then came the great time when I spent a whole day with Max Beerbohm and I asked him about Marzials. 'Theo Marzials,' he said, 'oh yes, wasn't he rediscovered by Henry Harland?' – *re*-discovered, mark you, so he must have been well-known as a poet and musician before the days of Wilde and the Yellow Book – 'And didn't he take stimulants in order to shine at Aubrey Beardsley's parties?' And then he told me how Marzials had been in the British Museum library as a clerk at the same time as Edmund Gosse when the great Panizzi, the librarian who founded the British Museum Reading Room, was in command there. Marzials was always a highly picturesque figure with flowing moustaches, long hair and a silk tie which fell in folds over the lapels of his coat. When out of doors he wore a wide-awake hat. He must indeed have been a picturesque figure in the British Museum Reading Room while Karl Marx was scratching away at *Das Kapital* and various mad antiquarians were hiding among pyramids of books. Anyhow, one day Marzials was in the gallery of that enormous, silent Reading Room – and if you have not seen it you can imagine it as something like the dome of St Paul's – when the great Panizzi came in. Suddenly, Marzials leant over the gallery and, in a loud voice, said 'Am I or am I not the darling of the Reading Room?'

With these tit-bits of information I went to see my friend Martin Secker, the publisher, who knows more about the nineties than most people, and he was so interested that he put a letter in the *Sunday Times* asking for information about Marzials, poet and eccentric. He had some fascinating replies. To begin with, Marzials was not dead in 1911 as a result of drink and drugs in Paris. No. He had spent most of the time in the West of England living first in Blandford, Dorset, and then with his sister in Colyton, Devon. She predeceased him by many years and he died in 1920 at Mrs Power's farm of Elm Grove, Colyton. He was aged seventy. I wondered how he had gone on all those years between when he was a famous singer and poet, the flashing centre of Bohemian parties and drawing-room concerts, and those last years when he was living outside a tiny Devonshire town as a paying guest in a farmhouse.

Mr Zealley, who had been a boy at Colyton when Marzials was an old man there, has allowed me to take this extract from his letter:

He lived quite alone, and it is certainly true that he was a most eccentric and striking figure in the rural community in which he lived. His interest in music was the outstanding feature which made him known to the villagers. He attended all concerts that were held, and almost inevitably caused consternation by standing up in the audience and declaiming, in his very strong accent, most outspoken, not to say rude, criticisms of the efforts of the performers. This was particularly the case if he thought he detected any form of affectation or musical insincerity. I remember on one occasion a lady, who really sang quite well, and who had a great affection for Italy in which she travelled a great deal, singing a song to a village audience in Italian and in the operatic style of that country. Brushing aside (not without physical violence) all efforts to dissuade him, Marzials got himself on the platform and sang 'Madam will you walk?' in the Italian manner, with every sort of trill and musical exaggeration.

The most interesting letter of all comes from Mr F. G. Skinner who had known him well in his declining years. Really, I must read you nearly all of it. Mr Skinner stayed with Marzials at Elm Grove farmhouse and says:

Theo had one fair-sized room on the ground floor with a single bed in one corner, occupying it day and night. By his bedside was a small table on which there always seemed to be a saucer containing sliced beetroot in vinegar so that the room continually smelt of this, together with the odour of chlorodyne (which he took to induce sleep), with, at night, the fumes of an enormous oil-lamp. During conversation, he would often fish out a slice of beetroot on the end of a fork and drop it into his mouth most elegantly – it was almost a joy to watch him. In another corner of the room, he kept a huge stockpot on a stove, into which he threw all sorts of odds and ends so that he had a kind of perpetual stew. What he did with it I do not know, but we thought he gave it to some of the poorer farmhands elsewhere.

As to his appearance, he was certainly the most striking figure I have met, fairly tall and of huge girth. When he sat down at the piano he dominated it by his size as well as by his genius. His hair was snow-white, his complexion as pink and clear as a healthy child's and although his clothes were odd and often the worse for wear, his person was always very well groomed. When I used to call and ask him to come out for a drink, he would slide out of bed, put on a tie, boots with no laces, no socks (he seldom wore socks) and join me with gusto. He seemed to love it. If we went to certain pubs he would go in with me to the bar-parlour and drink a pint or two of old-and-mild: but once I suggested going into the Colcombe Castle Hotel and he said 'All right' but made me go into the Lounge while he went into the public bar with the locals, I passing his beer through a kind of hatchway. He said he wasn't dressed for the Saloon Lounge – and he was the most important man in my mind for miles around!

He often seemed to have no money and would occasionally beg me, as I was a Christian, to give him sixpence or a shilling. I knew that he went later to the confectioners and bought lollipops for the village children. I believe that his income was sent direct to his landlady and that most of it went for board and lodging so that very little was left for pocket money.

He used to go mostly to Ye Olde Bear Inn, where I often stayed, and where in an upper room he would play and sing, even when nearly seventy, in a fine, rich, deep baritone – oh! splendid, splendid. His speaking voice, too, was a delight to hear – magnificently rich, and when he was roused in any way it was like thunder.

While speaking of his voice, I must mention another habit. He was sometimes seen and heard walking barefooted in the garden of Elm Grove in the small hours – one or two o'clock in the morning. He would sing in a very soft, low voice and now and then take a flower between his fingers, bend down and kiss it, and murmur 'O my pretty!' Theo Marzials – poet and eccentric!

He was ravenous for reading matter and annotated the books I used to send him with many interesting scribblings. Here is a sample – written under a picture of George Meredith:

'He was audience to my first singing of "Summer Shower". Mrs M. (No. 2) a tall, dignified, comely, sympathetic French woman, loving and by G. M. most beloved, used to be most kind about my speciality of French very old songs. I first met her at Mendelssohn's cousin's (Box Hill). I was the hired singer – 25 gns. for 3 songs – a lot in the 70s.'

I remember that sometimes after a long evening at Ye Olde Bear I would walk back to Elm Grove with Theo. He insisted on taking my arm – no easy thing for me as I weighed only eight stone while he must have turned fifteen stone – and although I could have walked the distance in three minutes, it generally took us twenty minutes or half an hour. He would keep on stopping and talking – books, music, art, local gossip, anything.

One conversation has always lingered with me. I started it by asking him whether he had seen that Mr Alfred Noyes had written that he (Noyes) considered the finest single line in English poetry to be Shakespeare's

Following darkness like a dream.

That was enough to keep us up till about two in the morning, with Theo quoting, quoting from Chaucer to Newbolt. He had a marvellous memory and could roll off passage after passage with ease and splendour. But what I most remember is that when I rose to go to bed that night, he put his hand on my shoulder and said, 'Well, Fred, my boy, you can take it or leave it, but as far as my judgement is worth anything, *I* say that the finest single *verse* in English poetry, Shakespeare, Milton and all the rest of 'em included, is Mrs Alexander's

> There is a green hill far away,
> Without a city wall,
> Where our dear Lord was crucified
> Who died to save us all.

Theophile Jules Henri Marzials – poet, and *not* so eccentric perhaps, after all!

The last person who wrote to us, and whom I must mention, is Mrs Belt. She is the daughter of Cyril Davenport, the great friend of Marzials's youth who drew the picture of him in a wide-awake hat which I mentioned earlier. This letter from Marzials to Mrs Belt is very touching. It was written from Colyton in 1918, two years before his death and when he had had a stroke which had paralysed him down one side:

... I kept my voice almost intact until this last 'breaking up.' But who cares to hear an old man sing? This is a rambling Dairy-farm. Folk come in summer and take rooms and some used to pay-guest or board, but since the war and rations &c. they don't. It is all very clean. The head is a wonderful old woman and she and I live here. She in her part and I in mine. I sup with them. The niece housekeeps. Her husband does for me – and in his way is very like Cyril and me – in fact it is very like the situation of when your mama and papa and me were all just married, as it were. Of the folk who come and go in the house, I don't often mix up with them. Cyril knows my fits of retirement and since all this dying and the war I make no new friends – oh, I couldn't. Cyril is a bit of me – of course, and always was and ever will be. We just meet and are side by side, arm in arm, heart to heart, as if he had gone into a shop and

I was waiting outside. Dear old Squirrel. This is a most beautiful place, of endless and immediate variety. I have never known a place like it, in this respect. Seaton is the ugliest sea-side I have ever seen, too commonplace to be odious – but the seventeen odd miles of wildlandslip just off Seaton is quite perfection – and quite undescribable. And your wonderful letter. And oh what a gentle-woman you must be . . .

On a lovely day in the spring of this year, I went to Colyton to find Marzials's grave. I had never been to this unspoiled and beautiful little Devonshire town before. It is a huddle of cream and pink-washed thatched cottages collected round a silver-grey church tower and it lies in a little lush Devonshire valley with small hills around it. The cemetery is high above the town and looks down towards the farm where Marzials lived, over a landscape, as he describes it, 'of endless and immediate variety'. There was the grave with his sister's name above and his own below on a stone cross –

'Theophile Jules Henri Marzials. Born at Bagnères de Bigorre, Hautes-Pyrénées, France, December 20th, 1850. Died at Colyton, February 2nd, 1920. Fight the Good Fight of Faith.'

Let us go back to that evening party where we started. The refreshments are over and only one more song is to be sung. Let it be that most famous of all his songs and lyrics 'The River of Years' – once sung by throaty tenors at village concerts and evening parties all over the English-speaking world, and even joked about in *Punch* by Phil May. And as we listen – if it isn't too inappropriate at a party – let us remember him whose body has been lying so long forgotten in that Devonshire hillside and whose soul is, I pray, in that fair daylight of his song.

[SONG: 'The River of Years']

Polzeath

I suppose coming down the road from Saint Endellion is the most exciting bit. There are high hedges stuffed with pennywort, foxglove, scabious, mallow – every Cornish hedge is what would be a rock garden anywhere else. The windswept aloe bushes lean inland. Another downhill bend, some hideous electric light poles and suddenly there is Polzeath and the wide Atlantic. The island of Newland stands like a huge rock-cake on the horizon. And Polzeath Bay is a watery field of tumbling waves – waves and waves of surf, one behind another, fifty acres of foam and fifty more of hard and silvery sand.

Before I describe Polzeath let me bathe. For the moment it's not Polzeath that matters, but the surf. Change on the beach or in a motor car if you have one. Clasp your surf board and then race across this hard sand, splashing through the drying stream-bed to meet the bounding, overwhelming sea. The first waves don't strike cold as they lap around my ankles. The water has been warmed by hot sand for it is an incoming tide. It's a little colder by the time the waves are knee-high then, slap! A breaker sends salt water shooting up my middle. Now for it. I wade forward, nearly knocked down each time by every oncoming breaker. I dive through one that is higher than I am. In the trough of water behind it I am only up to my knees. Now, ready! Turn to face the land! I poise the surf board in front of me ready to fling myself down on it as the next wave approaches. Now! No, not that one, I wasn't ready. Now! Flop! There is a roar of surf behind me and I am shot forward on this board all along the crest of the wave. Forward, forward gliding fast. I seem to have become the racing wave. Oh, no! I've timed it wrong, the wave goes on in front of me and someone on my right goes shooting forward too, right up to where the wave flattens to a wavelet and she grounds on the sand itself. After half an hour of surfing, I am ready to enjoy anything.

Rock climbing is not the best thing to do after a bathe. I can never balance properly. I don't know about you. But the rocks at Polzeath – along the Pentire or up the Camel to Greenway – are almost as good as the surf.

Bend down and look into a rock pool. The colours are brighter than the tropics. The veined rock itself, in which the warm salt water lies, is purple with white lines and then green, then purple again.

Warm forests of red seaweed grow, green seaweed which looks like trees if there is sand on the bottom of the pool. You may see a huge prawn gliding – and shooting backwards – gliding and shooting backwards and the sudden dash of a small fish too quick for eye to see more than the sudden cloud of sand it raises. Or the rock pool may be one with shells and shrimps at the bottom and perhaps those rose-tinted cowries, the pearls of this coast – and a huge starfish, magnified by the water in all its pink and grey and purple colouring. Never was such colour, never is the wonder of God's creation more brought home to me than when I see the strange, merciless bright-coloured world of these Cornish rock pools.

Looking inland from the car park here on the shore I remember Polzeath of thirty years ago when there was no big road and only a wooden footbridge over the stream. Three or four old slate cottages climbed the curving hills either side of the valley. They are still there and so is the terrace of Welsh-looking boarding houses on the cliff. Then came Fred Male's new Post Office down by the stream, the only really nice-looking modern building in Polzeath, and since then the place has become all wires and poles and bungalows of every shape and size.

But walk inland to Shilla Mill out of the roar of the surf. The lane is slatey. Brambles, wood nightshade and convolvulus are on either side of it. Woods hang down the further hill, woods of those thin, Cornish elms with mossy hedges below them and here and there forgotten apple trees. And here, by the Old Mill cottage, the stream is deep and edged with iris and forget-me-not, there is a smell of mint and dragon-flies flash about.

Or walk seawards to the Rumps and Pentire where paths are steep tracks and you must go single-file. Sloe and gorse bushes below the level of the bracken scratch your legs. The cliffs are wild and tremendous. Rocks rising from green cliff slopes look like ruined castles. Go to the edge and throw a huge stone down to the deep, dark, crawling water. The stone floats like a feather, it has so far to go and bursts in powder on the boulders down at the sea's edge.

These lonely, terrifying cliffs with trembling sea pinks, blow-holes shooting spray a hundred feet in air, caves where seals bask, and the whole shadowy coast-line from Hartland Point to Trevose – the sea itself an emerald green in summer, with cloud reflections in purple patches on the moving water – I have known and loved them all my life. However many poles and wires and bungalows, luxury coaches and ice-cream cartons man may load upon Polzeath, up here on the cliffs, down there by the surf, inland in the valley, nature will show through. The sweet-smelling wildness of the Cornish coast will triumph when we are all forgotten.

BBC broadcast

St Endellion

Saint Endellion! Saint Endellion! The name is like a ring of bells. I travelled late one summer evening to Cornwall in a motor car. The road was growing familiar, Delabole with its slate quarry passed, then Pendogget. Gateways in the high fern-stuffed hedges showed sudden glimpses of the sea. Port Isaac Bay with its sweep of shadowy cliffs stretched all along to Tintagel. The wrinkled Atlantic Ocean had the evening light upon it. The stone and granite manor house of Tresungers with its tower and battlements was tucked away out of the wind on the slope of a valley and there on the top of the hill was the old church of St Endellion. It looked, and still looks, just like a hare. The ears are the pinnacles of the tower and the rest of the hare, the church, crouches among wind-slashed firs.

On that evening the light bells with their sweet tone were being rung for practice. There's a Ringer's rhyme in the tower, painted on a board. It shows Georgian ringers in knee breeches and underneath is written a rhyme which ends with these fine four lines:

> Let's all in love and Friendship hither come
> Whilst the shrill treble calls to thundering Tom
> And since bells are for modest recreation
> Let's rise and ring and fall to admiration.

They were ringing rounds on all six bells. But as we drew near the tower – a grand, granite, fifteenth-century tower looking across half Cornwall – as we climbed the hill the bells sounded louder even than the car. 'St Endellion! St Endellion!' they seemed to say. 'St Endellion!' Their music was scattered from the rough lichened openings over foxgloves, over grey slate roofs, lonely farms and feathery tamarisks, down to that cluster of whitewashed houses known as Trelights, the only village in the parish, and to Roscarrock and Trehaverock and Trefreock, heard perhaps, if the wind was right where lanes run steep and narrow to that ruined, forgotten fishing place of Port Quin, 'St Endellion!' It was a welcome to Cornwall and in front of us the sun was setting over Gulland and making the Atlantic at Polzeath and Pentire glow like a copper shield.

Ora pro nobis Sancta Endelienta! The words are carved in strangely effective lettering on two of the new oak benches in the church. Incidentally, those carved benches, which incorporate some of the old Tudor ones, are very decent-looking for modern pews. They were designed by the present rector and carved by a local sculptress. But who was St Endellion? She was a sixth-century Celtic saint, daughter of a Welsh king, who with her sisters Minver and Teath and many other holy relations came to North Cornwall with the Gospel.

There was an Elizabethan writer who lived in the parish, Nicholas Roscarrock. He loved the old religion and was imprisoned in the Tower and put on the rack and then imprisoned again. He wrote the life of his parish saint. 'St Endelient' he called her and said she lived only on the milk of a cow:

> which cowe the lord of Trenteny kild as she strayed into his grounds; and as olde people speaking by tradition, doe report, she had a great man to her godfather, which they also say was King Arthure, whoe took the killing of the cowe in such sort, as he killed or caus'd the Man to be slaine, whom she miraculously revived.

Nicholas Roscarrock also wrote a hymn in her praise:

> To emitate in part thy vertues rare
> Thy Faith, Hope, Charitie, thy humble mynde,
> Thy chasteness, meekness, and thy dyet spare
> And that which in this Worlde is hard to finde
> The love which thou to enemye didst showe
> Reviving him who sought thy overthrowe.

When she was dying Endelient asked her friends to lay her dead body on a sledge and to bury her where certain young Scots bullocks or calves of a year old should of their own accord draw her. This they did and the Scots bullocks drew the body up to the windy hilltop where the church now stands.

The churchyard is a forest of upright Delabole slate headstones, a rich grey-blue stone, inscribed with epitaphs – the art of engraving lettering on slate continued in this district into the present century – names and rhymes set out on the stone spaciously, letters delicate and beautiful. From the outside it's the usual Cornish church – a long low building of elvan stone, most of it built in Tudor times. But the tower is extra special. It is of huge blocks of granite brought, they say, from Lundy Island. The ground stage of the tower is strongly moulded but the builders seem to have grown tired and to have taken less trouble with the detail higher up, though the blocks of granite are still enormous.

I can remember Endellion before its present restoration. There's a photograph of what it used to look like in the porch – pitch pine pews, pitch pine pulpit, swamping with their yellow shine the clustered granite columns of the aisles. Be careful as you open the door not to fall over. Three steps *down* and there it is, long and wide and light and simple with no pitch pine anywhere except a lectern. A nave and two aisles with barrel roofs carved with bosses, some of them old but most of them done twelve years ago by a local joiner, the village postman and the sculptress. The floor is slate. The walls are stone lightly plastered blueish-grey. There is no stained glass. Old oak and new oak benches, strong and firm and simple, fill, but do not crowd, the church. They do not hide the full length of these granite columns. The high altar is long and vast. At the end of the south aisle is the sculptured base of St Endelienta's shrine, in a blue-black slate called Cataclewse, a boxwood among stones. The church reveals itself at once. Though at first glance it is unmysterious, its mystery grows. It is the mystery of satisfying proportion – and no, not just that, nor yet the feeling of age, for the present church is almost wholly early Tudor, not very old as churches go, nor is the loving use of local materials all to do with it. Why does St Endellion seem to go on praying when there is no one in it? The Blessed Sacrament is not reserved here, yet the building is alive.

There is something strange and exalting about this windy Cornish hilltop looking over miles of distant cliffs, that cannot be put into words.

Down a path from the north door, bordered with fuchsias, is the Rectory. The Rector of St Endellion is also a Prebendary. This church is run by a college of priests like St George's Chapel, Windsor. There are four prebends in the college, though their building is gone and they live elsewhere. They are the prebends of Marny, Trehaverock, Endellion and Bodmin. Each of the Prebendal stalls has a little income attached to it and is held by local priests. The money is given to Christian causes. For instance, the Parish of Port Isaac, formed out of St Endellion in 1913, is financed with the income of the Bodmin Prebendary. How this heavenly medieval arrangement of a college of prebendary clergymen survived the Reformation and Commonwealth and Victorian interferers is another mystery of St Endellion for which we must thank God. It was certainly saved from extinction by the late Athelstan Riley and Lord Clifden. Episcopal attacks have been made on it; but long live St Endellion, Trehaverock, Marny and Bodmin! Hold fast. *Sancta Endelienta, ora pro nobis!* . . .

I take a last look at St Endellion standing on a cliff top of this Atlantic coast. The sun turns the water into moving green. In November weather, if the day is bright, the cliffs here are in shadow. The sun cannot rise high enough to strike them. The bracken is dead and brown, the grassy cliff tops vivid green; red berries glow in bushes. Ice-cream cartons and cigarette packets left by summer visitors have been blown into crevices and soaked to pulp. The visitors are there for a season. Man's life on earth will last for seventy years perhaps. But this sea will go on swirling against these green and purple rocks for centuries. Long after we are dead it will rush up in waterfalls of whiteness that seem to hang half-way up the cliff face and then come pouring down with tons of ginger-beery foam. Yet compared with the age of these rocks, the sea's life is nothing. And even the age of rocks is nothing compared with the eternal life of man. And up there on the hill in St Endellion church, eternal man comes week by week in the Eucharist. That is the supreme mystery of all the mysteries of St Endellion.

BBC broadcast

High Frecklesby

INTRODUCTION

The parish of Frecklesby, for the time being in the county of Rutland,* has been chosen for this survey and plan because it represents a particularly wasteful rural unit which, by economic development and the co-operation of local authorities with enlightened surveyors, sanitary inspectors and planners, might be transformed into a model community of national significance, thus contributing to the progressive crusade towards a world target of planned production, without which, etc., etc.

THE PROBLEM STATED

Frecklesby is a parish of three thousand acres and five hundred people approx., in a rural area infested with trees, wild flowers, vermin, birds and needlessly tortuous lanes. The land is irregularly partitioned by unhygienic hedges. There are four large farms foolishly competing with one another, two of them some distance from the village. Frecklesby Hall was scheduled as a building of historic interest, but it has fallen into such a state of decay that it is not worthy of preservation now that the Ministry of Supply has relinquished its tenancy.

The village itself, at the Hall gates, consists of obsolete family units built of local stone and of some obsolescence. They are arranged in what can only be described as a rural sprawl around the antiquated church. This building, though ancient, will have to be demolished as it is in the very centre of the area to be replanned. Though we may regret its departure as an historic relic, the compensatory saving of space and the provision of an inter-denominational meeting room at the top of High Frecklesby should satisfy any dissentients. Nor must it be forgotten that those who utilise the two Nonconformist chapels in Frecklesby for religious purposes will also be permitted to avail themselves of the privileges of inter-denominational assembly.

* This distressingly rural county will, it is hoped, soon be merged into its more important and industrialised neighbour of Leicestershire.

Moreover, the village atheists, a considerable body at present without a place of worship, will also find themselves catered for in the High Frecklesby meeting room. The present village is serviced by only one shop and a smithy, the latter still in demand owing to the as yet incomplete mechanisation of agriculture in this backward area. The village lacks at present such essential services as a cinema, greyhound track, clinic, youth parliament and amenity rockery.

THE SOLUTION

1. Agriculture

In order to ensure maximum land utilisation, all hedges are to be uprooted, all traffic highways, major and minor, are to be straightened. Trees, with their inevitable load of disease-carrying birds and flies, will be reduced to the minimum necessary for amenity purposes, i.e. two flowering cherries and a prunus of maximum height of four feet (in order not to endanger ratepayers) will be planted amid crazy paving at the base of High Frecklesby.

The common weal of livestock will be serviced in concrete sheds immediately adjoining High Frecklesby, and within easy reach of the farm helps. Grazing and arable will be safely partitioned by fences constructed of concrete posts and wire mesh, varying in height in accordance with the dangerous nature of the cattle or crops enclosed. Stock which keeps awake at night will be provided with concrete lamp standards and a roof at the base of the standards should they desire shelter.

2. Housing

The elevation should explain itself, and High Frecklesby can easily be made high enough to embrace outlying hamlets. A ceiling of one thousand inhabitants is envisaged. The walls are of glass, and the ceilings of an opaque plastic material so as to ensure privacy between one flatlet and those above and below it. Farm helps are domiciled in the lower storeys so as to be more easily available for attending on crops and livestock, while the farmers can supervise the work from their higher flatlets. Every room in High Frecklesby is provided with television.

3. Education

A school, under expert Government control, has been built out of glass at the base of High Frecklesby with an attractive view on to the amenity, and also to the livestock enclosures (for biology classes). All furniture is plastic and washable.

4. Transport

   a. Vertical. Lifts and escalators to all floors.
   b. Horizontal. A bypass, efficiently illuminated by concrete stand-ards, between two industrial towns, has been diverted to pass High Frecklesby and thus ensure the community of easy access to neighbouring culture centres.

CONCLUSION

If all English villages can only be rehabilitated on these lines, we may sing, with the Women's Institute:

> *We have built Jerusalem*
> *In England's green and pleasant land.*

J. BETJEMAN
Town Planner, Borough Surveyor,
Sanitary Inspector, Phil. D.(Art. Hist.).

Punch

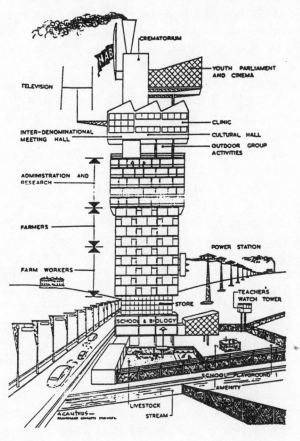

Childhood Days

Outside life was a see-saw when I was young. I expect it was the same with you. One moment ecstatic, rested, friendly, warm, unafraid. The next terrified, alone, ready to be hurt, secrets likely to be extracted by physical force. And over all there brooded the loneliness of Eternity.

'World without end, Amen.' That was the first phrase I can remember which really struck amazed terror to my heart. Something without an end. It was an appalling idea. And stars going on without stopping for millions of miles behind one another.

Lying in bed of a late summer evening I remember hearing the bells ring out from St Anne's Highgate Rise – the church where I was christened – they poured their sound, deep and sorrowful, over the chestnuts of the Burdett Coutts estate, through the hornbeam leaves I could see from bed. Maud, the nurse, was looking out of the open window. Crossed in love, I suppose, and for once fairly gentle with me. I remember asking her if I should go to Heaven. 'You will, but I won't' she said. I remember recognising even then that she spoke from her heart about herself. I did not recognise this, at the time, as any sign of grace in Maud. Nor did I really believe I would go to Heaven. Still less do I think so now.

Then I had a clear vision of the Devil. I used to go up in a black lift made of wood. We would arrive at the top where it was blindingly white and I would be in this little wooden lift one side of which was open and showed that we were floating on a limitless white sea. But I was not alone in the lift. Oh no! There rose up from the corner a tall thin-faced man with ram's horns springing out of his forehead. He was the Devil. His horns were outlined black against the sky. He was coming nearer. There was no escape.

As dreams became less real people became more so. Friends were important. Bill, Mary and Betty lived next door. They were my chief friends. Bill was, my mother told me 'easily led'. Perhaps this was why I liked him so much. Mary had freckles and blue eyes. I have always loved people with freckles and blue eyes since. I think the saddest moment of my life, as numbing as any subsequent loss, was the time when Bill, Mary and Betty left the district. I was about seven years old.

The pavements outside our houses on West Hill, the Heath, our little gardens seemed empty for ever.

As early as I can remember I wanted to be a poet. Even today when I am not writing poetry, I feel I am not fully justifying my existence. I used to take Bill out on to Parliament Hill Fields and say 'We will write poetry'. I would sit on a seat on top of one of those two little hills above Highgate Ponds and wait for inspiration, pencil and paper on my knees. What he did I can't remember, except that I made him bring pencil and paper too.

My father used to talk to me about the 'muse' and told me always to be original. And, of course, like all precocious children, I was derivative without realising it. Only healthy, normal children not afraid to be themselves, are truly original. I wasn't at all healthy. Always in love. I mean even when I was seven and eight. Generally girls with red or gold hair and always with blue eyes.

The enjoyable things of childhood one takes for granted. My mother making my old teddy bear Archie talk, my father taking me for silent, deeply contented walks, old Mrs Wallis letting me read poetry to her while we ate slices of hot buttered toast. And now while I'm on them – those enjoyable things, let me remember them – while *you* remember people who were kind to you when you were a child.

There wasn't any reason for people to be kind to me. I wasn't attractive. I was a toothy yellow-faced little boy with a strong tendency to show off. Yet lots of people were – always. It is so hard to be kind to children without being frightening (as I am) – or unconsciously cruel. For I now recollect the shameful and cruel incident of Miss Tunstead. She was a governess down in Cornwall. Whatever she said was right. And she said Miss Fisher was coming to stay. All of us children must try to please Miss Fisher. Miss Fisher was very nice indeed. Well, I went hell for leather to please Miss Fisher. I had something to say all the time. 'Did Miss Fisher like me?' I asked after she had gone. 'Shall I tell you what Miss Fisher said, John? – *pause* – she said she thought you were rather a common little boy.'

Why did I mind? Heaven knows. But I still do and I bet you would too. Silly Miss Tunstead, that wasn't the way to make me improve my manners! The enjoyable things I took for granted – it's the first signs that people aren't perfect that stick in my memory. They come as such a shock.

I knew I wasn't perfect myself. But I had always assumed that everyone else was and there was something wrong with me – I mean that strong desire to smash the faces of china dolls, locking a little girl into the lavatory and waiting outside until she cried – things of that sort, I thought were peculiar to me. Being an only child I didn't compare notes. I preferred my own company to that of other children always. I preferred electric trains and maps of the underground railways to people any day. I believed inanimate objects could feel and think. (I say, we *are* on the Third Programme aren't we, not on the Home Service? – for aren't I getting a bit introspective? Anyway, don't switch off now, I don't like being interrupted when I'm talking.) I felt very sorry for horse chestnuts if they were left on the road. I picked them up and took them home. A wooden train I had gave me a lot of trouble. It was badly smashed, but I thought it would be offended if I threw it away. I kissed it good night every night so that it should not be offended. If you are a psychoanalyst listening you can probably explain all this. But I've since discovered that most young children are animists so it's not so unusual after all.

Growing out of this private world of trains, maps, flags of all nations, poems and church bells was painful. I recollect Jack Drayton, a dissenting minister's son. He asked me to tea. He was very nice to me. He showed off at tea and made me laugh. Then he grew thick with Willie Dunlop, a fat little boy who even when he was seven looked like the beefy business man he probably now is. Together they waited for me after school one afternoon. 'You come down Fitzroy Avenue,' they said. I did. But they seemed a bit strange. 'Stand here,' said Drayton and stood me against a wall. 'You're not to speak to us, see?' 'Yes.' 'Promise.' 'Yes.' 'Punch him, Willie.' Willie punched. It winded me a bit. I started to blub. They ran away. I had no idea why they had suddenly turned nasty. I don't know to this day. Perhaps one of their parents had said 'You're not to know that horrid little Betjeman boy'. That happened going home from a kindergarten – Byron House, Highgate. It was an enlightened, happy place. Jack and Willie were its only blots.

Then I went on to another day school, this detestable couple had got there first. The 1914 war had just broken out. I was eight. One of the most hellish things then was having a foreign name. Though any educated person knows that a name with 'etje' must be Dutch or Flemish, all foreign names were German in those days. So I was greeted by Jack Drayton and Willie Dunlop, and some others they had gathered round, with 'Betjeman's a German spy! Betjeman's a German spy!' They shouted and danced round me in rings. Oh, would to God I were called Smith or Brown! I blubbed until the bell rang for school.

Merciful school bell. The dullest lessons were preferable to the company of the boys in the breaks. 'Booting' was the great thing at that school. Two boys held you and another took a running kick at your bottom to see how far he could boot you down an asphalt slope.

The school was so bad that when a boy with a withered arm was admitted, the headmaster had to come round and tell us not to laugh at him for it. All boys are self-righteous prigs, so of course we didn't – once we were told. And the headmaster of this London day school terrified us. He used to stand us round in a ring in class and ask us questions. When we couldn't answer he shook us till we cried. One good thing he did was to stop the throwing of steel-pointed darts dipped in ink. One stuck in my head and raised a lump.

Worst of all was returning from that day school in the afternoon. I used to be set on by another, even nastier, pair than Drayton and Dunlop. 'Come with us down Swain's Lane,' they used to say. It was a mile out of my way. 'We won't do anything to you – honestly we won't.' 'Cross my heart.' 'Honestly.' 'Oh why d'you want me then?' 'We like you. We want you to come with us.' Always the same thing happened. There was a hole in the fence of either Waterlow Park or Highgate Cemetery in a deserted part of that lane – it was unmetalled and tree-hung then – they dragged me through it, took off most of my clothes and threw me into a holly bush. I can't think why I went with them. I think it was a deep-seated terror of having to fight if I didn't go with them.

I am eternally grateful to my parents for taking me away from the place to Hum Lynam and his preparatory school at Oxford where I found refuge. But I learned a lot at that tough London boys' school. I learned how to get round people, how to lie, how to show off just enough to attract attention but not so much as to attract unwelcome attention, how to bribe bullies with sweets (four ounces a penny in those days) – and I learned my first lessons in mistrusting my fellow beings.

People tell me schools are happier places now and boys are much kinder to one another. I used to hear old people talking like that too. I knew it wasn't true then. I don't believe it now. Has sin suddenly stopped then, and is no one ever unkind to anyone else? Has evil been charmed or psychoanalysed out of all children? I don't believe it. Childhood days! They aren't all sunny smiles on the municipal swing as shown in the education officer's brochure. There's the dark corner in the locker room, the yard at the back of the coal shed – they're still there too. If bullying doesn't take one form, it'll take another. You can't stamp it out in a generation.

BBC broadcast

Pleasures and Palaces

If there is one word which can safely be applied to almost all the constructions for entertainment it is the adjective *impermanent*. Fire consumes and fashion changes; new and more hideous structures arise on the sites of older and less hideous, as we continue to slide into deeper depths of barbarism. One day, no doubt, something more blatant than the tower of the Odeon Cinema in Leicester Square will challenge comparison with the steeple of St Martin-in-the-Fields. For the present we must gaze at the pseudo-functional monument of the 'serious thirties', watching it grow more and more dated every week, while the steeple of St Martin's glows in its white Portland stone perfection, a dateless memorial of more settled days.

The architecture of entertainment, of fairs, exhibitions, concert halls and theatres may be considered alongside church building. Like churches, places of entertainment are where people go for short spells only – that is to say all except the cleaners and permanent staff who may be compared to the nuns and priests of churches and very heartily they may laugh at the comparison. But the difference is this. Churches are built to last, places of entertainment are not.

Nothing is more empty than a deserted fairground. A walk through the White City with no one about, the baroque sculpture collapsing, the plaster façades damp-stained, the halls echoing and dusty, the railway lines, for special trains which carried long-dead merrymakers, rusty and grass-grown, is macabre even in broad daylight, and empty race-courses seem emptier than that. But an empty church is full, especially one in which the Consecrated Host is reserved in tabernacle or cupboard in the wall, with a light before it. Such a building may be alarming. One may feel oneself elbowed out by angels, but the emptiness is awe-inspiring, not desolate.

For the truth is that in England and Scotland and Wales fairs and entertainments are the cast-offs of the church. Their ancestors were hurled out of churches when the religious plays acted in naves were considered too secular. They waltzed away into the churchyard and then into a field near the church. And on the date of the patronal feast of the church, in many an English village today, a fair is held in a neighbouring field. When I look at the roundabouts and swings and hoop-la canopies gaily coloured in King's Lynn in the same style as barges are coloured at Braunston and as some old-fashioned waggons are still painted, when I see these traditional colours of red and blue and gold and green twisting round the flashing mirrors which hide the steam organ, when I catch sight of flares or electric bulbs reflected in barley-sugar rods of polished brass, I think how near the church these really are. I remember they must be derived from the trappings of images carried with a mixture of reverence and guffaws, centuries ago in English sunlight. And I wish that this people's art would come back to churches – a little more vulgarity of painted wood, a little less of the church furnisher and the art expert and a little more of the fairground. For this colour decoration of old-fashioned fairs is the oldest and most permanent feature of the architecture of entertainment.

English visitors are often shocked by the garishness of patronal feasts and processions in the towns and villages of Italy and Spain. There fair and church, entertainment and worship, are undivided. We are shocked because we have still such a Puritan sense of sin about pleasure, that we drive it out into the open fields of the world. From these outcast fairs, from strolling players and booths and competitions grew up the entertainment business whose structures are the subject of this article.

Churches are built on reality, in the mystical sense of that word. Fairs, exhibitions, theatres and cinemas are built for day-dreams of personal wish-fulfilment, which is a phrase for pride. No wonder then that, unlike churches, impermanence pervades them.

Architecturally, the most impermanent, the most quickly dated of entertainment buildings are exhibitions and cinemas. The first great exhibition of 1851 was undoubtedly beautiful within its limits. I have a peep-show perspective of it. Under a bright light the eye looks down long glass avenues whose cast-iron columns are painted with bright reds and blues under the direction of Mr Owen Jones (the same man who later designed the pleasant colours of Paddington Station roof which have recently been changed for the worse). The eye is stayed by crystal fountains, statues and hangings, flags of all nations, the great elm trees of the Park which the palace enclosed, statuary, ormolu lamp standards and hundreds of ladies walking about in coloured crinolines. All seem bathed in old sunlight. One does really, in this Victorian perspective, recapture the idea current at the time that everything was getting better and better and that this exhibition of the flowers of Industrial Art was the beginning of a material millennium of peace on earth and goodwill towards men. But Ruskin, who saw through most things, was suspicious: 'We used to have a fair in our neighbourhood – and a very fine one we thought it,' he writes in *The Ethics of the Dust*. 'You never saw such a one; but if you look at the engraving of Turner's "St Catherine's Hill" you will see what it was like. There were curious booths, carried on poles; and peep-shows; and music, with plenty of drums and cymbals; and much barley sugar and ginger-bread and the like; and in the alleys of this fair the London populace would enjoy themselves, after their fashion, very thoroughly. Well, the little Pthah set to work on it one day; he made the wooden poles into iron ones, and put them across, like his own crooked legs, so that you always fall over them if you don't look where you are going; and he turned all the canvas into panes of glass, and put it up on his iron cross-poles; and made all the little booths into one great booth; – and people said it was very fine, and a new style of architecture, and Mr Dickens said nothing was ever like it in Fairyland, which was very true.' And he then proceeds to pour scorn on the exhibits. The Crystal Palace was indeed a new style of architecture. It was the first prefab, brought in numbered pieces in carts from the factories and erected swiftly in a public park. There is something ironic in the way this impermanent architecture, so well suited to an exhibition of lifeless industrial products, should have been resurrected in this century to make buildings which of all should be most permanent – homes for families.

The impermanent, utilitarian style of the Crystal Palace was, despite Ruskin's strictures, just the thing if industrial exhibitions were to continue. Yet later exhibitions – the Alexandra Palace, Earl's Court, the White City, Wembley, to cite London alone – seem to have been inspired by an over-confidence in material success. They are perma-nent buildings without that flimsy semi-rurality which must have been the charm of pleasure gardens like Vauxhall, Cremorne and Rosher-ville which preceded them. Not that I would condemn them. All lovers of the useless – and they must be increasing in Britain hourly with each 'utility' object that comes on the market – could hardly have failed to delight in the Alexandra Palace before the war. What a pleasure it was to tread acres of echoing boards past disused slot machines in search of the roller-skating rink where the huge steam-organ would be playing to a few swirling couples; what a pleasure to open a wrong door, as I once did, to find Gracie Fields with a full chorus behind her, singing to an empty theatre. Gas, brickwork, silent, dark towers, wet and windy amusement parks, bandstands where no silver band has played for twenty years, all these are associated with deserted exhibitions. What terrible crimes, hinted at by Denton Welch or invented by Graham Greene, may not be perpetrated in the dark, deserted refreshment rooms or cloakrooms where water drips everlastingly into stained, cracked and no longer hygienic porcelain. That is part of the romance of decay.

As soon as exhibitions become permanent buildings like those I have mentioned, they quickly look out of date. Their appeal is in being in the very latest style when they are erected. Decoration, to convey the latest style, even if it is a coating of chromium pseudo-simplicity as at the Glasgow Exhibition of the nineteen-thirties, must predominate. Hence the sad wilderness of the White City, hence that mysterious area of inner Metroland around the Wembley Stadium where, for all I know, those concrete temples of Empire may still be standing among thin poplars and rusty railway lines.

Cinemas too have their origin in fairs. They were, in living memory, booths where people paid a few pence to see the phenomenon of moving photographs. The exaggerated language of the huckster ('the most daring, stupendous, thrilling spectacle ever staged in the history of the Universe') applies as much to the architecture of the cinema as it does to the language of the play-bills, trailers and advertisements of films in the daily prints. However much the film, so far as producers and directors are concerned, may progress towards an art, the exhibiting side is still in the hands of those who have the mentality of the old fairs. There is hardly a cinema in Britain, except for a high-brow exception like the Curzon, which is not architecturally on its outside a showy attempt to be up to date. The interiors, whether designed to look like the Garden of Allah, a Moorish mosque, a Spanish palace, Stockholm Town Hall or Imperial Rome, are designed as an exotic daydream. That daydream looks still more pitiful in daylight when the place is being swept of old cigarette ends and cartons, and the manager has not yet assumed his boiled shirt. The earliest cinemas to be erected as permanent buildings may still be seen in some surburban and provincial high roads, the words *ELECTRIC PALACE* done in plaster among baroque twirls reminiscent of the White City, and a little pay-box in mahogany protruding out below the colossal entrance arch. They are survivals of the days when the cinema needed to attract people to go in. There is no need for a flashy entrance now, for the cinemas are the chapels of most of our people who feel it a sin not to attend each change of programme. The chief problem is to hold their increasingly sophisticated attention once they are inside. Slap-up-to-date decoration may help to hold it. There seems to be more sense in the comparatively modest façades of the Granada cinemas whose wildly fantastic interior decoration may, possibly, be changed as different styles come in to suit another popular mood.

Music halls come half-way between the cinema and the theatre. Their origin is older and more homely and permanent than the first. They started as entertainments in public houses and they ended as theatres with the single difference that the bar opened straight into the auditorium as at dear old Collins's on Islington Green.

Theatres themselves are an older and more respectable form of architecture, Renaissance in origin – it would be absurd to connect them with the theatres of ancient Greece and Rome since, in this country at any rate, theatres did not exist until after the Reformation. Nor do many of the older ones survive. The round and open wooden theatres of Shakespeare's time, Wren's Drury Lane, the magic effects created by de Loutherbourg with real waterfalls at Sadler's Wells, not all the water in the New River has saved. They were destroyed by fire or fashion. The most complete survival is the Theatre Royal at Bristol and even that is mostly 1800 in date. Mr John Summerson, that most learned and caustically entertaining of architectural writers, says, 'The theatres of this country have never been much studied as architecture, though many books have been written on their owners, lessees and managers and the men and women whom their audiences have applauded.' And this is surprising, for when great dramatists were alive, and actors like Garrick were known to all the world of intellect, the best architects were proud to design theatres. James Wyatt and Henry Holland both built Drury Lane theatres, Nash designed the Haymarket, Smirke did Covent Garden and Foulston designed Plymouth's Theatre Royal. All these buildings, except Covent Garden, have been destroyed or altered out of recognition 'by successive generations of profit-eager lessees', once again to quote Mr Summerson.

Many fine Victorian theatres survive, of which the best is the Theatre Royal at Newcastle (Benjamin Green architect). It is almost a Georgian building and mercifully preserved from successive generations of fashion. In London the noblest surviving building – in my opinion more impressive within and without than Covent Garden – is the Royal English Opera House (1892; Thomas Collcutt architect) now called the Palace Theatre. This is on an irregularly shaped island site. Its main façade on Cambridge Circus is concave and the awkwardness of the corners of such a façade is overcome by graceful octagonal turrets. The dressing rooms are all along the Shaftesbury Avenue side of the building and serve as a buffer against the noise of that main thoroughfare, just as the entrance-hall stairs keep out the sound of Cambridge Circus. The building slopes inwards from the auditorium and is acoustically a great success, though it is built on opposite principles to those generally employed in theatre design. The three tiers of galleries are cantilevered out – a revolution at the time – so that no columns obstruct the view of the audience. The decoration throughout is scholarly Flemish renaissance. Nothing is skimped on the entrance hall and staircase, which are rich in those contrasting marbles Collcutt delighted to use and which he employed so effectively in the Holborn Restaurant. The Palace is the only theatre architecture in London – or for that matter in the provinces – of the last sixty years which climbs into the regions of a work of art. But many have a splendid richness, as those by Charles John Phipps (1835–97), notably His Majesty's which was completed in the year of his death. Phipps designed some elegant, exuberant provincial theatres, of which the Gaiety, Dublin, is a still unspoiled example.

Some of London's smaller theatres preserved a charming quality of an Edwardian or late Victorian drawing-room with their whitewood or mahogany, plush seats, watered silk panels and electroliers. In the cheaper parts of these houses Dickensian fishtail gaslights in wire cages lit long stone staircases and passages. But most little theatres, of which the Criterion and the Comedy were outstanding examples, have been stripped, pickled, shaved, sprayed, chromiumed or simplified according to DIA rules of good taste so as to have lost most of their original character. The St James's survives as a charming period piece.

It would have been fun to have traced the architecture of cast-iron bandstands, of piers and their pavilions, of tea-rooms and restaurants and other phases of the architecture of entertainment.

Fire is, until the next war, better controlled than before. The enemy of old-fashioned theatres today is fashion. Fashion has about it that impermanence which suits the impermanent architecture of entertainment. But if ever a man wants to study a popular style exaggerated to its vulgarest, let him look at the decoration of the buildings of entertainment. Cherubs will have chubbier cheeks and bottoms, caryatids have more protuberant breasts, *art nouveau* water-lilies will be more attenuated, cubes and triangles outstrip the ugliest followers of the worst of the imitators of Picasso's cubist period; and if the word goes round, 'be functional', wall spaces will be plainer, chromium shinier, off-white be more off-white in or upon the theatres, cinemas, music halls, exhibition buildings, bandstands, piers and restaurants of the Kingdom. Only the fairs survive.

From *Diversion: Twenty-two Authors on the Lively Arts*

South Kentish Town

This is a story about a very unimportant station on the Underground railway in London. It was devastatingly unimportant. I remember it quite well. It was called 'South Kentish Town'* and its entrance was on the Kentish Town Road, a busy street full of shops. Omnibuses and tramcars passed the entrance every minute, but they never stopped. True, there was a notice saying 'STOP HERE IF REQUIRED' outside the station. But no one required, so nothing stopped.

Hardly anyone used the station at all. I should think about three people a day. Every other train on the Underground railway went through without stopping: 'Passing South Kentish Town!' Passengers used Camden Town Station to the south of it, and Kentish Town to the north of it, but South Kentish Town they regarded as an unnecessary interpolation, like a comma in the wrong place in a sentence, or an uncalled-for remark in the middle of an interesting story. When trains stopped at South Kentish Town the passengers were annoyed.

Poor South Kentish Town. But we need not be very sorry for it. It had its uses. It was a rest-home for tired ticket-collectors who were also liftmen: in those days there were no moving stairways as they had not been invented. 'George,' the Station Master at Leicester Square would say, 'you've been collecting a thousand tickets an hour here for the last six months. You can go and have a rest at South Kentish Town.' And gratefully George went.

Then progress came along, as, alas, it so often does: and progress, as you know, means doing away with anything restful and useless. There was an amalgamation of the Underground railways and progressive officials decided that South Kentish Town should be shut. So the lifts were wheeled out of their gates and taken away by road in lorries. The great black shafts were boarded over at the top; as was the winding spiral staircase up from the Underground station. This staircase had been built in case the lifts went wrong – all old Underground stations

* South Kentish Town Station opened on the Northern Line in 1907. It closed on 5 June 1924 as the result of a strike at Lots Road Power Station and never re-opened.

have them. The whole entrance part of the station was turned into shops. All you noticed as you rolled by in a tramcar down the Kentish Town Road was something that looked like an Underground station, but when you looked again it was two shops, a tobacconist's and a coal-merchant's. Down below they switched off the lights on the platforms and in the passages leading to the lifts, and then they left the station to itself. The only way you could know, if you were in an Underground train, that there had ever been a South Kentish Town Station, was that the train made a different noise as it rushed through the dark and empty platform. It went quieter with a sort of swoosh instead of a roar and if you looked out of the window you could see the lights of the carriages reflected in the white tiles of the station wall.

Well now comes the terrible story I have to tell. You must imagine for a moment Mr Basil Green. He was an income tax official who lived in N6 which was what he called that part of London where he and Mrs Green had a house. He worked in Whitehall from where he sent out letters asking for money (with threat of imprisonment if it was not paid). Some of this money he kept himself, but most of it he gave to politicians to spend on progress. Of course it was quite all right, Mr Green writing these threatening letters as people felt they ought to have them. That is democracy. Every weekday morning of his life Mr Green travelled from Kentish Town to the Strand reading the *News Chronicle*. Every weekday evening of his life he travelled back from the Strand to Kentish Town reading the *Evening Standard*. He always caught exactly the same train. He always wore exactly the same sort of black clothes and carried an umbrella. He did not smoke and only drank lime-juice or cocoa. He always sent out exactly the same letters to strangers, demanding money with threats. He had been very pleased when they shut South Kentish Town Station because it shortened his journey home by one stop. And the nice thing about Mr Basil Green was that he loved Mrs Green his wife and was always pleased to come back to her in their little house, where she had a nice hot meal ready for him.

Mr Basil Green was such a methodical man, always doing the same thing every day, that he did not have to look up from his newspaper on the Underground journey. A sort of clock inside his head told him when he had reached the Strand in the morning. The same clock told him he had reached Kentish Town in the evening.

Then one Friday night two extraordinary things happened. First there was a hitch on the line so that the train stopped in the tunnel exactly beside the deserted and empty platform of South Kentish

Town Station. Second, the man who worked the automatic doors of the Underground carriages pushed a button and opened them. I suppose he wanted to see what was wrong. Anyhow, Mr Green, his eyes intent on the *Evening Standard*, got up from his seat. The clock in his head said 'First stop after Camden Town, Kentish Town.' Still reading the *Evening Standard* he got up and stepped out of the open door on to what he thought was going to be Kentish Town platform, without looking about him. And before anyone could call Mr Green back, the man at the other end of the train who worked the automatic doors, shut them and the train moved on. Mr Green found himself standing on a totally dark platform, ALONE.

'My hat!' said Mr Green. 'Wrong station. No lights? Where am I? This must be *South* Kentish Town. Lordy! I must stop the next train. I'll be at least three minutes late!'

So there in the darkness he waited. Presently he heard the rumble of an oncoming train, so he put his newspaper into his pocket, straightened himself up and waved his umbrella up and down in front of the train.

The train whooshed past without taking any notice and disappeared into the tunnel towards Kentish Town with a diminishing roar. 'I know,' thought Mr Green, 'my umbrella's black so the driver could not see it. Next time I'll wave my *Evening Standard*. It's white and he'll see that.'

The next train came along. He waved the newspaper, but nothing happened. What was he to do? Six minutes late now. Mrs Green would be getting worried. So he decided to cross through the dark tunnel to the other platform. 'They may be less in a hurry over there', he thought. But he tried to stop two trains and still no one would take any notice of him. 'Quite half an hour late now! Oh dear, this is awful. I know – there must be a staircase out of this empty station. I wish I had a torch. I wish I smoked and had a box of matches. As it is I will have to feel my way.' So carefully he walked along until the light of a passing train showed him an opening off the platform.

In utter darkness he mounted some stairs and, feeling along the shiny tiled walls of the passage at the top of the short flight, came to the spiral staircase of the old emergency exit of South Kentish Town Station. Up and up and up he climbed; up and up and round and round for two hundred and ninety-four steps. Then he hit his head a terrific whack. He had bumped it against the floor of one of the shops, and through the boards he could hear the roar of traffic on the Kentish Town Road. Oh how he wished he were out of all this darkness and up in the friendly noisy street. But there seemed to be nobody in the shop above, which was natural as it was the coal-merchant's and there wasn't any coal. He banged at the floorboards with his umbrella with all his might, but he banged in vain, so there was nothing for it but to climb all the way down those two hundred and ninety-four steps again. And when he reached the bottom Mr Green heard the trains roaring through the dark station and he felt hopeless.

He decided next to explore the lift shafts. Soon he found them, and there at the top, as though from the bottom of a deep, deep well, was a tiny chink of light. It was shining through the floorboards of the tobacconist's shop. But how was he to reach it?

I don't know whether you know what the lift shafts of London's Underground railways are like. They are enormous – twice as big as this room where I am sitting and round instead of square. All the way round them are iron ledges jutting out about six inches from the iron walls and each ledge is about two feet above the next. A brave man could swing himself on to one of these and climb up hand over hand, if he were sensible enough not to look down and make himself giddy.

By now Mr Basil Green was desperate. He *must* get home to dear Mrs Green. That ray of light in the floorboards away up at the top of the shaft was his chance of attracting attention and getting home. So deliberately and calmly he laid down his evening paper and his umbrella at the entrance to the shaft and swung himself on to the bottom ledge. And slowly he began to climb. As he went higher and higher, the rumble of the trains passing through the station hundreds of feet below grew fainter. He thought he heard once again the friendly noise of traffic up in the Kentish Town Road. Yes, he *did* hear it, for the shop door was, presumably, open. He heard it distinctly and there was the light clear enough. He was nearly there, nearly at the top, but not quite. For just as he was about to knock the floorboard with his knuckles while he held desperately on to the iron ledge with his other hand there was a click and the light went out. Feet above his head trod away from him and a door banged. The noise of the traffic was deadened, and far, far away below him he caught the rumble, now loud and now disappearing, of the distant, heedless trains.

I will not pain you with a description of how Mr Green climbed very slowly down the lift shaft again. You will know how much harder it is to climb down anything than it is to climb up it. All I will tell you is that when he eventually arrived at the bottom, two hours later, he was wet with sweat and he had been sweating as much with fright as with exertion.

And when he did get to the bottom, Mr Green felt for his umbrella and his *Evening Standard* and crawled slowly to the station where he lay down on the dark empty platform. The trains rushed through to Kentish Town as he made a pillow for his head from the newspaper and placed his umbrella by his side. He cried a little with relief that he was at any rate still alive, but mostly with sorrow for thinking of how terribly worried Mrs Green would be. The meal would be cold. She would be thinking he was killed and ringing up the police. 'Oh Violette!' he sobbed, 'Violette!' He pronounced her name Veeohlet because it was a French name though Mrs Green was English. 'Oh Violette! Shall I ever see you again?'

It was now about half past ten at night and the trains were getting fewer and fewer and the empty station seemed emptier and darker so that he almost welcomed the oncoming rumble of those cruel trains which still rushed past. They were at any rate kinder than the dreadful silence in the station when they had gone away and he could imagine huge hairy spiders or reptiles in the dark passages by which he had so vainly tried to make his escape ...

BBC broadcast

City and Suburban (1)

A series of articles written for The Spectator

I have been looking through old photographs of London and also at precise watercolours of towns made at the end of the last century. I cannot help noticing posters advertising Pears Soap, Epps's Cocoa, Mellins Food, Lyceum Dramas and other old favourites stuck on to the sides of houses and on temporary wooden fences so that they are prominent and agreeable features in the pictures. Indeed, the old posters, with the lines of the brick walls behind them showing through and the slap-dash bill-posting on untidy fences, accorded well with the temporary nature of popular advertising. The point of posters remains the same, namely that their appeal, though it should be immediate, is also temporary. When we see them today along main roads and at the entrances to towns the permanent nature of their hoardings makes them ridiculous. These hoardings, by the way, no longer go by that time honoured name. They are called 'advertisement stations'. A 'station' is a thing shaped like a modernistic mass-produced fireplace, and this magnified two hundred times with the name of the advertising agents at the top. In front there is a pathetic little 'amenity,' with some floodlights set among the antirrhinums, and all this fuss is for telling us the qualities of a new soap or some new ingredients in our petrol. I look forward to the time when there is less pomposity about advertising and we go back to the gayer and more vulgar days of bill-posting. Posters on the sides of bombed buildings, pasted directly on to the brick, would look pleasanter than gaping fireplaces and peeling wallpaper.

*

The decision of the Paddington Borough Council to ignore the protests of the people it represents is nothing new in local politics. But its further decision to disregard the advice it sought from the Royal Fine Art Commission creates an interesting precedent. There is a part of Paddington known as 'Little Venice,' a place of classic stucco houses either side of the canal, overhung with trees and forming what has now become a famous colony of artists and writers in London. Paddington is not only notable for crime, slums and houses of ill-fame; it has in other parts of it, not least around 'Little Venice,' the most impressive late-Georgian and early-Victorian stucco squares, crescents and terraces in London.

Architecturally it is the London equivalent of Brighton, the best-lit borough in the country, where the Corporation has taken care to produce main-road lighting which in daytime is not an offence to the eye. Paddington, on the other hand, has defaced itself with triangular concrete gibbets from which hang lunch baskets shedding an odious coloured light and known as 'chastity' lights in the trade, because they make people look so unattractive. These are probably very useful in the Bayswater Road, but there is no need for such lights in 'Little Venice' which, even if it is to become a main road for traffic, is still not one of the places in Paddington where fatal road accidents occur. Concrete columns will be out of scale and out of texture with their surroundings – surroundings which another department of the Borough Council has taken the trouble to beautify by a well-planned public garden. The Royal Fine Art Commission advised against the columns with that hideous curve, so alien to all street skylines. What, one wonders, is the purpose of the Commission if its advice is sought and ignored?

*

How heartening it is to see protests against the destruction of the St James's and the Stoll Theatres. But of all the theatres in London, the one I like best, after Covent Garden, is the Palace, which was designed for D'Oyly Carte by T. E. Colcutt in 1891. Its gay and thoughtful terracotta exterior is defaced with signs and an ironwork marquee, but its elegant turrets still dominate Cambridge Circus and Shaftesbury Avenue. Inside it is most ingeniously planned and perfect for sound. Every detail in the Palace Theatre is of fine craftsmanship. It was copied by other architects, and variations on its theme may still be found in such places as the Wood Green Empire, the Hackney Empire, the Chiswick Empire, the Finsbury Park Empire and the Chelsea Palace. How long, one wonders, will these meritorious buildings be safe from the claw of the land-grabbing property trusts?

*

I have not seen it written down or published anywhere, but at least half a dozen people have told me that London University intends to pull down Colcutt's masterpiece, the Imperial Institute in South Kensington. If you are ever in that district, do go and look at it with an impartial eye. Forget that the Flemish Renaissance manner in which it was built (1887–93) is not at the moment fashionable, and just notice how its varied exterior moves as you walk past it, turrets and projections grouping themselves differently every few yards. Notice how it fulfils the London requirement of outline, and compare its tower with Bentley's too-thin campanile to Westminster Cathedral. Colcutt's Imperial Institute tower has always seemed to me, along with St Paul's and the Houses of Parliament, one of the three great additions to the London skyline.

*

I went into an enterprising London pet shop last week where they sell baby crocodiles. But this is not the season for buying crocodiles. They become available in April and May, as do snakes. So I asked instead for a nice big centipede about ten inches long, such as has so often bitten Strix. But the assistant had not got one. He said there was no demand.

*

I would not like to give the impression that I like things just because they are old. I think too much attention is devoted, in overcrowded Britain today, to the preservation of archaelogical sites, those mounds and those dreary foundations, which look like unfinished drainage schemes. Not half enough attention is paid to noble architecture, whatever its date. I can sympathise with the workmen on the site of the Temple of Mithras in the City, who are said to have been so annoyed at being held up by that discovery that they say that if they find anything old again it will go straight into the concrete mixer.

*

Now is the time when, stepping down the beach to bathe, your foot sticks in a soft black pebble of oil. You take if off with your hands and find brown grease all over your fingers. You wipe your fingers on your bathing dress and find brown streaks on your belly. You go to your hotel and leave brown blobs on the carpets. This is due to oil pollution, which kills thousands of sea birds cruelly and makes our shores unendurable. Tankers discharge millions of tons of oil sludge into the sea every year. In 1954 there was an international conference held in London in which forty-two nations took part. Twenty of these signed a convention to prohibit and control the discharge of oil into the sea. So far none of the nations has passed it into law. All we can do is to report cases of it to the local council and write to the newspapers until something is done.

*

One of the most glorious things about the railway strike has been the virtual silencing of station announcers. Those cultural accents which pronounce all names as they are spelt were gradually doing away with local pronunciations. Wilfred Scawen Blunt and Belloc went to much trouble to keep alive Horse-ham for Horsham, but they lost the battle when station or wireless announcers were invented. I dare say Bosham was never pronounced Bosom, and I dare say places on the Celtic fringe like Kirkoobry and Kinyaha will never be pronounced as they are spelt, but we have now time to remember English station names. The following lists from the main termini of London are submitted to Sir Brian Robertson:

Paddington	*Victoria*	*Euston*
Didcót	Margit	Daintry
Chipnem	Ramsgit	Cuventry
Tarnton	Brumley	
Weston-super-Marry	East Grinstid	
Froom		
St Ostle		
Larnston		
Wadebridge	*Liverpool Street*	*King's Cross*
Glorster	Rumford	Burlington
Cheltnem	Britlingsea or	
Ciren	Brittlesea	
Foy		
Redruth		

Of course, some of these may be wrong. If I have to be a station announcer at Waterloo after the Revolution, I shall never be sure whether it's Bornmuth or Boornemouth, and I dare say nobody now, outside Beverley, knows where Burlington is. But I foresee the time when we talk about Har-wich and Nor-wich and Reeding.

Augustus Welby Pugin

Pugin was one of the most entertaining men of the last century. And after his death the doctors said that in the forty years of his life he had done enough work to last a man a century.

Pugin was an architect and I am going to start with the least interesting thing about him – his buildings, and these were nearly all churches and convents. In the Midlands and the West I suppose these are his chief buildings, see if you know any of them – St Chad's Roman Catholic Cathedral in Birmingham; St Mary's, Derby; St Barnabas Roman Catholic Cathedral, Nottingham; St Osmund's Roman Catholic Church at Salisbury; St Mary's Grange – a Gothic house he built for himself – at Salisbury; the Church of England parish church of Tubney near Abingdon in Berkshire; St Augustine's, Kenilworth. (His biggest buildings that I have seen are Scarisbrook, Lancashire; Alton Towers, Staffordshire; the Roman Catholic Cathedral of St George's, Southwark, London, now bombed out of recognition; the students' buildings at Maynooth, the famous College for training priests in Ireland; and the Cathedral at Enniscorthy, Ireland. The two buildings Pugin himself liked best of all he built were St Giles', Cheadle, and the church he built for himself with his own house beside it, St Augustine's Roman Catholic Church, a flint and stone structure on the West cliff at Ramsgate.

Now I don't think it matters very much to your liking of this great and remarkable man, if you have never seen his buildings. All the same, if you do go to Cheadle or Ramsgate, have a look in at his churches there. Whenever I am in Birmingham and have a little time to spare, negotiating that awful and inconvenient change of stations from Birmingham New Street to Birmingham Snow Hill, I leave my luggage at Snow Hill and step across the few yards from the station to see Pugin's Cathedral. It is of red brick with twin spires and it stands on a hilly site. It is not much to look at outside. But inside, it fairly takes the breath – it soars to the heavens, its long thin pillars are like being in a mighty forest. The roof is a bit flimsy-looking – all Pugin's buildings are a bit flimsy-looking as though he couldn't get away from the stage scenery in which he was so interested as a youth, – but the flimsiness is redeemed by the brilliant colours. The stained glass glows like jewels, the great rood screen in front of the altar adds mystery to what would otherwise be a rather obvious place, the altars blaze with gilding and colour. I think Pugin liked the place very much, for he buried his second wife there. He buried his first wife in Christ Church Priory, Hampshire, but that was in the days before he became a Roman Catholic. His third wife survived him and indeed she had him buried in his own loved church of St Augustine, Ramsgate.

There is one more building ascribed to Pugin and it's one of the loveliest buildings in England and we all know it – the Houses of Parliament, London. I have said 'ascribed' to Pugin, because I really don't think it is by Pugin at all. I am quite sure it is by the architect who was knighted for designing it, the great Sir Charles Barry. (There may be several people listening to this who remember the old King Edward School in Birmingham. Well, that was designed by Barry and it always seemed to me to be a foretaste of the Houses of Parliament he designed several years later.) People try to make out that Barry, who designed many fine classical style buildings which exceed in beauty many of the works of Wren, couldn't design a medieval-style building and had to call in Pugin to help him. But that is untrue. What is quite true is that Pugin helped over the details. (He designed the shiny tiles made by Minton, the stained glass enamelwork made by the Birmingham firm of Hardman, the furniture and inkstands and locks and metalwork.) Pugin himself, always a truthful man, never claimed to have designed the Houses of Parliament. (He liked Barry as a man and he admired his architecture. When Barry won the competition Pugin said: 'Barry's grand plan was immeasurably superior to any that could at that time have been designed – (this was in 1836) – and had it been otherwise, the commissioners (they were the people who set the competition) would have killed me in a twelvemonth. No sir, Barry is the right man in the right place, what more could we wish?' And recently, evidence has come to light to show that Barry did undoubtedly design almost all the Houses of Parliament except for some detailed decorative work by Pugin.)

And now we come to the most important things – Pugin as a man and a writer and caricaturist. He was the son of a French émigré who had married a Miss Welby, known as the 'Belle' of Islington. His father was an architectural artist. He did the coloured plates of those beautiful books called the 'Microcosm of London' and Rowlandson the caricaturist put in the human figures. Pugin's mother was a forbidding woman. She went to bed at nine and rose at four in the morning and rang the bell to rouse the maids. Then she rang a bell to rouse Pugin Senior's pupils, including young Pugin himself, out of bed. They were made to work before breakfast until eight-thirty when they came in and bowed to Mrs Pugin.

They ate in silence, and bowed and went out to work until eight at night, with short intervals for meals. The only leisure allowed was between eight and ten in the evening. On Sundays Mrs Pugin took her son to hear long sermons by the celebrated Edward Irving. Old Pugin avoided going to chapel with them. He was a dear old man, very French and very humorous.

As soon as he was old enough young Pugin seems to have shaken himself free from his mother's influence. He became very downright and unconventional. Beside his passion for the theatre (which his mother hated), he had a passion for the sea. This lasted all his life. He often made his drawings in an open boat. He would even etch on a copper plate in a choppy sea. (The motion of the boat never disturbed him.) He founded a home for destitute sailors at Ramsgate. He dressed as a sailor himself. His biographer Benjamin Ferrey tells us 'He was in the habit of wearing a sailor's jacket, loose pilot trousers, jack-boots and a wide-a-wake hat. In such a costume, landing on one occasion from the Calais boat, he entered, as was his custom, a first class railway carriage and was accosted with a "Halloa, my man, you have mistaken, I think, your carriage." "By Jove" was his reply, "I think you are right; I thought I was in the company of gentlemen." This cutting repartee at once called forth an apology. (The remainder of the journey was most agreeably passed in examining his portfolio filled with sketches just taken in Normandy.)' He was indeed a man who stood on his dignity and was no respecter of persons. Once Lord Radnor called on him at Salisbury when Pugin was standing in his partially built house. Lord Radnor didn't take off his hat as the house was only half-finished, and started to talk at once. Pugin looked at him in astonishment. Then he rang the bell and ordered his hat. Placing it on his head, he said 'Now, my lord, I am ready.' He didn't mind who he offended. His rebukes were sharp. Once a Roman Catholic Bishop sent asking for designs for a new church of the following description. 'It was to be "*very* large" – the neighbourhood being *very* populous; it must be *very* handsome, – a fine new church had been built close by; it must be *very* cheap, – they were very poor, in fact had only £– ; when could they expect the design?' Pugin wrote in reply 'My dear Lord – Say *thirty shillings* more, and have a tower and a spire at once.'

So you see the sort of man Pugin was – unconventional, downright, and humorous, not the sort of person who would do well for himself in a Government Department of the Slave State. He was an intense individualist. The one thing he loved more than the sea was architecture. From his earliest years he had been taught to draw it. The only style he liked was the ancient Gothic. Pointed arches, old churches, ruined abbeys and ruined castles, ancient cathedrals and manor houses with mullioned windows. He hated anything new and anything he considered a sham. He hated workhouses and contrasted them with the almshouses attached to old abbeys for aged pilgrims; he hated Euston Station because it had a Greek Portico, he said it ought to be Gothic and pointed. He loathed St Paul's Cathedral because the flying buttresses which support its roofs are concealed from the outside – he thought this a pagan sham; he hated terrace houses in stucco or villas in stucco with little pointed windows – those graceful, cheerful little places we see in towns like Sidmouth, Cheltenham, Bath, Clifton and Brighton and admire because they are 'Regency' – he liked things to be built of local materials and to be absolutely honest.

His two great principles of Pointed or 'Christian architecture' – as he called Gothic – were these – 'First that there should be no features about a building which are not necessary for convenience, construction or propriety; second, that all ornament should consist of enrichment of the essential construction of the building.' And how forcibly and funnily he expressed himself. I must read you a bit of Pugin writing about the sham castles rich people used to build for themselves in parks and on hills and by the sea about one hundred and twenty years ago. 'What absurdities, what anomalies, what utter contradictions do not the builders of modern castles perpetrate! How many portcullises which will not lower down, a drawbridge which will not draw up! – how many loopholes in turrets so small that the most diminutive sweep could not ascend them! – On one side of the house machicolated parapets, embrasures, bastions, and all the show of strong defence, and round the corner of the building a conservatory leading to the principal rooms, through which a whole company of horsemen might penetrate at one smash into the very heart of the mansion! for who would hammer against nailed portals, when he could kick his way through the greenhouse?'

In his two most famous books, *True Principles* and *Contrasts*, both published at his own expense in 1841, he illustrated his arguments with extremely funny caricatures. Mr Goodhart-Rendell has described *Contrasts* as the most entertaining book on architecture ever written! I am sure he is right. It is angry, prejudiced, eloquent and uproariously funny. Very unfair and very funny they are. But it is impossible to describe them to you. He chose the worst classical-style buildings in the manner of ancient Greeks and Romans and stuck little chimney pots on them and fat lazy ruffians lurking about in the foreground and he pasted advertisements on them; then with infinite care and with beautiful shading he showed a contrasting building of his beloved Middle Ages, and images of knights in armour walking about. He loved good craftsmanship so much that he would not tolerate anything which was not made by hand.

Had he been just a funny man or just a dull pedant who liked dates and put F.S.A. after his name Pugin would not have been the great man he is. And, don't forget that there were architectural caricaturists as funny as Pugin before him.

Pugin could not separate buildings from their use and from the people who lived in them. He loved the Middle Ages. He loved people. He lived at a time when narrow brick slums were going up beside gloomy mills where there was child slavery, before the Factory Acts were passed. He saw pale, dulled mechanics dazed by the monotony of their work, thinking only of wages and escape to ease from the grindstone. He saw belching smoke and steam trains and the growing wealth of the Midlands, the ostentation of the new rich, the worldliness of manufacturers, the heartlessness of employers, the enforced depravity of the employed. And then, away from the towns, in still, quiet country where he sketched among grassy lanes the old churches of unpolluted villages, he saw the relics of the Middle Ages. He thought about his soul and how everything was under God and how machines were the devil because they killed the joy of craftsmanship. So he idealised the Middle Ages. He did not copy them. He lived in this dream world, with the church in charge of everything and all craftsmanship done by hand on looms, in smithies, in glass stainers, in carpenters' shops to the glory of God. He thought the Middle Ages were perfect and he wanted England to go back to his dream of what they were like.

He thought the Church of Rome was the True Church of those old days and in 1834 he joined, partly out of a desire to save his soul, and partly out of disgust at modern industrialism and the laziness of many of Church of England clergy in these days. At Ramsgate he lived a medieval life. His wife had to do his hair in a Gothic style, he ate off Gothic plates of his own design. He went to his chapel at six in the morning and said his prayers. He then worked in his library until seven-thirty and then the bell tolled for morning prayers which he said dressed in cassock and surplice. He heard mass at eight. He then worked till one when he dined very simply, without wine or beer, for quarter of an hour. Then he looked at his buildings and saw his one assistant – his son-in-law. He worked all the afternoon and then wrote letters until nine in the evening. He designed buildings till ten when he went to his chapel to say compline. Then he read theology till he went to sleep, – it was a sort of Roman Catholic version of his Protestant youth.

A man's religion colours his work. I only wish his buildings were as wonderful as his writings and drawings and as his own lovable downright self. But they aren't. His colour and his detail are beautiful. But he lacks that essential of all great architecture, a sense of proportion. Much of his work is a little unreal and dreamlike, not very solid, as though he was trying to bring an illuminated manuscript to life. They are an escape rather than a challenge.

Pugin was a dreamer. He was shocked, as all sensitive artists were, by modern barbarism. He built himself a never-never-land of the past, all colour and kindness and honest craftsmanship. He forgot the smells, disease, cruelty and injustices of the Middle Ages. He could only see modern evils. As Sir Kenneth Clark in his brilliant chapter on Pugin in *The Gothic Revival* realised, he was really a prototype of William Morris. Both invented false Middle Ages of perfection.

Pugin clung to his church, and I fear the Roman Catholic Church of those days did not think so well of Pugin as did the Church of England to which in his later years he became increasingly friendly. Morris clung to aesthetic socialism. Both dreamed of an unreal Middle Ages. Both dearly loved what is beautifully made and honestly done. Both loved their fellow men. Both were intolerant of shams. Both were energetic and singleminded artists of great talent. Both had their enemies. Ruskin disliked Pugin. Many more than Ruskin have disliked Morris. The worst legacy that Pugin has left us is much dull copying done in the name of 'restoration' and 'Gothic architecture' by his followers who believed the palpably untrue maxim that only Gothic is Christian architecture. And Morris has left us a legacy of dull economists. I don't know which is worse. The greatness of the two men survives in their love of the beautiful. That, the vigour of Pugin's personality implants on everyone who sees his drawings or reads his books or the books written about him. I have only given you the briefest sketch in this talk, of a man who set England reverberating a century ago with the church bells of his fancy. But if you can find any of his books or buildings, imbibe them and then go out into the world again, prejudiced maybe, but certainly invigorated and inspired by a man who loved God and his creatures.

BBC broadcast

The Festival Buildings

Sun shone on the South Bank site. Over their teas and their strip cartoons and sports pages the busy workers were resting in threes and fours, as they had been before when I visited the site with the illustrator of these pages. As before, some of their mates were hard at it. All honour to these mates. They have built the gayest and best of exhibitions. Modern artists and sculptors have been given a chance, so have modern architects. Hugh Casson has collected a team of talent and guided it with genius. The South Bank is treated with imagination and happiness: for the first time Londoners will realise the river in their midst. For the first time for a long time they will see things done for the fun of the thing. The Festival lacks the ponderousness of Wembley, the elaboration of White City, and it is a bigger affair altogether than Earl's Court. Though the site is small and thundered through by the Southern electric it would take days to see all the exhibits.

These were the highlights of what I saw.

The Regatta Restaurant by Messrs Black & Gibson. It seems built of crystal and planks. It surveys the lovely outline of the Royal Palace of Westminster, Shaw's Scotland Yard and the domes and turrets of Colonel Edis' Whitehall Court across the sliding water. The details of the restaurant are thoughtful and simple, not fussily modern as they are in the Thames-Side Cafeteria. I like the door handles which are brass hands with fingers open to clutch on the pull side. On the push side is the brass back of a hand.

The seaside section with its model town by Reginald Brill and nets and buckets and kiosks, arranged round it by the Simpson's window-dresser.

Eric Brown's seaside promenade with masts.

The 1851 Centenary Pavilion designed by Hugh Casson. It is made of cast iron from moulds still in stock at Macfarlane's. It is far the prettiest building in the exhibitions.

The wall of coloured balls on the Waterloo side, through which the chimney pots of dead old London look like a backcloth in pantomime.

Illustrated by Peter Fleetwood-Hesketh

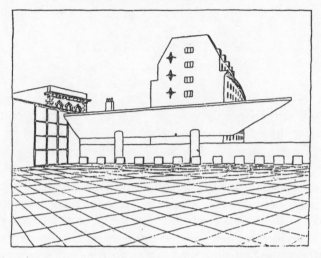

S. E. & C. R.

Acoustics

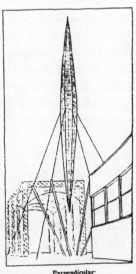

Perpendicular

The skylon, though it is best at night. In the day I am for ever wanting to pull it by its end on elastic and see if it shoots to the moon.

The landscape gardening by Mr G. Sheppard as seen from the Lion and Unicorn pavilion.

The roof of that pavilion and flight of doves from a wicker cage. Much of the other decoration there makes me think of Heath.

In the more solemn, permanent style of the thirties is Wells Coates' Telecinema.

The one certainly permanent feature of the exhibition, the Festival Hall, is forbidding outside. The outline of the roof is very ugly, the side elevations are decorated to look like the Tote. Because they had to be permanent the architects, Messrs Matthew & Martin, seem to have lost their nerve and missed the gaiety of the merry exhibitionists outside in the sun. But the interior of the Hall is amazing. Again, its decoration is rather self-consciously severe or modishly modernistic, but the scale, size and complete efficiency of the building make one realise that here one is standing in what must be the finest Concert Hall in the world. Sitting in the front row and looking through the *open* doors, I saw a Southern train pass outside not a hundred yards away, but I could hear no sound of it.

The Dome of Discovery by Ralph Tubbs is another partial success. Outside it looks well from across the river. Inside it is a disappointment and this is no fault of the architect, I am sure. The structure of the dome would have been unusual and impressive if left alone, but the numerous exhibits and decorations put it out of scale. I felt I might just as well have been in Olympia or any other large covered area. The interior is the most prominent example of the chief failing of the exhibition. Science seems to have obsessed the decorators. There are patterns in coloured tubes of nuclear whatever they are. There are bits of ships and engines and aeroplanes and patterns of them and patterns of plans and plans of patterns. In many parts of the exhibition I was not sure whether an objective science made it look like art or vice versa and that convinced me, that neither was either.

There are few really ugly objects so far as buildings are concerned. The most notable are the kiosks illustrated here and the hideous walls on the Homes and Gardens' pavilion, which are snail-pointed like a scraped Victorian church. If they are meant to illustrate methods of stonewalling they are warnings of how not to do it. All the walls are wrongly pointed and painfully insensitive.

I went to the Festival Buildings expecting to find gambolling functionalists trying to be funny. I returned over that endless Bailey bridge exhausted but enchanted.

Time and Tide

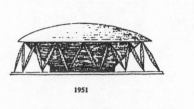

1951

Art

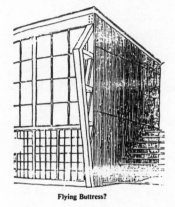

Flying Buttress?

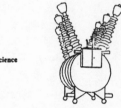

Science

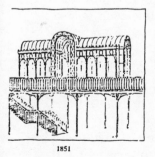

1851

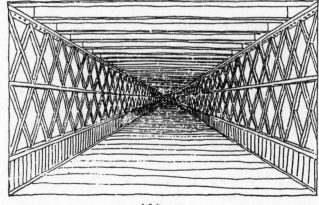

Infinity

Outline and Skyline

Outline is a most important part of British scenery. Those who walk or bicycle have the best opportunity of seeing it. Perhaps because most of us are bus or motor-borne and see half a thing through a rectangle of glass, we are beginning to forget the skyline.

Or perhaps because we so often see favourite views scrawled across by poles and wires, retched over by gigantic concrete lamp standards, and blocked by huge slices of packing-case building, we are deliberately blinding ourselves to the beauty of outline.

Consider how important outline is in the places where it survives. Our gentle hills were planted with trees in the eighteenth and the last century, subtly planted to make them beautiful from a variety of angles – Wittenham clumps in Berkshire, the 'forest fleece' of the Wrekin, Shropshire, Beechen Cliff in Bath, and the gentle undulations of Midland country parks planted with clumps and giving a sense of endlessness.

Consider the billowy globes of elm tree shapes, the feathered lanes of Essex willows, the homely elegance of church towers and spires rising out of cottages and orchards, the folly towers with which landowners adorned the distant heights of their demesnes. Remember Salisbury spire gathering the Downs around it, and the dome of the Radcliffe Camera at Oxford floating above the pinnacled colleges and brooding over them like a hen.

Into the gentlest, flattest country scenery, the Minister of Fuel and Power can introduce enormous power stations, three times as big as anything around, out of scale and out of texture with surroundings and higher than the little hills. The Minister of Supply can poison the downs at Harwell with ill-proportioned chimneys and the spreading acres of his human poultry farm. Neither pays any regard to aesthetic objections. As with the worst of Victorians, so with them, utility is the only consideration.

Outline is as important in our towns as it is in the country. The buildings in England which we remember best are those whose outline sticks in our mind: St Paul's Cathedral with the lead and white stone steeples round it and the twin towers of Cannon Street Station below;

St Pancras Station; the superb group of the towers and spires of the Houses of Parliament, which changes in richness and variety as we move around it, so that each time it might be another building.

Then think of the romantic outline of the Tower Bridge; the solid grace of the Cathedral high over Liverpool; Manchester Town Hall; Pearson's noble spires in Kilburn and Croydon, and at Truro, Cornwall, rising from the little houses; Oatley's tower of Bristol University; the tower of the Imperial Institute, South Kensington; Whitehall Court from St James's Park; Ely Cathedral and Boston Stump, soaring over their East Anglian levels and the low uneven roofs of their protecting towns.

Perhaps one of the finest outlines is the austere ancient Cathedral of Glasgow with the John Knox column standing on the hill above it against the grey sky, high over the clustering gravestones of the Necropolis. On this island, we think of scenery largely in terms of outlines.

There are rules about preserving ancient buildings, about density of population, about drains, roads and open space; but there are no rules for skyline, beyond some vague and often disregarded by-laws about the height of building. How often do we see mean little villas set high on country hills; transformers and china orchards connected with electricity standing in prominent isolation, ruining the look of a village almost as much as the poles and wires knitted round the cottages?

In London the greatest crime perpetrated on the skyline before the war was Faraday House, built for the Post Office in the City and ruining the western view of St Paul's; beside that, the late Victorian monster, Queen Anne's Mansions, is almost decent. At the present moment the gables and corner turrets of Charing Cross Hotel are being destroyed in favour of some flat pseudo-classic upper storey.

Walk in Berkeley Square, or around Regent Street, or where vast office blocks have gone up near Shaftesbury Avenue and Holborn Circus; see the various tall blocks of flats in St Pancras, Paddington and South London. Desperate attempts are made to enliven these new cliffs which turn our streets into chasms, and dwarf the irregular London skyline of chimney pots, towers, spires, Edwardian and Victorian turrets.

The attempts at gaiety usually take the form of swell entrance doors, or bright slabs of colour on an outside wall, long windows for staircases, or a few scattered bits of sculpture. The skyline remains flat and ugly, and the decorations just a cynical chuckle.

I am not here going to argue the pros and cons of building

horizontally or upwards, the charm of the spacious new housing estate at Lansbury built of local stock bricks and kept in proportion with its surroundings, as opposed to the ground-saving Karl Marx Hofs of the St Pancras Borough Council. It is most important to find accommodation for people. But we do not spend all day in our dormitories.

The sole remaining charm of many square miles of big cities may be found by looking up to the heavens: what is outlined against them may uplift or oppress us. Packing-case architecture oppresses. For all the ingenuity of its construction and the grandeur of its interior, the outline of the Royal Festival Hall is an insult to the London skyline. The late lamented Skylon was far preferable, though it was useless and gay.

In considering skyline, our architects and their employers should not think solely in terms of utility. It is sentimental and old-fashioned to assume that because a thing is useful it is beautiful. If that were true, what is the purpose of Salisbury Spire, St Paul's Dome, or the Grey Column in Newcastle?

I have been thinking about why skyline is so important in this country, and how much it differs from skylines in sunnier lands. Packing-case architecture looks well when there are high mountains behind it. Large slabs of tiled wall look gay enough in the bright climates where the sun is high and light and shadow are sharply contrasted.

But here we live for three-quarters of the year in a mist or in greyish light. The beauty of our building depends on texture rather than colour, on the weathering of materials, on the breaking of flat surfaces with deep mouldings, the piercing of high features with carving and holes for shadows and for the light to show through. These lines from a poem by John Davidson describe the character of town architecture:

> The Palace and the Abbey lost
>   Their character of masonry,
> Transformed to glittering shadows tossed
>   And buoyant on a magic sea.
>
> Ghastly and foul, as Hecate's ban
>   Pernicious are our fogs; but sweet
> And wonderful the mists that can
>   Imparadise a London street.
>
> The tissued dawn that gems encrust,
>   The violet wreaths of noon, the haze

> Of emerald and topaz dust
> That shrouds the evening distances . . .

Our buildings are seldom dominated by hills. They are hills in themselves and therefore their outline is prominent. They are given solidity by variations of plane and surface, and a building is still only when the observer stands still. All the best British architecture moves with the observer.

Packing-cases are not suited to our gentle lights and shades. Let the architects look at the finer Victorian and late Georgian warehouses of Liverpool, London and Hull, the card mills of the North, the graceful factory chimneys of a century ago, to see how to vary surfaces and to create shapes suited to our atmosphere.

Somewhere in an office there must be an architect of genius who will build – please God, before it is too late – a high building with a beautiful skyline, for this has not appeared since Thomas Collcutt raised his tower on the Imperial Institute in 1887 and Norman Shaw a year later designed the first block of New Scotland Yard.

The Daily Telegraph

The Literary World

'Meadowcroft'
Bee's Acre Way
Welwyn Garden City
Herts.

Dear Mr Betjeman, – As one who borrowed your last book of verses
from the Hertfordshire County Library, let me say that I admire your
honesty in referring to your rhymed writing as 'verses' and I wish that
other so-called poets had your modesty. My own poems which I
enclose are the fruit of long study and have been commended by Janet
Peaslake and others whose names may be unknown to you. Incidentally I think some of the critics scarcely did you justice because they
did not realise that you always write with your tongue in your cheek
and judged you consequently by too high a standard. I send you my
poetry for your considered opinion for a double motive. First I think it
is the duty of the older generation to lend a helping hand to less
established but essentially creative writers. I also want your advice and
help in getting them published. I am nineteen and sitting for the
General Post Office examination. If I am successful in passing this I
shall have to choose between a career as a Civil Servant and being a
free-lance poet. An early reply will oblige as I sit for the exam next
week.

Incidentally if you ever care to address our poetry group here at any
time I should be pleased to try to scrape up an audience.

Yours sincerely,
T. Atkins

St Etheldreda's Sanctuary
Spiggots
Ditchling, Sussex

Dear Mr Betzamin, – What am I to do? The manuscript novel which I
am sending by railway to you – I'm afraid it's COD because one never
knows what freightage charges 'British Railways' (!) are going to

charge and it is too bulky for the ordinary post – has been turned down by seventeen publishers. I ask you to read it because I know a word from a man of your influence in the right quarter will work wonders. Ten of the publishers said that while they admired it they thought it was too long and I'm sure someone with your experience will know where, if anywhere, it can be 'cut,' to use a rather horrible technical expression. If I were not sure that there was merit in the book I would not be troubling you. I so much admire your writing and I know you will be able to persuade a publisher to consider it. You might even like to give a preview of it, as it were, in the *Daily Telegraph*. Of course I know historical novels are out of fashion just now. I look forward to your opinion of my version of *Friar Tuck*. He seemed to write himself for me! I should add that I am not one of you literary pundits – not even a professional writer but just a simple hardworking housewife.

Sincerely yours,
Etheldreda Mary
Barraclough

17 Pedants' Lane
Cambridge

Dear Dr Betjeman, – You may remember me because when you gave a lecture on Charles Rennie Mackintosh in Hartlepool seven years ago I had occasion to correct one of the dates which you mentioned. You said the house at Helensburgh was 1903 when it was not actually begun until the spring of 1904. I am now at Cambridge with a ten years' Research Fellowship to write a thesis for my Doctorate on 'The Development of Norman Revival into Early and Middle Pointed Revival in the South Midlands in 1854.' This somewhat formidable task involves me in extensive travel to study documents at first hand in diocesan registries and public and private libraries. Dr Pevbrich, my professor, has been as encouraging as his time permits and Dr Bosegarden at Oxford has also been helpful, while one of the doctors in charge of the Warburg Institute has placed a table there at my disposal. I cannot personally examine the buildings which I am studying as there is so much to do with looking up illustrations of them and verifying references. Thus I am forced to depend on laymen such as yourself for a certain amount of the work. Would you mind looking at the south wing of St Mary's Convalescent Home (Street

1854) in Wantage and telling me whether it has been added to or altered since the time when the engraving I am sending you was made? The engraving is coming under separate cover by registered post. Please send me a telegram to announce its safe arrival as it is the property of the Arthur W. Doppelganger Kunst-Lieber Research Foundation of Illinois whose rules require that it must always be sent by registered post. I will, of course, acknowledge your valuable assistance in the preface of my thesis when it is published.

Yours very truly,

Percy Minge

Punch

City and Suburban (2)
A series of articles written for The Spectator

The current (June) number of the *Architectural Review* is called 'Outrage,' and is the most damning illustrated indictment of concrete lamp standards, 'Keep Left' signs, municipal rockeries, chain-link fences, truncated trees, garish shop fronts, pretentious hoardings, wires, poles, pylons and ill-sited power stations, that has yet been published. I hope that it will go to every borough engineer and surveyor in this island, as well as to all Government departments which leave disused Nissen huts and blockhouses about and string the sky with wires. As its opening editorial says, 'This issue is less of a warning than a prophecy of doom; the prophecy that if what is called development is allowed to multiply at the present rate, then by the end of the century Great Britain will consist of isolated oases of preserved monuments in a desert of wire, concrete roads, cosy plots and bungalows.'

*

Heatwave Fashion Note
During the hot weather I have been wearing a straw boater and a bow-tie in London. In Bond Street the glances of the women and men were so contemptuous at this ageing Teddy Boy that I had to take off my hat and expose my bald head to the sun. But in the City old faces beamed with joy to see a straw boater again, and two strangers stopped me to ask where I had bought it. I can't tell you because that would be advertising, but the hat is cheap and cool.

*

I was walking down Newgate Street with a girl in the hot weather of last week. She remarked on how unattractive men were. Looking at their clothes, I realised she was right – retired tea-planters bursting out of linen suits; youths with rows of pens and pencils in their pockets, and badges and combs and tubular grey-flannel trousers; businessmen in dark suits minus the waistcoat, with the sweat showing through their shirts. But perhaps this prejudice is induced by contrast, for there is no doubt that hideous as the fronts of chain stores are, the cheap cotton dresses for women that come out of them are simply delightful. I cannot believe that English women have ever looked prettier than they have done in the summer weather of this year.

*

The public relations officers of the incompetent British Transport Commission are always very vocal when they can answer a question. I wonder if they will have any reply to these about canals? Why is the British Transport Commission removing paddle gear from the Kennet and Avon Canal and removing cranes and lowering weirs on the Macclesfield Canal in advance of abandonment? Has the Bill been passed in Parliament yet? Was a single visit of a few hours, including lunch at Marlborough, a sufficient basis for the Board of Survey to recommend the immediate abandonment of the Kennet and Avon Canal, which is a broad one, fourteen feet wide and eighty-six miles long? Did this Board of Survey, which was set up by the Commission, consist of three men, none of whom had any experience of smaller inland waterways? Did this Board of Survey recommend exactly the same programme for shutting down canals which the British Transport Commission had publicised before the Board was set up? Why was there not an independent inquiry?

*

The Air Ministry is proposing to erect a mast, 350 feet high, on the top of the Berkshire Downs at Sparsholt Firs, near the famous Uffington White Horse. The Berkshire County Council's Planning Committee has protested against this decision. It will be remembered that when the Post Office decided to put wireless masts on near-by White Horse Hill, the Postmaster-General of the Labour Government, which was in power at the time, personally visited the site and ordered the scheme to be abandoned. Is there any hope that the Minister for Air will have the same sense of reverence due to one of the most beautiful stretches of downland in England?

*

This is the saddest week of all on railway stations. It is the beginning of the school year. Sons stand embarrassed by their parents outside the school special train, and still more embarrassed by their younger brothers. Parents look suspiciously at other parents or are over-jolly.

'We don't care. Ha, ha! It'll soon be Christmas.' Tears are near eyes. Hearts are in boots. How soon will the names of Hillard and Botting, North and Hillard, Godfrey and Siddons, Abbot and Mansfield, and all those other pairs led by the single lone figure of Benjamin Hall Kennedy, become more familiar than those of home. Oh Eric, Eric, how glad I am I am not at school any more! I hold him a hyprocrite or a pathetic case of arrested development who ever says schooldays are the happiest of your life. And as for *Eric* and *St Winifred's*, those despised school stories by Dean Farrar, they have always seemed to me more like school than any of the more realistic novels of a later age. Their language may be mawkish, their characters over-painted, their situations absurd, but the impending sense of doom which hangs over all school life, boarding or day, is caught as it has never been caught since.

*

It must be an unenviable task to be the editor of *Waterways*, whose first number has just appeared under the aegis of the British Transport Commission. It is a shamefaced and sad little periodical designed to pep up the bewildered remaining employees on our canals. The cat is let out of the bag surreptitiously here and there. The Report of the Board of Survey, which has condemned 771 miles of canals to become stagnant ditches and nuisances, 'sets the pattern,' we are told, 'for our future development.' God forbid! Elsewhere, in a list of canals 'to be retained for the present,' we find Kennet and Avon (River Avon section). This is like closing Barking Creek but allowing the Thames to remain navigable between Barking and Southend. It is, of course, sheer casuistry. The editor, luckless man, says he 'will welcome photographs, etc., on any subject connected with British waterways.' I wonder whether he would publish a photograph of the rally at Bath last April, in which that splendid character, Ted Leather, MP took part, when they actually cut the lock-chain which the British Transport Commission had illegally put on the first lock-gate to make the Kennet and Avon Canal unnavigable. I wonder whether he would publish views of the Macclesfield Canal, which has been illegally stripped of much of its gear by the Commission. I wonder whether he would publish anything I wrote.

Oxford and Suburban

More damage has been done to Oxford within living memory than at any time in its long history. I have known Oxford since 1915 when I went as a boy to Lynam's. I knew it during my chequered career as an undergraduate and for the last twenty years it has been the nearest big shopping town for my wife and me. In 1915 one could picnic on the Cumnor Hills, find fritillaries in the Cherwell water meadows, before the upper reaches of that river became a drainage ditch for farmers, wobble over cobbles in the Broad on one's bicycle and see the lines of horse-trams in some of the streets. The City of Oxford was still a country market town. The country came creeping unexpectedly up to the ends of wide late-Victorian suburban roads in North Oxford. Today all that is gone and an anonymous sprawl which might be Slough or Luton defaces all outskirts but Wytham. There are distant shopping arcades, clusters of concrete lamp standards, arid housing estates, telly masts and tinned food, all used by people who probably are unaware of the old colleges and their beauties, and who are poor things, chained to the conveyor belt for most of their lives. To them the fuss in the papers about Oxford traffic is only a problem of how quickest to get to the chain stores in the Corn and if the silly old university is in the way, then pull it down. Yet there are other citizens, and some of the most enlightened being from these new estates themselves, who know that Oxford could still be the most beautiful city in England. For the heart of the place is still there, contained in that tiny area bordered by St Giles, the Corn and St Aldate's on the west, by the Broad and Holywell on the north, by Magdalen on the east and by Merton Street and Christ Church on the south.

Any plan for Oxford must have as its first consideration the preservation of the beauty and character of this old heart of the place. To preserve this Oxford will not be to turn it into a museum, for the dons can continue bawling the Absolute across the hall and the undergraduates can continue cramming their heads with facts or releasing their inhibitions by breaking glass whether the beauty and character of their buildings are preserved or not.

The university and colleges of Oxford are not merely of local but of

national and even international importance. They are still used for the
purposes for which they were built centuries ago and there seems no
reason why they should not continue to fulfil their function, giving to
life at Oxford a background that can hardly fail to influence even the
most unseeing economist or philologist. But the character of the
buildings is preserved not only by tenants, but by quiet and by the
green girdle of gardens and meadows. The first has been destroyed
and the second is threatened.

If one looks at Oxford today what, apart from a few dreary blocks in
Bursar's Georgian and clumsy stone patching, destroys the beauty?
The answer comes in three words – the internal combustion engine.
Parked cars make the streets hideous by the garish and untidy contrast
they make against old buildings. The roar of moving cars destroys the
peace. Those adjuncts of the motor car, a tarmac surface replacing
cobbles and a smell of petrol drowning that of burning leaves or damp
earth, take away from Oxford's beauty too.

Plenty of solutions have been offered, from tunnels under the High
to bridges over the meadows or roads along the river bed. Each
suggestion has its local supporters, and the disunity about it all is
natural among local people. For no local resident can be wholly
disinterested, even if he thinks he is. Each college will favour whatever
plan suggests a road which does not cross its own property. Each
college will be further subdivided by Fellows who own houses in parts
of Oxford which may be affected by one or other suggestion. Nor do I
wholly trust the aesthetic judgement of most dons, judging by most of
the new buildings that have gone up in the university and the trivial
little rose garden, like a bit of Waterer's floral mile, with which
Magdalen planted its piece of Thames meadowland which once came
right up to the High. The city will be concerned about matters of
trade and keeping Cowley as part of Oxford and not letting it become
a separate borough. Nor, for all the symbolic burying of hatchets, do
city and university wholly trust one another. This is a good thing and
keeps both parties on their toes. The city, we must remember, is far
older than the university, and it is the county town of a big shire. But
all parties seem to regard Oxford primarily as a traffic problem and
only secondarily as a beautiful place whose future is in danger.

Before anyone can decide whether the preservation of Oxford is
wholly a traffic problem or not, a detailed analysis of the traffic, its
origin, type and destination, must be made. This has not been done.
Some years ago vehicles passing through or parking in the city were

counted, but such numbers convey nothing, because a fifty-foot lorry is equal to twenty motor bicycles in size, if not in noise.

As soon as a thorough traffic census is taken, Oxford will be able to discover which, if any, of its outer bypasses should be completed. It may even find that the one below Boar's Hill to Botley need never have been built at all. And after the traffic census, adequate car parks must be provided. No one knows now whether space for a thousand or for ten thousand cars is needed. But everyone must know that the present parking arrangements are inadequate and ugly. I should think personally that the solution will have to be in multi-storey car parks on the outskirts of the city. All these problems can be solved, at any rate temporarily, from information obtained from a traffic census. At present everyone is working in the dark. One thing is perfectly certain, and that is that Mr Duncan Sandys has done a public service by spurring on city and university to action.

The Spectator

The Isle of Man

Not long ago I stepped out of an Edwardian electric tramcar on to the grassy height of Snaefell, two thousand feet above sea-level. The day was clear and I could see Snowdon seventy-three miles away to the south-west and, much nearer, the mountains of Cumberland, the Mull of Galloway and, in the west, the mountains of Mourne – four countries in bluish outline beneath a sky of mother-of-pearl and a wrinkled sea all round us, cloud-patched with streaks of purple.

Four countries seen from a fifth – this ancient kingdom of Man which once owned the Sodor or southern islands of Scotland. The tramcar returned down the mountainside. Many who had landed at the top went into the café for tea or beer and I had, for a moment, the whole island to myself, thirty-two miles long and twelve wide at my feet; brown moorland and mountain in the middle with tiny fields on the lower slopes, green slate and blue slate, silver limestone and red sandstone, gorse and blaeberries and ling, gigantic cliffs and hidden, wooded glens, foxgloves, fern and scabious on Cornish-looking hedges, whitewashed cottages thatched with straw and drowned in fuchsia bushes. It is a bit of Ulster set down in the sea, a bit of England, Scotland, Wales and Cornwall too, a place as ancient as them all, a separate country, Norse and Celtic at once.

The Isle of Man, like Shakespeare, has something memorable for everyone. It is a place of strong contrasts and great variety. Yet in southern England it is hardly known at all.

Yet from June to September half a million people cross from the coast of Lancashire, whole towns at a time. Then lodging-houses are stuffed to capacity, then bathing things hang from the sixth floor downwards, then the main road round the island, the famous TT track, hums with 'charas', and still there is room. Each time I have visited the Isle of Man it has been at the height of the season and each time I have been able to lose myself in the country. I have tramped knee-deep in blaeberry bushes on the wild west coast of the island, looking in vain for the ruins of a Celtic chapel and never seeing a soul till I turned inland and walked down rutty farm lanes between foxgloves and knapweed to the narrow-gauge railway. And on the same evening I have been able to lose myself again in the crowds on Douglas front, to see Norman Evans in variety at the Palace and afterwards to watch a thousand couples dance in one of the big halls. All this in so small a kingdom, such wildness and such sophistication, such oldness and such newness. The trams, the farms, the switchback railways, the mountain sheep, the fairy lights and the wood-smoke curing kippers – how can I cram them all in? The clearest way of describing the island is to divide it into the two peoples of which it consists, the Manx and the visitors.

And the Manx come first. When the last boat of holiday-makers has steamed out of Douglas harbour back to Lancashire, about fifty thousand Manx are left behind: the Christians, Quayles, Crellins, Kewleys, Caines, Kermodes, Clucases, Kellys, Cregeens – Manx names seem almost all to begin with C, K or Q. They are a shy, poetical people. The look of their country is Celtic. There are small-holdings and plenty of *antiquities*, but not much ancient architecture. The island looks like Cornwall, Wales and Ireland mixed. But Man is Norse as well as Celtic. Until 1266 it belonged to Norway. Race enthusiasts see in the long, tall Manxmen with their fair hair and blue eyes and long moustaches, the descendants of the Vikings. Man was the capital of a Viking kingdom of islands, and very well the Vikings ran it and very slowly they adopted the Christian religion of the conquered Celts. Then the Scots took it over and finally Edward III, the strong man of the time, made England overlord. In 1405 Henry IV gave it to the Stanley family. The Stanleys became not only Earls of Derby but Kings of Man. And when that line of Stanleys died out, the kingship passed to a descendant, the Duke of Atholl. Late in the eighteenth century Man was still an independent country, an unknown island of mists and cliffs and smugglers with a king who was usually non-resident. Spain and France and Portugal shipped dutiable goods to Douglas and Castletown and other Manx ports. Manx sailors would run specially designed fast ships to England. By their own laws they were doing nothing illegal. They were only breaking British laws.

The island was also a place of refuge for debtors at this time when, by the laws of England and Ireland, a person could still be imprisoned for debt. I believe that Sir William Hillary, founder of the National Lifeboat Institution, who lived at Falcon Cliff, Douglas, was one of these debtors, though he did nothing but good to the Isle of Man. On the other side of Douglas Bay the ruined rake 'Buck Whaley' built himself Fort Anne, now an hotel, where, safe from his creditors, he wrote his memoirs. He died in 1800.

Assuming much moral indignation about the smugglers and debtors who had settled on Man, as well as seeing that the island might be both profitable financially and useful in times of war, the British Government bought out the last claims of the Duke of Atholl to kingship of Man in 1828 for nearly half a million pounds. This was an immense sum for the period, but the British Government gained in the long run. The only people who did not do well out of this sale were the Manx.

He who has not seen the Tynwald on Tynwald Day does not know how ancient and independent Man is. Of course the feel of another country is in the air as soon as one lands. It is an island, it has generous licensing hours, it has its own flag of three armoured legs on a red background, its own language (half Scottish, half Northern-Irish Gaelic), its own customs in both senses of that word. But the full Manxness shines on 5 July, the annual holiday of Tynwald Day. The centre of the island is St John's. Here most valleys meet and here surrounding mountains hide the sea. Carts from all the sheadings, tall men from Rushen in the south, small men from the white fuchsia-hidden farms of Ayre in the north, from forgotten holdings deep in the primeval forests of the Curraghs, from cottages in sycamore-shaded glens, from lonely houses on the sides of mountains, and from the narrow lanes of Peel that smell of wood-smoke and kippers, from the stately old capital of Castletown with its silver limestone castle, from the noble Welch Gothic range of King William's College, from Ramsey with its delicate Georgian Court House, from Douglas, that Naples of the North, from forgotten hamlets like Ronague on the slopes of South Barrule, from the stricken terraces by deserted lead-mines of Foxdale, from Laxey where the greatest water-wheel in the world stands idle for ever, and from the sheltered lanes of Port St Mary, the Manxmen come to Tynwald fair. The little railway runs extra trains. All sorts of extraordinary rolling stock, made in the nineties and as good as ever, is drawn by little engines past creamy meadowsweet and brown mountain streams to the curious junction of St John's. And there not far from the station is Tynwald Hill itself, an artificial mound of grass, eighty feet high with four circular terraces around it.

On 5 July, a cream canopy tops the mound to shelter the Governor of Man who will represent the King, and down the straight avenue that leads to the church white masts fly alternately the flags of Britain and of Man. St John's Chapel is a golden granite-spired building in that dashing and original style of romantic Gothic invented by John

Welch which characterizes almost all Manx established churches and
which is Georgian in origin, though often Victorian in execution. The
path to the church is strewn with rushes, offerings to a pagan sea god
older than the Viking Tynwald mound. As eleven strikes, the sun
streams down, a hymn from A and M is relayed from the church; the
chief people in the island are assembled for public worship. The
Coroners, the Captains of the Parishes, the Clergy in their robes, the
Chairmen of the Town Commissioners of Peel, Ramsey and Castletown in frock coats, the Mayor of Douglas all in red and ermine; they
step out into the sunlight from the west door. And so do the Vicar-
General, the Archdeacon, the High Bailiff – all these legal-clerical-
looking men – the Members of the House of Keys, their Chaplain and
their Speaker, the Government Secretary, the Members of the
Legislative Council, the Attorney-General, the two Deemsters in their
robes of red who are the judges of the island, and the Lord Bishop of
Sodor and Man – that luckless Bishop whose cathedral is a beautiful
ruin of green slate and red sandstone on an islet overlooking Peel, that
luckless Bishop who has a seat in the English House of Lords but no
vote in it – who is second in command of the island. And now comes
the Sword of State, a thirteenth-century Scandinavian relic, and
behind it the Lieutenant-Governor himself with a posse of police and
the Surgeon to the Household keeping up the rear. Slowly they ascend
to Tynwald Hill, the Governor to the top and the rest in order of
importance on terraces below. The Coroner fences the court. Then
the Deemster reads out the latest laws in English and a priest reads
them out again in Manx. It is all beautifully organised and it goes on
for a long time. But here in this ancient circle of the hills time seems
nothing. As the old Manx language is read out, the sun shines down on
us, although the peaks of every mountain round us are hidden in
clouds. It is always fine, I am told, at St John's on Tynwald Day. The
magician who lived in the island up to the fifth century used to make a
mist to hide the island from its invaders, and it is certainly true that
whenever Man has been visited by English king or queen it has been
shrouded in mist, even at a recent visit of King George VI.

Fishing and farming were once the chief industries of the Manx.
Fishing has dwindled so that there are now only nine boats Manx-
manned and owned among all the little drifters that set out into the
evening for herrings. The other hundred are mostly Scottish. And
even farming takes second place to the greatest Manx industry, which
is catering.

This brings me to the most enjoyable thing in all the enjoyment of

Man – the visitors. I wish I knew when it was that these mass migrations from Lancashire started. Perhaps I can tell most easily from looking at Douglas. If I stand on Douglas Head and look across that noble sweep to Onchan Head, before the fairy lights are on and while the sun setting behind the mountains still lets me see the outline of the houses on the front, I can trace the recent history of the island.

The original Douglas at my feet, around the harbour, is a small fishing port, not half so beautiful as Castletown further down this eastern coast – Castletown with its magnificent medieval-moated and turreted castle, its box-pewed, three-deckered, still unspoilt church, its exciting stone police station by Baillie Scott, and its Doric column to Governor Smelt. What made Douglas grow was its natural scenery, but people did not notice natural scenery until Georgian times. The last Duke of Atholl to be governor had the Shrewsbury architect George Stewart design him, in 1804, a palace on this noble sweep of bay. It is known today in its smooth, silvery stone as Castle Mona Hotel. Its dining-room is the finest room on the island, the Adam style at its simplest and most graceful. Only that exquisite country house the Nunnery, in Walter Scott Gothic by John Pinch, compares with it. And after the Duke, the debtors escaping to Mona with some cash, and other visitors, built themselves romantic castles on these heights above the bay – Falcon Cliff, Fort Anne, Derby Castle. These are late Georgian castellated buildings designed to look like romantic ruins by John Welch who also built in 1832 the Tower of Refuge on a rock in the middle of the water in Douglas Bay and so turned a looming danger into the semblance of an ancient castle. Then in the reign of William IV the gaps between the castles were filled in with stately stucco terraces, Brighton fashion (Windsor Terrace and Mount Pleasant are the best) sometimes high on the cliffs and here and there on the sea shore. The effect was and is magically beautiful. These Georgian terraces and Walter Scott, Peveril-of-the-Peak style castles flash out upon the cliff side. But this exclusive and romantic watering place cannot originally have been designed for half a million north-country folk – more likely for a few hundred half-pay officers eking out their pensions here where taxes are low.

I think the man of genius who turned the island into what it is, and saved it from ruin so that it is now financially prosperous, was Governor Loch. He improved the harbours and built the Loch Promenade in the sixties and seventies. Thereafter Douglas-style boarding-houses appeared in rows wherever there were gaps between the old terraces. They are innocent enough five-storeyed, bay-

windowed, gabled buildings, gloomy behind, sea-gazing in front, rows
and rows and rows of them so that the distant effect is of white paper
folded into a concertina and perched here and there and everywhere
along the shore. They are not as disfiguring as the modern bungalows
and clumsily arranged electric light poles which ruin so much of the
country part of Man. And now what with the TT, the motor races, the
improved harbours, the way everybody is out to be gay, *however*
gloomy you are feeling you cannot be ill-humoured in Douglas. The
boats arrive, the aeroplanes come down, young men and old in open
shirts, sports coats and grey flannels, young girls and old in cheerful
summer dresses, queue for ices, queue for shrimps, crowd round bars
for glasses of delicious dry champagne, gaze from horse-trams over
municipal flowerbeds to the Tower of Refuge and the sea, travel in
luxury coaches round the island half asleep in one another's arms till
the sun sets behind the boarding-houses of Douglas and all the lights
go up and the dance halls begin to fill. It is nine o'clock. There is still
light in the sky. Father and mother, basking in one another's love, are
sitting in chairs on the steps of the boarding-house; behind the front
door peeps the inevitable castor oil plant in its china pot. Beside them
sit the younger children, unnaturally good and quiet for fear they shall
be sent up to bed while it is still light and while the moon rises huge
and yellow above the purple bay. The elder children, grown up now,
are off to the dance halls. Only a few rejected young men sit sadly on
the steps among the ancients and the infants. The girls wear white
dancing shoes and that is how you know whither they are bound. Two
shillings or four-and-six, somewhere round that, is the cost of a ticket
to dance. I like the Palace dance hall best. It has a parquet floor of
sixteen thousand square feet and room for five thousand people. It is in
a gay baroque style, cream and pink inside, and from the graceful roof
hang Japanese lanterns out of a dangling forest of flags. A small and
perfect dance band strikes up – ah, the dance bands of the Isle of Man!
Soon a thousand couples are moving beautifully, the cotton dresses of
the girls like vivid tulips in all this pale cream and pink, the sports
coats and dark suits of the men a background to so much airy colour.
The rhythmic dance is almost tribal, so that even a middle-aged
spectator like me is caught up in mass excitement, pure and thrilling
and profound.

And while the dance bands are playing in Douglas and the yellow
moon is rising in its bay, on the western, wilder coast the herring fleet
is setting out from Peel. The sun sets behind the rugged outline of the
Castle and the ruined Cathedral and Round Tower enclosed within its

walls. A stiffish west wind is blowing and the sea beyond the breakwater is dark green and choppy. The herring boats are disappearing into the sunset. Out of the harbour, round the castle island, the dying sun shines gold upon their polished sides. I stand alone upon a rock by Peel Castle. The smell of salt and wet earth is in my nostrils, the dark green slate of those old castle walls is at my side. Inland, the last rays of sun are lighting the winding lanes of Peel, the red sandstone of its church towers, and the soft protecting mountains behind it of the Isle of Man. Here, salt spray, seagulls, wild rocks and cavernous cliffs. Beyond those mountains the dance halls of Douglas and the dance-band leader in his faultless tails. An isle of contrasts! A miniature of all the Western world.

From *Portraits of Islands*

Kelmscott

The best way of all to approach Kelmscott is the way William Morris, the poet, craftsman and Socialist, used to come to this house of his dreams – by the river. Kelmscott Manor House is on the banks of the upper Thames. It's not the sort of Thames of Boulter's Lock and Maidenhead night-clubs, not those used and wide waters, but a Thames that is almost a stream up between the last locks. There are more kingfishers than boats, and many dragon-flies like gleaming aeroplanes, and meadowsweet and willows and irises, and flat, almost Lincolnshire landscape on the Oxfordshire bank where Kelmscott stands. The roads round here are like streams themselves, winding among unfenced or low hedged fields, past greyish-golden cottages of stone, and barns and dovecots and little churches. It is all like England was in the sixteenth century when the Turners first built themselves this gabled manor house. Their descendants, the Hobbes family, still farm most of the land round it.

Now here is William Morris coming to the house as he describes it in *News from Nowhere*:

> Over the meadow I could see the mingled gables of a building where I knew the lock must be, and which now seemed to combine a mill with it. A low wooded ridge bounded the river-plain to the south and south-east, whence we had come, and a few low houses lay about its feet and up its slope. I turned a little to my right, and through the hawthorn sprays and long shoots of the wild roses I could see the flat country spreading out far away under the sun of the calm evening, till something that might be called hills with a look of sheep-pastures about them bounded it with a soft blue line. Before me, the elm-boughs still hid most of what houses there might be in this river-side dwelling of men; but to the right of the cart-road a few grey buildings of the simplest kind showed here and there ... We crossed the road, and again almost without my will my hand raised the latch of a door in the wall, and we stood presently on a stone path which led up to the old house.

It's not a very big house, and I think that why anybody likes it so much is because it is small and something they feel they could live in and love themselves. If you weren't sure, you would say this old stone house–purple when wet with rain, gold in sunlight when seen against dark green trees or approaching storm clouds – if you weren't sure, and like me, you were someone who thought he knew about architecture, you would say it was mostly Tudor. But I believe it is later – more like Charles I's time; for the tradition of stone masonry lingered on in this remote place even until well into the last century. And you will notice that one wing on the north is grander than the rest of the house with carvings on the outside which are a hundred years later than Tudor. And while we are outside look at the farm buildings: barns as big as churches all in the local stone, and high stone walls. They all seem to have grown with the landscape. 'If you touched them,' Janey Morris said to Rossetti, 'you would expect them to be alive.'

The house inside is very much as it was except that electric light has been introduced, there are water closets, and two bathrooms with immersion heaters. As Morris said, 'Everywhere there was but little furniture, and that only the most necessary, and of the simplest forms.' And I must say that today, you could not say Kelmscott was disappointing inside. The furniture is solid stuff, some of it heavily hand-made and painted by Morris and Rossetti. And some of it is Elizabethan. There is a great four-poster Elizabethan bed in which William Morris used to sleep – an inconvenient place, and not a very comfortable bed either. Anyone going into the tapestry room had to make their way past him lying in his bed. Round the posts at the top of the bed is a border with words embroidered by May Morris. It begins like this:

> The wind's on the wold
> And the night is a-cold,
> And Thames runs chill
> Twixt mead and hill
> But kind and dear
> Is the old house here
>
> And my heart is warm
> Midst winter's harm.

The ornaments in the house are mostly blue pottery, collected I believe by Rossetti. There are drawings of Mrs William Morris by

Rossetti – Janey Morris with her long, long neck and chin, her full lips and sleepy eyes and flaming hair, who was so adored by Rossetti from the days he first met her at Oxford when he and Morris and others were painting the roof of the Library of the Oxford Union. I suppose the grandest room is the drawing-room with its white Georgian panelling on the ground floor in that north wing of the house I described when we were outside. And about equally grand is the tapestry room above it – though I could, like Rossetti, do without the tapestry which has been there since the seventeenth century. It depicts the life of Samson, and one particularly gruesome scene shows Samson having his eyes gouged out. The rooms I like best are the older ones at the west end; the ground floor room which Rossetti moved into for a studio when he painted Janey Morris. His palette and paints are still there. Above it is a bedroom all papered in that green willowy pattern paper Morris designed which is so like the willowy lanes round here, and seems to be made almost of living branches. Throughout the house there are Morris papers, and Morris chintzes – the Strawberry Thief, the Daisy, and so on – flowered chintzes and papers which make it seem as though the beautiful garden outside had walked into the house and stylised itself on the walls and chairs and curtains.

I have not bothered you with a detailed tour of this rambling little manor house. What you cannot fail to notice and what is worth mentioning last and emphasising most, is its atmosphere. It haunts one. I know of no house with so strong an atmosphere. There is no other place which is kept as it was and yet so clearly is not a museum but a home. Come up to the first floor and look out of one of the windows over the tops of the yews and the flowering trees, through the great elms and into the wide upper Thames meadows. Winter and summer for three centuries while the Turner family lived here this stone grew lichened and from those water spouts the heavy rain fell on to the deep green grass of the garden from between the gables. Never did you hear such a noise of English wet as when the rain pours off Kelmscott Manor roof and splashes on to the grass and garden paths! And sometimes the Thames would rise and flood the garden.

Yet I think the chief atmosphere here is of those Pre-Raphaelite tenants, William Morris and Dante Gabriel Rossetti. Rossetti, in love with Mrs Morris, remained at Kelmscott, getting more and more moody, imagining plots against him, staying awake till five in the morning, taking chloral, and only going out when he would meet few villagers. But he had his moments of loving the place, and since he was in love, he produced some fine poems.

In 1877 Rossetti left Kelmscott never to return. Thereafter Morris came back, but used it chiefly as a country retreat, a holiday house for his wife and children, while he remained in London at his Hammersmith house which he also called Kelmscott House after his country manor. There in Hammersmith he did his printing and made his Socialist speeches and tore bits out of his black beard when he grew angry.

I like to think of him in a summer of 1880 setting out with three near friends and his wife to row from Kelmscott, Hammersmith, to Kelmscott, Oxon. The boat looked like a horse bus on water with a pair of oars in the prow. They reached Oxford after seven days:

> ... Janey the next day (Monday) went on by rail to Kelmscott: while we got up early and by dint of great exertions started from Medley Lock at 9 a.m., with Bossom and another man to tow us as far as New Bridge, where we sent them off, and muddled ourselves home somehow, dining at a lovely place about a mile above New Bridge, where I have stopped twice before for that end. One thing was very pleasant: they were hay-making on the flat flood-washed spits of ground and islets all about Tadpole; and the hay was gathered on punts and the like; odd stuff to look at, mostly sedge, but they told us it was the best stuff for milk ... Charles was waiting for us with a lantern at our bridge by the corner at 10 p.m., and presently the ancient house had me in its arms again: J. had lighted up all brilliantly, and sweet it all looked you may be sure ...

Sixteen years later in the early autumn of 1896 William Morris died. His body was carried to the little churchyard from Kelmscott Manor House in a yellow farm waggon with red wheels, wreathed with vine and willow boughs.

My own happiest memories of Kelmscott date from as late as the thirties, when May, Morris's surviving daughter, and her friend Miss Lobb lived in the Manor House. My wife and I used to drive there by pony cart and were always welcomed with a huge tea and a feed for the pony, for May Morris loved anything that was not to do with this mechanised age. She used to show us the beautiful vellum books her father decorated, and give us roses from trees he had planted in the garden. At any moment one would not have been surprised to see the burly form of Morris himself, and the thin bearded Burne-Jones beside him, and perhaps William de Morgan walk in over the sunlit flagstones into the drawing-room. They were about the house and their memory was loved by dear May Morris. And then the aerodromes came, and the pylons and wire of electric light and the noisome dredging of the upper Thames by the Thames Conservancy, and she and Miss Lobb liked being alive less and less. Just before the war they went to Iceland together – Morris, you will remember, always went to Iceland – and soon after they returned May Morris faded out of life, and Miss Lobb soon followed her. The Manor House was left by May to Oxford University as a memorial to her father.

One final story I heard from a recent tenant of Kelmscott. This lady was sitting on a still autumn night about five years ago up on the first floor in the room which has Morris's bed in it and which leads to the tapestry room. She was alone in the house. In the silence she heard two men talking amicably in this room. She opened the door of the tapestry room to see who they were – there was no one in it. Morris? Burne-Jones? Rossetti? Philip Webb? Who knows. The place is haunting and haunted, for it has been loved as only an old house can be loved.

BBC broadcast

Lamp-Posts and Landscape

I think it is useless to consider the design of street lamps first and the streets in which they are to go afterwards. England is far too varied and delicate in her building materials to have standardised designs plumped down in her towns regardless of local scale, colour and texture. I think it must have been this inhuman, standardising attitude to our beautiful country which resulted some years ago in the Royal Fine Art Commission choosing some of the less hideous designs of concrete standard and passing them, if not approving them. Some manufacturers have been so unscrupulous as to put in their catalogues 'approved by the Royal Fine Art Commission' against certain designs. Gullible, if well-intentioned, Borough Engineers have as a consequence put down many monstrosities, much too large, thick, ponderous and coarse for the old towns and villages for which they are responsible and they have permanently ruined their main streets by daytime. It is no use looking at a design for a lamp standard in a catalogue unless one sees it in the mind's eye set up in the street.

Luckily today there is excellent liaison between the Ministry of Transport and the Royal Fine Art Commission, so that where trunk roads go through old towns and villages, the Royal Fine Art Commission is consulted and each case is treated on its individual merits. Borough Engineers have always been helpful, and many a town has been saved from a fate even worse than Salisbury or Chippenham or Devizes, to quote three of eighty-seven instances of towns made hideous by ill-designed jazz-modernistic concrete standards. But side streets and others which are not trunk roads are still a local responsibility only.

Everyone has a favourite town or village. Let me choose a few favourites of mine and consider their qualities as street architecture. Launceston is, I think, the most beautiful town in Cornwall. It has narrow streets of high houses, Georgian and earlier, most of them built of slate, that feathery grey slate of Cornwall, varied here and there with Georgian red-brick. It has a magnificent church with a carved granite exterior, and the whole town is high on a hill and dominated by castle ruins. Like all old English towns its growth has been gradual and haphazard. Now that it is complete it looks from the distance like a hilltop fortress, and the first thing one notices about it is its skyline and the next the pale weathered silvery-grey of most of its buildings. As the skyline is so much a feature of this town it would obviously be a crime to dominate the place with the thick necks of sick concrete serpents reaching over the castle gardens and the chimney stacks. Since the houses are mostly comparatively high, wherever possible iron brackets should be used, if there *must* be new street lighting, and as the pavements are narrow the thinnest possible columns should be used if there must be twenty-five-foot columns.

Louth, in Lincolnshire, is one of the less known, but most attractive towns we possess. It stands at the foot of the chalk wolds, a cluster of dark, old red-brick houses with lighter red-tiled roofs gathered round the magnificent golden-grey spire of its parish church. Viewed from the wolds above it, it is like an old sea-port and the sea, instead of being water, is composed of long miles of grassy marsh, intersected by dykes and canals and far away is the low sandy shore of the North Sea itself. To walk in the streets of Louth is to walk among the mellow brick walls of a Dutch picture. How hideously inappropriate a thick concrete standard looks here may be judged from the example, fortunately unique in the town at the time of writing, close to the parish church. If I try to analyse why concrete looks so ugly in Louth I would say that it is for these reasons – the town is full of good woodwork Georgian windows, delicately moulded cornices, well-proportioned street doors. But there can be no delicate moulding on concrete. Next, the texture of the brick is varied, some dark red, some pale pink, some glazed, some orange. Against this concrete, whatever its colour, is unvaried and obtrusive. Finally there is again the all important question of skyline.

Burford, in Oxfordshire, is mostly one broad street descending a steep hill to the River Windrush. The houses are of all shapes and sizes and their harmony is one of material. The limestone of Burford is a golden honey colour, sometimes varying to silver-grey. Stone is used in these parts and worked as easily as wood in places where there are not local quarries. The windows have stone mullions and transoms, stone arches give glimpses of cobbled yards where hollyhocks rise above stone garden walls, stone tombstones carved in a rich Baroque style surround the golden-grey stone church, the green of the Windrush Valley, the distant elms and beeches intensify the gold of the stone, and almost every building is worn and weathered by time. The mouldings of its stone dressings most exquisitely hold the shadows. How could anyone put into this town the staring, glass-facia of a modern chain store, let alone the towering triangular, concrete serpent of a modern lamp standard? Here, if anywhere, flood lighting would be the best form of street lighting, for the main street is broad and there is room for it.

Finally let me consider a leafy and attractive part of the sad Borough of Paddington, where these words are written. Here we have not the unconcious artistry of our old towns, but consciously planned streets and planned vistas, mostly Victorian, but in a Renaissance tradition of town planning. Stucco houses, a little later and more Italianate than the earlier Georgian crescents and terraces of such Spas as Cheltenham and Leamington, stand well back among limes and plane trees in orderly semi-detachment, either side of broad streets. The lamp-posts everywhere are a delight, and related in scale to the houses. Unfortunately they have been painted aluminium but one is still able to appreciate the Georgian dignity of their proportions. The bases of some of the older lamp-posts in Paddington seem to be old canons, the next oldest have the vestry of Paddington recorded on them in cast iron, and the Borough of Paddington maintains the same design, with its own arms and initials. A tapering column sprouts from two acanthus leaves and flowers into a circular lantern crested at the top. The lantern is neither too large nor too small for the column which supports it, and the whole thing is well designed for the width of the pavement and the road. Mr Peter Varnon, that pioneer for decent modern street lighting, has pointed out to me how anyone can tell from a photograph, or could tell until standardisation – what town or borough was illustrated by the design of lamp-posts, for different towns and boroughs have different designs, sometimes named after them in the catalogues, of steel and cast-iron lamp-post manufacturers.

Now the point of all this has been to show that England's street architecture is full of variety. Indeed, England's beauty is in her variety. In no other country can you travel so quickly from one sort of scenery to another. Before the war there was a disastrous tendency to try and make all our towns look the same. Burton, the Tailor-of-Taste, Stones' Radios, Dorothy Perkins and Woolworths for examples did not care so much where they were, as that you should know who they were. There may be a commercial argument to justify the desecration that commerce has wrought in our old towns. But there is no justification for a non-commercial public authority spoiling what remains to us of this once beautiful country. More damage has been done since the war by lighting authorities to our landscape than ever was done by German bombs or greedy commercialism. I suggest that all public authorities consider their town first by what it will look like by day, because it is by day that it will be most seen, and secondly what it will look like by night. No town, however new, however rebuilt, in England, deserves triangular, jazz-modern lamp-posts with lunch baskets hanging off gallows and giants' match-strikes at the base, the half-baked designs of half-trained engineers who have never looked at the remains of our civilisation as exemplified in our street architecture. I do not condemn concrete as a material, though I prefer steel and cast iron. Concrete *can* be made slender and graceful. Cast-iron and steel standards should be painted grey, with either a little yellow or a little blue in it, so that they may be less obstrusive than when painted the dismal green which is meant to look like nature, and doesn't. On the whole, however, I think that whenever possible old lamp-posts should be retained. We are used to them. They are part of our street landscape and most of them are well proportioned in themselves and are related to the human figure as are the houses in which we live.

Light and Lighting

On Lewis Carroll and Edward Lear

There are those whose chief pleasure is in what they can touch and see, who think in terms of scenery and pictures, who remember every turn of a road, its colour, trees and houses. There are those who never see anything, whose private rooms are bleak as a public office, who remember nothing of the look of a place but who can grasp at a glance a list of statistics, a theory or an argument. The two sorts of people may be called visuals and non-visuals. The word 'intellectual' so loosely used now, really applies to non-visual people. A new book* of unpublished nonsense verse by Edward Lear will be a delight to the non-intellectual visual-minded person such as your reviewer, just as a new book for children by Lewis Carroll will delight the intellectual which your reviewer is not.

It is worth making this distinction because Carroll and Lear are so often mentioned together, whereas they have nothing more in common than being Victorian, being eccentric, and being writers of nonsense verse and prose in their spare time. The author of *Alice in Wonderland* was a mathematical Oxford don, his work for children has an intellectual basis – witness the game of chess in *Through the Looking Glass* – and his poetry, even such nonsense as the Jabberwocky, displays an effort which is noticeably absent from the poetry of Edward Lear. Lear was an animal painter who turned a landscape artist. It is too easy to say his paintings are unimportant compared with his nonsense verse, as does the American writer of one of the two Introductions to this book. More true is the remark of Angus Davidson in the longer Introduction to the same work. Speaking of those impressive watercolours with their brown ink lines, exact delineations of landscape and humorous descriptive remarks jotted down over their foregrounds, their great distances and wide skies and deep olive-woods, later to be beautifully interpreted in stone- and in wood-engraving in travel books, he says 'he evolved a personal style which gave him complete liberty to express spontaneously the feeling of a true artist, undistracted by superfluous detail, unfettered by the

---

* *Teapots and Quails:* Edward Lear. *John Murray.* 12s 6d.

Pre-Raphaelite influence . . .' This same personal style comes out in
the drawings in this book. Besides having an awed sense of the wonder
of creation whether in the wing of a bird or the shape of a mountain,
he also could imply an extremely funny line in drawing them. He can
make a bear lovable, funny and pathetic. He can make a pair of scissors
into a personality without drawing a face on it or trying to twist it into
semblance of the human form. He can draw a tree blooming with
clothes-brushes so that it looks like something in a botany book.

But what is the chief revelation of this book, is Lear's gift as a poet.
For the most successful series in the book, little four-lined stanzas, he
wrote the words first and did the drawings afterwards.

> Teapots and Quails
> Snuffers and Snails
> Set him a sailing
> And see how he sails!

He draws pairs of each of the first four articles and a single yacht for
the last two lines. The words were written for their sound first and
their incongruity second. The drawings bring out the latter. The
nonsense botany is drawing first and the subsequent prose is a
delightful parody of botanical writing and illustration. The limericks
and remaining poems are none of them so good as those published in
Lear's lifetime. He must have had a high sense of the quality of his
nonsense work.

Undoubtedly his friend Alfred Tennyson was Lear's chief inspiration as a poet. Tennyson and he had much in common; both were
visual men, awed by the vastness and detail of created things, both
were profoundly melancholy, both had a most musical delight in the
English language and poetic metre, both enjoyed staying in country
houses. Some of Lear's poetry is so near Tennyson(!) as almost to be
the Laureate. Compare

> O my aged Uncle Arley
> Sitting on a heap of barley
> In the silent hours of night

with:

> Only reapers reaping early
> In among the bearded barley

Hear a song that echoes clearly
Down to still Shalott.

Mr Davidson makes the perceptive observation that one serious piece of nonsense at the end of this book called 'Cold on the Crabs' is also influenced by Matthew Arnold. Lear's animism is like that of Hans Andersen, his poetry is like Tennyson's, his combination of nonsense and drawing is all his own. Apart from his sense of the ludicrous, of melody and metre, Lear appeals to most children because they are as awed and melancholy as he is. It is not for most of us until we are adult, that social glitter and intellectual argument stifle our sense of the tears of things. His only successor in nonsense poetry is Sandys Wason who has long been hopelessly out of print. Certainly, Lear is not like Lewis Carroll, nor that remarkable man's imitators.

Time and Tide

The Lecture

So you're the lecturer, are you? Glad you've got here at last. For my sins, I'm supposed to be your chairman tonight. I hope you won't mind my slipping away as soon as I've introduced you. The fact is, I've got a lot on tonight – a meeting of the Sanitary Committee at the Town Hall, then judging a Fancy Dress Parade at the Victoria Rooms. That's the worst of being in what people are pleased to call 'public life'. You never have a moment to yourself. I suppose I've got a name for being an easy-going, good-natured sort of chap with a gift of the gab, and one gets all sorts of odd jobs landed on one that other people seem to fight shy of. All the odds and bods ask you to preside at this and open that and judge what have you.

Now forgive my asking you, what's your name? Sorry what? Say it again, will you? Benjamin? Oh, Benchman. Any prefix, title or anything? Sounds good if I can say 'Dr' or 'Professor' or 'Sir Alfred' or what have you. Oh, just plain Mr. Very well then. Now I know you'll forgive me: I ought to know, but what are you talking about? Architecture! Well I've been in tighter corners than this at sea, though I can't say I have the faintest inkling about architecture or architects except that they generally forget to put the staircases in the houses they build. Still, I'll manage to say something.

Oh, Mr Baychmarn – there you are. I see you've met your chairman, our deputy Mayor. He's a frightfully busy person. So nice of him to come. Now wouldn't you like to put your things down, Mr Baychmarn? Did you have to walk all the way from the station? I'm so sorry and on a wet night too. I expect there were no taxis. Oh, are these your slides? I hope they're the right size for our projector. I must tell you you've struck a rather unlucky night. There's a dance at the Victoria Rooms, and there's just been a big bazaar at the Conservative Association and I fear that many of our members will be too tired to turn out again today, and then there's the weather. If I had known it was going to turn out like this I would have hired a smaller hall. But still, having advertised your lecture in the main hall, it would have been too late to change the *venue* at the last minute. The first two rows are nearly filled and we generally allow people ten minutes or so grace.

So you may get a few more. Do let me introduce you to Mrs Pytchely. She is the wife of one of our most progressive councillors.

As a matter of fact, Miss Linthwaite, I wanted a word with our deputy Mayor ...

Oh, here is Miss Staddlestone, Mr Baychmarn, who I'm sure is longing to meet you. She is most interested in all old things, so you will have a lot in common.

I did want to speak to you *before* your lecture, Mr Bergman. It's about the iniquitous proposal by our town council here to turn Sisam's barn into a county library. Sisam's barn is one of the gems of the place. It was built in 1455 by one Dubritius de Whaplode – I can show you a copy of the title deeds afterwards if you'd care to come to my cottage for coffee, and I think it more than probable that it is on the site of the very midden Rawlinson refers to in his two-volume history of the town – you will know it, of course, an invaluable work, though it has its inaccuracies – so that its history goes back even beyond its present building – if you can get anything in about it in your lecture I'm sure all the friends of what is really beautiful in this town ...

Oh, Mr Baychmarn, I'm sorry to say the lantern operator tells me your slides are the wrong size for his instrument. Now what are we going to do? It is too late to get another lantern. I'm afraid there's been a slip-up somewhere. I'm afraid you'll have to lecture without slides and I will ask your chairman to make his apologies to the audience.

Are we ready to begin? It doesn't look as though there'll be any more coming and I must get along to the Town Hall. Ladies and gentlemen, this is not the first time, as your deputy-Mayor, that I have appeared before the Literary and Philosophical Institute of our historic town, and it gives me great pleasure to be here this evening to introduce the Lecturer Mr Bletchington, I beg his pardon, Mr Betchington, who is going to speak to you on the subject of architecture. Now there's only one thing I know about architects, and that is that if you employ one he designs you a slap-up house but then forgets to put in the staircase (*laughter*). No doubt Mr Bletchington will be able to put you right on this point and I only wish I could stay to listen to him. But I must look after your interests in another quarter, namely at the Sanitary Committee in the Town Hall. There's one notice your indefatigable secretary asks me to give out. As Mr Bletchington has brought the wrong size slides for our magic-lantern there will be no slides this evening. In fact it will be all talk and no

pictures, and now without more ado I will ask our lecturer to
commence his lecture.

Punch

Six:

1955 to 1959

Six

1955–1959

By the time he was fifty in 1956, JB was in full swing. His collection of poems *A Few Late Chrysanthemums* had been well received. He was in the public eye as a result of his broadcasting, as well as his books and journalism. His name was everywhere. He was established. His reviews in the *Daily Telegraph* favoured lives of lost heroes like Thomas Telford, the engineer, or the painter Joshua Reynolds. And his fiery and informative pieces in *The Spectator* continued to annoy his detractors and enthuse his followers. 'The Central Electricity Authority, England's premier landscape destroyer,' he wrote, 'is pursuing the same course for driving its line of 130-foot pylons from Hampshire to Derbyshire as it used for destroying the Cotswolds. It takes one county at a time and bullies the weakest counties first....'[1]

Through this column JB had become the people's campaigner, not so much for preservation, although they wrote to him about buildings being pulled down in their towns and villages, but as a champion of Englishness. They wrote to him about saving woods from bypasses, and meadows from roundabouts, and because he was such a familiar figure and had such a good relationship with people through his radio and television work, he began to be taken seriously – or at any rate considered to be an important, rather than unimportant, nuisance – by the powers that be.

The miscellaneous comic relief between his tirades in *The Spectator* went on: 'Few things are more delightful than peculiar public positions. The City Remembrancer – for instance – what does he have to remember? I rang him up to ask. He was founded by Queen Elizabeth because he was able to write and remind the Queen (from his notes I suppose) of what she was to do. He is a lawyer and has free access to all the lobbies in Parliament and a special seat behind the Serjeant-at-Arms in the House....'[2] JB wrote advice to mothers visiting their children at school, '(1) Do not try to look young, look dowdy but not poor. (2) Show affection for your children, and on no account be seen kissing them. (3) Do not speak to other mothers you know. Their children may be unpopular in the school. (4) Do not talk to any masters or mistresses if you want to retain your child's confidence. On the other hand, to be on good terms with the headmaster or mistress is all right. . . .'³

In private, behind the view of the wider public, he was becoming president of more and more of the 'conservation' societies which began to burgeon throughout the country. They had been born by necessity as both the private and public sectors were putting forward more and more building schemes. JB himself was responsible with Anne Rosse for founding the Victorian Society which eventually came into being in 1958 as a result of so many Victorian buildings being threatened. As late as that few saw any merit in Victorian architecture. Sir John Summerson, the distinguished architectural historian, thought JB was mad to defend St Pancras Station. JB had been singing the praises of great nineteenth- and early twentieth-century Victorian architects from the late twenties onwards and had written scholarly pieces on those then disregarded figures like Pugin, Scott and Butterfield. Thirty years later he was well trained to defend their work.

He was doing more and more work for television. He made a series of films for BP and Shell about National Trust properties called 'Beauty in Trust', for which he wrote and spoke the commentaries. He was also contributing to an increasing number of anthologies and writing prefaces for friends. He worked with the great photographer Edwin Smith on an anthology of buildings for *The Saturday Book* which came out yearly under the auspices of his friend John Hadfield, and when he had time he still wrote articles for periodicals like *The Listener* on his favourite subjects. 'I have two hobbies in my life: collecting old books and looking at buildings. The former costs more than it used to do and the second is free and can be indulged in all places except deserts, forests, prairies and mountain heights. . . .'⁴

In 1958, when he was fifty-two, he finally published *Collins Guide to English Parish Churches* which had taken him fourteen years to compile. The process had been slow because his immense load of journalistic work had never left him with a stretch of time during which to galvanise himself. Instead the book had come together in dribs and drabs as he travelled about the country. Into his introduction he put much of what he had always felt for English churches, a subject which moved him deeply. He was able to convey this in a strong and simple way. When trying to imagine the Church of five centuries ago he wrote: 'So when we walk down a green lane like an ancient cart track towards the ringing church-bells, we can see the power of God in the blossom and trees, remember legends of the saints about birds and stones, and recall miracles that happened in the parish at this or that spot. And on a feast day we can see the churchyard set out with tables for the church ale when mass is over, and as we enter the nave we can see it thronged below the painted roof and walls with people in the village, young and old, and the rest of the parish crowding in with us. Human nature may not have been better. Life was as full, no doubt, of wrong and terror as it is today.'[5]

In the same year, his *Collected Poems* were published by John Murray and sold like hot cakes. Pessimistic as he was, JB was sometimes emboldened by praise and felt annoyed at various times by the barrage of complaints he was getting about his column in *The Spectator*. He found the weekly production of several paragraphs a strain and would always be in a bad temper the day before he had to produce it. He felt he had started seeing everything he did in terms of a *Spectator* piece and by the end of his stint he had become desperate, sometimes finding it hard to enjoy life for its own sake. He decided instead to take on a monthly column in the *Daily Telegraph* entitled, 'Men and Buildings' and this was to continue throughout the sixties.

1. *The Spectator*, 16 November 1956.
2. 'City and Suburban', *The Spectator*, 11 October 1957.
3. *The Spectator*.
4. *The Spectator*, 12 July 1957.
5. *The Listener*, 5 March 1959.
6. Extract from *Collins Guide to English Parish Churches* (1958).

R. S. Thomas

The poems of R. S. Thomas have been increasingly appreciated. They are easy to understand and they improve on re-reading, a sure sign of lasting quality. One of the first people to recognise the poet's merit was Mr Keidrych Rhys and Thomas's first volume, *The Stones of the Field* (1946), was published by the Druid Press, Carmarthen. That book contained the perfect lyric, 'Night and Morning'. Sixteen of the thirty-seven poems in *The Stones of the Field* have been omitted by the poet from the present volume. From his next book, *An Acre of Land* (1952), published by the Montgomery Printing Company, Newtown, the poet has omitted seven poems, while *The Minister* (1953) is reprinted in full, together with nineteen new poems.

Song at the Year's Turning therefore represents what R. S. Thomas considers the best of his work and makes those who are lucky enough to have the original locally-printed volumes anxious to hold on to them. It is worth mentioning here that all three slim books were attractively printed and produced.

In 1952 Mr Alan Pryce-Jones commended the poetry of R. S. Thomas on The Critics programme of the BBC and the effect was to sell out the remaining copies of the poet's work. It is rare enough for wireless commendation appreciably to affect the sale of any book: that it should sell out a book of poems must be unique.

Though he is essentially a local poet, the appeal of R. S. Thomas goes beyond the Welsh border. There certainly have been local descriptive poets whose work will be fully enjoyed only by those who know the locality they describe, for instance the parson poets of the eighteenth century who wrote heroic couplets or Thomsonian blank verse in praise of hills and ruins in their own and neighbouring parishes. R. S. Thomas is himself a parson, the rector of a parish in Wales. He is of Welsh origin and was born in Cardiff. He taught himself Welsh when adult and his knowledge of the language helped him to understand the remote hill people who appear so clearly in these poems.

Though R. S. Thomas is a local nature poet he is not one of the escapist kind. The 'wain and stook' pastoral poetry of the neo-

Georgians, good as much of it was, was literary and one associates it with thick paper and woodcuts of the home counties. R. S. Thomas is not at all literary and even remoter from the neo-Georgians than he is from the pastoral poets of the eighteenth century.

Having said so much about what sort of a nature poet he is not, makes it easier to describe the man revealed in the poems. R. S. Thomas is a country priest. He went to his parish not to bury himself in literature and take only the statutory services, but to learn all about his inarticulate and no doubt sometimes suspicious parishioners. He went with a keen interest in natural history and birds, in scenery, agriculture and the agricultural way of life. By talking to his parishioners in their own language about the things they knew, he would win the souls to the Christian faith and the sacraments. This much is implicit in many of his poems, though in none of them is it explicitly stated. This is what makes him look at man and nature in the light of eternity. Consider his description of 'The Village':

> So little happens; the black dog
> Cracking his fleas in the hot sun
> Is history. Yet the girl who crosses
> From door to door moves to a scale
> Beyond the bland day's two dimensions.
>
> Stay, then, village, for round you spins
> On slow axis a world as vast
> And meaningful as any poised
> By great Plato's solitary mind.

Compare that with Samuel Lewis's description of Manafon where R. S. Thomas was rector from 1942 until last year when he accepted a living in another country part of Wales. Lewis published his topographical dictionary of Wales in 1840, but the village of Manafon is likely to have changed little since Lewis's day. Then as now it is 'in a mountainous district nearly in the centre of the county, and intersected by the river Rhiw, and also by the road leading from Llanvair to Newtown and Montgomery: it comprises an extensive tract of land of which a considerable portion is uncultivated, and of the remainder, one half consists of old enclosures, and the other has been enclosed and brought into a state of cultivation under the provision of an act of parliament obtained in 1796. The surrounding scenery is strikingly diversified, and from the higher grounds are obtained

extensive and pleasingly varied prospects.' R. S. Thomas breathes the
wind and the wild flowers into this estate agent's language. What
sweat went to bringing those enclosures into cultivation may be
gathered from 'The Airy Tomb'. What pathos there is in the hard hill
life may be seen in a poem like 'Farm Child'.

A feeling for Dissent in R. S. Thomas's poetry gives it a peculiar
Welshness. Because he identifies the wild beauty of his parish with the
lives and work of its parishioners whom he loves, he cannot disregard
that nonconformity which is still stronger in Wales than the Church.
Under 'Manafon', Samuel Lewis mentions that a Sunday school run
by the Church has from thirty to sixty children according to the season
of the year, of whom four are educated free and the rest pay. On the
other hand, 'the Calvinistic Methodists gratuitously teach from a
hundred to two hundred males and females in three Sunday schools'.
R. S. Thomas describes the fruit of that teaching in his long poem
'The Minister' which was written for broadcasting. Here, one feels,
but for the fact that he loved the beauty of Welsh scenery and pitied
rather than despised those who cannot look up from the barren soil
and their hard tasks, goes R. S. Thomas. There have been good Welsh
writers driven to satire and contempt by the narrow Calvinism of a
mercenary peasantry. Poor Morgan, the minister of this poem, was
well versed in Calvin's theology and mistrusted beauty in scenery or
women. So he fell to railing against sin and leaving out charity until
his heart was twisted and he died defeated by his own fierce creed.

> Is there no passion in Wales? There is none
> Except in the racked hearts of men like Morgan
> Condemned to wither and starve in the cramped cell
> Of thought their fathers made them.
> Protestantism – the adroit castrator
> Of art; the bitter negation
> Of song and dance and the heart's innocent joy –
> You have botched our flesh and left us only the soul's
> Terrible impotence in a warm world.

W. B. Yeats seems to have been the only recent writer to have made
an acknowledged impression on R. S. Thomas's style. He thinks that
poetry should be read to oneself not out loud and that it is heard by an
inner ear. He does not read nineteenth-century poems because he
thinks that their obvious and jingly rhythms might upset his own sense
of metre.

This retiring poet had no wish for an introduction to be written to his poems, but his publisher believed that a 'name' was needed to help sell the book. The 'name' which has the honour to introduce this fine poet to a wider public will be forgotten long before that of R. S. Thomas.

Introduction to *Song at the Year's Turning*

City and Suburban (3)

A series of articles written for The Spectator

I have not been able to sleep lately for thinking of Monmouth. Is it Welsh or English? If a Welsh Nationalist puts up for it in the coming election, how will the Men of Gwent, as Monmouth people are called, receive him? James Hanley told me that every year, by an old treaty, the conquered country of Wales yields up a certain amount of acres to England and that these acres are taken from Monmouthshire. I rang up the Welsh Department of the Home Office to find out if this were true. They were most courteous and said they would let me know later. When they did so, it was that they could discover no record of such a treaty but they would be pleased to hear whether I could. So I telephoned to the Clerk's office of the Monmouth County Council. 'Is Monmouth Wales or England?' I asked. He said it was a very difficult question to answer and put me on to the County Archivist. I asked him about the treaty, which he said was a popular belief with no signatories. He said Monmouth was neither Wales nor England, but the county motto was *Utrique Fidelis*. In order to get the Welsh view, I spoke to the London offices of the *South Wales Evening Post* and the *South Wales Echo*. The former, after waiting for a bit, definitely said Monmouth was part of Wales. The latter said that culturally it was Welsh, but that the Men of Gwent regarded themselves as neither Welsh nor English. Ecclesiastically it is Welsh. As a keen Manx Nationalist I am in favour of total independence for Monmouth, Berwick-upon-Tweed and the Soke of Peterborough.

*

I am distressed about Lord Salisbury's motion to reform the House of Lords by excluding some of those delightful Peers who never put in an appearance. The less known a Peer is, the more he interests me: Lord Gardner, for instance, who may or may not exist somewhere in India: Lord Aylmer who rarely leaves British Columbia, that home of quiet baronets: Lord Carberry who changed his name by deed poll to Mr Carberry and lives in Kenya: Lord Egmont happy in Alberta: all the retiring Peers who live in country places doing their local duty on farm and bench or working for their livings in smoky cities. And how pleasant it would be if the Irish Peers formed themselves into an Irish House of Lords and governed that country. Some of the ablest Irishmen are Peers. I suppose all this is hopelessly romantic and snobbish. All the same it is true to say that hereditary Peers are more likely to be agreeable people than commoners as they have had less occasion to feel inferior. Some of them may be gloriously eccentric, but what is wrong with that endearing characteristic?

*

Whenever an English monarch visits the Isle of Man, a mist hangs over the island. The late King had to be diverted from Douglas, where he was expected to land. I write this while the Queen is on the high seas, and have telephoned to the Isle of Man Tourist Office, that friendly haven in Trafalgar Square, to find out whether the Manxmen expect a mist. They do, and alternative landing arrangements have been made at Peel and Port St Mary. It has long been my ambition to be made Lieutenant-Governor of the Isle of Man, that most beautiful and varied of our islands, with its own laws and licensing hours. I would live in the Governor's fine house above Douglas Bay, the Naples of the North, with a nice motor car and a salary of £3,000, and once a year I would sit on the grassy Tynwald Mound on St John the Baptist's Day and hear the laws recited in Manx and English. The rest of the time I would visit the churches, dance-halls and wild cliffs and valleys, travel on the trains and trams, and read Hall Caine and T. E. Brown in the evenings. As almost all the native Manx names begin with Q, C or K, I would change my name to Ewan Quetjeman and work for Manx Independence. With these happy ideas in mind, I telephoned to the Home Office this morning and offered my services. They were not accepted, and I was told that the Lieutenant-Governor was also head of the Manx Police and was Chancellor of the Exchequer, and was kept busy. I would sever the island's connections with the Home Office if the post were offered to me.

*

Contrary to my expectations, I found myself in Cowes this year during Cowes Week, and actually visited the Squadron lawn, wrongly dressed in a London suit and a yachting cap. What was worse, I visibly flinched when a gun went off at the end of a race. But the beauty of the scene, the Solent almost lapis in the sunlight and darker than the green and blue nylon spinnakers on some of the yachts, made me forget my social solecisms. People think of the Isle of Wight as crowded, but I bathed during August Bank Holiday week under the brown cliffs east of Freshwater on a sandy beach looking across to the gleaming white cliffs by the Needles, and there was not a soul in sight. This western part of the island is like Dorset, but even more exciting in its variety of colouring and contour.

*

I received a letter from *The Tail-Wagger* magazine asking me to send a picture of my favourite pet, be it dog, cat or budgerigar, enclosing particulars. Apparently Sir Winston Churchill and Sir Malcolm Sargent had already contributed to the series. As the Editor has not answered the letter I sent in reply, and which I publish below, I take this opportunity of making the correspondence public:

> My favourite pets are an old teddy bear called Archie, and his friend, an elephant. I have had them all my life. Archie has a very dreary, Nonconformist face, and I am convinced he is alive. He has the great advantage of not having to be exercised or fed, and staying where he is put and making no noise. He has not a tail, so I do not think he would be at all suitable for inclusion in your magazine.

I am surprised at the lack of enterprise shown by pet-buyers. I had the privilege of being introduced to two enormous millepedes, about nine inches long and half an inch in diameter, by Miriam Rothschild in a country house drawing-room in Oxfordshire a few days ago. They do not move very fast, and the flow of their two hundred jointed legs is as elegant, varied and fascinating to watch as the flounce of a long wave on the seashore. They are perfectly harmless and eat vegetables. I took one on to the back of my hand, and the feel of its legs, a sort of deep tickle, remained on my hand after the creature, which seemed to weigh about a pound, had left my hand for my coat-sleeve. The assembled company, once it had overcome the shock at the rarity of these pets, was as fascinated as I was. Provided they can be kept in an equal temperature of sixty degrees, millepedes will live for some years. They are invertebrates and the specimens I saw were a dark reddish-brown.

*

I attended one day of the inquiry held last week by the Ministry of

Fuel and Power at Maldon, in Essex, about the atomic power station
the Central Electricity Board has decided to erect on the Blackwater
Estuary at Bradwell. It seems odd that the Minister should be the
judge of the activities of one of his own departments, and that
Ministries like Agriculture and Fisheries and Housing and Local
Government should not be the judges. At this inquiry I should have
thought either of them would have been entitled to that position. But
that is something to do with law and I realise my ignorance of it when
I attend an inquiry like this. The skill of the lawyers is amazing,
particularly the way they lead a witness into a trap and pounce. The
Central Electricity Board, of course, has its professional witnesses, but
for us members of the public the ordeal is terrifying.

You must imagine the crowded hall beside the Congregational
Church in Maldon, the amiable inspector and his two assistants on the
platform. Below him on his right, the men from the Central
Electricity Board; there seemed to be about twenty-five of them in
dark, neat suits, hard collars and horn-rimmed spectacles, with files
and papers (first-class fares and time paid). They reminded me of men
from *1984*, or the novel by C. S. Lewis, *That Hideous Strength*. On the
other side were we, the mad-eyed preservationists, the shrewd farmers
and representatives of the fishing and oyster interests, all giving up
time and money voluntarily to save the Dengie Peninsula. I hope this
does not sound smug, but it is the truth, and it is worth noting that
counsel appearing on behalf of objectors to Government schemes
generally do so free or for very low fees. Between us sat the Essex
country people, some thinking the atomic station would bring them
riches, others wanting to continue the way of life their fathers lived
before them.

My own passion for the Dengie Peninsula is of long standing. It is a
place of narrow lanes which take sudden right-angle bends revealing
rows of weather-boarded cottages, small hills with elms on them, and
finally the great salt marshes, with their birds and sea lavender, so
superbly described by Baring Gould in his novel *Mehala*. It is the
remotest possible country, and the only sea coast near London which
has not been exploited. I went there first by bicycle years ago to attend
the chapels of the Peculiar People, that Essex sect which goes in for
healing, whose women wear black bonnets and whose hymn book, I
recollect, has the delightful couplet:

> Shall chapel doors rattle and umbrellas move
> To show how you the service disapprove?

And I went more recently to make a television film of the little Adam-style gem, Bradwell Lodge (1781–6, architect John Johnson), which is open to the public. The lawyer for the Electricity Board tried to imply that I had made this film knowing that this inquiry was to be held. I wish that had been true, for I could have got a remark or two into the script. In the luncheon interval I stood on the top of the tower of Maldon's Moot Hall, looking over the tiled roofs and elegant Georgian houses of that extremely attractive hilltop town – a sort of Rye in Essex – and saw the great sweep of mild pastoral landscape and the gleaming water. It seemed impossible to me there that these electricity officials, with their technical jargon, their 'implements', 'in principles' and their evasive answers to direct questions, should really be indifferent to the beauty of the place. Yet to mention beauty at that inquiry seemed rather like talking about religion at a canasta party, essentially bad form.

*

Last week I passed through the concrete and chain-link fence which surrounds Harwell AERE (pronounced 'eerie' locally) for an Open Day, when the atomic piles were on view to specially selected members of the public. Perhaps I was not quite the person to ask, for though the scientists explained things to me as simply as they could and with the greatest courtesy, I could only pretend to understand what they were saying. I left with an impression that immense power was being generated somewhere, with no sparks, no explosions, no wheels and no noise. My idea of science is retorts, bunsen burners and a stuffed crocodile hanging from the ceiling, and I must confess Harwell was a disappointment to one so behind the times as I am. Certainly the ladders, walls, and things containing uranium, plutonium and heavy water were painted in bright festival colours. All the other visitors seemed to understand what they were looking at and one of them made my flesh creep by telling me of what will shortly be revealed in a Government White Paper about the effects on health all over the world from the recent letting-off of hydrogen bombs. I was pleased to see the wind waving over the grass of the Berkshire Downs when I stepped out of that strange, fluorescent kingdom.

Glasgow

The splendour of Edinburgh none will dispute. For skyline, for situation, for history, for contrast – the multi-storeyed ancientness of the Royal Mile descending in grey stone from the Castle to Holyrood, the spacious gleaming silver-grey of the New Town with squares, crescents and terraces which are unrivalled in the world – the steeples, the follies, the porticoes, the statues, the craggy outlines, these make it the finest capital city in these islands if not in Europe. I who write this have never seen Prague, its only possible rival.

While all praise Edinburgh, there are few to hymn Glasgow. To visit Glasgow after Edinburgh is rather like meeting a red-faced Lord Mayor after a session with a desiccated and long-lineaged Scottish peer. They are both magnificent in their ways, but so different that there is no comparison.

'Let Glasgow flourish . . .' are said to have been the words of St Mungo, the seventh-century Celtic saint who is buried under the Cathedral: '. . . by the preaching of the Word', which is the rest of the city's motto, is usually omitted. But the fulfilment of St Mungo's prophecy is evidenced by the many spires and steeples of the locked Church of Scotland and its offshoots which enliven the Glasgow skyline between the factories, the chimneys and the domed commercial buildings.

The pillar with John Knox on top dominates the Necropolis, that hill to the east of the Cathedral. Around it the tombs of Glasgow merchants in Egyptian, Greek and Gothic styles pressing down their Presbyterian bones give the Cathedral so fantastic and unforgettable a setting that it is hard to believe that here was once a grassy hollow in the hills where a Celtic saint had set his cell beside the burn.

As for the ancient Cathedral of Glasgow, I know of no finer thirteenth-century Gothic structure in these islands. Its soot-blackened exterior gives the impression of rather a small building. Inside the effect is enormous. The clerestoried nave, which lacks the stone-vaulted roof which would have completed it, leads to a choir of majesty unparalleled. The triple-arched eastern vista has four chapels at its square, substantial end.

Below the choir is the Crypt, or more properly the Lower Church, where repose the bones of St Mungo, and this building, with its many-vaulted vistas leading the eye to the central burial place, is one of those superb and inevitable compositions which make one realise that there is such a thing as architecture as distinct from building.

It is a Gothic masterpiece, as impressive in its way as King's College Chapel. But it has no colour and woodwork to heighten its effect. It impresses by the perfection of its proportion. Glasgow Cathedral is one of the least appreciated glories of Gothic architecture.

On the whole the Scots are subdued, austere and three-dimensional in their architecture. They seldom attract with an ornate façade, but suddenly, as in Roslin Chapel and the Barclay Church, Edinburgh, they let themselves go with an exuberance which amazes and dumbfounds the beholder.

For instance, the simple late eighteenth-century façade of twin buildings known as Lauriston House in the Gorbals on the south bank of the Clyde and now occupied by a department of the Glasgow Corporation, gives little promise of the interior. But inside are domed staircases, oval rooms, plaster ceilings all in the Adam style which no building in that manner I have seen can rival in richness of detail.

Though this great city is ancient in origin, most of its buildings of note belong to the last century. Alexander ('Greek') Thomson produced in Glasgow a simple architecture, solid and so perfectly proportioned that though none of his buildings are very big, they command a respect which the least observant cannot help giving them. His Presbyterian churches in St Vincent Street and Queen's Park, his terraces – Great Western Terrace and Moray Place, Strathbungo – display a delicacy of detail and a perfection of proportion which are a Greek answer to St Mungo's Cathedral so many centuries earlier.

All over Glasgow there is distinguished cast iron in lamp-posts, fences and balcony railings, in conservatories and railway station roofs. Possibly the best example of the last is the great semi-circular roof of Queen Street Station.

And then, at the end of the century, to go with the interest in art which the merchant princes of this vigorous city showed, there are both the collections of pictures in the public galleries and the Glasgow School of Art, by some considered the origin of what is today known as 'contemporary' architecture.

The pictures, Italian, Dutch and French Impressionist in the Glasgow Art Gallery, together with the Whistlers in the University, make up what must be our finest collection of paintings outside London.

The Glasgow School of Art (1897–9) designed by Charles Rennie Mackintosh, is in its delicately mannered simplicity one of the most original buildings in Britain. It is as though Scottish Baronial had been translated into stone and wood and glass by Aubrey Beardsley. Glasgow is rightly proud of Mackintosh, and a dress-shop in Sauchiehall Street still wisely preserves a room for its brides which Mackintosh originally designed for Glaswegians to drink tea in and eat baps and bannocks.

This is the bright side of a great city. But there can be no city in these islands which has darker spots. Out of a population of over a million, about 400,000 are not satisfactorily housed.

At Anderston Cross, built in the middle of the last century, I visited the worst slums I have ever seen. The stone buildings, four and five storeys high, looked solid enough on their street faces.

Enter one of the archways to the court-yards which they enclose, and you will see the squalor.

Small children with no park or green space for miles play in rubbish bins with dead cats and mutilated artificial flowers for toys. Spiral stone stairs, up which prams and bicycles have to be carried, lead to two-storey tenements with one lavatory for four families.

One such tenement I saw housed five children and the parents. The coal and the marmalade and bread were in the same cupboard. There was one sink with a single cold tap. There was a hole in the roof and a hole in the wall, and the only heat was from an old-fashioned kitchen range on which was a gas ring for cooking.

Yet these people, though they complained, were not bitter and I was told that there were 150,000 such houses in Glasgow. The Gorbals is by no means Glasgow's worst district. The Corporation has a slum clearance problem far greater and more complicated than that of any other city. Politics no doubt hamper its being carried out. But Christian charity must overrule political expediency.

The Daily Telegraph

The Outer Isles

How wise some of the thousands who cross the Channel to the Continent of Europe would be to turn back and cross the Atlantic to the Shetlands. The islands are nearer to Norway than to Edinburgh, and because they are put in an inset in our atlases we do not realise their remarkable position in the British group of islands.

We think of them vaguely as Scottish and cold, but they are neither. They and the Orkneys were Danish until 1468, when they fell to the Scottish crown as a pledge for the unpaid dowry of Margaret of Denmark, wife of James III of Scotland. Their people are mostly Scandinavian, as are their place-names and many of the words in their vocabulary.

The Scots became landlords of the Orkneys and Shetlands and upset the Scandinavian system of land tenure and were generally resented. Even today people from Scotland are referred to as Southerners.

The great red sandstone Cathedral of St Magnus rises above the grey stepped gables of Kirkwall, the Orkney capital. It is a vast and stone-vaulted building in an early Gothic strange to us because it is Scandinavian.

Both groups of islands are studded with the settlements of that mysterious race the Picts, who lived here in the first century AD before the Vikings landed. They were a small people who dwelt underground and built brochs which look like miniature condenser towers made of dry stone, and which, with their internal passages, seem to have been used for shelter and defence. According to Norse legend they were a people who did marvels at dawn and in the dark, but whose strength waned in the middle of the day.

Before the Picts the Stone Age lingered on in the Orkneys and Shetlands long after it had died out in the rest of Europe. Today at Scara Brae in Orkney and Jarlshof in Shetland there are complete monuments of pre-history. So ancient is the surface of these marvellous, varied and windswept isles that our own age's tinny contribution of poles and wires, corrugated iron, motor cars and wireless masts (but no television poles) seems but a trivial though prominent scratch.

The islands, though so northerly, are not so cold in winter as the Midlands of England. Probably the best time to see them is early spring, before the summer mists arise and the mosquitoes and earwigs hatch. For colour – the sea 'a peacock's neck in hue', the hills gold and brown and green, with occasional grey lichened walls of crofts and outbuildings, the cliffs of red and yellow sandstone, or black and purple slate, the constantly changing light, all colours of the rainbow – the Orkneys and Shetlands can compare in vividness with the west coast of Scotland.

The Orkneys, which except for the island of Hoy are rather flat, hold a prosperous farming community of about 26,000 people. There are ninety islands, a third of which are inhabited. The Shetlands, fifty miles north of them, are less prosperous since they are dependent on fishing and more rugged and impressive in scenery. There are more than one hundred islands, of which twenty-nine are inhabited, and they take up the first four sheets of the one inch Ordnance Survey map. Their population is about 25,000.

The people are hospitable, intelligent and generous. Every Shetlander is an encyclopaedia of legend and folklore. An Englishman feels himself at home here, whereas in the Highlands of Scotland he can feel foreign through not being a Celt.

It has been my privilege for the past two years to visit our outermost Northern Islands with the National Trust for Scotland, that most vigorous of all voluntary bodies. Our motor ship the Meteor, of the Bergen line, was commanded by an intrepid Norwegian, Captain Knud Maurer, who enabled us to land on islands which rarely see a stranger. Our party consisted mostly of weatherbeaten bird-watchers, Scottish peers and baronets in tweeds, botanists and archaeologists. I, who am none of these things, profited from their company.

The first island on which we spent a whole day on this year's cruise was Fair Isle, half-way between the Orkneys and the Shetlands and an epitome of the two groups. It is about three miles long and two wide. The southern end, where the houses are, is farm land, and like Orkney; the north and west coasts have gigantic cliffs and are like Shetland.

The first thing one notices when one steps ashore at North Haven, where is the new pier with the islanders' 27-ton boat the Good Shepherd, is the freshness of the air. And suddenly above the whisper

of the waves and the wail of sea birds comes the unexpected note of a
song bird, the Fair Isle wren.

The sixty islanders are a friendly people, Sabbath-keeping, with two
simple kirks used on alternate Sundays. The coast is surrounded by
natural arches where seals play. In the north of the island is an
enormous hole called the Kirn of Skroo, and far below in its inky
blackness one can faintly hear the sea washing in.

Lerwick, the Shetland capital, is about as big as Basingstoke. It is
Dutch in origin and its older houses jut out into the harbour. The
older streets are all slate pavement. On the opposite island of Bressay
the Adam-style Georgian house of a Scottish laird surveys the town.
We tried to land at Out Skerries, one of the few Shetland islands
which is not becoming depopulated. But there was too much of a
swell; we saw the islanders outlined against the sky, waiting to
welcome us, and sadly we waved farewell.

We rounded the northernmost point of Britain at Herma Ness,
where the cliffs are black and vast. Here flew those sinister birds the
bonxies, whose disgusting habit it is to chase smaller birds and frighten
them so much that they are sick, and the bonxies swoop down and eat
the vomit.

We landed on Papa Stour, the least visited of the inhabited Shetland
Isles. Here are caves where one can row in a boat for half a mile. The
Post Office is in a field with no road to it. We saw men ploughing the
rich green earth with Shetland ponies and sowing the seed by hand.

One evening we landed on Foula, the most westerly of the
Shetlands, where a visitor might find himself stranded for weeks if the
weather changed, for there is no proper harbour. The hills on its west
coast, where the cliffs fall sheer into the Atlantic and are the second
highest in Britain, were shrouded in mist.

In 1900 there were two hundred people on this fertile and varied
isle. Today there are only fifty. All over the Shetlands one sees ruined
crofts, with rushes invading the once tilled strips and kingcups in the
garden. 'Gone to New Zealand' is a good name for such a scene,
because that is where many Shetlanders go, and there are, I am told,
two streets in Wellington almost wholly Shetland.

I looked at a 'black house' with its windowless stone walls and its
thatched roof held down against the wind by weighted cords. Peat
smoke was coming from the chimney, but the front door was
padlocked and the old man who had kept the peat fire alive all his life
was standing far off on the hillside.

Below in the pasture the primitive stone mill which had ground his corn stood over the burn among the rushes. The mist began to lift, and down a valley I saw peak beyond peak of those tremendous cliffs rise sheer in golden light and disappear as the mist once more descended.

The kirk, with its Georgian pulpit and simple benches, had a hole in the roof. The strong stone school house now serves as kirk on the Sabbath and school for four pupils in the week.

The houses on Foula seem better built than those on other Shetland isles, and except for a telephone kiosk there is nothing ugly on the island. The people are tall and handsome, and the place is like an independent kingdom.

We left the Shetlands to land on Rona and St Kilda, but this is leaving Scandinavia for that other world of the west.

The Daily Telegraph

City and Suburban (4)

A series of articles written for The Spectator

This week I had my fiftieth birthday. I had felt it coming on for some time. Standing nude in the bathroom two months ago, I suddenly realised I could not see my toes any more because my stomach was in the way. I started reviewing my past life first through a magnifying mist of self-pity – never quite made the grade, not taken seriously by the *Times Literary Supplement*, Penguin Books, the Courtauld, the Warburg, the *Listener*, the University Appointments Board, the Museums Association, the Library Association, the Institute of Sanitary Engineers. I thought of the many people at school with me who were now knights and politicians. I wanted to cry. Then I thought of my many friends who are now dead, and terror of eternity made me want to scream. Fifty. Not much longer for this world, every day more precious. I must begin cleaning up this earthly house so as to leave things tidy for my wife and children. And there it was that real frustration set in. I don't know whether it is the same with you as it is with me, but every time, as a self-employed person, I have income tax demands, I have to sell a little more of my dwindling capital. And what surprises me is that the Income Tax Commissioners, who are most charming and helpful about suggesting ways I can pay them what they demand, never tell me whether their demands are legal. Still less do they tell me about legal ways by which I may avoid their incursions into my capital. I would like to know, for instance, the answers to the following questions:

1. Is it legal for me to turn myself into a company with my family as shareholders and me as a paid managing director?
2. Is it legal for me to make a reciprocal arrangement with a friend whereby I pay an allowance to his children and he pays one to mine?
3. Am I entitled to a clothes allowance because I sometimes appear on television and often lecture on behalf of old churches, and how much allowance am I permitted?

I am not asking the Commissioners their opinion of the morality of my actions if I were to turn myself into a company, make a reciprocal agreement and claim a clothes allowance, just as I am not questioning the State's moral right to erect a huge new school in contemporary sprawling geometric cubes of glass on the hill above Wadebridge where the road turns off to Polzeath. I merely call out from my rowing boat of the individual for help to the State liner as she sails out into the night, or is it into the dawn?

*

Last week's golden October weather has made me think of Surrey and what a beautiful county it once was, and in some places still is. Sunset behind Sutton Palmer pine trees, brilliant fungi on brown pine needles, and here and there a sleepy valley between the heaths, with a few thatched cottages out of the sound of Southern Electric – if Tennyson is the poet of Lincs, Hardy of Dorset and Arnold of Oxon, then Meredith is the poet of Surrey. The winds, wet woods and vast sunsets are the stuff of his nature poetry.

> Now seems none but the spider lord;
> Star in circle his web waits prey,
> Silvering bush-mounds, blue brushing sward;
> Slow runs the hour, swift flits the ray.

*

I am told that anti-Semitism is strong in America, and that one golf club near New York does not allow Jews to play on it. A man playing on it lately was suspected. The secretary was sent to interrogate him, and said that he was very sorry but this club had its rules, and he understood that the player was a Jew and therefore he must ask him to play somewhere else. The man replied: 'My father was not Jewish, but my mother was. Suppose I play nine holes?'

*

Last week I travelled with my wife more than forty miles out of Berkshire into Oxfordshire in an American gig, pulled by a chestnut cob. As soon as we were off the main roads we were in a paradise of rain-washed scents and sights, and experienced the new thrill of slowness. From a gig you can smell and see again meadowsweet, honeysuckle, roses and grass. You can understand why in the horse-drawn age so many more people were botanists. Nothing could equal the beauty of some giant thistles I saw, or the blue stalks of the barley with the pale green heads above them. Motorists were fairly considerate. We felt they had a right to the main roads, but that they were not justified in cutting across the horse's head in country lanes.

*

It is not the fall of the leaf that makes me sad about autumn, but the thought that it is the beginning of term. There are still those smells of warm gym shoes in the changing room, of old biscuits and margarine in the dining-hall, of polished oilcloth and carbolic in the dormitories. The masters you liked have left, and those you do not like remain. There is a new matron, but that is no consolation. All sorts of unlikely people have been made prefects (have you ever noticed how those who become prefects at school become either knights, politicians or both in later life?). There stretch before you weeks and weeks of games of football in cold fields, and no hot water left when you return to the changing room, and at these games you must appear keen for the honour of the house. Meanwhile, the curtains are drawn in seaside residences and sea mist dulls the windows and rusts the metal casements, and waves crash over empty sands where once were love and life and Portuguese Men-of-War. The new year really begins in September, or at any rate in Advent when the Church's year starts and all holidays are done. I was speaking to Charles Letts, the diary firm, about why diaries must always begin on January 1. It is because of the Christmas trade and nothing to do with the Church's year, the school year or any of the other years by which most of us live.

*

'Excuse me,' said a lady to me when I was crossing Hammersmith Broadway. She elbowed me off the traffic island and asserted her rights on the zebra crossing in front of a bus. When people say 'Excuse me' I always reply 'No', and they look round, as this lady did, risking her life in doing so, in pained amazement. 'Excuse me' is only one of the phrases current today which has lost its original meaning. Today it means 'Get out of the way.' 'Can I help you, sir?' means 'What the hell are you doing here?' 'With due respect' or 'In all respect' means 'I have no respect for your opinions at all.' For years now 'To be frank' has meant 'To be unpardonably rude.' As our language loses its meaning (a Post Office official told a friend of mine the other day that he would 'organise' a telephone for him), so local accents disappear and clichés take their place. There is technological jargon, education jargon, church jargon and so on. I was in Bristol on Sunday exploring

Kingsdown, a leafy Georgian suburb of cobbled lanes, steps, pear trees and bow-windowed houses, all threatened with destruction on an airy hilltop in that wonderful city. But I listened in vain as I talked to people for the intrusive liquid which used to be a feature of that part of Bristol. Ernest Bevin had it. He used to put 'l's' on to words ending with an 'a' or an 'o' – 'idea-l', 'banana-l'; and, of course, 'Bristol' was originally 'Bristowe'. But there is still in the City of London, among older brokers and company directors, that delightful thing the 'City accent' which went with an Italianate house with a gravel drive and lamp-posts in Streatham or Lewisham and has now migrated to Esher and Sussex. The vowels are rather broad and flat. The speech is slow and shrewdly thoughtful.

*

Many authors, when one meets them for the first time, are comparatively unimpressive compared with their books. But Lord Dunsany, who died last week, never disappointed. He was every inch a poet, playwright, storyteller, Irish peer, big-game hunter, painter, modeller in clay, Conservative politician, soldier and country gentleman, all of which occupations he followed in the busiest and most-enjoyed life I have seen. He was a tall, splendid-looking man with a young voice, decided opinions and boundless energy. He was very happily married and had the good manners of an Edwardian autocrat. Unexpected things roused his anger. One of them was manufactured salt in advertised brands (he mistrusted everything that was branded and advertised) – if he found this on a dinner table, no matter whose house it was, he would say, 'Send for some ordinary kitchen salt and bring two glasses of water.' He would then pour some of the branded salt into one glass and the kitchen salt into another. The kitchen salt dissolved, but the branded salt left a white deposit at the bottom of the other glass which he said was either chalk or ground-up bones. He was one of those people who made you feel on top of the world and that all those who disagreed with you were petty crooks who would be beaten in the end. He talked with all the fantasy of his own Jorkens stories.

*

Another author who never disappoints when one meets him is Sir Compton Mackenzie. I think this is because his approach to strangers is the other way round to that of most people. He is prejudiced in their favour, whatever they might have done in the past, until they say or do something in his presence which damns them. I remember him once telling me that he did not regard himself as a literary man but as an entertainer, as he came from a family of entertainers. And he entertained me last week in Edinburgh with an example of Henry James's conversation which I will find it difficult to put into words. James was criticising Mackenzie's novel *Carnival* to him, saying that perhaps the lady delineated in that book was too delicately modelled for the vast structure in which she was set, and ending, 'but then I said the same to Flaubert about *Madame Bovary.*' Mackenzie, flattered, said that he was intending to rewrite the book. 'Never do that,' said James, 'I have wasted twelve precious years of my life doing such things. You are the one member of your generation who can throw up the ball and receive it back into his hands. But when I throw up the ball it hits first one wall, bounces to another and then another, until it finally rolls slowly to my feet and with my aching, ageing limbs I struggle to bend down and pick it up.' He told me that James used to send résumés of his novels before he wrote them to his agent Pinker and that these were marvellous short stories. I wonder what has become of them.

*

Edina, the Athens of the North, Caledonia's sternest city, is without doubt the finest capital in these islands, and I am told by those who know their Europe better than I that only Prague approaches it for romance of outline. And what makes Edinburgh so distinguished a capital is a variety of assets: the excellence of Scottish architects whether Georgian or earlier; the historical associations of places like Holyrood and St Giles and the Castle; the durability of the building stone admirably adapted to receive the strong mouldings and sculpture in which the Scots delight; the excellence of all details such as granite setts in the roads, paving stones, old lamp-posts where they survive, iron railings, street nameplates, front doors and windows with the original glazing bars; the brooding presence of Arthur's Seat and, above everything, the contrast between the Old Town with its narrow wynds and gables on one hill and the New Town with its superbly proportioned streets, crescents, terraces and squares. These last proclaim the Scottish genius for classic architecture in Georgian and early Victorian times.

It seems almost incredible that the town council of so glorious a city as this should deliberately plan to murder its greatest asset as it is going to do on January 9, unless wiser counsels on the council prevail, by diverting heavy traffic such as buses and lorries through the quiet streets of the New Town from Randolph Crescent (near the Waters of

Leith village) to London Road via Ainslie, Moray and Drummond Places. The first step in this programme is the destruction of the trees in Randolph Crescent. Local protests have been made by Moray McLaren, Sir Compton Mackenzie and Mr Fenwick, who is a member of the Randolph Crescent Proprietors' Committee. This scheme really amounts to taking all the quiet, the dignity and the character from a residential quarter. It is the equivalent of making Regent's Park in London open to buses.

But the traffic problem in Edinburgh is nothing like so great as it is in London. And I would advise those who think Edinburgh traffic is great to come down to London before Christmas next year and see what real traffic blocks are like. More than Bath, Cheltenham, Brighton, Stratford-on-Avon, Ludlow, Bristol, Dublin or Cork, Edinburgh is *the* most beautiful town in these islands. It is unique in having in its centre acres of magnificent Georgian residential streets whose charm comes from the very fact that they are exempt from buses and heavy traffic. Perhaps the Edinburgh Town Council may even now decide to preserve a chief part of their city from such disturbance, for noise and out-of-proportion buses and lorries are every bit as much murderers of landscape as are concrete lamp standards and ill-shaped buildings.

T. S. Eliot the Londoner

The yellow fog that rubs its back upon the window-panes may well have been a Boston fog, if they have them there: the four wax candles in the darkened room, which look to me so like somewhere in Bloomsbury (now bombed by Germans or demolished by London University), may well be in New England: the damp souls of housemaids sprouted for me at area gates in South Kensington, though New York may have been where the poet saw them: still I have the impression that Eliot is not only a town poet, but above all a London poet. Topography may not be an important element in a poem, there is little in Shelley, none in the seventeenth-century religious poems so much admired by Eliot, and yet London percolates most of his poems, and though he may call one *East Coker* and another *Burt Norton*, London is in them both. Love of place may not be essential to the full enjoyment of his poetry, yet it is a noticeable part of it, especially love of London. It is a part of his character, too. A friend of mine recalls his saying 'Speaking precisely as an air-raid warden of South Kensington . . .'

He is associated in my mind very much with London. He is the first poet that I ever met. This was in 1916 when I was at Highgate Junior School and he was known there as the 'American Master'. He looked then very much as he does today and he spoke with the same slowness and exactitude. It was known among us then that he wrote poetry, although *Prufrock* did not appear until a year later.

A love for London starts with a feeling for the City which is the heart of London and its oldest part. No poet has described the smells and noises of the City of London so well as Eliot since the days of Langland and 'the London Lyckpenny'. I imagine Eliot getting out of the District Railway at Monument Station and seeing the crowds walking over London Bridge and joining them as he moves towards the Bank to where St Mary Woolnoth kept the hours. And in the lunch hour I see him walking down to look at the Thames at London Bridge and catching that smell of fish by Billingsgate.

> O City city, I can sometimes hear
> Beside a public bar in Lower Thames Street,
> The pleasant whining of a mandoline
> And a clatter and a chatter from within
> Where fishermen lounge at noon: where the walls
> Of Magnus Martyr hold
> Inexplicable splendour of Ionian white and gold.*

The City of London and its river are the chief topographical backgrounds to *The Waste Land*.

Eliot's love of London extends to the suburbs and home counties. His appreciation of Sherlock Holmes, that essentially London and Home County man, is largely concerned with those subtle details of Norwood, Reigate and Charing Cross which are part of the delight we have in the stories today. Addresses in London very much please Eliot. I remember his telling me how Miss Swan at Fabers, the publishers, of which he is a director, lived in Trossachs Road, Dulwich, and I remember the pleasure he had himself in living in Bina Gardens, SW5. Who but someone who had worked in the City as a clerk could have written:

> But where is the penny world I bought
>   To eat with Pipit behind the screen?
> The red-eyed scavengers are creeping
>   From Kentish Town and Golders Green.

And how well he understands the pathos of those thousands who droop in a hundred ABC's:

> Highbury bore me. Richmond and Kew
> Undid me.

The subtle class distinctions of outer London are in his poetry, too. This quotation from *The Rock* is redolent of Esher and Wentworth:

> In the land of lobelias and tennis flannels
> The rabbit shall burrow and the thorn revisit,

JB's footnote:

* He must have entered St Magnus not earlier than 1921, the year when the present rector, Father Fynes-Clinton, was appointed. Before that St Magnus was low church, locked, box-pewed, dead and dusty. The Ionic white and gold must refer to the redecoration under Father Fynes Clinton by Martin Travers.

The nettle shall flourish on the gravel court
And the wind shall say: 'Here were godless people:
Their only monument the asphalt road
And a thousand lost golf balls.'

Whether it is the public transport of London:

Or as, when an underground train, in the tube, stops too long between
    stations
And the conversation rises and slowly fades into silence
And you see behind every face the mental emptiness deepen
Leaving only the growing terror of nothing to think about;

or in what he loves best, the churches of our own beloved Church of
England, it is London which inspires him, the London where he has
lived for the last forty years:

> Ill done and undone,
> London so fair
> We will build London
> Bright in dark air,
> With new bricks and mortar
> Beside the Thames bord
> Queen of Island and Water,
> A House of our Lord.

From *T.S. Eliot: A Symposium*

Elusive Ralph Hodgson

No living English poets have written more well-known poems than Ralph Hodgson. 'The Bull', 'The Song of Honour', 'Stupidity Street', and the short lyrics beginning: "'T would ring the bells of heaven', 'Time, you old gypsy man', are some of them.

Few well-known poets have published less. That slim volume 'Poems' appeared in 1917. Poems from it have been reprinted in countless anthologies and chanted out in thousands of classrooms.

What happened to Ralph Hodgson, that most elusive of famous men? *Who's Who* tells me he was born in 1871, that he was in Japan from 1924 to 1938, and that he has received various prizes for his poems. I have been told that he lives in the state of Ohio in the United States. Beyond that I knew nothing about him except his poetry and that he bred pedigree dogs many years ago when I met him in London.

His poems have a quality of memorability which keep them in one's head long after one's interest in what they expressed, and one's sympathy with the style and mood in which they were written, have disappeared. Before reading *The Skylark and Other Poems* by Ralph Hodgson I turned to that earlier volume. I recaptured the exaltation the poems gave me years ago. They stood the test of time, though I could see that 'The Song of Honour' is not so magnificent as Christopher Smart's 'Song to David' of which it reminds me.

There are a clarity, directness and love of animals in Hodgson which if he were not a true poet would make his verse trite. What that quality is which keeps him from toppling over into artiness and the sentimental, I cannot define. But it is there.

Thus the new volume of Hodgson, of ninety spacious pages handsomely printed in a large italic, and with wood-engravings by Reynolds Stone, is an event. Some of the poems here were included in his book published in 1917. Others were subsequently printed in defunct periodicals and yet more in rare chap-books published in America.

The new volume shows little change in the poet and that is a good thing. He started mature, and he has continued so. There is a certain tendency to obscurity in a long poem called 'The Muse and the Mastiff', which is still unfinished, and which probably requires a knowledge of mastiffs I do not possess. But there are other poems here every bit as good and memorable as those already famous. One, for instance, on 'Time' appraising its qualities and concluding thus:

> Comparing it for poise;
> The tops we spun to sleep
> Seemingly so deep
> Stockstill when we were boys
> No more than stumbled round.
> Boxwoods though they were
> The best we ever wound
> Or whipped of all such toys;
> Comparing it for sound:
> The wisp of gossamer
> Caught in a squirrel's fur
> Groans like a ship aground;
> Shadow makes more noise.

The book concludes with some gnomic utterances, sometimes no more than a single line, which are characteristic of all Ralph Hodgson's work. On the surface they seem obvious and then another meaning comes to life as the line goes on reverberating in the ear:

> 'Only the Eskimo,
> Staring at his dusty snow.
> Will ever know.'

I imagine this refers to the world after an atomic war.

The Daily Telegraph

A New Westminster

When I first learned that Westminster Abbey was to be demolished in the foreseeable future I was as dumbfounded as, no doubt, will be the readers of these words. I sought permission on the very highest level to present the case for demolition to an intelligent public in the favourable light in which I now myself see it and received an express intimation from my Minister himself via the deputy comptroller that I could do so. Neither my Minister nor the London County Council Planning Committee nor the works and buildings committee of the Westminister City Council, all of whom are of course directly and indirectly concerned with the proposed demolition, wished the matter to be discussed yet in the national press. It was considered that what my Minister calls 'a feeler' might be put out in the *Spectator* or the *Manchester Guardian*, to test the more enlightened reaction of an exclusive and cultivated public to a scheme the benefits of which might not at first seem to outweigh the somewhat sentimental losses. Both my Minister, the LCC and any local planning committees have always found that in practice it is best to present the general public with a *fait accompli* when a scheme is ultimately for its own good. I must, therefore, ask my readers not to pass on the information they read here to their lady helps, domestic science assistants, public cleansing officers, etc., but to confine their information to administrative grades.

For some time now the Minister of Transport has been concerned by the increase of traffic between Victoria and Parliament Square and notably by the bottleneck caused by the projection of the western towers of the Abbey into the roadway. In the near future it is proposed to erect on the site of the old Westminster Hospital a much-needed block of government offices, with the result that the bottleneck will be further intensified. My Minister was reluctant to take the drastic course of demolishing the Abbey without first examining all possible alternatives. The most obvious of these was the setting back of the proposed new government offices so as to secure a consistent width of roadway the whole way down Victoria Street to Parliament Square. To this there were insuperable objections: the plans for the new offices were already in an advanced state and could not be altered except at prohibitive cost to the public funds; the roadway itself would make an unnecessary curve to avoid the Abbey and interrupt a fine vista the LCC planning authorities had, with imaginative foresight, arranged whereby Big Ben would be visible with the Houses of Parliament from as far away down Victoria Street as the Army and Navy Stores. Another course to be taken was that of leaving things as they are, which *prima facie*, is impossible.

My Minister had then to consider the pros and cons of the Abbey itself. It has undoubted historic associations going back as far as Saxon times, though the vestiges of these interesting days are so slight as to cause very little trouble in their preservation, if it is envisaged, in the new scheme for developing the site. Then there are the memorials of eminent persons in the political, scientific, economic and artistic worlds whose bones are interred in the Abbey. By arrangement with the development company which is to erect the fine new building on the site, my Minister has arranged that these shall be moved and re-erected in a suitable cloister or close at Brookwood Cemetery, where they will be open to those members of the public who still enjoy the rather morbid occupation of examining gravestones.

Next my Minister was faced with finding alternative accommodation for the purposes for which the Abbey is used at present. There is still a certain amount of religious services carried on there, though, we may confidently expect, as material progress continues, rapidly diminishing numbers. By arrangement with neighbouring vicars of the Church of England and with the full assurance of the authorities of the adjacent Roman Catholic Cathedral at Westminster that they will receive any members of the existing congregation of the Abbey who may care to join them, it should be possible to cater for these persons without undue inconvenience. Finally, there are the rare occasions when the building is used for Coronations, and we must assume, for the present, that the monarchy will continue to exist. All will agree that the present building is too small, too inconvenient and too ill-planned to enable those many thousands who may wish to witness this quaint and historic ceremony to see it. It is suggested that a place with better visibility, say, the Festival Hall or Wembley Stadium, be used for future Coronations. This will have the additional advantage of being non-sectarian.

As to the fabric itself, my Minister has given this careful consideration. He has consulted acknowledged experts and learns that the building, though ancient in origin, was not all built at one period and therefore lacks the consistency of a single unit of architecture such as is envisaged on its site. The controversial western towers are indeed a fake, having been ascribed to Sir Christopher Wren and being in a Gothic which, if my readers will pardon the phrase, can only be called 'bastard'. The exterior was largely refaced by the Victorians, who notably lacked artistic taste. The only feature which all are agreed as being of exceptional merit is the Henry VII chapel, which, though very late and decadent Gothic, has a certain charm. The developers have expressed themselves as willing to retain a portion of this, if possible, in their new building, since they maintain that as it is the best the Middle Ages could do in the way of glass and stone (stainless steel not then having been discovered) it can be made to harmonise with the simpler and more honest expression of our own age in steel and glass which they are proposing to erect. But if they keep a part of this chapel they will have, for economic reasons, to develop on the site of the somewhat redundant church of St Margaret, Westminster.

Finally, there come the advantages of the proposed scheme, which may be summarised under the following heads.

Practical: London's traffic problem will be materially eased by a free passage of transport between the busy stations of Victoria and Waterloo and buses and cars will be able to travel much faster from the South-West to Whitehall. A more suitable building will be provided elsewhere for Coronations. Much needed government and commercial offices will be provided in Westminster which, in the neighbourhood of the existing Abbey, lags far behind the City of London in commercial development.

Economic: The development company is willing to pay a high enough sum for this key site to offset the cost of the road improvements and gain in public parking space which will result, thus putting no burden on the ratepayers.

Artistic: The very best architects are to be employed by the company and the design will of course be submitted to the LCC, the Westminster Corporation and possibly even to the Royal Fine Art Commission. The resulting achievement, to be in the form of a glass and steel tower hung with specially designed curtain walling and three hundred feet high with subsidiary light and airy blocks rising to not more than one hundred feet, will challenge, as our own age should if we have any faith in it, the Houses of Parliament to which it will act as a vast foil. A new vista will be opened from Victoria Street. A worthy contribution to a famous skyline will at last be added in a part too long dominated by the obsolescent buildings of past eras.

As a Government servant and Public Relations Officer I cannot, for obvious reasons, subscribe my name to this article, but have paid a journalist to do so who has pleasure in signing himself

J. Betjeman

The Spectator

English Parish
Churches

An extract from the Introduction to
English Parish Churches

THE OLD CHURCHES

To atheists inadequately developed building sites; and often, alas, to
Anglicans but visible symbols of disagreement with the incumbent:
'the man there is "too high", "too low", "too lazy", "too interfering"
– still they stand, the churches of England, their towers grey above
billowy globes of elm trees, the red cross of St George flying over
their battlements, the Duplex Envelope System employed for collections, schoolmistress at the organ, incumbent in the chancel, scattered
worshippers in the nave, Tortoise stove slowly consuming its ration as
the familiar seventeenth-century phrases come echoing down arcades
of ancient stone.

Odi et amo. This sums up the general opinion of the Church of
England among the few who are not apathetic. One bright autumn
morning I visited the church of the little silver limestone town of
Somerton in Somerset. Hanging midway from a rich-timbered roof,
on chains from which were suspended branched and brassy-gleaming
chandeliers, were oval boards painted black. In gold letters on each
these words were inscribed:

TO GOD'S
GLORY
&
THE HONOR OF
THE
CHURCH OF
ENGLAND
1782

They served me as an inspiration towards compiling this book.

The Parish Churches of England are even more varied than the
landscape. The tall town church, smelling of furniture polish and hotwater pipes, a shadow of the medieval marvel it once was, so

assiduously have Victorian and even later restorers renewed every-thing old; the little weather-beaten hamlet church standing in a farmyard down a narrow lane, bat-droppings over the pews and one service a month; the church of a once prosperous village, a relic of the fifteenth-century wool trade, whose soaring splendour of stone and glass subsequent generations have had neither the energy nor the money to destroy; the suburban church with Northamptonshire-style steeple rising unexpectedly above slate roofs of London and calling with mid-Victorian bells to the ghosts of merchant carriage folk for whom it was built; the tin chapel-of-ease on the edge of the industrial estate; the High, the Low, the Central churches, the alive and the dead ones, the churches that are easy to pray in and those that are not, the churches whose architecture brings you to your knees, the churches whose decorations affront the sight – all these come within the wide embrace of our Anglican Church, whose arms extend beyond the seas to many fabrics more.

From the first wooden church put up in a forest clearing or stone cell on windy moor to the newest social hall, with sanctuary and altar partitioned off, built on the latest industrial estate, our churches have existed chiefly for the celebration of what some call the Mass, or the Eucharist and others call Holy Communion or the Lord's Supper.

Between the early paganism of Britain and the present paganism there are nearly twenty thousand churches and well over a thousand years of Christianity. More than half the buildings are medieval. Many of those have been so severely restored in the last century that they could almost be called Victorian – new stone, new walls, new roofs, new pews. If there is anything old about them it is what one can discern through the detective work of the visual imagination.

It may be possible to generalise enough about the parish church of ancient origin to give an impression of how it is the history of its district in stone and wood and glass. Such generalisation can give only a superficial impression. Churches vary with their building materials and with the religious, social and economic history of their districts.

THE OUTSIDE OF THE CHURCH – GRAVESTONES

See on some village mound, in the mind's eye, the parish church of today. It is in the old part of the place. Near the church will be the few old houses of the parish, and almost for certain there will be an inn very near the church. A lych-gate built as a memorial at the beginning of this century indicates the entrance to the churchyard. Away on the outskirts of the town or village, if it is a place of any size, will be the arid new cemetery consecrated in 1910 when there was no more room in the churchyard.

Nearer to the church and almost always on the south side are to be found the older tombs, the examples of fine craftsmanship in local stone of the Queen Anne and Georgian periods. Wool merchants and big farmers, all those not entitled to an armorial monument on the walls inside the church, generally occupy the grandest graves. Their obelisks, urns and table-tombs are surrounded with Georgian iron-work. Parish clerks, smaller farmers and tradesmen lie below plainer stones. All their families are recorded in deep-cut lettering. Here is a flourish of eighteenth-century calligraphy; there is reproduced the typeface of Baskerville. It is extraordinary how long the tradition of fine lettering continued, especially when it is in a stone easily carved or engraved, whether limestone, ironstone or slate. The tradition lasted until the middle of the nineteenth century in those country places where stone was used as easily as wood. Some old craftsman was carving away while the young go-aheads in the nearest town were busy inserting machine-made letters into white Italian marble.

The elegance of the local stone carver's craft is not to be seen only in the lettering. In the eighteenth century it was the convention to carve symbols round the top of the headstone and down the sides. The earlier examples are in bold relief, cherubs with plough-boy faces and thick wings, and scythes, hour glasses and skulls and cross-bones diversify their tops. You will find in one or another country churchyard that there has been a local sculptor of unusual vigour and perhaps genius who has even carved a rural scene above some well-graven name. Towards the end of the eighteenth century the lettering becomes finer and more prominent, the decoration flatter and more conventional, usually in the Adam manner, as though a son had taken on his father's business and depended on architectural pattern-books. But the tops of all headstones varied in shape. At this time too it became the custom in some districts to paint the stones and to add a little gold leaf to the lettering. Paint and stone by now have acquired a varied pattern produced by weather and fungus, so that the stones are probably more beautiful than they were when they were new, splodged as they are with gold and silver and slightly overgrown with moss. On a sharp frosty day when the sun is in the south and throwing up the carving, or in the west and bringing out all the colour of the lichens, a country churchyard may bring back the lost ages of craftsmanship more effectively than the church which stands behind it. Those unknown carvers are of the same race as produced the vigorous inn signs which were such a feature of England before the brewers ruined them with artiness and standardisation. They belong to the world of wheelwrights and waggon-makers, and they had their local styles. In Kent the chief effect of variety was created by different-sized stones with elaborately-scalloped heads to them, and by shroud-like mummies of stone on top of the grave itself; in the Cotswolds by carving in strong relief; in slate districts by engraved lettering. In counties like Surrey and Sussex, where stone was rare, there were many wooden graveyard monuments, two posts with a board between them running down the length of the grave and painted in the way an old waggon is painted. But most of these wooden monuments have perished or decayed out of recognition.

'At rest', 'Fell asleep', 'Not dead but gone before' and other equally non-committal legends are on the newer tombs. In Georgian days it was the custom either to put only the name or to apply to the schoolmaster or parson for a rhyme. Many a graveyard contains beautiful stanzas which have not found their way to print and are disappearing under wind and weather. Two of these inscriptions have particularly struck my fancy. One is in Bideford and commemorates a retired sea-captain Henry Clark, 1836. It summarises for me a type of friendly and pathetic Englishman to be found hanging about, particularly at little seaports.

> For twenty years he scarce slept in a bed;
> Linhays and limekilns lull'd his weary head
> Because he would not to the poor house go,
> For his proud spirit would not let him to.
>
> The black bird's whistling notes at break of day
> Used to awake him from his bed of hay.
> Unto the bridge and quay he then repaired
> To see what shipping up the river stirr'd.
>
> Oft in the week he used to view the bay,
> To see what ships were coming in from sea,
> To captains' wives he brought the welcome news,
> And to the relatives of all the crews.
>
> At last poor Harry Clark was taken ill,
> And carried to the work house 'gainst his will:

And being of this mortal life quite tired,
He lived about a month and then expired.

The other is on an outside monument on the north wall of the church at Harefield, near Uxbridge, one of the last three villages left in Greater London. It is Robert Mossendew, servant of the Ashby family, who died in 1744. Had he been a gentleman his monument would at this time have been inside the church. He was a gamekeeper and is carved in relief with his gun above this inscription.

In frost and snow, thro' hail and rain
He scour'd the woods, and trudg'd the plain;
The steady pointer leads the way,
Stands at the scent, then springs the prey;
The timorous birds from stubble rise,
With pinions stretch'd divide the skies;
The scatter'd lead pursues the sight
And death in thunder stops their flight;
His spaniel, of true English kind,
With gratitude inflames his mind:
This servant in an honest way,
In all his actions copied Tray.

The churchyard indeed often contains cruder but more lively and loving verses than the polished tributes inscribed on marble tablets within the church to squires and peers and divines of the county hierarchy. The Dartmoor parish of Buckland Monachorum displays this popular epitaph to a blacksmith which may be found in other parishes:

My sledge and hammer both declin'd.
My bellows too have lost their wind.
My fire's extinct, my forge decay'd,
And in the dust my vice is laid,
My coal is spent, my iron's gone,
My nails are drove, my work is done.

Though such an epitaph can scarcely be called Christian, it is at least not an attempt to cover up in mawkish sentiment or in crematorial good taste the inevitability of death.

THE OUTSIDE

The church whose southern side we are approaching is probably little like the building which stood there even two centuries before, although it has not been rebuilt. The outside walls were probably plastered, unless the church is in a district where workable stone has long been used and it is faced with cut stone known as ashlar. Churches which are ashlar-faced all over are rare, but many have an ashlar-faced western tower, or aisle to the north-east or south-east, or a porch or transept built of cut stone in the fifteenth century by a rich family. Some have a guild chapel or private chantry where Mass was said for the souls of deceased members of the guild or family. This is usually ashlar-faced and has a carved parapet as well, and is in marked contrast with the humble masonry of the rest of the church.

Rubble or uneven flints were not considered beautiful to look at until the nineteenth century. People were ashamed of them and wished to see their churches smooth on the outside and inside walls, and weatherproof. At Barnack and Earl's Barton the Saxons have even gone so far as to imitate in stone the decorative effects of wooden construction. Plaster made of a mixture of hair or straw and sand and lime was from Saxon times applied as a covering to the walls. Only the cut stone round the windows and doors was left, and even this was lime-washed. The plaster was thin and uneven. It was beautifully coloured a pale yellow or pink or white according to the tradition of the district. And if it has now been stripped off the church, it may still be seen on old cottages of the village if any survive. The earlier the walls of a church are, the less likely they are to be ashlar-faced, for there was no widespread use of cut stone in villages until the late fourteenth century when transport was better, and attention which had formerly been expended on abbeys was paid to building and enlarging parish churches.

And this is the place to say that most of the old parish churches in England are buildings rather than architecture. They are gradual growths, as their outside walls will show; in their construction they partake of the character of cottages and barns and the early manor house, and not of the great abbey churches built for monks or secular canons. Their humble builders were inspired to copy what was to be seen in the nearest great church. The styles of Gothic came from these large buildings, but the village execution of them was later and could rarely rise to more than window tracery and roof timbering. Even these effects have a local flavour, they are a village voluntary compared with the music played on a great instrument by the cathedral organist. Of course here and there, when the abbeys declined, a famous mason from an abbey or cathedral might rebuild the church of his native place, and masons were employed in rich wool districts of East Anglia, the Midlands and parts of Yorkshire and Devon to build large churches which really are architecture and the product of a single brain, not the humble expression of a village community's worship. Much has been discovered about the names and work of medieval architects by Mr John Harvey in his book *Gothic England* and in the researches of Messrs Salzman, and Knoop and Jones.

These outside walls on which the sun shows up the mottled plaster, the sudden warm red of an eighteenth-century patching of brick, the gentle contrast with the ashlar, the lime-washed tracery of the windows, the heating chimney-stack in local brick climbing up the chancel wall or the stove pipe projecting from a window, these are more often seen today in old watercolours in the local museum, or in some affectionate and ill-executed painting hanging in the vestry showing the church 'before restoration in 1883'. Most of our old churches have been stripped of their plaster, some in living memory. The rubble has been exposed and then too often been repointed with grey cement, which is unyielding and instead of protecting the old stones causes them to crack and flake in frosty weather, for cement and stone have different rates of expansion. To make matters worse the cement itself has been snail pointed, that is to say pointed in hard, flat lines, so that the church wall looks like a crazy pavement.

Old paintings sometimes show the external roofs as they used to be. The church roof and chancel are scarcely distinguishable from the cottage roofs. If the original steep pitch survives, it is seen to be covered with the local tiles, stones or thatch of the old houses of the district. Fifteenth-century and Georgian raisings or lowerings of the roof and alterations to a flatter pitch generally meant a re-covering with lead, and the original pitch may be traced on the eastern face of the tower. Victorian restorers much enjoyed raising roofs to what they considered the original pitch, or putting on an altogether new roof in the cathedral manner. The effect of those re-roofings is generally the most obviously new feature on the outside of an old church. Red tiles and patterned slates from Wales or stone tiles which continually come down because they are set at a pitch too steep for their weight, are the usual materials. Instead of being graded in size, large at the eaves and getting smaller as they reach the ridge, the stone tiles are all of the same size so that the roof is not proportioned to the walls. The ridges are usually crowned with ridge tiles of an ornamental pattern which contrast in colour and texture with the rest. The gable ends are adorned with crosses. The drainage system is prominent and there will be pipes running down the wall to a gutter. On the rain-water heads at the top of these pipes there will probably be the date of the restoration. The old way of draining a roof was generally by leaden or wooden spouts rushing out of the fearsome mouths of gargoyles and carrying the water well beyond the walls of the church into the churchyard. If the water did drip on to the walls the plaster served as a protection from damp. Butterfield, a comparatively conservative and severely practical Victorian restorer, in his report on the restoration of Shottesbrooke church (1845) remarks of the flint walls of that elegant building 'There are no parapets to any part of the Church, and the water has continued to drip from the eaves for five centuries without any injury to the walls'. On the other hand the water has continued to drip from the eaves of Sir Edwin Lutyens' fine church of St Jude-on-the-Hill, Hampstead Garden Suburb, London, and over its Portland stone cornice with considerable injury to the brick walls in less than half a century. The nature of the wall surface, the pointing, and the means devised for draining the water clear from the wall foundations once it has reached the ground, have much to do with keeping out the damp.

Sometimes we may find on the outside walls a variety of scratches, marks and carvings. The only ones of any beauty will probably be the consecration crosses, where the Bishop anointed the walls with oil when the church was newly built. They are high up so that people should not brush them in going past. Similar crosses may be seen on stone altars inside the church. The small crosses which are cut roughly in the jambs of doorways were, according to the late E. A. Greening Lamborn, an angry antiquarian with a good prose style, probably put there not for consecration but 'to scare away evil spirits and prevent them crossing the threshold'. There is a whole literature devoted to masons' marks on the walls of churches, outside and in, and to the 'scratch dials' or 'mass clocks' which look like sundials lacking a gnomon, to be found on the outside south walls of many churches. The masons' marks are triangles, diamonds, bent arrows, circles, squares and other shapes looking rather like boy scout signs, cut into ashlar in some churches, notably the large ones, and surviving where stone has not been re-tooled by the Victorians. Often they may be only scribbles. But they seem to help some antiquaries to give an exact date to buildings or portions of a building. Scratch dials or mass clocks were used generally to show the time when Mass was to be said (usually 9 a.m. in medieval England). Others are primitive clocks. But they, like the parish registers, belong to the non-visual side of church history and it is with the look of a church that this book is primarily concerned.

Finally there are on the outsides of churches the gargoyles spouting water off the roof and the carved heads to be found either side of some windows and the figures in niches on tower or porch. Gargoyles can be fearsome, particularly on the north side of the church, and heads and statues, where they have survived Puritan outrage and Victorian zeal, are sometimes extremely beautiful or fantastic.

The church porch flapping with electoral rolls, notices of local acts, missionary appeals and church services (which will occupy us later) gives us a welcome. Though the powers of the parish vestry have been taken over by parish councils and local government, church doors or the porches which shelter them are often plastered with public announcements. Regularly will the village policeman nail to the church door some notice about Foot-and-Mouth Disease when the British Legion Notice Board has been denied him or the Post Office is shut. Most church porches in England are built on the south side, first as a protection for the door from prevailing south-west gales. Then they were used as places for baptism, bargains were made there, oaths sworn, and burial and marriage services conducted. Above some of them, from the fourteenth century onwards, a room was built, usually for keeping parish chests and records. In these places many a village school was started. At first they may have been inhabited by a watchman, who could look down into the church from an internal window. In counties where stone is rare there are often elaborate wooden porches, notably in Sussex, Surrey and Essex.

Professor E. A. Freeman, the great Victorian ecclesiologist, thought little of a man who went up the churchyard path to the main door, which is more or less what we have done, and did not go round the whole building first. But he was an antiquary who took his churches slowly, speculated on them and did detective work about dates of extensions. On a day when the wind is not too cold and the grass not too long and wet, a walk round the outside of the church is always worthwhile. On the farther side, which is generally the north, there may well be extensions, a family mausoleum for instance, of which there is no sign inside the church beyond a blocked archway. Mr John Piper and I had a peculiar experience through not going round the outside of the derelict church of Wolfhamcote near Daventry in

Warwickshire. The lovely building was locked, the windows smashed, and the sun was setting on its lichened stone. There was only one cottage near and we could make no one hear. So we climbed through a window in the south aisle. Bat-droppings were over rotting floors and damp stains on the ochre-plastered walls, and in the fading light we saw that the altar cloth had been raised and revealed a black tunnel with light at the end, a most peculiar thing to see beyond an altar. We approached and saw there were stairs going down under the table leading to a passage in which brass-studded coffins lay on shelves. When we went round the outside of the church we saw that beyond the east end was a Strawberry Hill Gothick extension, the mausoleum of the Tibbits family. Vestries are more usual on the north side of churches than mausolea, and very ugly most of them are, hard little stone sheds leant against the old walls. There will be almost for certain a north door blocked or bricked-up long ago, with the trace of its arch mouldings still there. There may even be a north porch. But unless the village and manor house are to the north of the church this side of the churchyard will be gloomy and its tombs will be, at the earliest, nineteenth century, except for a very few near the east end. And so round by the sexton's tool-shed and the anthracite dump and the west door of the tower, we return to the south porch.

Notice the stonework round the outside doors. Often it is round-headed and of Norman date, an elaborate affair of several concentric semi-circles of carved stone. It may even be the only Norman work left in the church and may originally have been the chancel arch before the chancel was enlarged and a screen put across its western end. The later medieval rebuilders respected the Norman craftsman-ship and often kept a Norman door inside their elaborate porches.

There is often difficulty in opening the door. This gives the less impatient of us a chance of looking at the door itself. Either because the business of transferring the huge church lock was too difficult, or because here was a good piece of wood older than any of the trees in the parish, church doors have survived from the middle ages while the interiors on to which they open have been repaired out of recognition. The wood of the door may be carved or be decorated with old local ironwork. If it is an old door it will invariably open inwards. So first turn the iron handle and push hard. Then if the door seems to be locked, turn the handle the other way and push hard. Then feel on the wall-plate of the porch for the key. Then look under the mat. Then lift the notice-board from the porch wall and look behind that. Then look inside the lamp bracket outside the porch. Church keys are usually six or eight inches long and easy to find. If there is no sign of the key and all vestry doors are locked, call at a house. If the path leading through the churchyard to a door in the vicarage wall is overgrown and looks unused, you may be sure the vicarage has been sold to wealthy unbelievers and there is no chance of getting the key from there. The houses to choose are those with pots of flowers in the window. Here will be living traditional villagers who even if they are chapel will probably know who it is who keeps the church key. Men are less likely to know than women, since men in villages are more rarely churchgoers. Villagers are all out on Saturday afternoons shopping in the local town. Only an idiot and the dog remain behind.

THE PORCH AND BELLS

Down one step – for the churchyard will have risen round an old building – and we are in the church itself.

The practised eye can tell at a glance how severe the restoration has been, and often indeed who has done the damage. For instance almost every other church in Cornwall, beside many farther east, was restored by Mr J. P. St Aubyn late in the last century, and he has left his mark at the church porch in the form of a scraper of his own design, as practical and unattractive as his work. We must remember, however much we deplore it, that the most cumbersome bit of panelling bought from a Birmingham firm without regard for the old church into which it is to go, the sentimental picture from the Art Shop, the banner with the dislocated saint, the Benares ware altar vases, the brass commemorative tablet, the greenish stained glass window with its sentimental Good Shepherd – often have been saved up for by some devout and penurious communicant. It must be admitted that spirituality and aesthetics rarely go together. 'Carnal delight even in the holiest things,' says Father R. M. Benson, founder of the Cowley Fathers '(habits of thought and philosophy, acquisition of knowledge, schemes of philanthropy, aesthetic propriety, influence in society) hinders the development of the Christ-life by strengthening the natural will.' So when one is inclined to lament lack of taste and seemingly wilful destruction of beauty in a church, it is wise to remember that the incumbent, even if he be that rarity a man of aesthetic appreciation, is probably not to blame for modern blemishes to the fabric. He is primarily a missioner and he cannot offend his parishioners on so unspiritual a matter. The reader who casts his mind back to his early worship as a child will remember that a hymn board, or a brass cross or a garish window were, from his customary gazing on them Sunday after Sunday, part of his religious life. If as an older and more informed person his taste and knowledge tell him these things are cheap and hideous, he will still regret their passing with a part of him which is neither his intellect nor his learning. How much more will an uninformed villager, whose feeling always runs higher where the church is concerned than a townsman's, cling to these objects he has known as a boy, however cheap they are. When the vicar or rector felt himself entitled to be a dictator, he could with more impunity and less offence than now, 'restore' the old church out of recognition. He could hack down the box pews, re-erect a screen across the chancel, put the choir into surplices and move it from the west gallery to the chancel, and substitute a pipe organ for the old instruments. Even in those days many a disgruntled villager left the church to try his voice in chapel or to play his instrument in the old village band. It is a tribute to the hold of our church that congregations continued to use their churches after restorations in Victorian times. Perhaps the reason for the continued hold is that the more ritualistic performance of the Church Services made church more interesting. There is no doubt that Evangelicals were worried at the success of Tractarian methods. But picture your own childhood's church whitewashed on the advice of the Diocesan Advisory Committee, your pew gone and a row of chairs in its place, the altar different, and the chancel cleared of choir-stalls and the choir non-existent as a consequence. Were it not your childhood's church, you would consider this an improvement. One part of you may consider it an improvement despite associations, but not the other. Conservatism is innate in ecclesiastical arrangement. It is what saves for us the history of the village or town in wood and glass and metal and stone.

Let us enter the church by the tower door and climb to the ringing chamber where the ropes hang through holes in the roof. Nowhere outside England except for a very few towers in the rest of the British Isles, America and the Dominions, are bells rung so well. The carillons of the Netherlands and of Bourneville and Atkinson's scent shop in London are not bell ringing as understood in England. Carillon ringing is done either by means of a cylinder worked on the barrel-organ and musical box principle, or by keyed notes played by a musician. Carillon bells are sounded by pulling the clapper to the rim of the bell. This is called chiming, and it is not ringing.

Bell ringing in England is known among ringers as 'the exercise', rather as the rearing and training of pigeons is known among the pigeon fraternity as 'the fancy'. It is a classless folk art which has survived in the church despite all arguments about doctrine and the diminution of congregations. In many a church when the parson opens with the words 'Dearly beloved brethren, the Scripture moveth us in sundry places ...' one may hear the tramp of the ringers descending the newel stair into the refreshing silence of the graveyard. Though in some churches they may come in later by the main door and sit in the pew marked 'Ringers Only', in others they will not be seen again, the sweet melancholy notes of 'the exercise' floating out over the Sunday chimney-pots having been their contribution to the glory of God. So full of interest and technicality is the exercise that there is a weekly paper devoted to it called *The Ringing World*.

A belfry where ringers are keen has the used and admired look of a social club. There, above the little bit of looking-glass in which the ringers slick their hair and straighten their ties before stepping down into the outside world, you will find blackboards with gilded lettering proclaiming past peals rung for hours at a stretch. In another place will be the rules of the tower written in a clerkly hand. A charming Georgian ringers' rhyme survives at St Endellion, Cornwall, on a board headed with a picture of ringers in knee-breeches:

> We ring the Quick to Church and dead to Grave,
> Good is our use, such usage let us have
> Who here therefore doth Damn, or Curse or Swear,
> Or strike in Quarrel thogh no Blood appear.
>
> Who wears a Hatt or Spurr or turns a Bell
> Or by unskilful handling spoils a Peal,
> Shall Sixpence pay for every single Crime
> 'Twill make him careful 'gainst another time.
> Let all in Love and Friendship hither come,
> Whilst the shrill Treble calls to Thundering Tom,
> And since bells are our modest Recreation
> Let's Rise and Ring and Fall to Admiration.

Many country towers have six bells. Not all these bells are medieval. Most were cast in the seventeenth, eighteenth or nineteenth centuries when change-ringing was becoming a country exercise. And the older bells will have been re-cast during that time, to bring them into tune with the new ones. They are likely to have been again re-cast in modern times, and the ancient inscription preserved and welded on to the re-cast bell. Most counties have elaborately produced monographs about their church bells. The older bells have beautiful lettering sometimes, as at Somerby, and South Somercotes in Lincolnshire, where they are inscribed with initial letters decorated with figures so that they look like illuminated initials from old manuscripts interpreted in relief on metal. The English love for Our Lady survived in inscriptions on church bells long after the Reformation, as did the use of Latin. Many eighteenth- and even early nineteenth-century bells have Latin inscriptions. A rich collection of varied dates may be seen by struggling about on the wooden cage in which the bells hang among the bat-droppings in the tower.

Many local customs survive in the use of bells. In some places a curfew is rung every evening; in others a bell is rung at five in the morning during Lent. Fanciful legends have grown up about why they are rung, but their origin can generally be traced to the divine offices. The passing bell is rung differently from district to district. Sometimes the years of the deceased are tolled, sometimes the ringing is three strokes in succession followed by a pause. There are instances of the survival of prayers for the departed where the bell is tolled as soon as the news of the death of a parishioner reaches the incumbent.

Who has heard a muffled peal and remained unmoved? Leather bags are tied to one side of the clapper and the bells ring alternately loud and soft, the soft being an echo, as though in the next world, of the music we hear on earth.

I make no apology for writing so much about church bells. They ring through our literature, as they do over our meadows and roofs and few remaining elms. Some may hate them for their melancholy, but they dislike them chiefly, I think, because they are reminders of Eternity. In an age of faith they were messengers of consolation.

The bells are rung down, the ting-tang will ring for five minutes, and now is the time to go into church.

Seven:

1960 to 1972

Seven
1960–1972

'I have never tried to make my living as a poet, nor expected to. I should dearly have liked to have done so as a young man, but I have always had to perform on the wireless as we are doing, write reviews – the most second-rate and miserable occupation, but it brings in a regular income – and do anything I am asked to do, however humiliating. . . .'[1]

By 1960, JB had at last been able to give up his 'miserable occupation' of regular book reviewing which he had done full tilt for almost twenty years. His television work, although freelance, brought home more pay than writing. He used his monthly 'Men and Buildings' article in the *Daily Telegraph* to further various crusades. The consequences of the property boom, which reverberated throughout the sixties, began to revolutionise the skyline of London and the face of Britain. In 1956, for instance, Charles Clore had bought an elegant row of bomb-damaged houses on the edge of Hyde Park for half a million pounds. Six years later the Hilton Hotel rose in their place, scraped the sky and dwarfed the park. High-rise buildings grew apace. More and more road and service schemes were funded by developers in exchange for planning permissions from local authorities. Further unplanned chaos ensued. JB had been on the Royal Fine Art Commission for twenty years and was only too aware of the political skulduggery and the treachery which led to corners of London being razed to the ground. The Houses of Parliament, Tower Bridge, the Foreign Office and the Tate Gallery Portico were all mooted for demolition but survived. The Euston Arch and the Coal Exchange, which stood for so much JB loved, were among the victims.

JB liked good modern architecture but hated the endless and relentless mediocrity of so many new buildings. 'Istanbul or Denver, Rotterdam or Mayfair, the new hotels are the same – a slab of cells perched over shops and offices, all excellently planned and calculated down to the last cubic inch to bring in a quick turnover. . . . Ants are always on the move. So is our age which has taken to wheels and wings and can never be still . . . and our latest hotels, instead of being glorifications of home, have become multi-storeyed nests for the shifting millions.'[2]

He built up a resentment towards the new breed of commercial architects. 'The remoteness of architects has given rise to a specialists' jargon, part-house agent, part-financier, part-planner, part-borough engineer, part-sociologist, part-critic and part-spec builder. Here are some of the current phrases and words, with their meaning as understood by members of the general public. They may help to explain the width of the gap between the public and those responsible for buildings . . .

Architect-designed – Copied by the builder, slightly wrong, from plans and elevations in an architectural journal.

Carport – Garage.

Chalet – Caravan without any wheels.

Comprehensive development – Total destruction.

Conference – Expedition to Torquay or Tokyo with the wife at the firm's expense or on the rates.

In conference – Asleep.

Contemporary – A few years out of date.

Dining area – Dining room in the kitchen.

Fence – Concrete posts and wire mesh.

Important – A building interesting to "art historians", and a possible subject for a thesis to entitle whoever writes it to a chair in one of the new universities.

Plot ratio – An official calculation to enable the "developer" to crowd the maximum number of people at minimum cost and maximum profit on any given site.

Sprinkling of light industry – Putting a noisy factory in a quiet part of the country and widening the lanes to reach it.

Townscaping – Doing away with the lines of old streets.'[3]

The Beeching Report in 1963, compiled by the infamous Dr Beeching, recommended the closure of a third of our railway network and wiped out hundreds of miles of branch lines. This tragic and gigantic error fired JB's pen. '. . . Railways are looked at by those who now govern them only from the point of view of a chartered accountant turned into a dictator,' he wrote. 'This money attitude ignores the human factor. In all our thickly populated places the railway is the only rapid and efficient means of transport. The more the number of motor cars increases, as does the population, the more essential an alternative to road transport becomes. . . .'[4]

As a result of JB's devotion to railways he was asked to make lots of films for British Transport. One was about the last steam train called *Railways For Ever*. 'I am told that in the mid seventies we will have trains going at 150 miles per hour or more, but I don't think it's the speed that matters. It's the release from tension and the thrill of seeing real country which you do from the train. And for some of us there will always remain memories of the hiss of steam, the sudden roar, the triumphant scream of the whistle, smuts and the grimy majesty of the whole thing. . . . Ah yes, Railways For Ever.'[5]

During the sixties JB made nearly a hundred film and t.v. appearances and fired the public's imagination about what was around them nobody had ever done before. He made a series for BBC Religious programmes with the director Kenneth Savage called 'The ABC of Churches' and with the young Jonathan Stedall, a series of films for HTV in the west country with commentary, more often than not in verse, to fit the picture.

'Tea time and Marlborough, youth's most magic hour
The clock strikes four, from grey St Mary's Tower . . .
For centuries too, these alleys have run down
To the broad High Street of the red-tiled town . . .'[6]

JB's films had an extra magic because he was involved with every aspect of them from helping to direct the shots of architecture and countryside to assisting in the editing, and sitting for hours alone in the studio writing a commentary while running the images through a Steinbeck.

In 1962 JB had gone on a lecture tour to Australia organised by the British Council and fell in love with the place. A few years later he returned to make a series of films called 'Betjeman in Australia'. 'The one thing that makes Australia different and makes me like it very much is that Nature is bigger than man,' he said, over a shot of spoonbills flying into the sunset. 'Whatever I do, I can only scratch at the surface.'[7]

1. 'Authors Talking', BBC, 1962.
2. *The Daily Telegraph*, 14 May 1962.
3. *The Daily Telegraph*, 15 June 1964.

4. *The Spectator*, 9 July 1965.
5. British Transport film, *Railways For Ever*, 1968.
6. *'Marlborough'*, HTV, 1962–4. Series of twelve films.
7. *Betjeman in Australia*, BBC, 1972.

Aspects of Australia

I spent six weeks in Australia jabbering away under the kind and capable protection of the British Council. Yet those six weeks have so enriched my life that even now, a year later, I have but to see a bit of news about Australia in the paper or to turn over the pages of any book in the two shelves of Australian books I have now acquired, to feel a longing to go back there which is almost a physical ache.

Why did I, in the first instance, accept an invitation to go? The air journey was even more formidable than I had been told and I strongly advise visitors to break the journey with two nights' rest on land on the way. One reason for going was the natural desire we all have to escape from Mr Marples' traffic problems and the depredations of 'developers'. Besides that, I was invited for November, which is springtime down under. Another reason was that I would have none of those language difficulties which make the continent of Europe so difficult for one who has had the advantage of a public school education. The overriding reason was to see what it was like. Sir Kenneth Clark and the late Neville Shute had long urged me to go there, telling me I would enjoy it. I had a suspicion it might be like America and I had spent a month of March in the Middle West when the land was brown and dry and robins as big as pheasants hopped about on the porch swings and the sun sank early behind Lutheran steeples in the land of Uncle Tom's Cabin. Australia was quite unknown to me and to most of my friends. I read the *Penguin Book of Australian Verse* on my way out, which was a better guide to the people and scenery than any official brochure.

All the same, I expected to find tin shacks, baked sand and clumps of eucalyptus. Everything was different from what I had expected. First there was the light, with its dazzling clearness everywhere. Next there was the brilliant colour of flowers, trees, rocks, birds, reptiles and insects. Australia is geologically one of the oldest parts of the earth's surface and the centuries, instead of fading its colours, seem to have intensified them. The gum-trees of Australia are of every shape and colour. Some look like British elms, others like oak or ash. There are hundreds of varieties of mimosa, or wattle, whose flowers vary from pale gold to deepest orange. The scarlet of the flame-tree flares on the mountain sides. The millions of flowers which appear everywhere after the rain give an impression of luxuriance like the tropics one reads about in *The Swiss Family Robinson*. There are trees of vast height, and some of the palms and pines look like the fossilised plants in coal. Never shall I forget flying in a small chartered aeroplane low over the sinister 'horizontal bush' in an unexplored part of Tasmania. Here men can walk over the tops of the trees, but if they fall down into the wood below there is said to be no way out, and there are stories of skeletons being found with manacles on them – skeletons of convicts who tried to escape from the cruel penal settlement of Port Arthur. We were flying to the forgotten city of Zeehan, once the third largest in Tasmania and now with only a few hundred people, a hospital, an opera house and scattered wooden houses and shops in a sea of sweet-scented white iris, with pink mineral mountains all round. Nor shall I forget standing in the rain forests below Mount Tamborine near Brisbane with Judith Wright, the poet. We heard cicadas loud as jet engines outside London Airport. They stopped suddenly and in the hush one could almost hear the jungle growing in the steamy depths below us where parasite climbed on parasite and strange and huge flowers burst from the greenness and the crack of the stock-whip bird and the chime of the bell-bird increased the strangeness. Then in Canberra, which is like an enormous Welwyn Garden City set down in southern Italian mountains, how odd it was to see pink parrots flying about the trim suburban avenues and find snakes slithering over the municipally mown grass between the footwalk and the road, which is seductively called 'the nature strip' in Australia. How pleasantly embarrassing, too, to be sitting in a drawing-room making polite conversation and suddenly to burst into giggles caught from the maniac laughter of the kookaburra birds on the lawn outside. I went to a party given by Douglas Stewart, the poet, in a suburb of Sydney and recall a spider's web as big as a sheet between the eaves of the verandah of his bungalow and the ground. In the middle of it was a beautiful green spider as big as one's hand which everyone took for granted as a common sight.

Though two-thirds of the people of Australia live in towns and most of these in the six state capitals, one has a sense even in so crowded a city as Sydney of nature being more powerful than man. One has a sense of the waiting forest and miles of bush and grassy plain and then that huge limitless uninhabitable desert in the centre of the continent. Vastness is so near all the time, life is so old when one sees primitive grass-eating marsupials that man falls into perspective. The sense of eternity out here under the Southern Cross gives Australians that sense of proportion which makes them the humorous, welcoming and kind people they are.

Man in Australia is so much newer than the animals that even the Aborigines, who are thought to have crossed from Asia several thousands of years ago, seem quite recent. They are a comparatively tall and distinguished nomadic people with great skill in hunting and trekking, and they live an entirely communal life. Their way of life is so different from that of the later settlers that I am sure they will come to harm if they are westernised and exploited as tourist attractions.

The greatest surprise to me in Australia was the splendour of the architecture, particularly of the last century. Its characteristic, until the coming of the American skyscraper, has been width – wide streets lined with trees, wide bungalows with the verandah round two or three sides supported on delicate cast iron which throws an intricate pattern on wooden walls in the strong light, and corrugated iron roofs bent into a graceful slope well proportioned to the walls. The origin of nearly all Australian towns is the same – a crossroads with two-storey shops and public houses with shady verandahs on three of the corners and a classical bank of stone on the fourth. The rest of the buildings are one storey high except for the classic court-house and town hall. There will probably be a sixties church in Gothic Revival style making good use of local brick or stone, for the Australians had in the last century architects who were even more field original and exciting than our own Butterfield and Burges, Street and Norman Shaw. All the same, the general impression of the towns, particularly Sydney in its older parts, Adelaide and Hobart and parts of Melbourne, is Georgian. Owing to slow communications until lately, the Georgian tradition of space, width and tree-planted landscape survived into this century. Its impetus came from Australia's first great architect, Francis Greenway, who was transported to Botany Bay for forgery at the beginning of the last century from Bristol. There he had designed the pleasant club and Mall at Clifton. In Sydney he excelled himself with work as strong and original as that of Soane.

I am hard put to it to say which state capital I preferred – Sydney with its oysters and delicate white wines, its old streets of verandahed terraces and its sudden glances of sea: Melbourne with its palatial public buildings in a classic style like the London clubs and its superbly laid out botanic garden and its great art gallery: Adelaide, which must be the best planned city in the world, a grid of wide streets surrounded by a green belt: Brisbane, where the houses are on stilts and toast-rack trams waft you in a warm breeze past banana trees and shops: Perth, where black swans glide on lapis blue water and immense parks of trees and flowers slope down to the river: or Hobart below its many-coloured mountains on the edge of the most beautifully landscaped harbour I have ever seen.

The further north you travel in Australia the hotter grows the weather and the slower comes the speech. All the states have distinct character. South Australia is the most English, New South Wales the most vigorous, Victoria the most official, Queensland the most countrified, Northern Territory the most primitive, while Western Australia and Tasmania seem to be separate leisurely countries.

An official of the British Council in London asked me to lunch before I went, to warn me not to patronise the Australians. Such had not been my intention, but I can see what he meant. It is a mistake to expect a welcome simply because one comes from England. The Technical College in Sydney occupies premises which were once a prison for the penal colony which was the origin of the city. The Principal showed me a yard outside his room where prisoners were once flogged. Forty-five lashes was the average sentence. There were rings in the walls to which the men were tied and channels in the stone floor leading to a hole where the blood drained away. A very small percentage now of Australians is descended from convicts, but the memory remains – particularly, of course in Celts. Many people, especially those from South Australia which was founded by free-settlers, may, as you get to know them, talk about their ancestry, which is nearly always from people who immigrated of their own free will. Since the war Australia has opened itself to the displaced of Europe, with great benefit to the arts and cookery. The resemblance to America in some of the hideous new petrol stations and commercial buildings is only superficial. Australia is now a civilisation of its own which, for its size and age, has contributed more to music, literature, the arts and sport than any other English-speaking country. It is a tonic which we all need and which can only be taken by a visit.

Vogue

Gilbert Harding

I've no fear of Hell, and Purgatory won't be all that bad.

Gilbert Harding

There were one or two lofty notices about Gilbert Harding in the papers after his death written with the cattiness and pseudo-impartiality of those who shelter under anonymity. He was described as a temporary phenomenon thrown up by television and it was to television only that his fame was accounted. The truth is that his fame was due to himself. He was shown, certainly to the best advantage, for the great entertainer and talker that he was, by able producers. No one I have met in television knew better than he how to get on with those he worked with in the studio. Cameramen and technicians on the floor enjoyed working with him. Perceptive producers knew just how long to leave the camera on him and from what angles. Gilbert himself worked in with them and his natural sense of the dramatic stood him in good stead so that he never went on talking too long. I used to enjoy, when on panels with him, watching him wait to bring in the telling sentence which would make what had, till then, been a dull programme, something memorable. He was a generous man to perform with because he did not monopolise a discussion nor did he necessarily wait to have the last word; he was so sensitive to the feelings of his fellow performers that he laboured to bring out the best in them either by provocation or by sympathy. He saw each programme in which he performed as a whole and thought of himself as a member of its team.

There were other ways in which he helped too. I remember how in a panel game called 'Who Said That?' we were made to seem more natural by being sat down in a drawing room with four walls and the cameras were hidden behind gauze on which pictures had been painted. Thus we could not see where the cameras were. Under the hot studio lights the room became very parching and Gilbert kindly concealed, in a vase of flowers and microphones on the low table in the middle of the room, a bottle of whisky for the performers. I remember too the exquisite courtesy he showed to ladies who were performing with him. He would usually present them with flowers before the performance. There was so different an atmosphere from the old competitive feeling of the 'Brains Trust' in the days of sound. There, people who had been polite to one another at the dinner beforehand suddenly struck out each for himself (like people boarding a crowded bus) when the performance started. In a Gilbert Harding programme, if there was an angry argument, you may be sure that he instigated it because he saw its dramatic possibility in terms of television, not because he was anxious to outshine everyone.

Nothing shows up falseness like a television camera. The smooth man out for himself, fails. The liar is shown up in his untruth. If what is said is said with honest conviction, even those who do not agree with it will see by television whether the speaker is sincere. The one thing that was patent about Gilbert was his complete honesty. Millions of people felt that they knew him because of this. What is more, they did know him. He was an expansive, irascible, intelligent and graphic talker in private life as well as on the screen. When the cameras started up, and the sound was switched on, Gilbert was just the same as he had been before and it was characteristic of his generosity that he took trouble at the beginning of a performance to put the new or nervous colleague at his ease by talking to him and drawing him out in those early awkward moments.

Gilbert Harding was a well-educated man. He won a scholarship to Cambridge and was enormously happy there discovering himself and what fun it was to be a welcome guest at entertaining luncheon and dinner parties. I have always thought that secretly he would like to have been a don. Like so many of his generation who went to the university and enjoyed themselves so much that they did not have time to do the requisite academic work, he became a schoolmaster. All those who have followed this profession know how essential it is not to be boring and how all ruses can be seen through by young pupils. His teaching experience was useful training for his sense of the dramatic and helped to give him his power of holding attention. His teaching career did not last long enough for him to become the bore that some elderly schoolmasters become who have laid down the law all their lives. It also taught him the value of honesty of expression. All the same that unfulfilled academic ambition at the university saddened him. It made him feel that he was no more than a public buffoon and he often sadly spoke of himself as this to me. He did not realise that his power over the spoken word, his gift for invective and his forceful form of expression would not have been what they were without his wide education and the sense of proportion that went with it. He was no pedant. His sense of proportion gave him humour. His true education, as opposed to the specialised knowledge which is sometimes mistaken for education, made him realise there was much he did not know and this gave him the humility which most endeared him to me.

He was, like many of us who are insecure, an ardent sacramentalist. He clung first to the sacraments of the Church of England when he was a student for the priesthood at Mirfield and later to those of the Church of Rome. Despite his sometimes violent pronouncements in public about the Church of England he was always, in private conversation with me, friendly to it and grateful to Mirfield for the Catholic faith he learned and practised there and interested to know about old friends in the kindly embrace of Canterbury. That embrace was a bit too wide for one who, though he was no heresy hunter, liked to be safely on the side of strict dogma. I think if it had not been for his religion success would have driven him mad, for success must be just as hard to live with as failure.

Finally I must touch on his generosity as a host and a friend. He gave his time and money freely to his church, to charitable institutions, to friends whatever their faith or misdoings.

On reading this through I fear I may have left the impression of a mild and unprejudiced man. All who remember him know he bristled with prejudice. They knew his feelings about American civilisation, the Irish Roman Catholic hierarchy, about so-called progress, about plastics, and his deep mistrust of majority opinions, civil servants and everything that goes with officialdom and the suppression of the individual. In his way Gilbert Harding, by being his irascible, generous self, did more to encourage the individual against domination by the State and heartless theorists than any television personality of his time.

From *Gilbert Harding By His Friends*

The Rhyme and Reason of Verse

When I was ten a family friend gave me a leather-bound book engraved with my initials. 'For your poems,' she wrote inside it. The book is by no means full. I think I kept it chiefly because it was a generous, well-bound present. When I look at its contents I am shocked at the weakness of the verses and wish I had never preserved them.

Certainly one of the pleasures of writing poetry is copying out the completed compositions, indenting the lines, leaving gaps between the stanzas and arranging the verses to look well on the page, leaving margins, right and left and at top and bottom. And then the poem . . . My heavens! It is dated November, 1918. Any boy of twelve today, provided he was literate, could do better.

> A Quiet Country Village
>
> Here is the inn, its signboard on the green
> Where now and then forgotten cattle stray
> Close by the pump where often may be seen
> The gossips talking weary hours away

Well at least it scans and rhymes correctly.

I had obviously been learning Gray's *Elegy in a Country Churchyard* by heart. And in the second stanza I note that I tried a little moralising as Gray does:

> In yonder trees peeps out that stately spire
> Of the lofty parish church. Within
> Is heard the singing of the village choir
> Giving joy – a good reward for sin.

I imagine that the last line was intended sarcastically – i.e. the village choir sings so beautifully that we dreadful sinners who are listening to it are getting more than we deserve. But then the rhythm seems to have gone wrong – and the sense.

Of course it is easy enough to pull one's own efforts to pieces many years later. I can do this to myself. But I would not do it to you. Everyone who has read thus far has written a poem. In fact there is no one living who has never composed two lines that he or she thinks are poetry. The reason why I would not criticise your poetry on any account, even if it were good, is that our poems are part of ourselves. They are our children and we do not like them to be made public fools of by strangers.

There are few exaltations greater than seeing your verse printed for the first time. It will probably be in a school or a house magazine. There is almost certain to be a misprint which will keep you awake all night, though no one else will have noticed it. When, after appearing in such magazines, you may assemble enough to get a book together, it is very unlikely you will find a publisher. Poetry does not pay. Most people find that they have to pay to have their first book of poems published.

Before you venture on this speculation, weigh up in your mind these two considerations: 1 You will have the glory of the feel of a book of your own writing between boards or stiff paper, a real book; 2 You will have to face cruel criticism or neglect, most likely the latter.

Here are some strict, dull rules for beginners. To write in rhyme and rhythm is easy. Rhymes in English are words which sound the same except for a different consonant at the beginning – 'sight' and 'light', 'breath' and 'death', 'way' and 'day'.

Vowel sounds do not have to be spelled the same to rhyme. 'Teeth' rhymes perfectly with 'sheath' and 'pie' with 'high'. There are, however, imperfect rhymes which purists avoid: 'shore' does not rhyme perfectly with 'raw' because there is a slight 'r' sound at the end of 'shore' which an Irishman would probably emphasise. 'Raw' rhymes with 'paw', 'shore' certainly rhymes perfectly with 'roar' as both have 'r' sounds at the end. 'June' does not rhyme with 'moon' unless you are writing Cockney, nor does 'dew' with 'blue'. 'Soon' rhymes with 'moon', 'tune' rhymes with 'June' and 'hew' with 'dew'. 'True' rhymes with 'blue'.

When the first syllable in a word is naturally stressed more than the others, then the rhyme is heard in the first syllable – as 'station' and 'nation', 'city' and 'pity', 'cheerfulness' and 'tearfulness'.

Rhyming dictionaries are not to be despised. They can often suggest a word one would not have immediately thought of oneself, and which is more effective from its unexpectedness than a much more obvious rhyme.

There are a variety of rhymes in English from the very simplest like

'Twinkle, twinkle little star.
How I wonder what you are'

to the rollicking alliteration of the chorus from Swinburne's *Atlanta*.

When the hounds of spring are on winter's traces,
The mother of months in meadow or plain
Fills the shadows and windy places
With lisp of leaves and ripple of rain;
And the brown bright nightingale amorous
Is half assuaged for Itylus
For the Thracian ships and the foreign faces
The tongueless vigil and all the pain.

In these lines he uses alliteration, words beginning with the same consonant, 'mother of months in meadow or plain'. The fifth line is a deliberate slowing down of the rhythm and so is the sixth; the last two lines take up the rhythm with which the verse started.

Rhythm in English poetry is produced by stress, that is to say where the accent falls when the word is spoken out loud. I would have to have a dictionary of classical mythology near me to find out who Itylus was and what the reference to Thracian ships means, and bird books with coloured plates to verify whether nightingales are brown and bright. The quality that matters more than meaning in this stanza is the sound of it. It must be spoken aloud, and rolled off the tongue, and marched to and danced to and learned by heart to be fully enjoyed.

Rhythm is best understood by reading out loud, or better still, learning by heart a few verses in familiar traditional metre.

The curfew tolls the knell of parting day
The lowing herd winds slowly o'er the lea
The plowman homeward plods his weary way
And leaves the world to darkness and to me.

Ten syllables in each line, as in simple blank verse. The second of each two syllables is stressed a little bit more than the first.

A good training for writing verse is to start with imitation or even parody, so that the rhythm is established in your ear and you write variants on it, rather as a musician can improvise on a tune.

> This colour supplement is out today
> The typists are not here to make the tea
> The Editor has gone down Wiltshire way
> And leaves the press to printers and to me.

These are simple rules for writing verse. Indeed, if you can write a quatrain (that is to say four lines) in the style of Gray's *Elegy* you are on your way to writing in more complicated rhythms. You may even be on the way to writing blank verse, which is verse that does not rhyme but which has rhythm.

Of all rhyming verse-forms the most succinct is the Petrarchan sonnet. It consists of fourteen lines. All lines have ten syllables and the words are stressed as they are spoken. The first eight lines are called the Octet and present the theme. The rhymes are:

$$A$$
$$B$$
$$B$$
$$A$$
$$A$$
$$B$$
$$B$$
$$A$$

The sestet, which sums up the theme, is of six lines and the rhymes can be:

$$C$$
$$D$$
$$E$$
$$C$$
$$D$$
$$E$$

The sestet summarises the theme or comments on it.

It is not until you have learned the rules of English verse that you know what free verse is. You must know the discipline before you can escape it, and escape, when it comes, must be voluntary.

Throughout all this please notice I have been writing about how to write *verse*, not about how to write poetry. What turns verse into poetry is something that comes into it from outside. It is variously called 'inspiration', 'the muse', 'the gift'. Others discover it in you, if you are lucky. You never are sure you have genius yourself.

Weekend Telegraph Magazine

Sir Henry Newbolt after a Hundred Years

How does Henry Newbolt stand as a poet today? There is 'Drake's Drum', a poem which everybody knows, and there are others with famous opening lines: 'Admirals all, for England's sake, Honour be yours and fame . . .'; and there is: 'Stand by to reckon up your battleships, Ten, twenty, thirty . . . there they go . . .'; and 'It was eight bells ringing For the morning watch was done . . .'; and 'He gave us all goodbye cheerily . . .'; and the famous

'Ye have robbed', said he, 'ye have slaughtered and made an end,
   Take your ill-got plunder, and bury the dead:
What will ye more of your guest and sometime friend?'
   'Blood for our blood', they said

and the most famous of all, I suppose:

   There's a breathless hush in the close tonight –
      Ten to make and the match to win –
   A bumping pitch and a blinding light,
      An hour to play and the last man in.
   And it's not for the sake of a ribboned coat,
      Or the selfish hope of a season's fame,
   But his Captain's hand on his shoulder smote –
      'Play up! Play up! and play the game!'

When Newbolt was lecturing in Canada in 1923 he said that that poem had become a Frankenstein monster to him, 'that I created thirty years ago and I find it falling on my neck at every street corner. In vain do I explain what is poetry; they roar for "play up!": they put it on their flags, and on their war memorials and tombstones: it's their National Anthem'. Those naval and school poems of his are as famous – or were as famous – as any poems in the language when I was young, and I am now fifty-five. He may not be so well known now because patriotism of that sort is out, and the school anthologies of the serious thirties and the frightened fifties and the sneering sixties would not want to include such unfashionable verse.

I find Newbolt himself asking the questions I have to answer: 'It is flattering to be liked for what you are, even if that is not what you wish you were', he wrote. '*Am* I just a ballad-monger who loves the sea and seamen? Probably. And of course I *know* that taste for the pavement. I can't honestly say like Robert Bridges: "I don't care whether they read me or not" . . . my real ambition is to leave some poems – enough of them – to make a lasting change in man's ideas of Time and Eternity'. Here are his own eight lines called 'Against Oblivion':

> Cities drowned in olden time
> Keep, they say, a magic chime,
> Rolling up from far below
> When the moonled waters flow.
>
> So within me, ocean deep
> Lies a sunken world asleep.
> Lest its bells forget to ring,
> Memory! set the tide a-swing!

The tide is deep and still over the world that Henry Newbolt knew and expressed in his poetry and prose. With memory let me try to set it swinging again.

Newbolt was born in the Black Country town of Bilston, Staffordshire, where his father was vicar a hundred years ago. He was educated at Clifton and then went to Corpus Christi College, Oxford, and from there into a lawyer's office in London. He married the daughter of a Somerset squire from Orchardleigh named Margaret Duckworth. He produced a family, and his life was, I think, always comfortable and happy because fame came to him in a flash when he was young.

One evening when he was a young man in that lawyer's office he went into Denny's bookshop, which was in one of the old streets where Aldwych now is and the Strand. 'Have you come for your book, sir?' said the assistant. 'You're just in time, we've hardly a copy left tonight.'

'How many had you this morning?' Newbolt asked in as unconcerned a way as he could manage.

'I don't know, but we shall have five hundred tomorrow if we can get them'.

That book was *Admirals All* – his first volume of verse.

Newbolt belonged to the professional classes at a time when England was top dog, and Britannia ruled the waves, and there had not even been a Boer War let alone the Great War of 1914. He died in 1938 before the final crash. His family and his wife's family were what used to be called the backbone of England. They had relations in the Services, the law, and the Church. The men went to public schools and universities. In a sense they were privileged but they gave themselves unflinchingly to patriotic causes and they kept their word. Newbolt himself was no hearty, bluff, slap-you-on-the-back sort of man, as you might suppose from his early poems. He was a quiet scholar with a deep knowledge of Latin and Greek and English poetry – the old and the new. He first drew public attention to the poetry of Walter de la Mare and Mary Coleridge. He knew all the great men of letters of his time – Yeats, Hardy, Kipling, Henry James, Hewlett, John Buchan, and Anthony Hope – and it was the last who gave me a letter of introduction to him. He lived to know and appreciate T. S. Eliot and Ezra Pound and Peter Quennell, Siegfried Sassoon and Raymond Mortimer.

I love the story Newbolt tells of the first appearance of 'Drake's Drum'. He was living in Yattendon, a Berkshire village still sleepy with the cawing of rooks and comfortable with the converted cottages of commuters. Next door lived Robert Bridges, one day to be Poet Laureate. Newbolt had just had a proof of 'Drake's Drum' sent him. He pasted it on to a card, went through the door in the garden wall, and found Bridges lying on the doormat of his house in the sun with his spaniel Ben beside him. Bridges was wearing lavender-coloured nankeen trousers, a slouch hat, and an old, well-cut coat. Nervously Newbolt gave the great man his poem. There was a long silence as he read it through, and then Bridges said, seemingly to himself: 'Awfully swell! awfully swell!' Then he read it through again with great deliberation and said: 'You'll never write anything better than that . . . it isn't given to a man to write anything better than that. I wish I had written anything half so good'. That is high praise from the poet of 'London Snow' and 'Whither Oh splendid ship, thy white sails crowding . . .'.

Maybe the world to which Newbolt belonged is gone, with its little dining clubs of the influential to which he also belonged. Newbolt was a friend of generals, admirals, and prime ministers as well as writers and artists. He really was a member of the Establishment when such a thing existed. And maybe today some people find his poetry of war ringing too much of headquarters and too full of abstract nouns like 'valour' and 'honour' and 'chivalry'. Perhaps we do prefer the more down-to-earth war poetry of Wilfred Owen, Siegfried Sassoon, and Edmund Blunden which came from the trenches rather than the study. Listen to Newbolt: 'Owen and the rest of the broken men' – for Newbolt thought Owen's poetry extremely good – 'Owen and the rest of the broken men rail at the old men who sent the young to die: they have suffered cruelly, but in the nerves and not the heart . . . they haven't the experience or the imagination to know the extreme agony'. (Newbolt had a son at the front.) '. . . Paternity apart, what Englishman of fifty wouldn't far rather stop the shot himself than see the boys do it for him?'

It is hard for us to appreciate our immediate forbears. Yet I think Newbolt will live for two reasons: one is for his very skilful technique. He knew exactly what he meant to say, he said it simply and shortly, and he always chose a metre which suited his theme. For instance, there is a poem of his, 'The Death of Admiral Blake', about August 7, 1657, and in its metre it is exactly like one of those great big, rather forgotten sea-pictures one sees on a staircase in a museum, not properly regarded today but well worth looking into. Savour this metre:

Laden with spoil of the South, fulfilled with the glory of achievement,
    And freshly crowned with never-dying fame,
Sweeping by shores where the names are the names of the victories of
                                                                England,
    Across the Bay the squadron homeward came.

And so it goes on in that metre, and you can see how it is like a sea-picture. The other example of his metrical skill suiting the theme I would like to take from one of his school poems. You know the fearful boredom one can go through on a sunny day in school chapel, when somebody is preaching and you are longing to get out and you are not listening properly. This is a description of such a thing in Clifton Chapel:

I sat by the granite pillar, and sunlight fell
    Where the sunlight fell of old,
And the hour was the hour my heart remembered well,
    And the sermon rolled and rolled
As it used to roll when the place was still unhaunted,
    And the strangest tale in the world was still untold.

> And I knew that of all this rushing of urgent sound
>   That I so clearly heard,
> The green young forest of saplings clustered round
>   Was heeding not one word:
> Their heads were bowed in a still serried patience
>   Such as an angel's breath could never have stirred.

You can hear that phrase 'still serried patience . . .', and can see the long lines of heads.

Finally, I think Newbolt will live because of his memorability. I do not think there is any poet of the present century who has written so many lines that are so easy to remember and that stick in one's mind even if one does not want to remember them. 'The dons on the dais serene . . .'; 'Capten, art tha sleepin' there below? . . .'; 'A bumping pitch and a blinding light . . .'; 'Play up! play up! and play the game!'

I think of Newbolt as the late Edith Olivier and I last saw him one summer day long before the war in Netherhampton Manor House, near Salisbury, where he lived. He was thin, clean-shaven, silver-haired; gentle and courteous. I remember him in his attic study lined with leather-bound books and looking out from the house over the flowery garden, and beyond the elm tops to the Wiltshire Downs. Like his poetry, Newbolt himself remains deep in the memory.

BBC broadcast

Edmund Blunden

I am so glad you are giving me the opportunity to express my admiration for the poetry and personality of Edmund Blunden. I first came across his poetry in the large, floppy pages of *The London Mercury* when I was a schoolboy at Marlborough in 1924. I was just moving out of the Swinburne and nineties phase through which most literary schoolboys in those days passed, and beginning to appreciate the English landscape poets of the late eighteenth and early nineteeth centuries. In Blunden's poems in *The London Mercury* and in his volume *English Poems*, which was the first book by a living poet I remember saving up to buy, I found that true tradition of pastoral verse carried on into the present century. Here, without any hint of artiness or escapism, the countryside of Kent was unrolled in mellifluous numbers. I learned many of his poems by heart and can still recite them with their autumn mists, summer cricket matches, sounds of church bells and recollections of eighteenth-century romantic poets.

Blunden puts new life into heroic couplets and uses the old conventional metres and ode forms of men like Gray and Collins to express the England he knew and loved as a boy. But he is never a pasticheur. He is always as original as he is true.

By the time I reached Oxford in 1926 'the Squirearchy', as those poets who contributed to *The London Mercury* edited by Sir John Squire were called, was going out of fashion. Like all undergraduates I bought the newest poets and fashionable prose works so as to impress people coming into my room. But I retained my volumes of Blunden, slim and spacious, with the splendid typography of their now extinct publisher, Richard Cobden-Sanderson. I remember Auden coming into my room and appraising my shelves with the sure and precocious literary judgement he had even in his teens. 'Ah! the usual stuff,' he said, 'but I see you have got *something* genuine.' And he picked out my volumes of Blunden, adding 'he's a good poet.'

Time has justified that judgement and Blunden's poems have widened with his reading and travel so that he has brought Japan and China to us in England in elegant lyrics. No one has done more than he in his books of criticism to recall the mood and outlook of writers he loves – such men as Lamb, Leigh Hunt, Cowper, Hurdis, Byron and Kirke White. On the grimmer side he has put down in lasting prose the reaction of a pastoral poet to the horrors of 1914–18 in his *Undertones of War*.

It was not until I had left Oxford that I met Edmund Blunden and found in his shy and gentle personality the embodiment of his poems. His generosity to me by letter and introductions when I was young I shall always remember and I can well understand the affection with which you at the University of Hong Kong must hold him. Give him my best wishes on his sixty-fifth birthday. May he live long enough to be our next Poet Laureate and enrich us again, as he is now enriching you.

From *Edmund Blunden – Sixty Five*

Philip Larkin: The Whitsun Weddings

The last of the thirty-two poems in this book is about two stone
effigies of an earl and countess of the Middle Ages. More than their
names, former fame, quarterings, or estates, is this fact – that the
sculptor who was paid to carve their recumbent forms took the liberty
of carving the left hand of the earl withdrawn from its gauntlet and
secretly clasping the right hand of his wife lying beside him. All the
poems in this volume are clear, disciplined, and well-formed, with
ultimate lines or stanzas giving a final pat, punch, or moulding into
shape of what has gone before. When he has seen 'with a sharp, tender
shock' these clasped hands, Philip Larkin concludes:

> The stone fidelity
> They hardly meant has come to be
> Their final blazon, and to prove
> Our almost-instinct almost true:
> What will survive of us is love.

That he is not sure of what truth is, that what is carved may be an
untruth, is characteristic of this compassionate poet of doubt, this least
smug and cocksure of men, the very reverse of the professional and
now slightly ageing prigs of a decade ago.

It is quite easy to be funny or satiric about the packaged era of the
housewife which most of us in England endure today, where
everything is washable, hygienic, of standard size, and in cheerful
shades approved by the Council of Industrial Design. The eating up of
the country by 'developers', the tearing down of the old streets to
make way for supermarkets and car parks, the huge lies on the huge
hoardings – Philip Larkin is aware of them all and puts them down
with a deadly and memorable accuracy easier to digest than the
Buchanan Report:

> And residents from raw estates, brought down
> The dead straight miles by stealing flat-faced trolleys
> Push through plate-glass swing doors to their desires –

> Cheap suits, red kitchen-ware, sharp shoes, iced lollies,
> Electric mixers, toasters, washers, driers ...

He epitomises the futility of advertising:

> In frames as large as rooms that face all ways
> And block the ends of streets with giant loaves,
> Screen graves with custard, cover slums with praise
> Of motor-oil and cuts of salmon, shine
> Perpetually these sharply-pictured groves
> Of how life should be. High above the gutter
> A silver knife sinks into golden butter ...

And instead of just describing, giving a cynical shrug and leaving it at that, he feels and puts down the bewilderment we all feel – Why were we born? What is the truth we should be finding out? And anyhow, we have not long to live and will soon die, and then what? 'What are days for?' he asks, and concludes:

> Ah, solving that question
> Brings the priest and the doctor
> In their long coats
> Running over the fields.

Or he will express the sudden shock of loneliness we feel at an everyday sight, as in his fine poem 'Ambulances', which begins:

> Closed like confessionals, they thread
> Loud noons of cities, giving back
> None of the glances they absorb.

He goes on to describe the white face seen above the hospital blanket before it is whisked off into private silence:

> All streets in time are visited.

This tenderly observant poet writes clearly, rhythmically, and thoughtfully about what all of us can understand:

> Home is so sad. It stays as it was left,
> Shaped to the comfort of the last to go ...

Being humane and personal, he cannot help revealing his own preferences and situation in life in his poems. He loves music, particularly jazz. Of Sidney Bechet he says:

> On me your voice falls as they say love should,
> Like an enormous yes.

He seems resigned to having no wife, no son, and to be living in furnished rooms:

> Whose window shows a strip of building land,
> Tussocky, littered. 'Mr Bleaney took
> My bit of garden properly in hand'.
> Bed, upright chair, sixty-watt bulb, no hook
>
> Behind the door, no room for books or bags –
> 'I'll take it.' So it happens that I lie
> Where Mr Bleaney lay, and stub my fags
> On the same saucer-souvenir, and try
>
> Stuffing my ears with cotton-wool, to drown
> The jabbering set he egged her on to buy.

Philip Larkin is the librarian of the university at Kingston-upon-Hull, and some of his most beautiful poems describe that remote strip of the East Riding where the Humber widens to the North Sea, and ships and church towers sail across the landscape under an enormous sky as the train curls out of Hull (Paragon) station, on its long journey to Doncaster and King's Cross. The superb title-poem of this book opens with a stanza whose ambling metre is exactly suited to what it describes:

> That Whitsun, I was late getting away:
>   Not till about
> One-twenty on the sunlit Saturday
> Did my three-quarters-empty train pull out,
> All windows down, all cushions hot, all sense
> Of being in a hurry gone.

This unperturbed, unenvious, and compassionate poet of doubt, common experience, and the search for truth has a reverence for the vastness around us and stands on the brink of eternity wondering whether it will be day, twilight, or night when we are dead. He is the John Clare of the building estates, and as true to them as was Clare to the fields and trees of Northamptonshire. He has certainly closed the gap between poetry and the public which the experiments and obscurity of the last fifty years have done so much to widen. It is to be hoped that these poems, together with those in *The Less Deceived* (1955), will be produced in a cheap paper edition so that those who really like poetry may read them.

The Listener

Men and Buildings

A series of articles written for The Daily Telegraph

Sheffield

I stood in Sheffield on a wet Saturday afternoon. I was in an industrial part of straight, two-storey brick streets wedged along the tall walls of silent factories.

No one was about, for it was the sacred hour of sport for the men and shopping for the ladies. Not a blade of grass was in sight. Smoke from railway sidings and the faint smells of gas and chemicals filled the air.

The worn little houses were scoured without and clean in their crowded front rooms, and through an archway that led to the backyard I could see a row of communal outdoor privies. On a working weekday I could visualise, with Sheffield's early industrial poet, Ebenezer Elliott, 'this bloodless Waterloo! this hell of wheels!' In memory's ear I could hear the:

> '. . . ceaseless roar
> Urging the heavy forge, the clanking mill.
> The rapid tilt and screaming, sparkling stone.
> Is this the spot where stoop'd the ash-crowned hill
> To meet the vale, when bee-lov'd banks o'ergrown
> With broom and woodbine heard the cushat lone
> Coo for her absent love?'

The nearest approach to nature was the polluted water of the River Don flowing under an iron bridge leading to the chain stores and flash shop-fronts of the Attercliffe Road. The church I had come to see was locked and many of its windows had been smashed. There was no decipherable board to say whether there were a vicar and services.

I thought of the leafy district of Broomhill on the western heights of Sheffield (why is the western side of an English city nearly always smarter than the eastern?), where gabled black stone houses rise above the ponticums and holly and private cast-iron lamp-posts light the gravelled drives.

Greek, Italian, Gothic, they stand in winding tree-shaded roads, these handsome mansions of the Victorian industrialists who had made their pile from steel and cutlery in the crowded mills and slums below. They lived in what is still the prettiest suburb in England, though now most of their houses are academies and offices. Here the churches are open and cared for and still reminiscent of the days of top hats and pew rents when church-going was respectable. The Noncomformist chapels, too, in this prosperous district, are larger and more church-like than those in the poor streets.

Here was the best and worst of Victorian England.

Sheffield today is a city of half-a-million people, the city of steel, a heavy industry which cannot move from the valleys where water power was used for grinding as long ago as 1624 when the Company of Cutlers was founded. The descendants of those who lived in the big houses of Broomhill are now 'executives' and come flashing in by Jaguar from converted cottages and farms and manor houses in the distant dales. The manual workers must remain near the mills which now work by steam and electric power.

Again Ebenezer Elliott came to mind in his famous hymn:

'When wilt thou save the people
O God of mercy, when?
The people, Lord, the people.
Not thrones and crowns, but men!'

The Lord seems to have swept the Sheffield Corporation (it became a city in 1893) into doing much for its people. There is not much fine architecture of the past in Sheffield – the marvellous Wicker Arch by Weightman (c. 1850), a few handsome industrial buildings like Green Lane Works (1860), the eighteenth-century Paradise Square, the Mappin Art Gallery (1886) by Flockton and Gibbs, the medieval Parish Church, now the Cathedral, the Town Hall (1897), and the neo-Georgian City Hall (1932) by Vincent Harris and the Students' Union (1936) by Stephen Welsh, some good Greek and Gothic revival by local Georgian and Victorian architects like W. Flockton, J. F. Gibbs and J. D. Webster. But it has not an architectural heritage like that of Halifax, Leeds or Huddersfield.

Sheffield's great advantage is its beautiful natural surroundings of hill and dale. Of these it has long been aware. It has left the spacious leafy suburbs of prosperity, already mentioned, fairly intact. The large gardens are as yet little built upon.

Best of all, the Corporation has bought up open spaces and received others from landowners, so that its parks, from the trim Georgian Botanical Gardens to the wild woods of Whirlow Brook Park, the extensive Graves Park, the spreading grass and woods around Beauchief Abbey, the tumbling streams, the open moors, and the many golf links, are unrivalled in England. And beyond them are always the blue hills of Yorkshire and Derbyshire.

From King Edward VII's reign to that of King George VI, you will remember that the theorists in English housing thought every man should have his own bit of garden and live in semi-rural surroundings – the garden suburb ideal. Move the people out of their dense, grassless streets into fresh air with a bit of garden, a row of shops, a cinema, a public hall and, possibly, a church. This Sheffield did, and many a healthy hill and pleasant pastoral slope, a long bus ride from the mills and factories, is now covered with crescents of semi-detached council houses, treeless and inexpensive versions of Hampstead Garden Suburb.

I stood in such a suburb of Sheffield on a hot day. Only about one garden in three was cultivated. Litter lay in the grass that bounded the road, with its inevitable smell of last night's fish and chips. Again the church was locked and some of its windows smashed. From the distance came the musical note of the ice-cream van.

A lady, obviously recently re-housed, asked me: 'Where are the shops?' I did not know. There were none in sight, only houses, houses.

This seemed to me a wasteful use of Sheffield's countryside. Then I went to look at the new blocks of flats rising near the city centre. The first sight of them was terrifying and inhuman, tier on tier of concrete with ugly 'contemprikit' detail rising on a steep slope called Park Hill. When you start to walk about among them and see the flats inside, you become acclimatised.

The City Architect has, as it were, taken the old two-storey streets and raised them one on top of the other. Sheffield people are beginning to live vertically instead of horizontally.

From far away below come the cries of children playing in their public playgrounds: far below, too, are the public-houses and shops. High up here the living-room windows look out on to the magnificent moorland and if you cannot make out which dot in the area below is your child, you are at least centrally heated and with hot water and proper sanitation. The planning is thoughtful and ingenious and people do not much miss the gardens they never had.

More successful aesthetically are the square tower blocks arising in the city and its outskirts. These are much better detailed than Park Hill and as ingeniously planned.

They stand in wide open spaces where once were crowded streets. They look out on to the moors. As blocks they are well-proportioned and even noble – a pale yellow brick facing with square green tower on top which really looks like a termination and not like a parcel left by mistake on the roof by the builders.

Who shall say what a race these new, churchless, communal blocks will breed? It is still too early to say. That they are kinder than the old streets and the sprawling mid-wars suburbs there can be little doubt. They are super-human additions to a new landscape.

I believe they suit the rugged hills of Sheffield and its people. The question is will they make a houseproud horizontal people apathetic and turn them into the machines they tend?

> Flowers of thy heart, O God, are they:
> Let them not pass, like woods, away –
> Their heritage a sunless day.
> God save the people!

The re-housed Sheffield people now have any sun that is shining.

The Buchanan Plan

We look nervously at the sky, fearing what may fall out of it. We ignore the earth at our feet where a monster is growing bigger, noisier and smellier every day.

The roads of England are at present more congested than anywhere in the world and within ten years are likely to have twice as much traffic.

Already you think twice about going to a town in a motor car because of parking difficulties. Already the quiet village you visited three years ago is now crowded with cars. What will it be like in ten years' time?

A thoughtful study of standards and values in the motor age was made recently by Mr C. D. Buchanan, a civil engineer and town planner, and published in the journal of the Royal Institute of British Architects.

Mr Buchanan offers two solutions. One is the American, and may be
described as the sprawl which recognises the motor car as master. This
means more and more suburbs with new shopping centres surrounded
by ample car parks, the whole system tied together by express-ways for
motor traffic which radiate from the chief cities. This will mean
abandoning any attempt to preserve the home counties round our
large cities and indeed giving up agriculture as a serious part of our
economy.

Even if this policy of turning England into a huge suburb is thought
to be disastrous, we must remember that, from the point of view of
motorists, it is excellent.

It will mean no parking problems and comparatively easy communications by car, though the distances travelled will be far greater.

Maybe the international situation will soon be such, or science will
have advanced so far, that there will be no need for us to grow any of
our own food. Maybe the side of us which enjoys the country and all
the varieties of English counties must be suppressed.

At least everyone will have a house of his own and his own bit of
garden, room for a garage to protect his beloved car in winter and to
wash it on Sunday mornings and a convenient shopping centre for
weekdays and an easy journey to work.

There is a lot to be said for sprawl from the point of view of the
private motorist.

But the private motorist is two people and here come the most
penetrating remarks in Mr Buchanan's study. He realises that the
motorist is a split personality.

'The mere act of being sealed up in a vehicle induces a change of
mentality characterised by indifference to all considerations other
than those relating to the journey in hand. To the homeward-
bound lorry driver, residential streets that offer short cuts are there
for his convenience; to the motorist, pedestrians have no function
other than to obstruct his progress; to the motor-cyclist, the noise
of his exhaust is music.'

Everyone has a pedestrian side to him. He likes to stand on a
footbridge and see shoals of minnows in a clear stream. He would like
walking between the colleges in Oxford and Cambridge or in the
closes of our cathedrals, noticing how the sun strikes the mouldings of
weathered stone if only he could see them without a foreground of
motor cars.

And with what relief he turns into the quiet of a trafficless quadrangle, court or cloister to hear again birdsong and to smell mown grass. And in a city what relaxation we all enjoy when we step out of the fumes and roar of the High Street into the quiet of an arcade or an alley of small shops.

What we have to decide is to which part of us must we give first place? The part that travels on wheels? Or the part that walks on foot? I believe that most of us prefer to use our eyes looking at skyline and scenery rather than at traffic signs and asphalt; I believe we would rather hear wind in trees and birds and running water than hootings and the roar of the internal combustion engine, and that we certainly prefer the scent of flowers to the smell of petrol.

At the present moment all that local authorities and the Ministry of Transport seem to be doing is trying to make the traffic move faster. In the end this is no solution, for if you open a bottleneck in one part of the road you only find you have created another farther on.

We carve our old cities and villages to pieces and still there is nowhere to park in them and they are no quieter, safer, less smelly or easier to use for shopping and recreation.

The possibility that Mr Buchanan sees as an alternative to sprawl is 'compactness'. This may well mean a limitation eventually in the number of motor cars on our overcrowded island. It will certainly mean segregating certain central and attractive parts of our existing towns from through traffic, and even parked traffic, so that people may once more walk about in them and enjoy them. It will mean that traffic essential to these segregated areas will have to go either underground or overhead.

It will cost millions, but unless it is done we had better give up our present way of life altogether and become a civilisation which spends most of its waking time travelling in tin boxes, watching traffic lights and decanting itself into the multi-storey boxes which are the architecture of the motor age.

Personally I think that uncontrolled motor traffic is the enemy of the most important side of our nature. The motor is only a means to find peace. It is too fraught with anxiety and too confining to be peace itself.

Nonconformist Architecture

The Nonconformist architecture of these islands has a tradition of over

three centuries. It dominates Birmingham, that centre of Unitarianism.
It dominates Wales. Indeed, Welsh Methodism has produced a native
style of chapel of whose textures, colours and shapes John Piper was
the first artist to see the pictorial possibilities.

The Methodism of Bristol, the city which has been the start of so
many great movements, produced another kind of Methodist architecture.

In the centres of big industrial towns a large porticoed building,
which one takes at first glance for the town hall, turns out to be a
Baptist, Congregational or Methodist place of worship.

Over 2,000 clergymen of the Church of England were ejected for
refusing to obey the Act of Uniformity in 1661. Many were
persecuted, and though they came into their own again for a short
time under the Commonwealth, at the Restoration they found
themselves out once more and had to found their own churches, of
which the Independents or Congregationalists, Baptists and Presby-
terians (many of whom in England became Unitarians) and the
Quakers, are the best known senior survivors.

Because their buildings have been written about in terms of their
founders, subsequent ministers and particular families, and because the
causes for which they stood represented struggles of conscience and
loss of property and privilege for the sake of religious conviction, the
architecture which they produced has not had the attention it
deserves.

The puritanism from which much Nonconformity sprang regarded
architectural adornment, rich carving and gilded organ pipes savour-
ing of worldliness Popery, the Established Church. Yet if there is such
a thing as an architecture of the people in the past three centuries, it is
to be found in nonconformist chapels.

The earliest seventeenth-century nonconformist churches were
meeting houses, usually cottage-like structures built by members
themselves, on the property of another member – down a back street
in a town, on somebody's garden, or in the country on the field of a
sympathetic farmer or landlord. Examples are the Strict Baptist chapel
(1695) hidden away in Winslow, Bucks, and the Blue Idol Quaker
meeting house (1682) in Surrey, which is a converted farmhouse.

The earliest buildings were places of assembly of those who
seriously disagreed with Episcopacy. They were built at a time when
theology was considered far more important and interesting than
economics. They must not be thought of as revivalist chapels, where
people shouted Alleluya and sang hymns, but as assemblies of

theologically-minded people who wrestled with the Word of God and practised forms of worship which suited them.

The first of these is the Congregational Church (1566) at Horningsham, Wilts. The simplest are Quaker meeting houses, such as Jordans (1688), Buckinghamshire, and the little thatched meeting house of Come-to-Good (1709) in Cornwall.

Outside, the building may look like a small farm or a cottage. Inside, the worn old floors, scrubbed benches, and plain walls hold an expectant quiet which seems to go on even after the meeting is finished. The furnishings are no more than benches, a gallery and a raised platform for the Elders.

In the towns, more elaborate chapels were built. Those which were not Quaker had a tall pulpit as the focus of attention and galleries, carved wood and twinkling brass chandeliers, for example: Mary Street Chapel (1721), Taunton, once Baptist, now Unitarian; Rook Lane Congregational Church (1707), Frome; the Unitarian chapel in Bury St Edmunds (1711–12); and the Octagon chapel, Norwich (1754–6); and Underbank Chapel, Stannington (1742), near Sheffield. There are a hundred or so more. Externally they are almost like Wren City churches, but without the steeple, for towers were illegal on Nonconformist churches until the last century.

The one thing these early chapels had in common was an absence of chancel and altar. The table some of those used for occasional celebrations of the Lord's Supper, a memorial service and not a sacrifice, was plain wood.

When John and Charles Wesley started the Methodist Revival in the early eighteenth century, the neglected poor of Bristol were the first of hundreds of thousands to be moved. John Wesley intended his 'meeting houses,' as he always called them, to supplement the work of the parish church. Even down to the present century it has been the custom in some villages for Methodists to go to their parish churches for Communion at Christmas and Easter.

But, because the Church of England mistrusted 'enthusiasm,' as it was called, in Wesley's followers, he ordained ministers himself and thus the movement, with its many subsequent offshoots, now mostly reunited as the Methodist Church, became separate from the Church of England. The first Methodist chapels are rectangular buildings like the New Room, Bristol (1739), with as many seats as possible fitted in for hearing sermons. John Wesley himself preferred an octagon shape.

Most Methodist, Baptist and Congregational churches throughout the country until towards the end of the last century were built on the rectangular plan. They have a large welcoming entrance on the main road. There are internal staircases to left and right to reach the galleries. The climax of the design inside is the raised pulpit with a Communion Table beneath it. The organ is either behind the pulpit or in the gallery at the back. They are buildings primarily designed for preaching and singing.

Most of the earlier nineteenth-century Nonconformist entrance façades were classical. Sometimes the front masks an older building behind, at other times the original chapel has become the Sunday School. Much ingenuity was used to produce interesting chapel façades: the Adam style, the Greek, the Roman and even the Norman. There was much variety of material; coloured bricks became popular to relieve dullness.

For a long time, the Gothic Revival was suspect, because it was associated with High Church and Popery, until Ruskin pointed out that it was the native style of the English working man.

Thereafter, many Nonconformist churches were rebuilt in Gothic by J. Tarring, the Gilbert Scott of the Nonconformists, and his followers. They still had the same rectangular plan but with pointed windows and coloured glass and, possibly, a thin spire. Sometimes a Gothic façade was clapped on to the front of an older building.

Daring and interesting experiments were made in the planning of churches – two-storey buildings with schools underneath; Baptist churches with built-in tanks; octagonal halls for preaching.

The most notable of the latter type in London are Alfred Waterhouse's Congregational church, Lyndhurst Road, Hampstead (1883–4) and Cubitt's Welsh Presbyterian church (1888) in Charing Cross Road. At the beginning of this century, a sort of art nouveau Gothic in brick and terracotta was very popular.

Today, as the population shifts to the South and to the new suburbs, many old chapels are being destroyed or converted to secular uses. For this reason it is well they should be looked at and the more comely and historical examples preserved. They are memorials to that freedom of conscience which has characterised our way of life.

The Ideal Town

The quietest Sunday walk today is in the heart of a big city. Traffic lights go red, orange and green at empty crossings; warehouses and Victorian and Edwardian offices rise like Venetian palaces either side of their asphalt canals. Shop windows, with no one to look at the display in them, seem pathetic and temporary.

Round the corner, down a curving cobbled alley, sounds the bell of a forgotten church, reminding us that people once lived here before steam, electric traction and internal combustion drew them out in increasing numbers to find a *rus in urbe*.

Now those first rural retreats for the Georgian and Victorian citizen are no longer rural. Their gardens long ago were built over with villas, and the descendants of those who strolled on their lawns have driven themselves yet farther from the cities.

So tedious and nerve-racking has become the daily journey back to work that many big firms are moving their offices and factories out into the suburbs. It may well be that in thirty years from now our old cities will become the best places to live, for a quiet, friendly life in which to breathe, smell, see and hear. That is to say if there are any old cities left after the do-goodery to which they are being subjected.

Last year there came out a book called 'The Italian Townscape' which was noticed in this paper by my colleague Ian Nairn. It was about the most important book on architecture that has appeared since the war. Its author, who delights in the extraordinary pseudonym of Ivor de Wolfe, has been the most influential figure in English architecture and planning for the past thirty-five years. His pleasure has been to work anonymously and behind the scenes.

He first battled for 'contemporary' architecture in England, though he must now deeply regret the misinterpretations of it with which this country is littered. He first fought against the academic planning in neo-Georgian and Paris *beaux-arts* style which created Kingsway in London and the Headrow in Leeds, and whose last expression is the wide, chilly and wind-swept openness of post-war Plymouth. He first introduced Osbert Lancaster, Sir Hugh Casson, J. M. Richards, Nikolaus Pevsner and Ian Nairn to architectural journalism.

In his book Ivor de Wolfe and his photographer wife go back to what a town ought to be, and why it is natural for most of us to live in one. The original walled cities of Europe served a treble purpose – they provided protection from the enemy outside, shelter from wind, rain and excessive heat, and congenial places in which to walk, talk, hold meetings, sell goods and worship the Creator. He has found an admirable example in Sabbioneta, a sixteenth-century walled town entered through gates, and deliberately designed with narrow streets, straight and short, each giving a promise of something beyond by means of a vista through an arch or a sudden patch of sunlight. In the end the visitor finds himself in the charming, low-scaled, wide, central piazza, with its campanile and church and colonnaded ducal palace.

This is no place for motor cars nor for grandiose straight avenues down which the eighteenth century liked to bowl in carriages. It is intimate and humane, the reverse of what architects and town planners have been doing for the past 200 years.

He has applied his principle of what he calls 'townscaping' to other old Italian towns as yet not burst open by the motor car, though they may be rendered hideous with the noise of motor scooters. He shows how an uphill curve can lead the eye and foot on to see what is beyond; how some buildings were designed to be seen sideways on, and how others are more subtly appreciated when partly hidden, so that there is an air of mystery and more to come.

The English town planner Dr Thomas Sharp, usually more ahead of his time than the 'with-it' boys, some years ago first pointed out that the tree between All Souls and Queen's College on the curve of Oxford's famous High was as important as the buildings. He went on to say that he thought that English builders, before conscious town planning was ever thought of, had always had an instinctive sense of where to put what in the streets and lanes of towns and villages – a high building there, a low one here, a wall, a tree, a building set back, another thrust forward, a mixture of textures, brick, stone, cob, thatch and tile.

What better place to start a townscape walk in England than the City of London – although York, Norwich, Bristol and even parts of Exeter may provide less multilated examples? It will have to be on a Sunday because cars are the enemies of a civilised city, and we are still too barbarous to realise they must be kept without the walls.

Notice how Ludgate Hill is not straight but curves as it approaches the West front of St Paul's, and how that West front is itself not square to the hill so that it is given depth by perspective. Follow the little cobbled alleys down to the Thames below Mansion House station, or in the neighbourhood of Billingsgate, and see how some towers and Wren steeples can still be seen on the skyline as he meant them to be seen.

Compare this with the arid, monotonous new cubes with their garish mosaics and crazy-paved patterning in post-war Gresham Street. See how the do-gooders have even insulted Wren by exposing the West front of St Lawrence Jewry and its tower, which is out of the straight, and was never meant to be seen except above house tops. Or walk farther north to the intimidating glass slabs along route 11.

Notice the windy, exposed platform, pompously called a 'podium', which is to be the shopping street of the Citizen of Tomorrow.

And lastly turn again to the river, to the cobbled square of Queenhithe off Lower Thames Street. Even today it seems like a port. Through an alley between the wharves you come to the ancient harbour of London. The water belches under the barges. Distant traffic noise is drowned. The twelve bells of Paul's ring out and there is a nearer tinkle from St Benet Paul's Wharf or maybe St James's Garlickhithe. We are back in the true City of London. It is to this unembanked side of the Thames and in the alleys and courts that slope down to it, now all warehouses and office, that the citizens should return. Here, perhaps, one day we will be allowed to eat and sleep and live in quiet. This is the real City of London which can yet be saved from mammon and the motor car. It is human townscape.

Garden Suburbs

The word suburb means an outlying district to a town. But no one in London in May, 1684, when Barbon laid out Red Lion Square, or when eighteenth-century squares such as Grosvenor, Cavendish and Smith were added to the Metropolis – not even someone living in the Old Town at Edinburgh when the New Town was rising clean and spacious on a nearby hill – would have thought of calling the dwellers in these places suburbanites.

The eighteenth-century idea of a suburb was an extension of the town into the fields.

A late and splendid example of this, which is too little regarded, is Birkenhead, where, beyond the Priory and the small village, a whole town of straight streets, broad squares and crescents enclosing a park, laid out by Paxton, was planned by two Scottish architects, Thomas Hamilton and Gillespie Graham, in 1844.

Hamilton Square is an impressive realisation of Hamilton's scheme, and although many other streets of Birkenhead today lack the gracious building their architects intended, breadth and straightness survive. Birkenhead is probably the last example of a consciously planned town spreading over the fields in the eighteenth-century grand manner.

What we have come to think of as suburbs, alas in a faintly derogatory sense, is the opposite idea to that in the heads of men like

Hamilton in Birkenhead, Wood in Bath, Playfair in Edinburgh, Papworth in Cheltenham, Foulston in Plymouth. These were classical men who wanted to extend the town into the country. The later suburb builder wanted to make country of towns.

The suburb as we think of it is a late eighteenth-century romantic idea. Instead of straight lines there were curves, instead of symmetry, irregularity. The dweller in the romantic suburb was to live in a detached house in a garden of his own. Neighbouring gardens were to give the illusion of being an extension of his own garden. Each man was his own squire with his own short carriage drive and park.

This exactly suited the merchant of the industrial towns of the North and the big cities of the South. Every town dweller in Britain in the last century was little more than one generation removed from some country village where his family originated. Instead of a cottage he could now afford a villa and if he was not entitled to a coat of arms on his carriage and over his front door he could at least have stained glass on the hall stairs and spikes and turrets on his roof.

The railway could take him to his work and he could be at home with his wife and children in the evenings in what seemed like country. The suburb was the fulfilment of every man's dream, a house of his own in the country.

A precedent for it had been set in Georgian times by such schemes as the layout of detached houses on the Eyre estate in St John's Wood, London, started in 1794, and John Nash's Park Villages circa 1830. But the houses here were too small for the suddenly enriched Victorian industrialists: consequently we have residential districts like Streatham and Lewisham in London, the Park in Nottingham, Jesmond Dene in Newcastle-upon-Tyne, Mossley Hill in Liverpool, Edgbaston in Birmingham, Roundhay in Leeds, Morningside in Edinburgh, Kelvinside in Glasgow and Whalley Range in Manchester.

Gas lamps and possibly a lodge at the entrance, laurels along the drive (in which Sherlock Holmes might be hiding with his bull's-eye lantern), red paper in the dining room and heavy mahogany chairs, green paper in the billiard room, pale silk on the drawing-room walls and armour in the hall, what are they now, these merchants' dreams of home? Clinics, branches of the public library, Ministry of Pensions offices, and their gardens filled with huts or new villas built in a feeble attempt to look like Frank Lloyd Wright.

And where are they now, the sons and grandsons of these merchant princes? Expenses farmers in the Home Counties or fishers in the Scottish lochs.

I think these mid-Victorian suburbs were jeered at because they were symbols of class distinction. The old land-owning classes despised them because they were not real country, the sweated-workers of the industrial towns envied them.

They themselves were built when the middle classes were riddled with subtle distinctions. The wholesaler looked down on the retailer, the attorney and the doctor looked down on the merchant whether wholesale or retail because he was in trade. Only clergymen and peers were above criticism; even bankers were suspect.

The most significant suburb built in the last century, probably the most significant in the Western world, is Bedford Park, Chiswick, laid out in 1876 by Norman Shaw. It was designed specially for 'artistic people of moderate incomes.' It stands in orchard land and the picturesque brick houses with their faintly Dutch look are late Victorian versions of the small parsonage houses which were built in the heyday of the Gothic revival a generation earlier.

Bedford Park was built to be self-contained: it has a church, and what was once a co-operative store. The Tabard Inn with William de Morgan tiles in the public bar and a hall panelled with cedar from a demolished city church, was where men could play the clavichord to ladies in tussore dresses, and where supporters of William Morris could learn of early Socialism.

Here Yeats as a young man lived with his artist father. Here until just before the war gentle craftsfolk survived making Celtic jewellery in their studios or weaving on hand looms among the faded sun flowers of a now forgotten cult.

It is sad that the winding roads of this leafy garden suburb are now cut through by heavy traffic and that the fences so carefully designed as part of the whole composition are dilapidated or altered. But the spirit of Bedford Park is still there and it is probably one of our most charming and important monuments: nor is its usefulness past. Many of its roads are very pleasant to live in.

Bedford Park was the origin of many another garden suburb. Enlightened manufacturers, spurred on by the ideals of early Socialism and with that social conscience which Nonconformity and Christian Socialism in the Church of England gave to the late Victorians, built garden suburbs for their workers.

Lord Leverhulme at the beginning of this century built an interdenominational church, an art gallery and a village of cottages by the best exponents of the arts and crafts style at Port Sunlight. Cadburys built Bournville, near Birmingham, and Reckitts built a garden suburb for their workers in Hull. There are several other examples.

In 1892, Ebenezer Howard started the idea of garden cities which were an extension of the Bedford Park experiment, and Letchworth was begun in 1903. Hampstead Garden Suburb was started in 1907 with its charming houses by Barry Parker and Raymond Unwin and the Lutyens churches. In these places the houses were more cottage-like than those of Bedford Park, the old village rather than its parsonage was the model. Welwyn begun in 1919 was an even bolder experiment with its own industries and houses in a Georgian style.

Today certain Government departments are building suburbs as may be seen in the well laid-out estates for atomic workers at Abingdon and Wantage. And I suppose that the New Towns themselves may originate from Bedford Park, though some of them are designed in the more grand manner of Birkenhead.

A suburb, provided it is not too consciously community centred, can be a pleasant place to live in – quiet, clean and full of vistas. Above everything it is human and respects the individual. This cannot be said of the tall blocks of workers' flats going up today which are conceived in terms of density, plot ratio and cost to the rates.

Just as there was a 'railway mania' in the last century there seems to be an 'office mania' today. In London for instance we learn that the LCC has a policy of decentralisation. This, it seems, is ignored by the speculators who continue to fill every bombed site or decent row of old houses which they can buy cheap with speculative blocks, particularly in the centre of London.

I notice that more and more of these are empty. No typists are bronzed behind their glass acres. No directors dictate in their low-ceilinged rooms. Perhaps the tide is turning and there is some hope that the faces of our big cities may not be further lifted into unrecognisability.

The Demolition of Euston Arch

The LCC has given permission to British Railways to demolish the Great Arch at Euston, and its attendant lodges. It has made the wise condition 'provided that they are re-erected on another site in an appropriate, dignified and open setting.'

The Arch was completed in 1837 from designs by Philip Hardwick and marked the arrival of the railway from Birmingham to London. It was a symbolic gateway heralding the new mode of transport and built with all the courage and swagger of a time which was convinced of a glorious future.

Its enormous granite blocks have withstood the London atmosphere, its proportions are vast and awe-inspiring and are given scale by the attendant lodges and railings. It was intended to be seen from the Euston Road but has since been obscured by an hotel and its lodges have been defaced by additions to the station.

I can think of no worthier memorial to the fact that Britain built the first railways than to re-construct this Arch, its lodges and railings on the Euston Road itself.

Railways were born in England. The early railway architecture of this country is therefore of more than merely national importance. It is the beginning of the whole history of the Railway Age.

If it were just *old*, I would not be so anxious to plead for its preservation. It is also often very fine, particularly in its stations, viaducts, bridges and tunnel entrances.

Large cast-iron roofs such as those at St Pancras and York Central are still among the engineering wonders of the world. The wooden roof of the original station at Temple Meads, Bristol, has a span exceeding that of Westminster Hall, the largest medieval wooden roof in existence. Not only for their engineering feats are the railways of the United Kingdom remarkable, but also for the architecture of their stations.

Unfortunately railway enthusiasts are mostly people interested in engines and speeds of trains and the history of railway development. There is very little written about railway buildings. The names of the architects of some of our grandest stations such as Temple Meads are forgotten.

Partly because of this and partly because of an incredible insensitivity to architecture on the part of the British Transport Commission in the past, a great many splendid buildings have been mutilated or allowed to decay.

Since the war, for instance, one of the earliest railway stations in the world, that at Nine Elms, Vauxhall, London (1837–8), with its arcaded entrance, has been partly demolished. The vista Brunel designed for Paddington Station, the only large London building with no exterior walls, has been obscured by a new and needless screen at the platform barriers. The roof of Edward Middleton Barry's railway hotel at Charing Cross with its mansard roof and spikes, so pleasant and prominent a feature of the Strand and Thames skyline, has been flattened and reconstructed in a feeble semi-Georgian manner.

The magnificent Cannon Street awaits no doubt a similar fate, with its enclosing walls now open to the sky. The tower top which lent unity to the buildings of Liverpool Street has been removed. Unworthy electric light fittings have been clamped haphazardly on to the brickwork of St Pancras Station's entrances. Holborn Viaduct, with its distinguished arcaded entrance and tiled refreshment room, is being destroyed. These examples come from London alone.

The history of railway stations is in itself interesting. The very first, of which Euston is an example, had arched entrances for road traffic which led to cast-iron sheds over the platforms. Later, protection for the passengers was demanded and a great hall, like the concourse in a modern airport, was constructed in which they could wait until a man came in and rang a bell to announce the departure of a train.

The finest of these survives, again at Euston. It was designed by Philip Hardwick and his son P. C. Hardwick ten years after the Arch and was rightly described by the late H. S. Goodhart-Rendel as 'one of the noblest rooms in London.'

Two other grand early stations come to my mind – that at Huddersfield (1850–4), by J. and C. Pritchett, which is like an enormous classical country house with central portico and arcades and wings on either side, and Central Station, Newcastle upon Tyne (1846–9) with its impressive classical entrance by J. Dobson.

The next phase in station development was for an hotel to be built as part of the station. The first was at York and one of the best to survive much as it was originally designed by T. G. Andrews (1847) is that at Paragon Station, Kingston-upon-Hull, in the Italianate manner.

The first railway stations to be built alongside the line between termini were thought of as lodge gates or tollhouses beside the iron road and were consequently in a cottage style. Many survive, notably in the neighbourhood of Derby. They were generally of local materials and harmonise well with their setting. South London and Surrey have several.

Stations are by no means the only good architecture with which the railways provided Britain. There are bridges: the Britannia Bridge over the Menai Strait, by Robert Stephenson and Francis Thompson (1845–50), with its enormous guardian lions and cyclopean piers and entrances; Conway Bridge in the Gothic style by the same architects, blending with the castle; Brunel's wonderful brick bridge over the Thames at Maidenhead with its nearly flat arches.

There are viaducts like the Wharncliff Viaduct at Hanwell, Middlesex, and that which carries the London and North Western northwards from Wolverton and those which carry the Midland through Rutland and Northants.

The railways were built by people who were proud of them and thought of their stations, bridges, viaducts and tunnel entrances as the additions to the landscape we now recognise them to be. Their present shoddy treatment is thus doubly distressing.

Pleasant, flimsy wayside stations of wood are allowed to rot and are then replaced with a less functional and infinitely more uncomfortable concrete, so that they are like cold public lavatories.

If ruined castles, decaying churches and country houses are part of our heritage worthy of preservation, so are many of the constructions of our railways. I hope that a survey will be made of our railway architecture and that its best examples will be preserved.

St Pancras

St Pancras was a fourteen-year-old Christian boy, who was martyred in Rome in AD 304 by the Emperor Diocletian. In England he is better known as a railway station. That station takes its name from the parish in which it stands. It is the terminus of the Midland Railway, the most mid-Victorian of all British lines. It wasn't the fastest line but it was the most comfortable, and was the first to introduce a dining car and upholstered seats for third-class passengers. Its livery was scarlet. Scarlet were the famous Kirtley engines with their black funnels; scarlet the carriages and scarlet enlivened with stone dressings and polished granite the walls of the mighty terminus and hotel of St Pancras. So strong is the personality of this station to a Londoner that he does not remember the medieval but mercilessly restored local church, nor the chaste Greek revival St Pancras church in the Euston Road, nor even St Pancras Town Hall opposite the station, now renamed Camden Town Hall. What he sees in his mind's eye is that cluster of towers and pinnacles seen from Pentonville Hill and outlined against a foggy sunset and the great arc of Barlow's train shed gaping to devour incoming engines, and the sudden burst of the exuberant Gothic of the hotel seen from gloomy Judd Street.

The Midland Railway did not reach London until 1867 for goods and 1868 for passengers. Its headquarters and its heart were always in Derby. It used to run trains into King's Cross by arrangement with the Great Northern Railway. Its other rival from the midlands was the long established London & North Western at Euston next door. This was always a belligerent and uncooperative company. If the Midland was to have a terminus in London, it must be a contrast with its neighbours – not old fashioned Greek and Graeco-Roman like Euston with its Doric portico and Great Hall, not mere engineering like grimy stock brick King's Cross, but something to show that the midlands and the Midland had plenty of brass and were not old-fashioned. Bringing the line to London avoiding its competitors was difficult enough, and when the outskirts of the metropolis were reached it was harder still. After burrowing through the Middlesex hills at Hampstead it had to cross a canal. Should it tunnel under this, as the Great Northern and the London & North Western had done, or should it cross it by a bridge? It decided to bridge the canal. In order to do this the very large and very crowded burial ground of old St Pancras would have to be levelled. When the work started, skulls and bones were seen lying about; a passer-by saw an open coffin staved in through which peeped a bright tress of hair. Great scandal was caused and the company was forced to arrange for reverent reburial. The architect in charge of the reburial was A. W. Blomfield, and he sent one of his assistants to watch the carrying away of the dead to see that it was reverently done. That assistant was Thomas Hardy, and his poems 'The Levelled Churchyard' and 'In the Cemetery' recall the fact. Once when he and Blomfield met on the site they found a coffin which contained two skulls.

> O Passenger, pray list and catch
> Our sighs and piteous groans,
> Half stifled in this jumbled patch
> Of wrenched memorial stones!
>
> We late-lamented, resting here,
> Are mixed to human jam,
> And each to each exclaims in fear,
> 'I know not which I am!'

Hardy never forgot the event.

The Midland also had to clear a horrible slum district at Agar Town and part of the equally depressed Somers Town. The inhabitants were not properly rehoused. Yet on came the Midland, full of brass and assurance. It tunnelled one line down to join the Metropolitan (steam) Underground Railway, which is now part of the Inner Circle, and, from Farringdon Street, trains could enter the City or cross the river at Blackfriars. Most of its lines at St Pancras stopped short at the Euston Road, but as it had had to cross the canal by a bridge, the station ended high in air above the Euston Road. This gave its engineer William Henry Barlow (1812–1902) a chance to build what remained for nearly a century, the largest station roof in the world without internal supports. It also inspired him to build what is still the most practical terminus in London. The great cast-iron arched ribs which support the roof were made by the Butterley Iron Company, whose name appears in white on a blue background on each rib above the platforms, reminding us of the Derbyshire origin of the line. The ribs are tied together by floor girders over which the trains run. To increase wind resistance the great curved arch of the station is slightly broken at its apex, so that it is almost a Gothic arch. This whole structure rests on a forest of iron columns under the station. The exterior fence of this forest is the brick wall of the station and hotel. The Midland made good use of the ground-floor level under its terminus. Much of the trade of the line was beer from Burton-on-Trent, and the distance between the iron columns was measured by the length of beer barrels, which were carried down here from the station above by hydraulic lifts, and taken by drays out into London. This gloomy area, when it ceased to be used for beer, became a lair of wild cats. It is now partly a National Car Park and partly the haunt of motor repairing firms. A few shops survive with Gothic windows to them along Euston Road and Pancras Road.

When Barlow designed the train shed, he made provision for an hotel to be built in front of it, above the Euston Road. The station and hotel are approached by ramps, one steep and the other a gentle double curve, so that to this day St Pancras is the most practically designed station for ambulances and certainly the most considerate and humane to mobile passengers. The station was completed in 1868 and Barlow constructed glass screens at either end of his train shed. That on the Euston Road side was designed to keep smoke and noise from the projected hotel. The hotel was started in the year the station was completed, and it was opened to the public in 1873. At the time it was easily the most magnificent of all London hotels. It was one of the first to have lifts, called 'ascending rooms' and worked by hydraulic power. It was also one of the first to have electric bells. It could be a fine hotel again. The architect was the most eminent man of his time, Sir Gilbert Scott (1811–78). Scott was of course the envy of his profession. This is one of the reasons why the *avant garde* architectural critics of the seventies condemned the building as a 'monster'. It may also be a reason for the totally false rumour which I once believed myself, that St Pancras was the Gothic design Scott made for the Foreign Office in 1856, and which Palmerston rejected. Having studied both designs and the plans for them, there is no resemblance except in style. It must be remembered that in the 1860s Gothic was the equivalent of what used to be called 'contemporary' in the 1950s. Any promising architect and go-ahead company would insist on Gothic if they wanted to be thought up to date.

For the last ninety years almost, Sir Gilbert Scott has had a bad press. He is condemned as facile, smart, aggressive, complacent and commercial. When at the top of his form Scott was as good as the best of his Gothic contemporaries. He was so firm a believer in the Gothic style as the only true 'Christian' style – Scott was a moderate High Churchman – that he was determined to adapt it for domestic and commercial purposes. St Pancras station hotel was his greatest chance in London and well he rose to the occasion.

I used to think that Scott was a rather dull architect, but the more I have looked at his work the more I have seen his merits. He had a thorough knowledge of construction, particularly in stone and brick. For St Pancras the bricks were specially made by Edward Gripper in Nottingham. The decorative ironwork for lamp standards and staircases and grilles was by Skidmore of Coventry, who designed the iron screens in some English cathedrals for Scott. The roofs of the hotel are of graded Leicestershire slates; the stone comes mostly from Ketton. Scott's buildings are so well-built they are difficult to pull down. He had a grand sense of plan and site. The hotel building consists of refreshment and dining rooms at station level on the ground floor, and wine cellars in the basement. The Grand Staircase, which alone survives of the hotel's chief interior features, ascends the whole height of the building, by an unbelievably rich cast-iron series of treads with stone vaulting and painted walls. The chief suites of rooms are on the first floor and the higher the building, the less important the rooms, until the quarters for the servants are reached in the gabled attics – men on one side, women on the other – and separate staircases. Yet even these are large and wide and compare favourably with more modern accommodation. The building has been chopped up and partitioned inside for offices. It is odd that it is not used again as an hotel especially now that hotels are so badly needed in London.

Scott had full confidence in being able to exploit the site. The chief rooms are on the front and look across to the once level plains of Bloomsbury and up and down the Euston Road. Even on the first floor they are sufficiently high to be out of the noise of traffic. For the external effect of his hotel Scott used the same technique as Barry had done for the Houses of Parliament, that is to say he increased the sense of height on the comparatively low setting by having a steep roof and many towers and spirelets. Such things always look well in our grey climate. He meant to put Euston and King's Cross to shame. For the rear of his hotel, where it faced the station, he put service rooms and backstairs and made the brick exterior plain, since it was mostly submerged in the train shed. Above the train shed it rises into gables.

There was at one time a serious threat to St Pancras, both as a station and an hotel. Puritans of the thirties were prepared to allow merit to Barlow's train shed, because it was simple and functional. Scott's hotel, however, filled them with horror, because its exterior was ornate and its style they considered sham medieval. If you look again at the hotel you will see it is not sham. It uses brick of the best quality and cast iron, and its proportions bear no resemblance to a medieval domestic building – no medieval building, not even an Hôtel de Ville, of that size was ever built. There still survive along the Euston Road some ingenious façades Scott has constructed for shop fronts in the low brick arches under the station. Today we can appreciate Sir Gilbert's masterpiece. For grandeur of scale it compares with that best work of Sir Gilbert's grandson Sir Giles, Liverpool Cathedral.

The architectural department of British Railways has not tried to have St Pancras station cleaned, and has allowed mean hoardings for advertisements to deface the interior of the station, and to be placed without any regard for the vertical lines created by Scott and Barlow. Mingy little notices and cumbersome new electric lamps are stuck about without regard to proportion or the façades. The now old-fashioned with-itry of the fifties, which has given us the slabs and cubes of high finance, and ruined most of London, has made St Pancras all the more important to us for the relief it brings. It shows that trouble was taken and money spent in its building.

There is one more most important thing to be said in favour of St Pancras station. This was said to me at a party I attended for the publication of Jack Simmons's readable, learned and inspiring book *St Pancras Station*. I was introduced to three former Station Masters of St Pancras, a succession going back to the 1914 war. They all said how magnificent the station was, how fond they were of it, and the last one added, 'moreover *it works*'.

Wheeler's Quarterly Review

Thank God it's Sunday

Broadcast by the BBC as the second of two television programmes.

Vision	Commentary
Aerial tracking shot of Fenchurch Street Station and along the line.	What do most Londoners do on Sunday? They leave it. Most comfortably of all of course by rail from Fenchurch Street
London houses and flats seen from the train.	over brick arches. Who would want to stay behind in an inhuman slab of council flats, built in the priggish . . .
People travelling in a bus. A bicycle on top of a car.	. . . 1960s, when sea and country call? We leave by every means we can.
A station and rail track seen from the train. Close-ups of a bus and car wheels.	Swift, swiftly eastwards through Stepney, Barking, Dagenham, Upminster. Electric railway, diesel, coach and bus. Car and motorbike, bypass and high road.
Outer London Suburbs seen from the train, revealing Essex.	Eastward and further east until the last brick box is out of sight, and then we see the wide enormous marsh of Essex,

*A boy on a motorbike and a
family in a car.*

London's nearest real
countryside, and join the
others speeding to Southend.

*Interior of a family in a
Southend Pier tram.
The sea from the window.*

Hold on, what's that?
A different sort of noise.
And now we're in a different
sort of train.
We're travelling down
Southend Pier by tram, for a
mile and a third towards the
coast of France.
The longest pier in the world.
Was it perhaps a mid-
Victorian dream of bringing
England close . . .

*A couple walking along the pier
in the wind.*

. . . to France at last, and
getting there on foot?
Or was it to build an
elongated jetty . . .

A man walking under the pier.

. . . for vessels making for the
Thames's mouth?

*Men walking under the pier.
Mid-shot of the pier end and
close-up of fishermen's faces and
tackle.*

At any rate, today upon the
pier they sell a map which
shows you where to find the
different kinds of fish the
estuary yields and what's the
bait to use.

To southward from Southend
across the Thames . . .

*Long shot of a boat against oil
refineries.*

. . . you faintly see along the
Kentish coast the oil refineries
which work on Sunday – give
me Sunday here,

A man sitting on the pier.
A child with a thermos flask and
men fishing.

sniffing the salt sea air
and salt sea water.

Sundays of patience waiting
for a bite.

A couple pushing a pram.
A courting couple.

Sunday the day when fathers
push the pram.

Sunday for lovers walking in
the wind.

A father running with two small
children.

Sunday for running to catch
the lunchtime tram.

A tram.

And missing it.

Leaving the terminus.

It doesn't matter here, time's
of no consequence in kind
Southend.
An unpretentious breezy
friendly place.
I like Southend.
East London on the sea.

The reverse of the tram
trundling back along the pier in
the sea.

Southend where Charlie
Chaplin as a child first saw
the real sea and thought it was
a wall of sky-blue water.

Mid-shot of a ferris wheel.

The rear of a bus travelling
along a country lane.

I can't like motor traffic on
the Sunday struggle out of
London south through the
Sussex Downs to the sea.
Motor traffic.
It smells nasty, ...

Traffic in a small village.

... it looks nasty.
It's out of place in a human-

scale village street, it's like a
poisonous snake, a killer too.

*A model dog nodding its head in
a car back window.*

Not even a bit of nonsense
like that makes a motor car
agreeable,

Cars in country lanes.

and driving a car makes the
mildest man competitive and
turns him into a fiend.

The sea glimpsed across fields.

All this for a first sight of the
sea.

*Brighton beach with the pier in
the distance.
Shot of a fisherman by the sea.
A man walking along the pier.
People sitting on the pier.*

Early-morning Brighton waits
in Sunday early-morning calm.
Waits for the inflow of the
human tide.

A deck chair attendant.

Seaside people are a friendly
race because their job is
looking after strangers and
trying to make them happy –
for a fee.

Heavy traffic.

*Shots of:
Man taking an awning off a
merry-go-round.
Close-up of the merry-go-round
horse and children's swings.*

I think that clever patron of
the Arts, the spendthrift
Prince Regent, later George
the Fourth, . . .

A man putting up deck chairs.

. . .with his pavilion, parties,
mistresses, gave Brighton the
cheerful smile which has never
left its face.

'Old ocean's bauble' it once
was called and the name still
suits it.

*Long shot of a couple in deck
chairs.
Mid shot of a couple walking.
Close-up of a man standing
beside a bus.*

*Women pushing a dog in
wheelchair.
Close-up of a woman reading a
newspaper.*

*A man carrying a deck chair
towards a group on the beach.
A lady reading a newspaper on
the beach.*

*Children paddling at the sea's
edge.*

*Children throwing pebbles into
the sea, a girl in the water.
An old lady on the beach.*

Brighton Pier.

*A dinghy under the pier.
The promenade.*

It's a toyshop for London,
open on Sunday, a place to lie
back in and to look around
and wonder who is who.

Of all things that this toyshop
has to show, the favourite's
the most dangerous toy of all,
the English Channel.

Oh, friendly and luxurious at
the edge, delightful to the lazy
and the tired.
Look at it, breathe it, listen to
it, but do not try to cross it.

How comfortable the roar that
rakes the shingle, the feel of
rounded pebbles underfoot.
The Brighton English
Channel seems a friend.

And most people have come
down for the day, swell
bookies, shorthand typists,
acrobats from Reigate, Purley
Oaks and Thornton Heath.

'Old ocean's bauble!' Yes,
indeed she is.
Confectionery Brighton in the
sun.

Two men talking.
People strolling.

Regardless of the sunlight on the sea the business man discusses stocks and shares. Regardless of the whisper of the waves ladies compare the prices at the sales.

An old lady being pushed in a wheelchair.
Close-up of twins in a pram.
Pan up to reveal the parents.

And some are old but still cling onto life, and some are young and wonder what it's for.

For some this is the first time they've been down.

A teenager leaning on a railing.
An Asian family having a meal.

For others, perhaps the last. For more and more, it's a first view of England and its coast.

Close-up of an old lady sitting in a deck chair next to a young man.

I wonder what that lady used to do, so unattracted to the sleeping youth.
A cook? A missionary? A woman don?
And is she self-sufficient or afraid?

People walking up steps towards the camera.

The joyous time of Sunday lunch is near – theirs is a set one in a private hotel.

Close-up of a man on a terrace.
The top of an open-topped bus.
Pan up to reveal the beach and the sea.

From this point we can survey the whole field of seaside sociology. Its income brackets and that sort of jargon.

A young couple on an easy-rider motorbike.

These can't have come far in that uncomfortable position or, if they've come from London, she must be absolutely mad about him.

An open bus travelling along the promenade.	And all of us would rather go by bus than sit frustrated in a stuffy car, and all of us will want to view the sea.
Close-up of girls on top of the bus, the pier in the distance.	What are the girlfriends talking of? Men or starfish? What the palmist said? Madam Gymkhana and her crystal ball?
A conductor collecting tickets on top of the bus travelling along the promenade.	How different this than the bus to work, the 19 for instance, or the 22.
	A day of recreation and of rest But oh, it still is travelling along.
The top of the church spire.	On Sunday morning, Matins or Morning Prayer, the Mass or Eucharist, whichever they like to call it, is over in Bosham Church.
Pull back to reveal a lady painting in water-colour. Close-ups of her face and her painting.	But still she paints, forgetful of the time and food and other people. Absorbed in what she sees. She puts it down. Happy, contented, quiet, competent.
A churchyard and a church exterior.	Under those stones the local farmers lie. Their old brick houses mostly have been bought ...
Pan up the church tower.	... by business men who mess about with boats. The old church looks forlornly from the shore.

A man walking something by the sea.
A boat being launched.

And a very curious thing it seems to see.
What explanation can there be of this?

A man in a wet suit, launching the boat.

I wonder why that man is wearing tails?

A boat trailer being pulled up the beach.

That's going to leave a trail of misery behind it in the country lanes.

Two old men walking to their boat.

Those two rugged workers may well be retired Admirals, such is the camaraderie of the sea.

Just to anticipate any trouble – 'Take a letter

A young man, climbing into a speed boat and setting off.

from Wheelhouse Grange
              Albatross Lane
                    Havant

to the Chairman of the Governors, BBC, London.

Sir,

I was disgusted to find the BBC had had the effrontery to turn its cameras onto the private marine activities of our English coast, and what is more, on a Sunday morning when they should all have been in Church.

An old lady paddling a small boat.

My aunt, who is not an expert oarswoman, was shown on the screen without her permission.

A woman eating a picnic and a group having fish and chips.	My own picnic party, with my niece and daughter, was also filmed without permission, as was the party of my staff who were on holiday at Burnham-on-Crouch.
Close-up of a poodle being fed with fish and chips.	How would you like to have the private moments of your family life shown to millions and commented on facetiously by a man with an unpronounceable name? Is nothing sacred?
A small sailing dinghy. Various shots of people drinking coffee, and beer.	There are many good sailors at the Yacht Club, why did you only select shots of incompetent amateurs? And why this emphasis on food and drink? Are you in the pay of the breweries, sir? What will foreigners think if this film is shown abroad as depicting the English way of life? Do we only live for pleasure – surely on Sunday at least a reverent expression might have been shown somewhere.
Shots of sailing boats interspersing these images.	And I have one final and very serious complaint to make. The wife of my managing director kindly came down to the shore to meet me, and your cameraman took the unpardonable liberty of filming her as she was getting ready for the bridge party to which we were going.
	Yours, etc.

A pleasure boat heading towards the camera.
Shots of a barge in a lock, and people around watching a man.

A happy Sunday slowness
haunts the Thames between
its Buckingham and Berkshire
banks.
The river of our contemplative
youth, river for family parties,
Cockney salts.
Who with such skill can push
the boat away and moor her
safely into Boulters Lock?
For Londoners are faithful to
the Thames as the Thames
has been to them for
centuries.
'Sweet Thames run softly till I
end my song'.
So Spenser said it, and we say
it still.

Children fishing on a little wooden pier, with a terrier.

River and London mingle into
one – riparian rights and lock-
keepers and locks, sluices and
weirs, punts and fishing
permits.
Sweet Thames, the sliding
wonder of our youth.
Fish on, fish on, until you find
yourself or find yourself again,
in years to come . . .

Cut to shots of top of a pleasure boat and a family, in a small boat trying to moor

. . . alone among the strangers
in the boat, or in the bosom
of your family who don't seem
quite to know what they
should do, with all those
awkward bits of coiling rope.

A pleasure boat passing the camera.

Bear us along the river of our
youth . . .

A steam train.

. . . into the long-remembered

world of steam down here in
Sussex, where from Sheffield
Park the Bluebell Railway runs
to Horstead Keynes.

*Little boys' watching steam
trains.*

Here middle-age remembers
joys of youth and youth can
share the joys of middle-age.

*Families boarding a train. The
train leaving the station.*

*Cut to a steam train approaching
the camera through green trees.*

Deep down in Sussex listen
for it here, the sound the
poets hated makes by now a
melancholy music in the hills.

*Motor traffic. Pan to reveal a
cricket game on a village green
and spectators.*

Whiter than the daisies are
the flannels on the field.
It's an heraldic game, and
cricket is the heraldry of
Sussex.
And cricketers are large, large-
hearted men, and boundaries
are waiting to be saved.
(Thank God it isn't I who
have to do it.)

*A bowls match – players and
game in progress.*

I like to watch the calculated
bowl, the subtle curve along
the cherished grass, the
hushed awaiting till the final
kiss of wood on wood,
directed from afar.

Motor traffic.

Some Londoners most
unwisely make for home,
thinking they ought to make
an early start.

A couple walking over a brick
bridge below Sussex Downs.

Now we can take the dog out
for a bark and Alfriston
becomes itself again under the
shadow of the Sussex Downs.

A terrier playing in the grass.

If I may quote two lines from
Thomas Gray, and leaving out
the one that's in between:

A herd of Guernsey cows in a
meadow.

'The lowing herd winds slowly
o'er the lea
And leaves the world to
darkness and to me'.

People in a churchyard, the
camera pulls back to reveal the
church.

Except for some late last
Londoners who still savour the
country quiet. At half past six
some villagers will go to
evensong. For evening is a
time when some of us are
thinking of the evening of our
lives and of the vastness into
which we go . . .

A rear view of a car facing the
sea and various shots of people
walking and playing on the beach
in the evening.

. . . or nothingness, or of
eternal bliss.
Whatever it is, for sure we've
got to go alone, alone, and
time will part us all and
somehow, somewhere waits
the love of God.

Sunday is sad. But Monday's
so much worse for those of us
who haven't any hope.
Faith, hope and charity.
Oh, give me hope.

The lady water-colourist walking
home with her easel and her dog.

Her brief accomplishment is
somewhere there,
the painting that she did and
tucked away.

The cricketers walking off the field, and a father changing his small son's shirt.
Father and son playing.

The match is over and the game they played was much more fun than work will be tomorrow.
Oh dear, oh dear, the agonies of youth.
Oh dear, oh dear, the trials of middle-age.
But do they matter? There's the mystery.

A car about to leave a picturesque view.
Motor traffic going home.

[The hymn 'The Day Thou Gavest Lord is ended ...' is played over the final shots.]

Eight:

1973 to 1977

Eight
1973-1977

JB did not realise how much he had done to awaken England to its self-destruction. He didn't appreciate that his long, slow battle against bad planning and development had had an enormous effect. He still felt that the bulldozers were in full flood. In 1971 he suggested to Richard Ingrams, the editor of *Private Eye*, that he launch a column called 'Nooks and Corners of the New Barbarism' which would pretend to glorify particularly ghastly buildings and expose their builders and architects to ridicule. JB felt like hitting below the belt. His first victim was Hillgate House on Ludgate Hill, followed by the Shepherd's Bush Centre and the new Paternoster Square. He suggested that people spend their holidays in the 'lovely' new Euston Station. 'Many choices are offered – paperbacks, cafeteria, warmed alcohol and souvenirs. Those in a hurry will want to join the taxi queue, or the almost equally long queue to the Underground. If you like fresh air, then the best you will find comes up from the moving stairs on the Underground. More sophisticated tourists will enjoy the diesel-scented corridors leading down to the taxi rank ...'[1]

JB was also writing 'Sunday with Betjeman' in the *Sunday Express* where he continued to lash out against concrete jungles, or extol the virtues of places like the Orkneys and Bury St Edmunds. Meanwhile his clear and untechnical articles on English architecture in the *Daily Telegraph Weekend* magazine were eventually published together as a book called *The Pictorial History of English Architecture*.

'... At the beginning of this century, Elizabethan became very popular. It was the homely style. Later it was associated with copper warming-pans, horse brasses, and electric log fires, and the novels of Dornford Yates, Jeffrey Farnol and Warwick Deeping ...'[2] JB's scepticism about 'antiquarians' which he had first felt in the twenties was still as fervent as ever. He determined to write in an unscholastic way. He saw this as a way of converting the unconverted. 'Higher than the forest trees, nobler than the barons' castles, the English monasteries of the thirteenth century soared heavenward in stone. They were the beginning of a national style. We call it Early English ...'[3]

JB had always thought his poetry sold by some fluke. He said it was luck. Until he became Poet Laureate in 1972, he didn't feel any pressure about writing it, as he did with journalism. The painful process of the latter had become a way of life which JB was used to; he was at heart a fighter and his sense that he had a duty to safeguard England never left him. But still there was time to write tributes, addresses, obituaries, and all the sad essays which grand old men like JB have to write as their friends begin to die. 'When I think of Randolph, I see him in terms of noise, light and laughter ...,'[4] he began his essay on Randolph Churchill for an anthology.

When in January 1973, his school friend Arthur Elton died, who had pioneered the documentary film in the early thirties, JB wrote in his obituary, 'Once, when he knew I was going to Denmark, he advised me not to bother too much about the Castle of Prince Hamlet at Elsinore, but to look at the railway station there, it was much more interesting. He was quite right, for the castle is carefully tended archaeology and the railway station is architecture ... What has not been mentioned is that the making of films, whether documentary or feature, and Arthur made both, is a co-operative effort and demands forbearance on all sides. Cameraman, sound man, editor, cutter, sound mixer and their assistants, and a person to be a successful film producer, such as Arthur was, must not only be a good mixer, but have a clear mind and an idea of the shape of the film right from the beginning. He must also be humane and humorous and prepared to change his opinions ...'[5]

Later that year JB's film *Metro-land* was screened for the first time, the triumph of a 'co-operative effort'. The following year he made *A Passion for Churches* with the same brilliant editor, director and cameraman. JB put everything into it that he could muster; the film was about all that he loved most about England – its people, its church and its architecture. Throughout his life he had been able to find poetry where others had never thought to look. In the end this is where it all began:

> 'What would you be, you wide East Anglian sky,
> Without church towers to recognise you by?
> What centuries of faith, in flint and stone,
> Wait in this watery landscape, all alone ...'

1. *Private Eye*, 10 September 1971.
2. *The Daily Telegraph*, Colour Supplement, 27 November 1970.
3. *The Daily Telegraph*, Colour Supplement, 6 November 1970.
4. From *Randolph Churchill the Young Pretender* (Heinemann, 1971).
5. *North Somerset Mercury*, January 1973.

Trebetherick

When I first knew Trebetherick it was 1908.

There was an old farm at the top of the hill owned by Francis Mably and another one, lower down, farmed by Tom Blake. Both farms had ponds in their yards, and geese which terrified me when I went to fetch the milk bare-foot from Whalley Cottage down near the shore.

Colonel LeMarchant was the nearest approach to a squire in his rambling modern house by the sand-dunes. Dr Hoskins lived at Bray House and would not let us walk on Bray Hill. Colonel LeMarchant would not let us take the short cut to Greenaway over the field, which is now a car park. No golf was allowed on Sunday on the holes round St Enodoc Church. Someone was employed by Dr Hoskins, and later by his widow, to remove the flags from the greens. Services were at 3 p.m. on Sundays. Tom Blake of Lower Farm pulled the bell. Mrs Blake was a friendly soul. Tom was not. Josh used to sail the ferry over to Padstow from Rock and back. He was succeeded by Bluey England, whose daughter Bess pulled an oar when the engine failed, which it often did.

All our shopping was done in Padstow and we carried it over the links from the ferry. The higher the tide, the shorter the walk.

Wadebridge was the nearest railway station. Its town did not play much part in our lives. Polzeath was a hamlet with a wooden plank bridge over the stream. The only new houses were the terrace, which looked like a bit of Plymouth stuck down by the Atlantic, and a few old cottages either side of the hills going down to the stream.

Though I did not realise it at the time, there were many Cornish still resident – Charlie Mably who collected golf balls on the course and lived in the oldest house; Tom Buse, who, with his wife and daughters ran the Haven Boarding House at which we first stayed, and drove a jingle to take us to the station. Francis Mably once drove me by farm cart to Wadebridge.

It took all day.

Picnics to Lundy Bay and Pentire were whole day expeditions. There was much scare of German spies in the '14 war. My family and I were considered to be such because of having a foreign name. Tom

Blake was annoyed when my father bought his farm from the squire at St Minver.

There was quite a large Scottish element in the people of comparative leisure who lived at Trebetherick down by the shore – Miss McCorkindale and her nephews the Adams boys, Captain Rendel at Polzeath Lodge and his wife and daughter. Then there were various families of an Empire-building type. The Stokes, the Oakleys, the Bents and their cousins. Above all there were the schoolmasters, heralded by Mr Alfred Roseveare from Plymouth, and his wife who made good sponge cakes. Their son was killed in the war. There were people there who came for the golf such as Mr Percy Savage, endlessly practising approaches and putts on the green near the beautiful slate-hung house he built himself, Daymer House 1911. Its architect, Archibald Allen, was a relation of his wife and the house was built of Bray Hill stone, the same material that Robert Atkinson used for Undertown, a house which he designed for my father.

This must all sound like a rather dull letter from home to a relation abroad. But that is what it is. We were a family, though not related. We were all equal, and the Cornish inhabitants – the Buses, the Mablys, the Coxes, the Males, the Champions, the Camps and many others in the shops and farms were all part of us. But more privileged than we were, because they could stay there all the year round and go to school at Tredrizzick, and never leave the parish except to cross by ferry to Padstow, or amble by cart to market-day at Wadebridge.

The cliffs at Pentire seemed enormous, and even those at Greenaway were too steep to scale. Stinging fish were in the ponds at low tide when we went prawning, and congers barked and shook our open dinghies. No one thought of bathing out of his depth and surfing was unknown. Vessels making for Padstow hugged the Padstow shore and at lowest spring tide, timbers of wrecks stuck up out of the sand of Doom Bar. When my father bought Blake's farm, we children used the fields along the cliffs to Greenaway for a golf course which was laid out by Mr Fred Glover, the club secretary. It was so full of rabbit scrapes that matches were well-nigh impossible because one was always losing balls in them.

It was the happiest place for childhood that anyone could have. The soft west-country voices after a London twang. The varieties of scene to suit every mood. The steep woods by Shillar Mill and the boding anger of Captain Rendel when he caught us disturbing the pheasants. The finding of extra-big cowries in Cowry Cove. The seaweeds to collect, wild flowers and blue butterflies. The tiny tinkle on a hot

Sunday afternoon from the crooked steeple of St Enodoc. The magic mournful call of Padstow bells across the Sunday estuary, and far inland the lovely ring from St Minver. Blackberry picking in the woods at Grogley. Collecting green seaweed that fringed the pools at the very lowest tides, and giving it to Aunt Ursula (Miss Warren) to send to the troops in Flanders.

It must sometimes have rained. But it did not matter. Rain water was no more cold-giving than sea water. Some grown-ups tried to organise us into games but the wisest didn't. Tom and Joan Larkworthy, Jock and Audrey Lynam, Ralph and Vasey Adams were our ring-leaders. Where they were was safety and laughter.

Bare feet were a sure indication of where one was walking. The lane down to the bay was unmetalled, and here and there smooth grey and purple slate jutted out, cooling and comfortable to the feet, and then it changed to broken bits of slate and granite before petering out into sand. Our feet grew so hard that our soles were their own leather.

I think it was tennis which first made me aware of the opposite sex, or rather that boys weren't the same as girls! Being an only child and being brought up in the days of bathing dresses, when one changed with one's back to the shore and rubbed down discreetly facing the cliff, I did not look at pudenda nor care about them. But tennis, and who one was partnered with on the bumpy grass court at Mr Roseveare's, and all the other little bumpy courts that people who had the room for them mowed and rolled into their gardens – tennis was where one's heart sang, and mine particularly if I had Biddy Walsham as partner, with her straight gold hair with a seductive wave in it; her laughing uselessness at the game which equalled mine.

Trebetherick ... it may have been a suburb by the sea and for all our crabbing, fishing and bathing, nothing to do with the real Cornish who regarded us as the foreigners we still are. But for me it was home for the eyes, the nose and the ears. The great, black half-moon of Bray Hill with its three cairns on the top, the long low stretch from Padstow to Stepper Point on the other side of the estuary. The regular cragginess of Newland's rocky island. The changing vegetation of the high-hedged lane ... all these for the eyes. For the nose there was the scent of seaweed and salty sand. Wild mint at one season, honeysuckle and thyme at another; and drying cow-dung always. For the ear there was the roar on the shore when the tide was high. The utter silence when it was low. The larks and oyster-catchers shrill and small, and sea-gulls wailing like angry babies. The rumble of wooden wheels over stony roads and the far-off puff and rumble of the London and South-

Western as it crossed the viaduct on its way to the Padstow terminus, the end of that long, slow journey of the ambitiously named Atlantic Coast Express.

This was my Trebetherick.

Its people are mostly elsewhere. Some in St Enodoc churchyard. The roads are all changed, and unless the motor car goes it will for ever be lost.

From *Both Sides of the Tamar*

Metro-land

Broadcast on BBC Television

Vision	Commentary
Close-up of Metro-land brochures.	Child of the First War, Forgotten by the Second, We called you Metro-land. We laid our schemes Lured by the lush brochure, down byways beckoned, To build at last the cottage of our dreams, A city clerk turned countryman again, And linked to the Metropolis by train.
Still of Quainton Road.	
Interior of Horsted Keynes Station. *JB walks from the bar on to the platform and gets into the Metropolitan Railway carriage.*	Metro-land – the creation of the Metropolitan Railway Which, as you know, was the first steam Underground in the world. In the tunnels, the smell of sulphur was awful.
Close-up of slogan: 'Live in Metro-land' on the carriage door.	When I was a boy, 'Live in Metro-land' was the slogan. It really meant getting out of the tunnels into the country.

*Interior of the carriage. JB
reading a newspaper.*

For the line had ambitions of
linking
Manchester and Paris,
And dropping in at London
on the way.
The grandiose scheme came
to nothing.
But then the Metropolitan had
a very good idea.

*Archive film: 'A Trip on the
Metro'.*

Look at these fields,
They were photographed in
1910, from the train;
'Why not,' said a clever
member of the Board, 'buy
these orchards and farms as
we go along, turn out the
cattle, and fill the meadow
land with houses?'
You could have a modern
home of quality and
distinction – you might even
buy an old one, if there was
one left.

Close-up of JB.

Archive film.

And over these mild home
county acres
Soon there will be the estate
agent, coal merchant,
Post Office, shops, and rows
of neat dwellings,
All within easy reach of
charming countryside.
Bucks, Herts and Middlesex
yielded to Metro-land.
And city men could breakfast
on the fast train to London
town.

Close-up of rails.

Exterior of Baker Street Station.	Is this Buckingham Palace?
Interior of Chiltern Court Restaurant. *JB sitting at a table.*	Are we at the Ritz? No. This is the Chiltern Court Restaurant, built above Baker Street Station, the gateway between Metro-land out there and London down there. The creation of the Metropolitan Railway.
Close-up of a brochure. *Mid-shot of JB.*	The brochure shows you how splendid this place was in 1913 which is about the year in which it was built. Here the wives from Pinner and Ruislip, after a day's shopping at Liberty's or Whiteley's, would sit waiting for their husbands to come up from Cheapside and Mincing Lane. While they waited they could listen to the strains of the band playing for the *Thé Dansant* before they took the train for home.
Archive film of 'Leaving Baker Street Station'. *High altitude shot of Marlborough Road Station.* *Train goes through the station.*	Early electric – punctual and prompt. Off to those cuttings in the Hampstead Hills, St John's Wood, Marlborough Road, No longer stations – and the trains rush through.
JB on the platform of Marlborough Road Station.	This is all that is left of Marlborough Road Station. Up there the iron brackets supported the glass and iron

	roof. And you see that white house up there? That was where Thomas
Thomas Hood's house.	Hood died. Thomas Hood the poet. He wrote: 'I remember, I remember, the house where I was born', and the railway cut through his garden.
Exterior of Marlborough Road Station.	I remember Marlborough Road Station because it was the nearest station to the house where lived my future parents-in-law.
JB exits from an Angus Steak House.	Farewell old booking hall, once grimy brick,
Houses in St John's Wood.	But leafy St John's Wood, which you served, remains, Forerunner of the suburbs yet to come With its broad avenues, Detached and semi-detached villas Where lived artists and writers and military men.

And here, screened by shrubs,
Walled-in from public view,
Lived the kept women.
What puritan arms have
stretched within these rooms
To touch what tender breasts,
As the cab-horse stamped in
the road outside.

Sweet secret suburb on the
City's rim,
St John's Wood.

12 Langford Place –
'Agapemone'.

Amidst all this frivolity, in one place
a sinister note is struck –
in that helmeted house where, rumour has it,
The Reverend John Hugh Smyth-Pigott lived,
An Anglican clergyman whose Clapton congregation declared him to be Christ,
a compliment he accepted.
His country house was called the Agapemone –
the abode of love –
and some were summoned to be brides of Christ.

Lilies in stained glass windows.

Did they strew their Lord with lilies?
I don't know.
But for some reason this house has an uncanny atmosphere – threatening and restless.
Someone seems to be looking over your shoulder.

The house reflected in a pond –
pan up to the house.

Who is it?

Rails.

Over the points by electrical traction,

Interior of a train, JB looking
out of the window.

Out of the chimney-pots into the openness,
'Til we come to the suburb that's thought to be commonplace,
Home of the gnome and the average citizen.
Sketchley and Unigate, Dolcis and Walpamur.

Exterior of a milk float,
Neasden.

Neasden Parade.
Rows of shops.
Houses and a milkman.

[*Sequence: Gladstone Park, Neasden. Mr Eric Simms speaks of the*
Neasden Nature Trail and bird-watching].

Metropolitan tube train
approaching slowly.

Beyond Neasden there was an
unimportant hamlet
Where for years the
Metropolitan didn't bother to
stop. Wembley.

Still of Wembley Tower.

Still of Sir Edward Watkin.

Slushy fields and grass farms,
Then, out of the mist arose
Sir Edward Watkin's dream –
An Eiffel Tower for London.
Sir Edward Watkin, Railway
King, and Chairman of the
Line,
Thousands he thought, would
pay to climb the Tower
Which would be higher than
the one in Paris.
He announced a competition –
500 guineas for the best
design.

Designs of towers.

Never were such flights of
Victorian fancy seen.
Civil engineers from Sweden
and Thornton Heath,
Rochdale and Constantinople,
entered designs.
Cast iron, concrete, glass,
granite and steel,
Lifts hydraulic and electric, a
spiral steam railway.
Theatres, chapels and sanatoria
in the air.

Front of a brochure with winning design.	In 1890 the lucky winner was announced. It had Turkish baths, arcades of shops, and Winter Gardens. Designed by a firm of Scots with a London office,
Still of base of the tower. Pan up. Still of the tower.	Stewart, McLaren and Dunn. It was to be one hundred and fifty feet higher Than the Eiffel Tower. But when at last it reached above the trees,
Still of the top of the tower.	And the first stage was opened to the crowds, The crowds weren't there. They didn't want to come.
Still: Wide shot of the tower with the lake.	Money ran out, The tower lingered on, resting and rusting Until it was dismembered in 1907.
Interior of Wembley Stadium. JB in the centre of the pitch.	This is where London's failed Eiffel Tower stood. Watkin's Folly as it was called. Here on this Middlesex turf, and since then the site has become quite well-known.
Archive film of trumpeters and horses. JB listening.	It was here, I can just remember the excitement and the hope, St George's Day, 1924.
Archive film of a gun salute. Flags unfurling.	The British Empire Exhibition at Wembley,

King George V and Queen Mary.	Opened by King George the Fifth.
Exterior of the pavilions.	Ah yes, those Imperial pavilions India, Sierra Leone, Fiji, With their sun-tanned sentinels of Empire outside. To me they were more interesting than
Interior of the Palace of Industry.	The Palaces of Industry and Engineering Which were too like my father's factory.
Exterior of the Palace of Arts (today).	That was the Palace of Arts where I used to wait While my father saw the living models in Pears' Palace of Beauty.
Exterior of the Palace of Arts (archive film).	How well I remember the Palace of Arts, Massive and simple outside, Almost pagan in its sombre strength, but inside ...
Interior of the Basilica and the Palace of Arts. Pan up. *JB in the Basilica and the Palace of Arts.*	This is the Basilica in the Palace of Arts. It was used for displaying the best Church art of 1924. A. K. Lawrence, Eric Gill, Mary Adshead, Colin Gill and so on. Today it's used for housing the props of the pantomime, 'Cinderella on Ice' and that kind of thing. And really it's quite right because Church and Stage have always been closely connected.

Archive film of the Pleasure Park.	The Pleasure Park was the best thing about the Exhibition.
King and Queen.	The King and Queen enjoyed it too – There they are.
Debris and desolation of the Exhibition site.	Oh bygone Wembley where's the pleasure now? The temples stare, the Empire passes by. This was the grandest Palace of them all.
JB outside the British Government Pavilion. Close-up of lion. Zoom out.	The British Government Pavilion and the famous Wembley lions. Now they guard an empty warehouse site.
Tracking shot along Oakington Road, Wembley.	But still people kept on coming to Wembley. The show-houses of the newly built estates. A younger, brighter, homelier Metro-land: 'Rusholme', 'Rustles', 'Rustlings', 'Rusty Tiles', 'Rose Hatch', 'Rose Hill', 'Rose Lea,' 'Rose Mount', 'Rose Roof'. Each one is slightly different from the next, A bastion of individual taste On fields that once were bright with buttercups.

JB at Highfort Court, Kingsbury.	Deep in rural Middlesex, the country that inspired Keats, magic casements opening on the dawn. A speculative builder here at Kingsbury let himself go, in the twenties.
High altitude shot of Harrow.	And look what a lot of country there is; fields and farms between the houses, oaks and elms above the roof tops.
Archive film of 'Classic Harrow'. Tube train approaching Harrow.	The smart suburban railway knew its place, And did not dare approach too near the Hill.
JB at Harrow Garden Estate.	Here at the foot of Harrow Hill, alongside the Metropolitan electric train, tradesmen from Harrow built in the eighties or nineties – I should think from the look of the buildings – these houses. And a nice little speculation they were. Quiet, near the railway station with their own Church and Public House; and they're named reverently after the great people of Harrow School, Drury, Vaughan and Butler.
Harrow schoolboys outside the school.	Valiantly that Elizabethan foundation at the top of the hill Has held the developers at bay;
A cricket match.	Harrow School fought to keep this hillside green,

But for all its tradition and
elegance,
It couldn't wholly stem
The rising tide of Metro-land.

JB in Harrow.   The healthy air of Harrow in
the 1920s and thirties when
these villas were built. You
paid a deposit and eventually
we hope you had your own
house with its garage and
front garden and back garden.

JB in Harrow.   A verge in front of your house
and grass and a tree for the
dog. Variety created in each
façade of the houses – in the
colouring of the trees. In fact,
the country had come to the
suburbs. Roses are blooming
in Metro-land just as they do
in the brochures.

*Close-up of the Metro-land
brochure.*
*Close-up of houses in the
brochure.*

Exterior of a house in Harrow.
Zoom in to stained glass window.

*Sequence of stained glass; sunsets,
bulrushes, bluebirds, etc.*

Exterior of Harrow houses.   Along the serried avenues of
Harrow's garden villages,
Households rise and shine and
settle down to the Sunday
morning rhythm.

   [Sequence: Sunday morning gardening, mowing lawns, washing

cars, etc. to the music of Family Favourites, Rod McNeil; and 'Down by the Lazy River', The Osmonds.]

Close-up of fast rails.

This is Grims Dyke in Harrow Weald. I've always regarded it as a prototype of all suburban homes in southern England. It was designed by the famous Norman Shaw a century ago.

Exterior of Grims Dyke, Harrow Weald.

JB goes in through the front door.

Merrie England outside, haunting and romantic within.

Interior of the Hall, Grims Dyke, with JB.

With Norman Shaw one thing leads to another. I came out of a low entrance hall into this bigger hall, and then, one doesn't know what is coming next. There's an arch and if I go up there, I'll see – goodness knows what. Let's go and look.

JB climbs the stairs.

There's a sense of mounting excitement.
Have I strayed into a Hitchcock film?

JB arrives at the dining-room.

Groups of ladies.

SECRETARY:
Ladies, good afternoon and welcome to the Byron Luncheon Club. I would like to give a very

Pan down from the ceiling to the groups of ladies.

warm welcome to our speaker, Mrs Elizabeth Cooper.
[*Applause.*]
MRS COOPER:
I would like to thank you, Madam Chairman, first of all

for inviting me to this
beautiful lunch, a beautiful
room and bevy of beautifully
dressed and beautifully hatted
ladies. I think it's the most
beautiful house in Harrow,
one of the most interesting
both architecturally and
historically.
BETJEMAN:
Dear things, indeed it is.

*Details of the exterior of Grims
Dyke; gables, windows, etc.*

Tall brick chimney stacks
Not hidden away but
prominent
And part of the design,
Local bricks, local tiles, local
timber.
No façade is the same,
Gabled windows gaze through
leaded lights down winding
lawns.
It isn't a fake – it's a new
practical house
For a newly-rich Victorian,
Strong, impressive, original.

The pool and the boathouse.

And yonder gloomy pool
contained on May 29th 1911,
the dead body of W. S.
Gilbert, Grims Dyke's most
famous owner and Sullivan's
partner in the Savoy Operas.
After a good luncheon he
went bathing with two girls,
Ruby Preece and Winifred
Emery. Ruby found she was
out of her depth, and in
rescuing her, Gilbert died, of
a heart attack, here – in this
pond.

Train slowly approaching Pinner.

Funereal from Harrow draws
the train,
On, on, north-westwards,
London far away,
And stations start to look
quite countrified.

*Archive film of 'Approaching
Pinner'.*

Pinner, a parish of a thousand
souls,
'Til the railways gave it many
thousands more.

*Long shot of a train at Pinner.
Pull out to show the High
Street and a Fair, a roundabout
and a Church.*

Pinner is famous for its village
Fair
Where once a year, St John
the Baptist's Day,
Shows all the climbing High
Street filled with stalls.

Ferris wheel, etc.

It is the Feast Day of the
Parish Saint,
A medieval Fair in Metro-
land.

*Archive film of approaching
Sandy Lodge.*

When I was young there
stood among the fields
A lonely station, once called
Sandy Lodge,
Its wooden platform crunched
by hobnailed shoes,
And this is where the healthier
got out.

Archive film of golfers.

*JB on the golf course at Moor
Park.*

One of the joys of Metro-land
was the nearness of golf to
London. And Moor Park,
Rickmansworth, was a great
attraction.

JB prepares to drive.

Now, eye on the ball
Left knee slightly bent,
    Slow back . . .
Missed it! [*Laughter.*]

Mid-shot of JB.

Well that wasn't up to much.
Perhaps the Clubhouse is
more exciting.

A group drinking outside the
Clubhouse.

Did ever Golf Club have a
nineteenth hole
So sumptuous as this?

Close-up 'Reserved for Chairman'
sign.
Pan along signs as JB walks up
to the entrance.

Interior of the Hall at Moor
Park: the ceiling, murals etc.

Did ever Golf Club have so
fine a hall?
Venetian decor, 1732.

And yonder dome is not a
dome at all
But painted in the semblance
of a dome;
The sculptured figures all are
done in paint
That lean towards us with so
rapt a look.
How skilfully the artist takes
us in.

Interior of Moor Park.

What Georgian wit these
classic Gods have heard,
Who now must listen to the
golfer's tale
Of holes in one and how I
missed that putt,
Hooked at the seventh, sliced
across the tenth
But ended on the seventeenth
all square.

Exterior of Moor Park.	Ye gods, ye gods, how comical we are! Would Jove have been appointed Captain here? See how exclusive thine Estate, Moor Park.

[Sequence: Gate-keeper chats to lady Member in car at entrance to Estate; admits her, but turns away non-Member at barrier.]

JB sitting in a train carriage looking at a brochure. Close-up of fast rails.	Onwards, onwards, North of the border, down Hertfordshire way.
A Pipe Band approaches and floats, etc.	The Croxley Green Revels – A tradition that stretches back to 1952. For pageantry is deep in all our hearts, And this, for many a girl, is her greatest day.

[Sequence with music: Croxley Green Revels. Procession of the Queen of the Revels. Crowd shots. The Queen is crowned. Speeches.]

Archive film of Chorleywood Village.	Large uneventful fields of dairy farm, Slowly winds the Chess brimful of trout, An unregarded part of Hertfordshire Awaits its fate.
	And in the heights above, Chorleywood village, Where in '89 the railway came, And wood smoke mingled with the sulphur fumes, And people now could catch

the early train
To London and be home just
after tea.

Metropolitan train on line – pan
left as horses come from under
the bridge and gallop across a
Common.

This is, I think, essential
Metro-land.
Much trouble has been taken
to preserve
The country quality surviving
here –
Oak, hazel, hawthorn, gorse
and sandy tracks,
Better for sport than farming,
I suspect.

The common with a Church and
a School in the background.
Children playing rounders in
foreground.

Exterior of 'The Orchard',
Chorleywood. JB goes through the
gate and up to the house.

Common and cricket pitch,
Church School and Church,
All are reminders of a country
past.

BOY: Mrs Hill, we've got eight
rounders now.
JB: In the orchards, beyond
the Common, one spring
morning in 1900 a young
architect, Charles Voysey, and
his wife decided to build
themselves a family home. I
think it was the parent of
thousands of simple English
houses.
'All must be plain and
practical' –
That sloping buttress wall is
to counteract

Details of the house.

the outward thrust of the

heavy slate roof.
Do you notice those stepped
tiles below the chimney-pots?

Details of 'The Orchard'.

They're there to throw off the
driving English rain,
And that lead roof ridge is
pinched up at the end for the
same reason.
Horizontal courses of red tiles
in the white walls protect
windows and openings. It's
hard to believe that so simple
and stalwart a house was built
in Queen Victoria's reign.

JB at the front door.

Voysey liked to design every
detail in his house. For
instance that knocker, Voysey.
A typical curious shaped
handle, Voysey. And this
handle or iron hinge with
what seems to be his signature
tune, the heart. It's there at
the end of the hinge, it's here
round the letterbox, it's also
round the keyhole and it
seems to be on the key.
That's a Voysey key, and in
the house he did everything

JB in the hall.

down to the knives and forks.
The plan of the house radiates
out from this hall. Extreme
simplicity is the keynote. No
unnecessary decoration. The
balusters here for the stairs,
straight verticals, giving an
impression of great height to
this simple hall. But as a
matter of fact, it isn't a
particularly high house; in fact,

it's rather small. I knew Mr
Voysey and I saw Mrs Voysey;
they were small people and in
case you think it's a large
house, I'll just walk – I'm fat I
know, but I'm not particularly
tall – and I'll stand by the
door here and you compare
my height with the ledge and
the door.

JB in the dining-room.

A round window on the
garden side of the house. A
typical Voysey detail.
This pane which opens to let
in the air from beechy Bucks,
which is just on the other side
of the road, over there.

Close-up of trees.
The River Chess.

Back to the simple life,
Back to nature,
To a shady retreat in the
reeds and rushes
Of the River Chess.
The lure of Metro-land was
remoteness and quiet,
This is what a brochure of the
twenties said:
'It's the trees, the fairy dingles
and a hundred and one things
in which Dame Nature's
fingers have lingered long in
setting out this beautiful array
of trout stream, wooded slope,
meadow and hill-top sites.

House names and houses at the
Loudwater Estate.

Send a postcard for the
homestead of your dreams, to
Loudwater Estate,
Chorleywood.'

Children in a swimming pool.

O happy outdoor life in
Chorleywood,

In Daddy's swim-pool, while
old Spot looks on
And Susan dreams of super
summer hols,
Whilst chlorinated wavelets
brush the banks.

*JB walks up to Len Rawle's
house.*

O happy indoor life in
Chorleywood
Where strangest dreams of all
are realised,

Interior shots of an organ.

Mellifluating out from modern
brick
The pipe-dream of a local
man, Len Rawle,
For pipe by pipe and stop by
stop he moved

Cutaways of pipes, effects, etc.

Out of the Empire Cinema,
Leicester Square,
The Mighty Wurlitzer
Till the huge instrument filled
half his house
With all its multitude of
sound effects.

*Stills of steam engines intercut
with an organ.*

Steam took us onwards,
through the ripening fields,
Ripe for development. Where
the landscape yields

*Archive film of a train to
Amersham, then the present day.*

Clay for warm brick, timber
for post and rail,
Through Amersham to
Aylesbury and the Vale.
In those wet fields the railway
didn't pay,
The Metro stops at Amersham
today.

*The pool at 'High & Over',
Amersham.*

In 1931 all Buckinghamshire
was scandalised by the
appearance high above

*Exterior various shots of 'High &
Over'.*

Amersham of a concrete house
in the shape of a letter Y. It
was built for a young
professor by a young architect,
Amyas Connell. They called it
'High & Over'.
'I am the home of a
twentieth-century family,' it
proclaimed, 'that loves air and
sunlight and open country.'
It started a style called
Moderne – perhaps rather old-
fashioned today.

Surrounding estate.

And one day, poor thing, it
woke up and found developers
in its back garden.
Goodbye, *High* hopes and
Over confidence –
In fact, it's probably goodbye
England.

*Exterior of Quainton Road
Station.
JB walks up the steps and leans
on the bridge.*

Where are the advertisements?
Where the shopping arcade,
the coal merchant and the
parked cars? This is a part of
the Metropolitan Railway
that's been entirely forgotten.
Beyond Aylesbury it lies in flat
fields with huge elms and
distant blue hills.

Long shot down the line.

Quainton Road sign.

Quainton Road Station. It was
to have been the Clapham
Junction of the rural part of
the Metropolitan.

*JB sitting on a bench on
Quainton Road Station.*

With what hopes this place
was built in 1890. They hoped
that trains would run down
the main line there from
London to the midlands and

the north.

They'd come from the midlands and the north rushing through here to London and a Channel Tunnel, and then on to Paris. But, alas, all that has happened is that there a line curves away to the last of the Metropolitan stations in the country in far Buckinghamshire, which was at Verney Junction.

Still of Verney Junction.

And I can remember sitting here on a warm autumn evening in 1929 and seeing the Brill tram from the platform on the other side with steam up ready to take two or three passengers through oil-lit halts and over level crossings, a rather bumpy journey to a station not far from the remote hill-top village of Brill.

Still of Quainton Road.

Still of a Brill tram.

JB leaning on a fence at Verney Junction.

The houses of Metro-land never got as far as Verney Junction.

JB turns to the camera.

Grass triumphs. And I must say I'm rather glad.

JB turns and looks down the line.

Superimposed: Closing credits. Fade to black.

Frederick Etchells

In the thirties (and in Paris), he was always called 'Etchells'. Even his wife Hester whom we called 'Aspidestra', called him 'Etchells'. Once a businessman started a letter to him 'Dear Mr Etchell' and after that we used to drop the 's' to irritate him. The point about Etchells was that he was an artist first and an architect *faute de mieux*. He used to tease me by using architectural terms I couldn't define. He was inspired, amusing and eloquent. His monologues against all forms of profes-sionalism were a joy to hear. When he was made a Fellow of the RIBA after translating Corbusier and designing Crawfords' building in Holborn, he said 'Well anyhow it's something to walk out of'.

I first met him when I was an assistant editor of the *AR* (which Baillie Scott always used to spell 'Revue') and used to have to go around to the architect's office to fetch drawings and photographs. The arbiter of what was to go into the *AR* was H. de C. Hastings. He was an enemy of jazz modern, which was typified for him by the works of Wallis Gilbert & Partners. I was told that one of the partners called at Queen Anne's Gate with a horsewhip but he never found the ever-elusive H. de C. Sometimes I used to have to go to architects of the neo-Renaissance school who in those days were disapproved of by advanced people. But as their buildings brought in advertisements for ironwork, Portland stone and electric light fittings, they were tolerated. They, however, could not tolerate the contents of the *AR*. For some reason Lutyens was considered all right.

When I arrived at the Crawfords building which was only just finished, my apprehensions about the architect – as I had been used to hostile ones – were dispelled. Etchells did not look like an architect. He was welcoming and friendly and there was no sense of a generation gap. He looked like J. C. Squire. I subsequently asked them both to lunch and found that Etchells was slighter and more talkative even than that large-hearted encouraging editor.

Etchells was extremely funny about architects who thought they were up-to-date, and were what H. de C. Hastings called *'moderne'*. He wrote to me some funny letters in the manner of a pompous would-be modern architect which alas I have lost. He was called in to correct the '*moderne*' of Welch, Cachemaille and Lander for Drage's building in Oxford Street, the furniture-hire people. I was then writing a book on architecture called *Ghastly Good Taste* and Etchells contributed some letters signed 'Batty Langley' in the manner of an eighteenth-century architect addressing his patron. They were clever parodies.

Just as I did, Etchells liked a few hereditary peers especially if they were eccentric. He found them a change from pompous professionalism. He preferred letters before a name to letters after it. He and Hester his wife, were the most friendly, unshockable and hospitable of hosts in their eighteenth-century brick house, France House, in East Hagbourne near Didcot, which Etchells had repaired. It was while he was restoring this that I became aware of his deep knowledge of the restoration of ancient buildings in the manner of the SPAB (which he always called 'Antiscrape'). Sometimes in his conversation, never to dazzle his friends but just because they were his friends of a previous generation, he would refer to 'Pound', 'Lewis' (Wyndham Lewis), and 'Fry' in whose Omega Workshop he had worked and helped reveal the Mantegnas at Hampton Court. At heart Etchells was a craftsman who enjoyed making things with his hands. He could go wrong. There was a time when he did not appear for lunch in West Challow where he was repairing his old cottage, because he had stuck to the wall by electricity. He did not think it at all funny. He very much enjoyed other jokes against himself particularly. A couplet which we used to sing to the tune of the *Volga Boatman*: 'The sunset sheds a horizontal ray/On Frederick Etchells, FRIBA.'

He preferred builders and surveyors and even journalists to professional architects.

The surprising thing about Etchells was his many-sidedness. He was proficient in whatever he undertook. He was a typographer and publisher (Etchells and Macdonald, the Haslewood Books). He was an artist, some of whose abstracts are in the Tate; he was much influenced when living in Paris by Braque. He was a musician and delighted in playing Tudor music on the harpsichord. He was a liturgiologist of high repute and wrote a classic book with the Dean of Chester (The Very Reverend G. W. O. Addleshaw, whom he referred to as 'young Addleshaw') called *The Architectural Setting of Anglican Worship*. It was really a Laudian answer to Anglo-Catholic Baroque, yet not a revival of Percy Dearmer. Although Etchells translated Corbusier and designed Crawfords' he was no opponent of neo-Georgian and much delighted in working in succession to Detmar

Blow on Grosvenor Estate buildings in London. He tried to make his buildings look as if they had always been there and he succeeded. He built a house for Lord Chetwode at 40 Avenue Road, St John's Wood, in a modern style, but of brick and without a pitched roof. Since then it has been Georgianised and lost its exterior distinction.

Etchells enjoyed being alive so much, especially talk, wine and food. I remember him punting Reggie Yorke, Thelma and me on the Cherwell after lunch talking about roodscreens uninterruptedly and then sinking slowly into the river on the punt pole, and continuing uninterruptedly while he was being dried at the Yorkes'. He did not bother very much about the afterlife. He delighted in ecclesiastical matters. 'Low in a cope' was how he described a bishop we knew. His friends when I knew him were P. Morton Shand, Lord Wicklow, Lord Kinross, Paul Nash and Cyril Sweett, my wife and I and John and Myfanwy Piper. He was loyal and generous to his friends. He had no self-pity but the death of Hester must have been a great loss. His daughter Susan and his son-in-law and their children looked after him to the end of his long, well-spent life.

Etchells had such powers of concentration that he could cut himself off entirely from whole circles of friends including those I have mentioned of the thirties. I once asked Clive Bell about him and he remembered him with a vividness that I do and added 'In my days he had red hair and was surrounded by suffragettes'.

I remember having a copy of *Blast* with drawings by Etchells in it, and when I showed it to him Etchells said: 'I hope you don't draw attention to that John, it would upset my little vicars'.

As a painter, an artist and tactful church restorer, as architect and talker Etchells was a genius. He was a life-enhancer and generous friend to many and Oh Lord; how we miss him!

Architectural Review

Hardy and Architecture

Anyone whose first introduction to Hardy was *Wessex Poems and Other Verses* (1898) might have supposed that the poet was an architect or architectural draughtsman by profession. The illustrations are distinctly architectural – a brick-built turret with a sundial on it and a conical tiled cap; a late fifteenth-century country church with square western tower; the cross-section of a church showing a Transitional Gothic arcade of two and a half bays furnished with box pews and at one end poppy-head bench-ends, underneath in section are shown coffins, a catacomb and various skulls and bones; fortification at Valenciennes; the High Street of Dorchester with Georgian buildings in sharp perspective; the market-place at Leipzig in evening light; the Georgian bay-window of an inn; some Jacobean panelling; the top stages of the twin Romanesque towers of Exeter Cathedral; an Empire-style couch with a dead body laid out on it; a Gothic church key such as might have been designed by Pugin; a Grecian urn containing dying wild flowers; an accurately and tenderly drawn perspective of the interior of the nave of Salisbury Cathedral looking eastward and with Sir Gilbert Scott's iron screen still there to add mystery and depth to the choir and sanctuary. There are certain quaint touches about these illustrations which even if the monogram T. H. was not on them would lead one to suppose that this was no ordinary architectural draughtsman. As for the meticulously drawn landscape, the rising swell of down; the outline of earth-works; prehistoric or Napoleonic ramparts; a winding foot-path; an hour glass with butterflies poised on it – they give the country an air of passivity as though it was waiting for some crime to be committed on it.

In 1856 before he had written any novels Hardy was apprenticed to a local Dorchester architect John Hicks. To be an architect in the nineteenth century was socially better than being a builder or a carpenter. Building and joinery were 'trade'; architecture was a 'profession' and enabled the architect to stay in the country houses of his clients – those who employ architects are 'clients' not 'customers'. Thus was Hardy able to stay in Cornwall with the rector of St Juliot and meet his first wife, the rector's sister-in-law. Parsons in those days were men of standing and second to the squire. Sometimes the rector was squire and parson in one.

The Architectural Notebook of Thomas Hardy (Dorset Natural History and Archaeological Society, 1966) is thought by its copious and painstaking editor, Dr C. J. B. Beatty, to contain work done mostly between 1866 and 1871, though there are earlier and later sketches. The drawings are very much those of any Victorian architect. That is to say there are sections of timber construction, profiles of mouldings, minute calculations and notes in ink about colour and materials. There are also plans roughly sketched out for a house and even quite a large house. Apart from Hicks and another local architect, Crickmay, Hardy also worked for a very distinguished church architect, Sir Arthur William Blomfield (1829–99), who had an office in London. Blomfield was himself the son of a bishop of London and possibly this church connection accounted for the immense amount of church work which went through Blomfield's office. Hardy was sent as clerk of the works on behalf of the London diocese to superintend the digging up of old St Pancras churchyard, a very full cemetery through which the Midland Railway had to pass on its way to a terminus in the parish of St Pancras. The experience deeply affected Hardy who was then twenty-six years old. Professor Jack Simmons quotes from Mrs Hardy's *Life of Thomas Hardy*:

> There after nightfall, within a high hoarding that could not be overlooked, and by the light of flare lamps, the exhumation went on continuously of the coffins that had been uncovered during the day, new coffins being provided for those that came apart in lifting, and for loose skeletons; and those that held together being carried to the new ground on a board merely.

The scene is described in one of Hardy's *Satires of Circumstance* called 'In the Cemetery'. It describes mothers squabbling over the graves:

> One says in tears, *''Tis mine lies here!'*
> Another, *'Nay, mine, you Pharisee!'*
> Another, *'How dare you move my flowers*
> *And put your own on this grave of ours!'*
> But all their children were laid therein
> At different times, like sprats in a tin.

And then the main drain had to cross,
And we moved the lot some nights ago,
And packed them away in the general foss
With hundreds more. But their folks don't know,
And as well cry over a new-laid drain
As anything else, to ease your pain!

Another poem on the same theme is 'The Levelled Churchyard'. Let it not be thought that Sir Arthur Blomfield was a hard and gloomy man who put his young assistant onto this task. The times were hard. And Hardy had a countryman's matter-of-fact point of view about death. He and Blomfield got on very well together. Mrs Hardy remarked in her biography fifteen years after he had left the office on how Hardy discussed with Blomfield the puzzle of a coffin that contained a skeleton with two skulls, Blomfield opening with the remark, 'Do you remember how we found the man with two heads in St Pancras?' One of his earlier poems, 'Heiress and Architect', was written while he was in Blomfield's office and describes a capricious lady who wants all sorts of dainty oddities in her new mansion and each time the architect puts her down with robust common sense. The poem is dedicated to Blomfield.

The *Notebook* shows that Hardy had a wide training in architecture and was not a wholly Gothic revival man. Nor was Blomfield, one of whose earliest churches was the Byzantine building St Barnabas, Oxford (1869). It was bringing the gospel to the poor in a part of West Oxford called Jericho where Hardy pictures Jude the Obscure having a room. St Barnabas, because it was of brick was condemned as a cheap church. Blomfield, as Canon Clarke quotes in his *Church Builders of the Nineteenth Century*, replies thus:

The idea usually conveyed by this term (cheap church) is that of a showy exterior, flimsy construction, and a mean and disappointing interior. Now, as the exact opposites of these are found in St Barnabas', I object to its being classed with cheap churches; it is true that no money was wasted on it, and it was in that sense economically designed and economically carried out; but, as I have before said, no expense was spared to secure strength and solidity of construction; the work was put without any competition into the hands of a thoroughly good contractor, and not one single item of the design from first to last was altered or cut down in the slightest to reduce the cost; everything was carried out as originally designed,

and this is more than can be said for many churches that have cost
three times as much.

Blomfield's best-known London buildings are the 'Lombardised'
interiors of St Mark's, North Audley Street and St Peter's, Eaton
Square. He also designed the fine Gothic nave of Southwark
Cathedral and Lower Chapel at Eton and many suburban churches,
some in brick and some in stone.

Hardy's house of Max Gate is of red brick and has a tower with a
conical cap, not unlike that shown in the illustration to *Wessex Poems*.
It is quite unlike any other house built in Dorchester before it. Most of
the larger houses were Italianate and stone or stucco. I wonder if he
was thinking of it in the second stanza of 'Architectural Masks':

> In blazing brick and plated show
> Not far away a 'villa' gleams,
> And here a family few may know,
> With book and pencil, viol and bow,
>   Lead inner lives of dreams.

Max Gate was designed on the 'L' plan which Hardy shows or
rather hints at in his notebooks. He used plate-glass and sash windows
and wooden glazing bars in sunny rooms to reduce glare. The house
was clearly designed to look out across the bleak pastoral landscape
west and south of Dorchester. It was comfortably contained in a long
brick garden wall within which was also a walled garden.

Hardy, like his master Blomfield, was not a rigid Gothicist. *The
Architectural Notebook* shows in the sketches and details Hardy's
knowledge of, and delight in, Gothic moulding and details of joinery
and ironwork as well as practical house plans for St Juliot rectory in
Cornwall. They also show his pleasure in what might be called 'late'
by rigid Gothic revivalists.

In north Cornwall Hardy had sole supervision of the restoration of
remote St Juliot church near Tintagel. Here he was working in the
early seventies and went to much trouble to preserve seventeenth-
century carved bench-ends which are still there and a medieval screen
at a time when screens were not approved of by purists. The screen is
rather a botched job, for the carpenter took it out of Hardy's hands
and produced his own version – to Hardy's dismay.

St Juliot is an interesting contrast with its adjoining parish
Lesnewth which was restored by J. P. St Aubyn, far more violently, in

1866, only five years earlier. There the walls were scraped of plaster, the pews destroyed and replaced by pitch pine as roofs and floors were altered and new windows inserted in a style considered correct by the architect. I do not think Hardy would have had much sympathy with St Aubyn as a church restorer.

Hardy would have been in sympathy with the advanced architects of his time, that is to say, Norman Shaw and Philip Webb. He would have approved of the Arts and Crafts as practised by William Morris. He admired craftsmen. In the touching story of the old workman who breaks his back carrying too heavy a load, the last stanza might be Hardy – and his works:

> 'Yes; that I fixed it firm up there I am proud,
> Facing the hail and snow and sun and cloud,
> And to stand storms for ages, beating round
>   When I lie underground.'

From *The Genius of Thomas Hardy*

My Oxford

For me, there were two Oxfords. There was the Oxford of 1916, when I was a boarder at the Oxford Preparatory School (as the Dragon School was still called by old folk) and there was the Oxford of 1925–28 when I was up at Magdalen College.

There was hardly anyone about in my first Oxford. Everyone was away at the Front. We were sent to visit the wounded soldiers who were occupying Somerville and the other women's colleges in bright blue flannel, and we knitted gloves out of string for the sailors on the minesweepers. At that time, the school seemed almost in the country – north of Linton Road there were manifold allotments; east of us, across the narrow Cherwell, were misty meadows and distant elms. To the south, hawthorn hedges made fields between us and Lady Margaret Hall. The way into the shops was westwards. The city was further than we went on foot. The nearest shops were in North Parade – 'N.P.', we called it – Gee's, and Twinings the grocers, and Ora Brown, the cheerful lady who sold us sweets.

There was very little traffic then. The infrequent wartime buses down the Banbury Road were worked by gas, housed in a balloon over the top deck. We went everywhere, when we were free, on bicycles, and I spent many a summer evening bicycling round 'the square', as Bardwell Road, Charlbury Road, Linton Road and Northmoor Road were then called. Most of us could bicycle with our hands in our pockets, slowly zigzagging past the railed-in gardens where tamarisk and forsythia grew; or we would lean against the cream-coloured lamp-posts with their terracotta coloured gas-lamps which were placed at infrequent intervals down all the leafy North Oxford roads.

The school was in the red-brick Anglo-Jackson part of North Oxford, which only burst into full beauty when the hawthorn and pink may was in flower. The inner North Oxford – Crick Road, Norham Gardens, Norham Road and the magic, winding Canterbury Road, the cottages and stables by North Parade, and those ecclesiastical-looking houses gathered round the motherly spire of St Philip and St James ('Phil-Jim') – was more haunting, and more daunting. Bicycling down those 'Phil-Jim' roads whose fenced-in gardens had speckled laurels and 'Beware of the Dog' and 'No Hawkers' on their gates, one could glimpse the front-room windows where the widows of Heads of Houses and famous professors sat writing letters in crowded, gaslit rooms. Flowered papers were on the walls and served as backgrounds to photographs in Oxford frames. Hansom cabs still trotted down these roads, taking the aged inhabitants to the dentist in Beaumont Street, or to one of the two railway stations, or shopping at Elliston & Cavell.

In all the wide-roaded silence, the deepest quiet was on Sunday afternoons, when I would bicycle to No. 4 Chalfont Road. There my father's Aunt Lizzie and her husband, John R. Wilkins, ever generous with tea and rock cakes and jam puffs, lived a life entirely unconnected with the university or the school, but closely bound up with the town. My great-uncle was architect to one of the breweries, and did some nice little public houses in a free, Tudor style. He also restored the Clarendon building, and supervised the construction of Professor Dicey's house on the corner of Bardwell and Banbury Roads on behalf of Colonel Edis.

The OPS, or Lynam's as we called the school, prided itself on its freedom. The boys did not have to wear Eton suits on Sundays and walk in a crocodile, as did the benighted pupils of Summerfields, further up Banbury Road. We could bicycle into the city and look at colleges. Together with my friend Ronnie Wright, the son of a barrister of Tractarian opinions and of a mother who had recently been converted to Rome, we bicycled off to Oxford churches, noticing their liturgical differences. My favourite was St Peter-le-Bailey, which was always empty and always open. I preferred it to the arid Norman revival of St Andrew's Church, which was also very evangelical. We usually ended our explorations at St Aloysius, the Roman Catholic church, where in a side chapel there was a relic of the True Cross, surrounded by candles, polished brass and jewels, which seemed to me very sacred and alarming, as, indeed, did the whole church, with its apse of coloured saints and its smell of incense and many *dévoués* crossing themselves and looking back at us while on their knees. One of our schoolmasters, Gerald Haynes, who had a passion for church architecture – if it was medieval – took us bicycling round the village churches near Oxford, and listened to our accounts of colleges we had explored and chapels we had visited in the university. He liked to take photographs of Norman features in churches, and it was from him that I learned to think that Norman was the only style that mattered, and that Iffley Church was far the most interesting building in Oxford or its vicinity.

Five years later, Oxford – outwardly very little changed, except for an increase in the number of motor cars, so that one had to look to right and left before crossing the Banbury Road or Magdalen Bridge – was a city of pleasure. Schoolfriends from Marlborough had gone to Oxford ahead of me, among them John Edward Bowle, the historian, who had won a Brackenbury Scholarship to Balliol. I was much affected by his outlook on Oxford. He regarded it as an infinitely superior place to Marlborough – and so did I. Dons were to him – as to me – cleverer and more learned than schoolmasters. He thought Balliol the cleverest college, and the Balliol dons therefore the cleverest in the world – I did, too.

I was at Magdalen, and had beautiful panelled eighteenth-century rooms on the second floor of New Buildings. From my bed I would hear the Magdalen bells 'sprinkle the quarters on the morning town'. They led the chorus of quarters chiming from Merton and New College. I would wait until the fourth quarter had struck and the bell announced the hour, before getting up. This was usually ten o'clock, and so I was too late for breakfast. That did not matter at all.

My tutor was the Reverend J. M. Thompson, a shy, kind, amusing man, and a distinguished authority on French history. Rumour had it that he had been defrocked for preaching in Magdalen Chapel that the miracles were performed by electricity. I later found out that he was an early modernist in theology.

By now I was more interested in the type of churchmanship in a church than in its architecture. I had no Ronnie Wright to accompany me on my expeditions; instead, one of my closest friends was Lord Clonmore (now Wicklow), who was an ordinand at St Stephen's House, Norham Road. We were both Anglo-Catholics. Through the offices of the Reverend Frederic Hood (who was then on the staff of Pusey House under the celebrated Dr Darwell Stone), I was instructed by the Reverend Miles Sargent in the Catholic faith, which was nothing like the abbreviated Matins I had enjoyed daily in the school chapel at Marlborough.

When I left the gentle charge of the Reverend J. M. Thompson, my tutor was C. S. Lewis, who was then in what he would have called his 'unregenerate days'. Breezy, tweedy, beer-drinking and jolly, he was very popular with extrovert undergraduates. He found the liturgy very funny, and delighted in pointing out *non sequiturs* in it; moreover, he ruined Coleridge's 'Kubla Khan' for me by wondering whether the pants in the line 'As if this earth in fast thick pants were breathing' were woollen or fur. Now I knew dons were cleverer than any schoolmaster, even than a headmaster, I realised that when Lewis asked me to read three books of 'Paradise Lost', he had not only read them all himself, but had enjoyed them and even knew what they meant.

Oxford was divided for me into two groups; hearties and aesthetes. Hearties were good college men who rowed in the college boat, ate in the college hall, and drank beer and shouted. Their regulation uniform was college tie, college pullover, tweed coat and grey flannel trousers. Aesthetes, on the other hand, wore whole suits, silk ties of a single colour, and sometimes – but only for about a week or two while they were fashionable – trousers of cream or strawberry-pink flannel. They let their hair grow long, and never found out, as I never found out, where the college playing fields were or which was the college barge. Aesthetes never dined in hall, but went instead to the George restaurant on the corner of Cornmarket and George Street, where there was a band consisting of three ladies, and where punkahs, suspended from the ceiling, swayed to and fro, dispelling the smoke of Egyptian and Balkan cigarettes. Mr Ehrsam, the perfect Swiss hotelier, and his wife kept order, and knew how much credit to allow us. I was an aesthete.

The chief Oxford aesthete when I went up in 1925 was Harold Acton who, with his brother William, was at Christ Church, but was never seen inside the college in my day. He was a frequenter of restaurants, and his own lodgings were somewhere in the High. Michael Dugdale, another aesthete and a friend of mine at Balliol, always used to walk into Brasenose – an entirely athletic college – with the aid of a stick and limping, because he knew that the athletes would be too sporting to attack a lame aesthete.

Aesthetes used to gather at the very fashionable sherry parties – largely attended by Anglo-Catholic and a certain number of Roman Catholic undergraduates – given on Sundays at noon by George Alfred Kolkhorst, lecturer in Spanish at Exeter College and later Reader in the university. He had been born in Chile, which would explain why he knew Spanish, as I cannot imagine him ever taking the trouble to learn it. We nicknamed him 'Colonel' Kolkhorst, as he was so little like a colonel. He was very tall with a slight stoop, and had rooms on the first floor at No. 38 Beaumont Street. When he first came up as an undergraduate, the Colonel had been known as G'ug –

the apostrophe, he thought, implied deference, and gave the impression of a slight yawn when pronounced. He wore a lump of sugar hung from his neck on a piece of cotton 'to sweeten his conversation', and at some of his parties would be dressed in a suit made entirely of white flannel, waistcoat and all. Though people never got drunk at the Colonel's parties, it was a habit to form a circle round him and slowly gyrate, calling out 'The Colonel's tight, the room's going round!' And we used to stick stamps on his ceiling by licking them and throwing them up on up-turned pennies. After one of his merrier sherry parties, the Colonel accompanied Robert Byron and Lord Clonmore and some other undergraduates to the top of St Mary Magdalen's Tower in the Cornmarket, where they sang hymns and began spitting on the people on the pavement. The Proctors were called and waited at the bottom of the Tower for the delinquents to descend, which they eventually did, headed by the Colonel in his white suit. As a graduate of the university and lecturer in Spanish, he was immune from punishment, but the others were fined.

The Colonel disliked dons, believing that they took themselves too seriously. He regarded Spanish as hardly a subject at all, and not worth learning. He thought Cervantes the only outstanding Spanish author, though he liked the Nicaraguan poet Ruben da Rio, whose name we would pronounce at sherry parties with a tremendous rolling of 'r's. The one thing the Colonel detested above all else was research. It might be justified in reputable subjects like 'Literae Humaniores' and biology and the physical sciences, he said, but in Modern Spanish, a subject with very little literary history, research meant nothing but scratching around inventing subjects to increase the self-esteem of examining professors, and did no one any good.

If anyone talked about their subject or held forth with a lot of facts at his parties, the Colonel would open his mouth to simulate a yawn, tapping his upper lip as he did so. He carried a little ear trumpet for 'catching clever remarks', but would swiftly put it away and yawn if they were not clever. I never heard of anyone seeing him in Exeter College, and it was a frequent practice of his friends to ask at the Lodge whether the Colonel had been in lately.

Magdalen College, to which I was admitted through the kindness of the President, Sir Herbert Warren, had been the best college – in the social sense – because Edward VIII had been an undergraduate there when Prince of Wales. It had a very famous steward of the Junior Common Room, named Gynes, who saw to it that the undergraduates had the best food and wine when they entertained in their rooms. I remember giving a luncheon party at which constant glasses of Tokay were the only drink from the hors d'oeuvre to the coffee. I must have seemed an impossible person to poor C. S. Lewis, but he had his revenge, for he wrote me a reference when I was trying to become a private schoolteacher which was so double-edged that I withdrew it after my first unsuccessful application for a post.

However, the best college in my time – it probably still is – was Christ Church, known as 'The House'. There, blue blood prevailed; it was the Mecca of all the socially ambitious. Indeed, one undergraduate who had rooms in the college backing on to a public highway, would let down a rope ladder from his windows after the bell in Tom Tower had finished striking its one hundred and one notes – which meant that all college gates were closed. This undergraduate allowed people from other colleges to use his rope ladder if they were acceptable to him. Thus it was said that he had climbed into society by a rope ladder.

There was always an atmosphere of leisure surrounding Christ Church undergraduates. They gave the impression that they were just dropping in at Oxford on their way to a seat in the House of Lords, shortly to be vacated on the decease of their fathers, or that they were coming in for a term or two, but mostly staying away from college in country houses. They hunted, fished and shot. They may even have rode. But I never heard of them playing football or hockey, or even cricket, though cricket was sometimes played in the grounds of country houses within motoring distance of Oxford, and men from 'the House' might have been called upon to swell a village team. Then it was not unusual for a rich undergraduate, and there were many such at the House, to chuck out the Bursar's furniture and all the humdrum college fittings in his rooms, and have the whole place redecorated at his mother's advice and expense. Edward James, for instance, had rooms in Canterbury Quad whose ceilings were black and whose walls were gold, and around the frieze in Trajan lettering ran the words 'Ars longa, vita brevis'. They outstayed Edward's tenure of the rooms.

Of course, there were also ordinary lay undergraduates – that is, those who were neither peers nor very rich – at Christ Church. There was the clever, bespectacled historian from Cornwall, A. L. Rowse, whom I was not to know till later. My chief friend among the laymen was a tow-haired boy from Greshams called Wystan Auden, who was reading English and was tutored by Nevill Coghill of Exeter College. Coghill was an inspiring tutor who rendered Chaucer into readable English, and was a keen producer of Shakespeare at the OUDS.

There must have been dons at Christ Church, too, though apart
from Professor Lindemann (later Lord Cherwell, the scientist, and
friend of Winston Churchill), and Gilbert Ryle the philosopher, and
J. C. Masterman, the Senior Censor and historian, I do not remember
them ... except for Roy Harrod, a young don who looked about my
own age. He, as Junior Censor, was in charge of undergraduates'
behaviour.

Balliol was, as I have mentioned, the cleverest college, but it was
more ascetic than aesthetic. Balliol was associated with brains. Our
hero Aldous Huxley had been there in rooms papered plain grey,
looking out on frosty stars above the Waterhouse block's Scottish
baronial turrets. The whole tone of the college was Scottish and
frugal, but like all things Scottish, it had a side of unbridled
exuberance, reserved for parties. Lampoons would be sung outside the
rooms of dons. Fortunately the dons at Balliol were far friendlier to
undergraduates than at most other colleges. The don who dominated
Balliol was 'Sligger' Urquhart, who held court in summer on a lawn of
the garden quad near the dining-hall. He liked people to be well-born,
and if possible, Roman Catholic, and he gave reading parties in
Switzerland. I only knew him well enough to touch my hat to him, or
to give him an oily smile.

Balliol had good scouts, the undergraduates gave good luncheons
and teas in their rooms, and it was the college where I had the most
friends. Balliol people whom I knew were, like me, not college men,
and therefore were to be found in restaurants and other people's
rooms. As well as John Edward Bowle, there was Wyndham Ketton-
Cremer, Norfolk squire, Old Harrovian, and a gentle pastoral poet
much admired by Bowle. An old distich (by Dennis Kincaid, a Balliol
wit who was the life and soul of the Colonel's parties) hath it:

> 'John Edward Bowle
> Had a superflux of soul.
> He was more beautiful than Rima,
> But not as beautiful as Ketton-Cremer.'

Exeter College was for me the headquarters of Anglo-Catholicism,
and I had many friends there, too. The dons were mostly approachable
and encouraging, like Professor R. M. Dawkins, who had rooms on
the ground floor, and appeared delighted to welcome anyone who
called on him, whatever his real feelings about the intruders. He
preferred, however, tough sporting men to aesthetes. He was an

unconventional man with a red walrus moustache, freckled bald head and gold wire spectacles. He was exactly one's idea of the absent-minded professor, yet nothing escaped him. He was generally called 'Dorks', and was reputed to have known Baron Corvo, though he never mentioned him to us undergraduates. The fact that he was Sotheby and Bywater Professor of Byzantine and Modern Greek was a matter of childlike wonder and delight to him. Although he was the son of a land-owning family with military traditions, he was the least military of men. He had been put into the electrical engineering business in Chelmsford, but had carried on with modern Greek, regardless. How he moved from electricity to a Fellowship at Emmanuel College, Cambridge, is a puzzle. He always thought of himself as a Cambridge man even after Oxford had made him a Professor. He once told me you could never depend on the aesthetic opinions of classical scholars or philosophers – scientists were far more reliable and humble-minded.

That was my second Oxford. It has lasted long. Still the colleges retain their individuality. I could have gone on through every college in Oxford and the halls and theological colleges, but time and the patience of readers press. I must conclude with a mention of what has always been my favourite college – Pembroke, where Dr Johnson's teapot was preserved in the library. In my day it was still a college you could enter if the dons liked you. Examinations were not all that important. Mr Drake, who was the senior tutor, was the greatest authority on port in England, and Pembroke had the best cellar. The last Lord Pembroke was at the college in my day and wrote excellent racing news for the *Cherwell* when I was an editor. I don't think he bothered much about exams. The Master was the great Dr Holmes Dudden, the most successful of all Vice-Chancellors. He had been a popular London preacher at the fashionable and beautiful Holy Trinity Church, Sloane Street. He and Mr Drake and Mr Salt, a High Churchman and Bursar, and dear old Doctor Ramsden, a scientist who kept silkworms on the mulberries in the Fellows' Garden, made the Pembroke Senior Common Room the most enviable of all. Clipped ivy still grew on the walls and in summer the window boxes were filled with pink geraniums, the college colour. Pembroke retained, of course, its barge when all the 'withits' were building boat houses of brick. With its creeper-hung walls, intimate quads and rich Chapel decorated by Kempe, Pembroke was the best-maintained and most romantic Oxford survival. Even today its new buildings have involved the restoration of little streets adjoining, and no flashy additions. Hurrah!

From My Oxford

W. H. Auden at Oxford

When we first met we were Oxford undergraduates. I was adolescent enough to think that learning was the accumulation of facts and getting dates right. I greatly reverenced dons and thought that schoolmasters were men who were not full enough of facts to be made fellows of an Oxford or Cambridge college. When at Marlborough I had had the run of a little-used part of the library which contained, bound in leather, the whole run of Alfred H. Miles' *Poets and Poetry of the Nineteenth Century*. The short biographies and clear criticisms of these excellent volumes, together with the selected examples of the poets, are still fresh in my mind. At school and at Oxford I generally had with me the *Oxford Book of English Verse* and Quiller-Couch's still unsurpassed *Oxford Book of Victorian Verse*. I felt I knew as much about poetry as a schoolmaster, nearly as much as a don and certainly much more than my fellow undergraduates. Witness then my horror on being introduced to a tall milky-skinned and coltish member of 'The House' (Christ Church), who contradicted all my statements about poetry, who did not think Lord Alfred Douglas was a better sonneteer than Shakespeare, who had read Ebenezer Elliott and Philip Bourke Marston and other poets whom I regarded as my special province and who was not in the least interested in the grand friends I had made in the House – such as John Dumfries, Christopher Sykes, Edward James, Harold and William Acton and Bryan Guinness; who dismissed the Sitwells in a sentence and really admired the boring Anglo-Saxon poets like Beowulf whom we had read in the English school; and who was a close friend of John Bryson and Nevill Coghill, real dons who read Anglo-Saxon, Gutnish, Finnish and probably Swedish and Faroese as easily as I read the gossip column of the *Cherwell* of which I was then an editor. And yet there was an oracular quality about this tough youth in corduroys that compelled my attention. He was very attractive and quite unselfconscious and already a born schoolmaster and lecturer.

He would not come to the fashionable luncheons with peers and baronets and a sprinkling of dons which I liked to attend and sometimes gave myself. He was not a member of the 'Georgeoisie' like

Alan Pryce-Jones and Mark Oglivie-Grant who dined every night at the George restaurant to the strains of a string band. (Mark Oglivie-Grant once came into the restaurant in a bathing dress with seaweed in his hair and carrying a looking-glass.) He didn't belong to the OUDS like Osbert Lancaster or Peter Fleming. He belonged to no clique. When he asked me to tea in his rooms high up in the north-west corner of Peck (Peckwater Quad) I felt I was district-visiting, so snobbish was I, so other-worldly he. There it was that I found out where his heart was. He had quite enjoyed his life at Gresham's School, but did not seem to have retained Greshamian friends in Oxford. At this time it was fashionable, in my set, for undergraduates to regard their parents as brutal philistines. Auden, on the other hand, much reverenced his father. They lived in Edgbaston and his mother was high church as I was. He often spoke with affection of his parents and brother, of Birmingham and the country around it and was very proud of a relation who had written the decidedly antiquarian Methuen *Little Guide to Shropshire*. He was interested in sanitation as his father had been and was, even after I had gone down from Oxford, always asking me for the return of a book with coloured illustrations of soil-pipes and domestic privies for the working classes which he had lent me and which I had lost.

Wystan (the name is that of a Saxon saint whose church Wistanstow is fully noted in Auden's *Little Guide to Shropshire*) was unaware that he represented the new type of Oxford undergraduate. I was the old type, trivial, baroque, incense-loving; a diner with a great admiration for the land-owning classes and the houses and parks in which they were lucky enough to live. Wystan was already aware of slum conditions in Birmingham and mining towns and docks. But he combined with this an intense interest in geology and natural history and topography of the British Isles. He liked railways and canals and had a knowledge of Bradshaw's timetables. He liked visiting churches old and new. He loved the Isle of Man, its railways, trams and trains, and first encouraged me to go there. Above all he liked poetry, chanting it aloud after tea. In this he enjoyed the complicated internal rhymes in Irish hedge poetry and the alliteration of Anglo-Saxon poetry. The alliteration of Swinburne seemed false by comparison. The two friends of his I recall meeting in his rooms at this time were Gabriel Carritt (later Bill Carritt the politician) and William McElwee who became a schoolmaster at Stowe. They must have been interested in the music, a side of Wystan's life I was never able to share except in the appreciation of verbal rhythm.

Wystan and I much enjoyed discovering unknown poets, preferably of the last century and the Edwardian age and reading out our discoveries to each other. This was how we stumbled on the works of the Reverend Doctor E. E. Bradford, DD, whose lyrics, innocent and touching about the love of 'lads', as boys were so often called by scoutmasters in those days, used to bring us uncontrollable mirth.

> Once a schoolboy newly come,
> Timid, frail and friendless,
> Feared to face a footer scrum
> Oh! the taunts were endless.
>
> Suddenly he drew apart
> Soon they heard him crying.
> With a penknife in his heart
> Home they brought him dying.

This was the Auden I knew at Oxford and whom I was to meet later in the documentary film world and at home, when I was first married, in Uffington, Berkshire, where he rapidly wrote in some parts for a village play which my wife was producing. We never lost touch with him. The last two times we met were in the Refreshment Room of the Great Central Railway on Marylebone Station, before it was ruined by re-decoration and, more conventionally, at a poetry recital given by the BBC.

From *W.H. Auden: A Tribute*

L. Moholy-Nagy

The distinct variety of English publishers was the chief charm of Edwardian book production. It continued into the twenties. The 'Chats' series by Arthur Hayden, an old friend of my father, published by T. Fisher Unwin *Chats on old Clocks*, *Chats on old Chafing Dishes*, *Chats* on anything. There were spaciously printed books of memoirs by doctors, lawyers, politicians and explorers, and hereditary peers, on thick paper with wide margins and large type, for dowagers to read without their spectacles. These were published by Eveleigh, Nash & Grayson.

Then there were my favourites, Seely Service & Co., who specialised in regimental uniforms and pond life. But one of the most mysterious of the publishers was John Miles. Whether he had a moustache or pince-nez I cannot be sure, and how he got on with the other members of his firm, who were Simpkin Marshall, I do not know. It had always been my ambition to appear under an obscure imprint, or with Rivingtons, originally High Church and later wholly educational.

So, when a letter came from John Miles, one of these obscure, polysyllabic firms, I could not resist the temptation offered me by its signatory, Mr Harry Paroissien, to write a book about Oxford, packed with illustrations. It was the illustrations which tempted me, for Harry had a gift for layout, and the look and feel of a book, and so, I thought, did I. There were to be photographs, and this, alas, meant shiny art paper, but the text could be on rough paper, and a variety of type faces displayed. There could be wide margins such as would have pleased Hamish Hamilton in his youth, and Eveleigh, Nash and Grayson in their middle age, and we were allowed the use of black letter type such as might have pleased Caxton, in the headings.

Osbert Lancaster did some particularly brilliant caricatures of Oxford types: learned lady dons on bicycles; swells in the Bullingdon Club, and scarved rowing men. Line drawings, which had illustrated *Verdant Green*, by the Reverend Edward Bradley (1853), mixed in very well with those of Osbert's drawings. But the chief illustrations were photographs taken by L. Moholy-Nagy, a member of the Bauhaus. He was a huge man with a constant smile and shaped like a large, oval water beetle which suddenly comes to the surface and dives out of sight. Moholy (Mowli-Wogie, as my wife called him) had a Leica and rushed about frenziedly photographing everything he saw. At Encaenia, when honorary degrees were given to distinguished persons, my father-in-law being one, he became particularly excited. The result of Moholy's clickings was hundreds of little prints measuring about one square inch, and from these he selected those which were to be enlarged.

That was where his genius lay. He knew just which to choose, showing the beauty of crumbling stone, the crispness of carved eighteenth-century urns, and members of the public who were quite unconscious they were being photographed: undergraduates scratching their spots; the master of Balliol waiting to post a letter; ladies flat on punts; people browsing in Blackwells; and everywhere bicycles. Where certain noble, and then unfashionable, buildings had been omitted, photographs were specially taken by Miss Joan Eyres Monsell (Mrs Leigh Fermor) and others. Which pictures should be big, and where placed in the text, was, I think, determined by Moholy and Harry Paroissien.

My own text was designed to be entertaining reading only, and useless in the examination industry. Now that I see it reprinted, I notice what an advantage it is to have the paper all the same quality and without that sickening introduction of shiny art, though the binding is distinctly inferior to the earlier book. In 1937 we were all very Left (Parlour Pink in my case) and of course Morris Cowley had to be mentioned and a special mention by Ernest J. Marsh called 'An Industrial Worker at Oxford' was included. Perhaps it greatly enhanced the book as a social document. At least there was the merit of early enthusiasm.

The Times

Maurice Bowra: A Formative Friend

Stand with me on a moonlit night in the late twenties in the front quad of Wadham College seen from the porter's lodge. At the top right-hand corner of this pleasant, three-storeyed manor-house of a quadrangle, the work of Somerset masons, are the rooms of the Dean. Raised and cheerful voices may be heard. Above them all, and louder, is the voice of Maurice, the Dean of Wadham, audible even from here. One did not have to look for Maurice, one only had to listen.

So lovable, loyal and formative a friend must be written about without a waste of words. Maurice despised journalism and pitied journalists. He was a stickler for grammar. There must be no hanging clauses, no verbless sentence in what I write about him here. He also despised television and refused to appear on it.

If one wants to hear an echo of Maurice's voice it may be heard sometimes in the conversation of Isaiah Berlin, Patrick Kinross and Osbert Lancaster – 'Couldn't agree with you more', 'Yers, yers – splendid!' But his resonant voice is needed and that 1914 army slang punctuated with 'old boy' and 'old man', to bring back the feeling of safe elation as the glass was thrust into one's hand and the introductions made to people one knew and liked already, but given different titles in the fantastic hierarchy Maurice invented for them.

And then there were his clothes. 'Why do you dress like an undergraduate, Betjeman?' he said to me some years after I had gone down. This was because I still wore a tweed coat and grey flannel trousers. Maurice himself was always in a suit, generally dark blue.

The Oxford of the late twenties, which was when I first came up, seemed to me to be divided, so far as undergraduates were concerned, between aesthetes and hearties. I was an aesthete. There would have been no hearties at the parties which I attended. Maurice's were always dinner parties. On the other hand we all knew he was a great 'college man' and was held in high favour by the rowing men of Wadham and he may have known Blues – provided they came from Wadham. But he kept us all as sets, and very much apart.

The guests I met at Maurice's dinner parties were generally intellectuals, with a few young peers who may have been sons of his friends of the 1914 war generation to which unexpectedly Maurice belonged. We could not believe that anyone so free and easy and unmilitary and scandalously entertaining could ever have fought the Huns in trench warfare. He never mentioned it in the twenties. We thought he was our own age.

I think his way of speaking with a strong emphasis on certain syllables partly came from Winchester. Maurice, though a Cheltonian, was at New College, which was then an Oxford branch of Winchester. I think it also came from Cambridge and such friends there as Dadie Rylands and Adrian Bishop. It was a King's Cambridge way of talking. Adrian Bishop was his closest and most reckless friend in the twenties. Under the pleasure-lover, as with Maurice, so with Adrian, there was the ascetic. Adrian, whose real name was Frank, became an Anglican-Benedictine monk and took the name of Brother Thomas More in religion. Maurice reconciled himself to this change by referring to Adrian as 'Brother Tom'. I still possess *A Sixteenth-Century Anthology* edited by Arthur Symons which Adrian gave me with this inscription: 'To John Betjeman, hoping that his thirty-first year may bring an increase in tact, wisdom and courage. With love, from Frank Bishop.' The censoriousness was characteristic of the stern self-discipline which Maurice, Adrian and many of that generation imposed on themselves.

Because Wadham had an Evangelical tradition going back to the time of Warden Symons who had arranged times of Chapel so that undergraduates could not attend Newman's sermons in St Mary's, Maurice also proclaimed himself an Evangelical. But his Evangelicalism was only skin deep. One of his closest friends among the Fellows of Wadham was Father Brabant, the Wadham chaplain for many years, who was most distinctly Anglo-Catholic. So were many of Maurice's friends. It was through one of these, Lord Clonmore, that I first met Maurice. Pierse Synnott, an Irish Roman Catholic, was about the only Papist friend of Maurice in these days. Maurice and I went to stay with both of these people and I remember on one occasion Maurice coming into my bedroom when we were changing for dinner and saying, 'I say, old boy, shall we roger the skivvies?' The gift of exceeding the bounds of good taste was to me one of his endearing characteristics. There was a streak of Gowing in *The Diary of a Nobody* about Maurice which either attracted or repelled.

So outspoken a man contracted enemies. Sometimes it may have been simply a matter of genes. The rival host to undergraduates in the late twenties was the University Lecturer in Spanish, G. A. Kolkhorst,

then known as 'G'ug' and later as 'Colonel' Kolkhorst because he was
so little like a colonel. 'Charming fellow, Kolkhorst,' said Maurice. 'A
pity he's got a touch of the tarbrush.' To which Colonel Kolkhorst,
who was wholly white, replied by always referring to Maurice as 'Mr
Borer'. It was a good early lesson in diplomacy to be acceptable to
both Maurice and the Colonel, as neither of them stood any nonsense
and exposed mockingly any pretension. Maurice, who was so alarming
on first acquaintance with his machine-gun fire of quips and sudden
slaying of popular idols, was kindness itself when one was in trouble.
When I was rusticated he commiserated and had me to dinner, and
even drove out with congenial friends to Thorpe House, Oval Way,
Gerrards Cross, where I was working my passage as a private
schoolmaster. He came to see my parents and induced them to
continue an allowance to me and he secured for me, through his
friendship with the owners of the Architectural Press, a position on
the *Architectural Review* which enabled me to keep myself independent
of my parents. What he did for me, who was not of his College, he did
for all the Wadham undergraduates. He was their adviser and friend
who gave practical help. During the last war he gave practical help to
the victims of the Nazi Government and found them positions in
England. Politically I should have said he was Left, but not
doctrinaire. Hugh Gaitskell was a close friend, and many a wrangle
over economics to which I did not listen did I hear at Maurice's table
in my undergraduate days.

His most endearing quality was his power to build one up in one's
own estimation. He did this by listening and either agreeing or
suggesting a similar train of thought.

In the same way he took one's own troubles on his shoulders.
Firmly and kindly he separated me from those he regarded as
unsuitable. Cautiously and slowly he made friends of the opposite sex
who then became as close as his own generation had been. I think
particularly of Enid Starkie, Audrey Beecham, Dame Janet Vaughan
and my wife, to whom he was devoted, and Pam Hartwell, Celli Clark
and Ann Fleming. He forgave because he understood. What he could
not forgive was disloyalty and ruthlessness. He was surprisingly kind
and unshockable.

Maurice continued his kindness to the children of his friends.

But his greatest loves were Oxford as a place and Wadham College
as a society. He liked their buildings. My life is emptier without those
afternoons when he would ring up and say, 'What about a look at
Hertford and some Anglo-Jackson?' We would set off in search of the

many works in Oxford of the architect Sir Thomas Jackson. Maurice would hear no word against him, for Jackson had been a Fellow of Wadham.

His favourite colleges to visit when in architectural mood were Hertford because of the Jackson work, Keble because of Butterfield and his friend Crab Owen, and Pembroke because he admired the members of its Common Room and Dr Holmes Dudden, its Master.

In the twenties and thirties Maurice would venture further afield in hired cars driven very fast and dangerously by undergraduates. He did not drive himself. He took us to Garsington and Lady Ottoline and Sezincote, and of course we went out very fast to dine at the Spread Eagle at Thame at Fothergill's.

Once, when the car I was driving waltzed around in the road near Moreton-in-Marsh and buckled its wheels, he was quite unmoved. But I remember once taking him to see the inside of the Cowley Fathers' Mission House in Marston Street. That was the only time I knew him alarmed.

In later life he liked walking in North Oxford, especially in places like Belbroughton Road where he would look at houses in which he might retire. Another favourite walk was Holywell Cemetery, where he looked at the headstones to great brains and Heads of Houses now dust in erstwhile meadowland. He is buried there himself.

Shall any of us who knew him enjoy life so much as we did in his company? I can hear him say 'Definitely *no*'.

From *Maurice Bowra: A Celebration*

Westminster Abbey

Westminster Abbey is different things to different people.

To the *dévoué* it is the shrine containing the bones of its founder, St Edward the Confessor. Annual pilgrimages are made to it not only by members of the Church of England but by Roman Catholics, whose Cathedral is Bentley's magnificent basilica further down the road towards Victoria Station. For all the English it is the place where every monarch since William the Conqueror (except for Edward V and Edward VIII) has been consecrated with oil and crowned. For antiquaries it is Thorney Island. There are stone vestiges of St Edward the Confessor's original Saxon Abbey. For architects the present church and its great octagonal Chapter House are an exemplar of the Gothic style. Here in Nave, Transept and Cloister is the tall French architecture of the reign of Henry III when England was an integral part of Christendom. It is purest Early English, started in 1376* and continuing to be used in the building of the Nave until 1528, a remarkable survival of a strong plain style triumphing over fashion. At the east end is the last exuberant Tudor outburst of Gothic in Henry VII's Chapel, fan-vaulted English Perpendicular within, sheltering elaborate early Renaissance coloured monuments and gilded ironwork. Outside from across the Thames, Henry VII's Chapel must have looked like an elaborate galleon, for its pinnacles were topped with little gold pennons and vanes.

To the boys of Westminster School 'up Abbey' means going to the Abbey for their school chapel. In it they have daily services. The monks who served St Peter's Abbey, which the Confessor founded, were Benedictines and a teaching order. Boys were first taught by the monks, it is said, in the Western Cloister. There was also a grammar school west of the Abbey in the precincts. Queen Elizabeth I refounded the two schools as a single institution which is the present Westminster School. The Dean is *ex officio* Chairman of its Governors. In the Abbey at Coronations its scholars have the right to

---

* 1376 was the date the building of the Nave was started but not the date of the start of the Abbey. The rebuilding of the church itself was started in 1245 by Henry III, continuing the Lady Chapel built earlier and now replaced by the new Lady Chapel of Henry VII.

acclaim the monarch first. In the eighteenth century it was the greatest public school in England, and it is still one of them. For those interested in monumental sculpture the Abbey is unrivalled in the kingdom. It has the handsomest tombs of every age from the medieval to the present. To the liturgiologist the services of the Abbey and its customs make it a unique survival. The late minor Canon and Sacrist, Jocelyn Perkins, wrote three volumes for the Alcuin Club on Westminster Abbey, its worship and ornaments (1938–52). The Dean, Canons, minor Canons, and Sacrist in their enviable houses about the precincts are the successors of the Benedictine monks. The surveyor, organist, vergers, masons and those concerned with the fabric are the equivalent of the lay-brothers of the medieval community.

For historians it is the burial place of our kings, queens, courtiers, statesmen, lawyers, writers, generals and particularly admirals and naval officers. Though one could not say that the poets buried in Poets' Corner run the whole gamut of Palgrave's *Golden Treasury*, they are a memorable group.

Joseph Addison in a paper to the *Spectator* for Friday 30 March 1711 said:

> Upon going into the Church, I entertained myself with the digging of a Grave; and saw in every Shovel-full of it that was thrown up, the Fragment of a Bone or Skull intermixt with a kind of fresh mouldering Earth that some time or other had a place in the Composition of an human Body. Upon this, I began to consider with myself what innumerable Multitudes of People lay confused together under the Pavement of that ancient Cathedral; how Men and Women, Friends and Enemies, Priests and Soldiers, Monks and Prebendaries, were crumbled amongst one another, and blended together in the same common Mass; how Beauty, Strength, and Youth, with Old-age, Weakness, and Deformity, lay undistinguished in the same promiscuous Heap of Matter.

Or there was Max Beerbohm's essay on the Abbey's wax effigies, 'The Ragged Regiment' from *Yet Again* (1909).

> Certainly, such of us as reside in London take Westminster Abbey as a matter of course. A few of us will be buried in it, but meanwhile we don't go to it, even as we don't go to the Tower, or the Mint, or the Monument. Only for some special purpose do we go – as to hear a sensational bishop preaching, or to see a monarch anointed.

And on these rare occasions we cast but a casual glance at the Abbey
– that close packed chaos of beautiful things and worthless vulgar
things. That the Abbey should be thus chaotic does not seem
strange to us; for lack of orderliness and discrimination is an
essential characteristic of English genius. But to the Frenchman,
with his passion for symmetry and harmony, how very strange it
must all seem!

I suppose I was five when I first saw it. At that age there was the
impression that it was only the South Transept. For most visitors,
until recently, this was the chief entrance open to the public. One
glanced in, the crowds were great, the place was tall and dark and
surprisingly short for something so tall. I did not walk as far as the
tower-crossing nor did I look down the Nave nor up to those three
exquisite arches behind the High Altar. It was not until I was nine or
ten that I was taken to the royal tombs and Henry VII's Chapel. These
did not seem as interesting to me then as the Tower of London and
Traitor's Gate. There were not enough ghosts. In those days I did not
know that the bodies of Cromwell's government had been disinterred
at the Restoration and thrown into a deep pit outside the Abbey and
their decapitated heads displayed over Westminster Hall. I thought
that anything really old and to be revered, had to be round-arched and
Norman. As for the kings and tombs and effigies, they were a spate of
words of vergers or schoolmasters or guides and too many to be taken
in.

At the age of sixteen or seventeen one reacts against the opinions of
one's parents. Mine admired the Gothic and the Abbey particularly,
because it was Gothic and historic, two qualities of perfection. I was
already tending towards the Georgian and had begun to admire the
Baroque sculpture of Roubiliac and the pioneer investigation by Mrs
Esdaile of eighteenth-century monuments. Partly to annoy my parents
and old-fashioned schoolmasters, and also partly within myself, I then
preferred St Paul's. When I came to work in London, after the usual
two year period of teaching in preparatory schools, my friend John
Edward Bowle, the historian, had been made sixth-form history
master at Westminster School. Thus I was able to discover the
Armoury and the Little Cloister with its splashing fountain and its
unforgettable view of Barry's Victoria Tower. I also discovered the
Main Cloisters. As to the Canons and clergy, I knew none of them;
they seemed to me semi-royal. The precincts of the Abbey, though

they are blessedly open during most of the day, still have a forbiddingly private look.

As a journalist on the *Architectural Review* in Queen Anne's Gate, I found the Abbey a dominating presence. Those two Western Towers completed by Nicholas Hawksmoor, in his own version of Gothic, were to be seen every day down Tothill Street. A reproach to them, we modernists must have felt, was Charles Holden's London Transport Building, built in 1929, with its plain square tower in the latest modern unadorned functional style, and carved insets by Henry Moore, Eric Gill and others. This seemed the true Gothic. All the same there was the deeper call of the truer Gothic, when all ten bells rolled out on state occasions and when the lesser smaller melodious ring could be heard after fashionable weddings in St Margaret's.

In those days the interior of the Abbey was dark and dingy. The great Lethaby seemed to have concentrated on keeping the structure standing, and I have been told that his only artistic contribution was the rather inadequate brass electroliers. There were many things for a forward-looking architectural journalist to criticise. For instance the lettering on the Unknown Warrior's grave seemed a very long way from Eric Gill. It still seems so, and must have come from a monumental mason and been ordered by the foot and acquiesced in by the Dean and Chapter, who were only interested in the wording. But now I do not know that art is all that important in an inspired idea like this. In a way, this famous slab typifies the Abbey and that touch of the commonplace and the numinous which makes it different from anywhere else.

Since the war the Abbey has been transformed inside and has flowered. The new Surveyor, Stephen Dykes Bower (appointed in 1951), first cleaned the stone and we realised that the grey Purbeck of the Henry III columns was designed to contrast with the cream-coloured Caen stone. The paintings on the vaulted roof became visible, including arabesques designed by Wren around the bosses. The early Renaissance monuments were startlingly restored to their full colour, which brought back the swagger and delightful vulgarity of the New Learning. The monument to Henry Carey, 1st Baron Hunsdon, in St John the Baptist's Chapel off the north ambulatory, must be the biggest in any church in England. The cleaning of the walls showed up the splendour of the eighteenth-century glass, particularly that in the West Window. The noble, white marble statues of Georgian and Victorian days were cleaned.

The internal glory has been almost wholly restored, yet the heart of the Abbey, the shrine of its founder, is a caricature of a shrine. It was despoiled in 1540, and though the relics are still inside it, the mosaics have been picked out from the stonework and its columns damaged. All this could easily be restored to what it was like when Henry III rebuilt the shrine. The Cosmati work with which it was adorned could be put back by modern craftsmen.

One of the first of the Victorian restorers of the Abbey was Edward Blore, who designed the Choir Screen in 1834. Greatly daring, the present Surveyor applied full colour to this screen and to the stalls within the Choir, which had later been restored by Sir Gilbert Scott, whose masterpiece is the restored Chapter House. This lightening of the former dinginess of the Abbey shows up how good Victorian work can be. Its proportions and detail are emphasised by bright-coloured paint and they are well suited to their surroundings, as is the restored stained glass in the Chapter House. Let us hope that this book will bring about the completion of the interior restoration of the Abbey. For the floors of Nave and Transepts, at present of inferior Portland stone, should be of more durable material, such as marble, to withstand the onslaught of thousands of shoes.

The chief delight of Westminster Abbey for the Londoner can be its daily services. I remember with embarrassment some satirical verses I wrote before the war on official religion connected with the Abbey. After the war, when I deteriorated into becoming a committee man, I sat on a Commission whose offices were close by. After these painful and often boring sessions, it was a relief to come out into the open air. More often than not the two bells were ringing for Evensong, then I would go in to the service and be ushered into a seat near the Choir. The evening light would fade from the stained glass. Softened electric light threw mysterious shadows. The well-known prayer-book phrases were read by priests in canopied stalls. An anthem by Lawes or Weelkes or some unrecognised Victorian musician soared to the vaulting. The Commission and the arguments fell into proportion and ceased to irritate. The traffic roar in Parliament Square, the 11s and the 24s, were muffled by the buttressed building. Even more than state occasions and memorial services, these weekday Evensongs have impressed me. The Abbey is more of an ancient abbey still at an 8 a.m. Communion Service in one of the side chapels, with only a few there.

For the purpose of writing this introduction, I was taken on a final tour of the place by the Archdeacon, Canon Carpenter. It was a summer evening after the church had been shut. I walked to his house just as the gas-lights were being turned on in the Cloisters and cobbled passages of the royal surroundings of the Abbey. I was in the London of Dickens. As we passed the Chapter House, I remarked on how strange it was that this building, so well restored by Sir Gilbert Scott, was in the care of the Department of the Environment, and not of the Dean and Chapter. He pointed out that it had been the scene of the first English Parliament in the Royal Palace of Westminster and that it represented what the Abbey stands for, the tension between the present and the past. As we came into the Nave by the South-West Door, someone was playing the organ. There was a lay brother (i.e. a verger) on duty. The stained glass in the West Window, gold, blue, dark red and silver was at its Georgian armorial grandest. I saw the point of those crystal chandeliers, which were presented to the Abbey by the Guinness family after the last war. The lay brother turned them on and they gradually swelled in brightness, though there was never a glare. We walked round the tombs, up to St Edward's shrine, over the engineer's new bridge leading to it. This is as inoffensive as it is practical. We went into Henry VII's Chapel, and had a look at the praying hands of Margaret Beaufort. The lights were turned down into semi-darkness as we came out into the gas-lit mystery of the Cloister and past the Hall of Westminster School close by the Deanery – that Hall inside looks like a Georgian aquatint of the hall of a Cambridge College.

As I write these final sentences in a City of London precinct near the Norman church of Rahere's Priory of St Bartholomew the Great, the Corporation of London dust-cart is making a hellish noise under my window. There is always a tension between the past and the present. In Westminster Abbey the tension for most of us is created by the thousands of tourists of all nations and faiths who queue, apparently without comprehension, through a place which means much to us. But do they not understand? I think they do. Their shuffling presence remains after the doors are shut. Finally, at the south end of the South Transept hidden away, is the chapel of St Faith. This is for me the part of the Abbey where tension between past and present ceases.

From Westminster Abbey

A Passion for Churches
Broadcast on BBC Television

Vision	Commentary
JB in a rowing boat.	I was eight or nine years when I used to come here to the Norfolk Broads on the river Bure, sailing and rowing with my father. And I think it was the outline of that church tower of Belaugh against the sky which gave me a passion for churches; so that every church I've been past since I've wanted to stop and look in.
Belaugh Church.	
JB walking towards Bressingham Church	
TITLE: A PASSION FOR CHURCHES	
Interior of a church.	
Sub-title: A Celebration of the Church of England.	
JB playing a Victorian barrel organ.	
	The air the Old Hundredth. The place: Bressingham. The diocese: Norwich, which includes most of Norfolk and a little bit of Suffolk.
A boat on the river.	

Montage of Norfolk Churches.

What would you be, you wide
East Anglian sky,
Without church towers to
recognise you by?
What centuries of faith, in
flint and stone,
Wait in this watery landscape,
all alone
To antiquaries, 'object of
research'
To the bored tourist 'just
another church'. The varied
Norfolk towers could also be
A soothing sight to mariners
at sea.

Cley Church.

Exterior: JB at Cley.

This is Cley-next-the-Sea. The
sea is now quite a long way
off. It is a tiny place but it's
got an enormous church. They
must have had hopes of it
being very much bigger. And
look at that porch – built I

The tower and the sundial.

should think about 1430. Very
delicately done, almost another
church in itself. And slapped
on to it very coarsely, a
sundial. Time suddenly stuck
into eternity.

JB inside Cley Church.

Look at that, for vastness and
light.

Interior of the Church.

*Bench-ends at Great
Walsingham Church.*

Light falling on carved
Norfolk oak.

Gone silvery-grey with age
And towards the light come
out
the nightmare figures of marsh

and forest
Earth-bound creatures
struggling up the bench-ends.

Interior of Knapton Church.

They know they can never
reach the winged celestial
hosts here in the roof at
Knapton

The angels in the roof.
Font cover at Trunch.

The finest of all the wood
carving
Is in the neighbouring Parish
of Trunch
It exalts the very first
sacrament.

Pan down to see a baptism
service.

Baptism sequence.

Baptism by water
the first armour we put on
against the assaults of hate,
greed and fear on our journey
back to eternity.

Cherry Ann
your Godparents make
promises on your behalf
And the village of Trunch
bears witness.

Children and mothers go to
Mattishall Church.

First steps on the journey
At Mattishall, they have
Sunday school on Wednesday
afternoon.
The 'Little People', as they
call them,
Clutching their tambourines
and triangles

Sunday school sequence.

come to hear the old story
told anew.

*The screen at Binham Church
and painted faces.*

Each generation makes itself
heard
The past cries out to us even
when we try to smother the
cries
Medieval saints peer at us

Through godly warnings put
over them by pious
Elizabethans
who had more use for the
written word

Than the painted picture.

*Pauline Plummer restoring the
rood screen at Ranworth Church.*

We can help the past come
through
A hundredth of an inch at a
time
Miss Pauline Plummer is
revealing
The secrets of the chancel
screen at Ranworth
And soon will show it in its
medieval glory.

*Paintings on the screen,
Ranworth Church.*

In the fifteenth century
Norwich was famous for its
painters
they delighted in herbs and
flowers
And living creatures.

The lithe and feathered figure
of the Archangel Michael

Is by no provincial hand
It's rather a masterpiece.

*Fifteenth-century painted glass at
Weston Longville, Bale, Warham
St Mary.*

The Norwich artists also
painted on glass and light

came in to every Norfolk
church through golden late
medieval windows. Men hate
beauty. They think it's wicked.
Self-righteous churchwardens
delighted in smashing it

Village boys flung stones
Storms did the rest.

Today the famous Norwich
glass is nearly all jumbled
fragments

East Harling.   A few whole windows survive.

Norwich.   Here's where the artists
JB in the foreground.   worked
                                      The City of Norwich down in
                                      the valley of the Wensum
Elm Hill.   It's a city of cobbled alleys
Churches.   and winding footpaths
                                      It has more medieval churches
                                      within its walls
                                      Than London, York and
                                      Bristol put together.
                                      Remember Norwich.
                                      Round the corner, down the
                                      steps, over the bridge, up the
                                      hill

St Margaret's.   There's always a church.
St Peter Mancroft.   And grandest of all, St Peter
                                      Mancroft – so large
                                      That sometimes people
                                      mistake it for the Cathedral.

Norwich Cathedral.   The city wears its cathedral
                                      like a crown.
                                      A coronal of flying buttresses
                                      Supporting the walls of glass.

The Normans started it
The stone was brought over
the sea from France
To build and adorn the
Cathedral church
Of the Holy and Undivided
Trinity.
It draws the whole Diocese
towards it.
And in its cloisters,
Made for contemplation,
Mothers and grandmothers
Vicars and rectors
From the towns and villages
Of the Diocese of Norwich
Gather together for the annual
festival
Of the Mothers' Union.

Pan down from the spire to reveal Mothers' Union in the cloisters.

Bawdeswell greets Stratton
Strawless,
Potter Heigham is on terms
with Little Snoring,
North Creake sits beside
Melton Constable,
And for everyone there's the
chance to meet the Bishop.

The Bishop and the Mothers' Union.

Maurice Wood, Diocesan
Bishop of Norwich
When not entertaining, he's
Maurice Norvic,
Father-in-God to the clergy.

The Bishop at the Induction Service – Holt.

The Induction Service.

The Bishop institutes a new
rector
To the living of Holt, in
North Norfolk.
By the laying on of hands,
The Bishop commits to the

priest
The spiritual care of the
Parish.

Great Snoring.

With every Parish church
There's a house
Rectory or vicarage
Usually beside the churchyard.
I think you probably need
Money of your own

The Rectory.

To be Rector of Great
Snoring
Because the Rectory house is a
Tudor Palace
With moulded autumn-
coloured brick
And elaborate chimney-stacks
And the date about 1525.

*A modern rectory at Weston
Longville.*

It's the usual practice now,
though,
To sell big rectories
And build labour-saving villas
in their place.

Weston Longville Church.

At Weston Longville, in
Georgian days
Parson Woodforde wrote his
worldly diaries
Full of good dinners.

The Rector of Weston Longville.

The present rector types the
parish magazine.

Reverend James: We send
belated birthday Greetings to
Mr Walter Pardon of Weston
Longville who reached the
splendid age of eighty-nine
years on February 17th. Little
Johnny Atherton aged three-

and-a-half years broke his leg
on February 17th – bad luck –
we hope you get well soon,
Johnny. It is only a rumour
but there is talk of a
sponsored streak for church
funds. By whom we wonder.

Exterior of Letheringsett Church.

Not, I think by members of
The Parochial Church Council
at Letheringsett
The PCC
It's meeting this evening in
the church hall

The PCC meeting.

With the Rector in the chair.

A fête at South Raynham.

If it isn't the tower, it's the
transept or the North Porch
And the answer is usually a
fête
To raise another few pounds.
We can rely on the parish to
rally round.

The fête.

God bless the Church of
England
The rectory lawn that gave
A trodden space for that
bazaar
That underpinned the nave.
We must dip into our pockets
For our hearts are full of
dread
At the thought of all the
damage
Since the roof was stripped of
lead.

An auction of a painting.

And it's always worth a try to
get the key

Exterior of Belaugh.

However remote the church

In fact, the remoter the better.
There's more chance of its
being left unspoiled.

St Mary Belaugh, in the valley
of the Wensum.
Look.

Interior and JB.

The pulpit.

This is a perfect example of a
church in a park in the time
of Jane Austen. The
woodwork is all of oak. Notice
that altar-piece with the
Creed, the Commandments
and the Lord's Prayer painted
on it and here is a three-
decker pulpit in full sail.

This is where the Parish Clerk
said Amen at the end of the
prayers and announced the
name of the hymn tune or the
psalm tune.

Here, a gentle staircase leads
to the middle deck. And this
is where the minister, as he
was called, read the holy
offices of morning and
evening prayer and the
lessons. And if he was in the
mood, or if it was the fourth
Sunday in the month, or
something like that, he would
ascend to the top deck to
preach a sermon.

And from here the parson
could survey his whole parish.
In the big box pew there the
squire from the hall
slumbering while a fire
crackled in the grate. The
large farmers in the pews in
front; the cottagers and lesser
tenantry behind; all by country
custom in their place in the
Church by law established.

Exterior of Felbrigg Church.

The cottagers and lesser
tenantry
Would have had a good long
walk,
By field and footpath,
To the isolated parish church
of St Margaret, Felbrigg.

The squire would have had a
gentle stroll.
It is in the park of the big
house.
I wonder who fall to their
knees here today?

*Interior of the church and zoom
out to discover brass rubbing.*

Oh – the new cottage industry
– brass-rubbing.

Memorial brasses to former
generations of Squires of
Felbrigg and their ladies.

Medieval effigies that tell us
nothing
Of the people they represent.
They're so calm and bland
and self-controlled
Outlined there, as large as life

Sir Simon and Lady Margaret
Felbrigg.

He, a Garter Knight, and she
a cousin of the Queen

It must have been the day of
days,
The day they took their vows.

*A wedding sequence – Lyng
Church.*

*Interior of the bell tower at
Wiveton Church.*

Ringing the changes, treble
bell to tenor
Unites young and old.
Captain of the Tower
And sixty years a ringer,
Billy West.

Billy West: Ah that's music in
your ear – that's music in the
ear. Once that gets hold of
you – I suppose that's like
smoking cigarettes – once that
gets a hold of you that, that's
a drug, you can't get rid of it.
There's something about it, I
don't know what it is, but
you'd go anywhere for it. If
there weren't somewhere
where there were some bells
I'd go crazy, I know I should.
Bells are life to me – I mean
it never seems a Sunday to me
if we don't hear the bells.
That never seems Sunday if
you can't hear church bells
going.

*The high street – view of the
Broads from Ranworth Church.*

I hear a deep sad undertone in
bells

Which calls the Middle Ages
back to me.
From prime to compline the
monastic hours
Echo in bells along the windy
marsh
And fade away. They leave me
to the ghosts

Exterior: JB walking.

Which seem to look from this
enormous sky
Upon the ruins of a grandeur
gone

St Benets Abbey.

St Benets Abbey by the river
Bure
Now but an archway and a
Georgian mill
A lone memorial of the
cloistered life.

*Exterior of All Hallows Convent,
Ditchingham.*

Alone? No, not alone. Serene,
secure,
The sisters of All Hallows,
Ditchingham
In this brick convent, for over
a century now
Have taught and trained the
young and nursed the sick

And founded rescue homes,

Wafer-making sequence.

A homely practical community.
Their souls are fed with daily
Eucharists
You see the impress there
upon the bread
You see the impress also in
their lives.

Gardening sequence.

Their motto – *semper orantes,
semper laborantes,*

	Always at prayer, and always at their work.
Feeding chickens.	An Anglican convent in East Anglia A place to think of when the world seems mad
Bee-keeping sequence.	With too much speed and noise A pleasant place to come to for retreat. There's really not much risk of being stung.
A steam train.	Just as some people are holy so are places
	They draw us to them whether we will or not.
JB in a train	In the misty past in the 1920s and 30s people came to Norfolk by train, by steam. By Great Eastern, and more locally by Midland and Great Northern Joint. They came on pilgrimage by train. Faith enlightened, full of hope and on the way to Walsingham.
JB at Walsingham station.	This is all that remains of the railway track that carried all those pilgrims to Walsingham. And what's become of the station? It's the Orthodox church. The Orient come to East Anglia.
Walsingham.	To this country town Where in 1061 (Forgive my mentioning dates)

The shrine at Walsingham.

The Lady of the Manor
Saw the Virgin Mary
Mother of God
Then medieval pilgrims,
peasants, kings,
In thousands thronged to
England's Nazareth,
The cult has been revived in
modern times;
Suburbanised, perhaps.

Exterior of the shrine and JB outside.

The Shrine of our Lady of
Walsingham.
1930s red brick romanesque.
But inside is the goal of all
the pilgrims. And very peculiar
it is.

Interior of the Shrine.

I wonder if you'd call it
superstitious
Here in this warm mysterious
holy house
The figure of our Lady and
Her Child
Or do you think that forces
are around
Strong, frightening, loving and
just out of reach,
But waiting, waiting,
somewhere to be asked –
And is that somewhere here at
Walsingham?

Pilgrims at the well.

The water bubbles from the
Holy Well
By water we were brought
into the church
By water we are blessed along
the way.

Exterior: the Pilgrims' procession.

I've seen processions like this

in Sicily
You can see them in the
streets of Malta, too.
But it's an exotic flowering of
the Church of England
Here in a Norfolk garden
The Anglican church has got
a bit of everything
It's very tolerant – and that is
part of its strength.

Pilgrims leaving by coach.   Farewell to the pilgrims
                                            Here come the tourists

JB arriving at Sandringham in   Sandringham is the Queen's
an old Bentley.   country estate
Exterior of the church.   The parish church is used
                                            both by the villagers
                                            And the Royal Family
                                            It seems appropriate to arrive
                                            in style

JB outside the church.   Originally, says the guide
                                            book, Sandringham Church
                                            had little or nothing to
                                            distinguish it from any village
                                            church in Norfolk – Well, ...

Interior of Sandringham Church.   At first glance it rather
                                            reminds me
                                            Of the Wee Kirk o' the
                                            Heather in Hollywood
                                            Those silver panels on the
                                            pulpit
                                            That jewel-encrusted bible
                                            But in fact it's very Edwardian
                                            For here worshipped King
                                            Edward VII
                                            And Queen Alexandra
                                            The ornate furnishings, this
                                            altar of solid silver,

Were given by Mr Rodman
Wanamaker, a very rich
American admirer of our
Royalty.

Sandringham Church has its
homely touches, too.

JB inside the church.

Of all the details in this
church I think this is my
favourite. You can tell from
the swirls and the curves who
the sculptor was. He was Sir
Alfred Gilbert who designed,
you'll remember, Eros in

The statue of St George.

Piccadilly Circus. In
Sandringham he's done the
figure of St George.

Exterior of Booton church

I wade my way alone, no
tourists near,
Through last year's autumn
leaves
To Booton's haunting weird
Victorian church.
It's pinnacles outlined against
the sky
Seem outsize pinnacles
Copies of others elsewhere,
But they look so big
I fear the church will topple
with their weight.

Interior: the windows.

A rich Victorian rector paid
for them
And paid for all the stained
glass windows too.
No painful crucifixions here
The heavenly choir
In Victorian dress

Choir practice at Martham.

Let everything that hath
breath
Praise the Lord –
But practice first
In the rectory at Martham
Between the Broads and the
sea.

Exterior of the rectory.

Meanwhile
In his room above
The Rector, Father Cooling,
model engineer,
Oils his parish wheels
And indeed they run
themselves most smoothly.

Exterior of Wymondham.

Everywhere church choirs
prepare for Easter
Wymondham's Norman Abbey
is the town's parish church
And in this century Sir Ninian
Comper made the East Wall

*Interior: zoom out to reveal the
choir and reredos.*

A lofty reredos of sculptured
gold
Scale is the secret of its
majesty.

Scale was Comper's secret
In 1914 they let him loose
In this plain old country
church
He turned it into a treasure
house.

JB inside Lound Church.

The golden church of Lound,
Suffolk, in the diocese of
Norwich. Gold on the font
cover, to emphasise the
sacrament of baptism, entry
into the church. Gold on the
screen to veil the mystery of

holy communion at the high altar.

I knew Comper. He died a few years ago and he looked rather like that advertisement for Colonel Sanders' Kentucky Chicken. Little white pointed beard; and he spoke in a very lah-di-dah manner. 'My wark doncha know in that charch'. And his wark in this charch is really marvellous.

Lound.

I think this is what a late medieval English church
Probably looked like when it was new
Colour very important
Saints, angels and symbolic figures everywhere.
Comper was much influenced
By the colour and decoration
Of Spanish, Sicilian and Greek churches
He didn't mind about style
Sometimes he mixed Classic with Gothic
That he called 'unity by inclusion'.

JB inside Lound.

As I look through this rood screen I can see the colours of the altar hangings. Pink predominates. It's called Comper Pink, and he had it specially made in Spain. He used to buy scarlet silk and there have it bleached in the sun till it was just the shade he wanted. 'Incomperable' as people used to say.

Exterior of Flordon Church.	'A church should pray of itself With its architecture', Said Comper. 'It is its own prayer And should bring you to your knees when you come in'.
The vicar rings a bell.	But there's another way. At his ordination Every Anglican priest promises to say Morning and Evening Prayer, daily. The Vicar of Flordon Has rung the bell for Matins
The vicar.	Each day for the past eleven years.
Exterior of Flordon.	It doesn't matter that there's no one there It doesn't matter when they do not come The villagers know the parson is praying for them in their church.
Norwich churches.	In some churches All prayer has ceased St Benedicts, Norwich is a tower alone But better let it stand A lighthouse beckoning to a changing world.
St Edmund Fishergate.	St Edmund Fishergate – a store for soles of shoes Once it was working for the souls of men

Churches are what make
Norwich different.
'A church for every Sunday of
the year'
They used to say of it
A use for every church is what
we say today.

St Lawrence the exterior and the interior.

St Lawrence here – spacious
and filled with mitigated light
The matchless words of the
Book of Common Prayer
Once rolled along these walls
Now young Artists use it for a
studio
Better that than let the
building fall

Exterior of St Mary's.

Artists come to St Mary
Coslany, too.

Interior.

In this church John Sell
Cotman the Norfolk water-
colour painter was baptised
and here Crome the artist was
married. The present
congregation is well
upholstered. It is all stored
here for charity.

Interior of St Helen's.

A use for every church – a
thought not new
Four hundred years ago St
Helen's Norwich
Became a hostel and a hospital
Men in the nave, ladies in the
chancel
The parish church in between.
This is the upper floor of the
Chancel, the Eagle Ward.

And here you can be cared for
till you die.

Derelict churches.

And should we let the poor
old churches die?
Do the stones speak? My
word, of course they do.
Here in the midst of life they
cry aloud.
'You've used us to build
houses for your prayer
You've left us here to die
beside the road'.

Exterior: the graveyard.

Christ son of God come down
to me and save
How fearful and how final
seems the grave.
Only through death can
resurrection come
Only from shadows can we see
the light
Only at our lowest comes the
gleam
Help us, we're all alone and
full of fear
Drowning, we stretch our
hands to you for aid,
And wholly unexpectedly you
come
Most tolerant and all
embracing church

*The Chaplain of the Missions to
Seamen.*

Wide is the compass of the
Church of England.

Lightship visit sequence.

The Smith's Knoll Lightship
is the farthest point
Of the Norwich diocese,
twenty-two miles out to sea.

The Reverend Maurice Chant
Chaplain of the Missions to
Seamen in Great Yarmouth,
Comes aboard to meet the
men,
See if there are any problems
And to be there just in case
he's needed.

He distributes the Mission's
magazine
And pastoral greetings.

Chaplain of the Broads and
Canon Blackburne.

On inland waters, Canon
Blackburne, Chaplain of the
Norfolk Broads,
Summons the floating
members of his flock to Easter
Service.

Dawn at Lowestoft.

Easter Day.
Dawn over the easternmost tip
of Britain
Ness Point, Lowestoft.

A service on the quay.

At six o'clock in the morning
Led by the band of the
Salvation Army
All churches join in the first
Easter Service
And greet the rising sun.

Exterior: Castle Rising sequence.

Peaceful their lives are, calm
                    and unsurprising
The almshouse ladies here at
                    Castle Rising
And suited to the little brick
                    built square
The Jacobean hats and cloaks
                    they wear
See from the separate rooms
                    in which they dwell
Each one process. The warden
                    pulls the bell
Fingers and knees not yet too
                    stiff to pray
And thank the Lord for life
                    this Easter Day.

Exterior of St Peter Mancroft.

Bells of St Peter Mancroft
                    loudly pealing
Fill the whole city with an
                    Easter feeling.

People going to church.

'Is risen today' 'Is risen today'
                    they plead
Where footpath, lane and
                    steep-up alley lead.

Haydon – people going to church.

Across the diocese from tower
                    to tower
The church bells exercise
                    compelling power.
'Come all to church, good
                    people', hear them say,
'Come all to church, today is
                    Easter Day'
Over our vicar we may not
                    agree
He seems too high to you, too
                    low to me.

But still the faith of centuries
     is seen
In those who walk to church
     across the green.
The faith of centuries is in the
     sound
Of Easter bells, that ring all
     Norfolk round
And though for church we
     may not seem to care
It's deeply part of us. Thank
     God it's there.

John Betjeman – A Chronology
1906 to 1984

1906	Born Highgate, London, 28 August, son of Ernest and Mabel Bess (née Dawson) Betjemann.
1911	Byron House Montessori School, Highgate.
1915	Highgate Junior School.
1917	Dragon School, Oxford.
1920	Marlborough College, Wiltshire.
1925	Magdalen College, Oxford.
1928	Schoolmaster at Thorpe House Prep. School, Gerrards Cross, for one term.
1929	Private Secretary to Sir Horace Plunkett for two months.
1929–30	Schoolmaster at Heddon Court Prep. School, East Barnet.
1930–34	Assistant Editor, *Architectural Review*.
1931	*Mount Zion* (The James Press).
1932	Conceives *Shell Guides* for Shell Oil Company. *Cornwall Illustrated* (Shell). Lifetime involvement with BBC begins.
1933	*Ghastly Good Taste* (Chapman and Hall). Marries Penelope Chetwode, 29 July.
1934	Moves to Garrards Farm, Uffington, Berkshire.
1934–35	Film critic to *Evening Standard*.
1935–39	Works in Shell Publicity Department, Shell-Mex House.
1936	*Devon: A Shell Guide* (The Architectural Press).
1937	*Continual Dew* (John Murray). Son Paul born.
1938	*An Oxford University Chest* (John Miles).
1939	*Antiquarian Prejudice* (Hogarth Press).
1940	Works for Ministry of Information. *Old Lights for New Chancels* (John Murray).
1941	United Kingdom Press Attaché, Dublin, Ireland.
1942	*Vintage London* (Collins). Daughter Candida born.

1943	Returns to Uffington from Ireland.
	English Cities and Small Towns (William Collins).
	Resumes job with Ministry of Information.
1944	Serves with Publications Branch of the Admiralty in Bath.
	English Scottish and Welsh Landscape with Geoffrey Taylor and illustrated by John Piper (Frederick Muller).
1944–51	Regular book reviewer for *Daily Herald*.
1945	Moves to Farnborough, Wantage, Berkshire.
	Works for British Council in Oxford and Blenheim.
	New Bats in Old Belfries (John Murray).
1946–48	Secretary of Oxford Preservation Trust three days a week.
1946–78	Serves on the Oxford Diocesan Advisory Committee.
1947	*Slick, But Not Streamlined* (Doubleday, New York).
1947–50	Edits *Watergate Children's Classics* for Sidgwick & Jackson.
1948	*Selected Poems* (John Murray).
	Murray's Buckinghamshire Architectural Guide.
1948–63	Serves on the London Diocesan Advisory Committee.
1949	*Murray's Berkshire Architectural Guide.*
1949–54	Literary Adviser/Editor to *Time and Tide*.
1950	*Collected Poems* (John Murray).
1951	Moves to The Mead, Wantage, Berkshire.
	The English Scene (Cambridge University Press).
	Shropshire: A Shell Guide (Faber and Faber) with John Piper.
1951–59	Weekly book reviews for *Daily Telegraph*.
1952	*First and Last Loves* (John Murray).
1952–62	'Men and Buildings' column for *Daily Telegraph*.
1952–70	Serves on Royal Fine Art Commission.
1954	*Poems in the Porch* (John Murray).
	A Few Late Chrysanthemums (John Murray).
	Rents 43 Cloth Fair, London.
1954–58	Weekly column 'City and Suburban' for *Spectator*.
1954–77	Serves on committee of the Society for the Protection of Ancient Buildings.
1955	'Discovering Britain', a series of twenty-six short films (Shell).
	Foyle Poetry Prize for *A Few Late Chrysanthemums*.
1956	*The English Town in the Last Hundred Years.*

'Our National Heritage: Stained Glass at Fairford' (BP/Shell).

Loines Award for poetry.

1957   *English Love Poems* edited with Geoffrey Taylor (Faber and Faber).

'Beauty in Trust' (BP/Shell).

Poet in Residence at the University of Cincinnati, Ohio, USA.

Honorary Associate, Royal Institute of British Architects.

1958   *Collins Guide to English Parish Churches* (Collins).

Collected Poems (John Murray).

Duff Cooper Memorial Prize for *Collected Poems*.

Founds the Victorian Society with Anne Rosse.

1958–84   Vice-chairman and committee member of the Victorian Society.

1959   *Altar and Pew* (John Murray).

Foyle Poetry Prize for *Collected Poems*.

Honorary D. Litt., Reading University.

1960   *Summoned by Bells* (John Murray).

A Hundred Sonnets by Charles Tennyson Turner, selected in collaboration with Sir Charles Tennyson (Hart-Davis).

'Our National Heritage: journey into the Weald of Kent' (BP/Shell).

Queen's Gold Medal for Poetry (for *Collected Poems*).

Commander, Order of the British Empire.

Buys Treen, Trebetherick, Cornwall.

1960–68   'ABC of Churches', a series of twenty-six films (BBC).

1961   Visits Australia (five weeks).

1961–62   Euston Arch demolished.

Collected Poems (with additional poems, John Murray).

A Ring of Bells (John Murray).

'Steam and Stained Glass' (ATV).

'Wales and the West', a series of six films (TWW).

Coal Exchange demolished.

1963   'A Hundred Years Underground' (London Transport).

'Wales and the West', a further series of four films (TWW)

1964   *Cornwall: A Shell Guide* (updated, Faber and Faber).

'Discovering Britain with John Betjeman', a series of five films (BP/shell).

1964–67   Regular feature for *Weekend Telegraph*.

1965   *The City of London Churches* (Pitkin Pictorials).
        Honorary LL.D, Aberdeen University.
1966   *High and Low* (John Murray).
        'Journey to Bethlehem' (BBC).
        'Betjeman at Random', a series of four films (BBC).
1967   'The Picture Theatre' (BBC).
        'Tale of Canterbury' (Rediffusion).
        'Betjeman's London', a series of six films (Rediffusion).
        Six Betjeman Songs (Duckworth).
1968   'Contrasts: Tennyson: A Beginning and an End' (BBC).
        'Footprints: the Finest Work in England: Isambard
        Kingdom Brunel' (BBC).
        Companion of Literature, Royal Society of Literature.
1969   *Victorian and Edwardian London* (Batsford).
        'Bird's Eye View: Beside the Seaside' (BBC).
        'Bird's Eye View: The Englishman's Home' (BBC).
        Knight Bachelor.
        Commissioner of the Royal Commission on Historical
        Monuments.
1970   *Collected Poems* (enlarged third edition, John Murray).
        Ghastly Good Taste (second edition, Anthony Blond).
        Ten Wren Churches (Editions Alecto).
        'Four with Betjeman: Victorian Architects and
        Architecture'.
        'Look Stranger: John Betjeman on the Isle of Man'.
        'Railways For Ever'.
1971   *Victorian and Edwardian Oxford* (Batsford).
        'That Well Known Store in Knightsbridge' (BBC).
        'The Isle of Wight' (BBC).
        'Bird's Eye View: A Land for All Seasons' (BBC).
        Honorary Fellow, Royal Institute of British Architects.
        Visits Australia (three months).
1972   *Victorian and Edwardian Brighton* (Batsford).
        London's Historic Railway Stations (John Murray).
        A Pictorial History of English Architecture (John Murray).
        'Betjeman in Australia', a series of four films (BBC/ABC).
        'Thank God it's Sunday', a series of two films (BBC).
        Poet Laureate, 10 October.
        The Mead sold.
1973   'Metro-land' (BBC).
        Rents 29 Radnor Walk, London.

1974	*A Nip in the Air* (John Murray).
	Victorian and Edwardian Cornwall (Batsford).
	'A Passion for Churches' (BBC).
1975	Visits Canada for Macdonald Stuart Foundation.
1976	'Summoned by Bells' (BBC).
	'Vicar of this Parish: Betjeman on Kilvert' (BBC).
1977	*Metroland* (Warren).
	Archie and the Strict Baptists, illustrated by Phillida Gili (John Murray).
	'The Queen's Realm' (BBC).
1978	*The Best of Betjeman* (John Murray).
1979	'John Betjeman's Dublin' (BBC).
	'John Betjeman's Belfast' (BBC).
1980	*Church Poems* (John Murray).
	'Nationwide: Southend Pier' (BBC).
	'Betjeman's Britain' (Anglia TV).
	'Late Flowering Love' (Charles Wallace Picture Co).
1981	'Nationwide: St Mary le Strand' (BBC).
1982	*Uncollected Poems* (John Murray).
1983	'Time with Betjeman', a series of seven films (BBC).
1984	Dies, Trebetherick, 19 May.

Index